F. SCOTT FITZGERALD'S
THE BEAUTIFUL AND DAMNED

F. SCOTT FITZGERALD'S
THE BEAUTIFUL AND DAMNED

NEW CRITICAL ESSAYS

EDITED BY
WILLIAM BLAZEK
DAVID W. ULLRICH
& KIRK CURNUTT

LOUISIANA STATE UNIVERSITY PRESS   BATON ROUGE

Published by Louisiana State University Press
lsupress.org

Designer: Barbara Neely Bourgoyne
Typeface: Minion Pro

Cover illustration: *Study for Butterfly Couple,* by J. C. Leyendecker, 1923.

Library of Congress Cataloging-in-Publication Data
Names: Blazek, William, editor. | Ullrich, David W., editor. | Curnutt,
  Kirk, editor.
Title: F. Scott Fitzgerald's "The beautiful and damned" : new critical
  essays / edited by William Blazek, David W. Ullrich, and Kirk Curnutt.
Description: Baton Rouge : Louisiana State University Press, 2022. |
  Includes bibliographical references and index.
Identifiers: LCCN 2022009107 (print) | LCCN 2022009108 (ebook) | ISBN
  978-0-8071-7857-7 (paperback) | ISBN 978-0-8071-7773-0 (cloth) | ISBN
  978-0-8071-7861-4 (pdf) | ISBN 978-0-8071-7860-7 (epub)
Subjects: LCSH: Fitzgerald, F. Scott (Francis Scott), 1896–1940. Beautiful
  and damned. | LCGFT: Literary criticism. | Essays.
Classification: LCC PS3511.I9 B434 2022 (print) | LCC PS3511.I9 (ebook) |
  DDC 813/.52—dc23/eng/20220310
LC record available at https://lccn.loc.gov/2022009107
LC ebook record available at https://lccn.loc.gov/2022009108

CONTENTS

ABBREVIATIONS

Please note: Because the essays in this collection focus on *The Beautiful and Damned,* we do not use the standard abbreviation in Fitzgerald studies for this 1922 novel (*B&D*) in parenthetical page references to avoid redundancy and repetition. Unless otherwise noted, all citations are to the 2008 Cambridge edition of the novel edited by James L. W. West III. All other references to entries in the Cambridge Edition of the Works of F. Scott Fitzgerald are cited using the abbreviations below. This includes West's variorum edition of *The Great Gatsby* (2019), which, because it corrects some controversial editing choices Matthew J. Bruccoli made in the original 1991 Cambridge edition of that novel, has become the standard citation source in Fitzgerald studies. Although there it is abbreviated as *GGVar* to distinguish it from Bruccoli's text, here for simplicity's sake we employ *GG*.

ASYM	*All the Sad Young Men*
BJG	*The Basil, Josephine, and Gwen Stories*
CC	*A Change of Class*
F&P	*Flappers and Philosophers*
GG	*The Great Gatsby: A Variorum Edition*
LD	*The Lost Decade: Short Stories from "Esquire," 1936–1941*
LK	*Last Kiss*
LLT	*The Love of the Last Tycoon*
MLC	*My Lost City: Personal Essays, 1920–1940*
S&G	*Spires and Gargoyles: Early Writings, 1909–1919*
TAR	*Taps at Reveille*
TITN	*Tender Is the Night*

TJA   *Tales of the Jazz Age*
TSOP   *This Side of Paradise*

Complete bibliographical information on these Cambridge editions is included in the Works Cited at the end of this collection.

F. SCOTT FITZGERALD'S
THE BEAUTIFUL AND DAMNED

INTRODUCTION
REDEEMING THE SOPHOMORE SLUMP

William Blazek, David W. Ullrich, and Kirk Curnutt

On 7 July 1920 F. Scott Fitzgerald wrote his editor at Charles Scribner's Sons, Maxwell Perkins, with a forecast: "My novel ought to be finished about Sept 15 & I will send you a copy. The Metropolitan"—a leading periodical of the day—"will probably begin to serialize it right off after that so if you care to I imagine it will be eligible for book publication in the spring" (Kuehl and Bryer 31). As with most claims from the twenty-three-year-old writer in this earliest, headiest period of his career, his words radiate both audacity and insecurity. The project to which he refers would become his second novel. His first, *This Side of Paradise,* had arrived in bookstores only three months earlier but was already a succès de scandale. Since its publication on 26 March, Fitzgerald's name had appeared in national newspapers more than one hundred times, and Scribner's was primed for the autumn publication of a first collection of short stories, *Flappers and Philosophers,* featuring tales fresh from the pages of prominent weeklies and monthlies, including the *Saturday Evening Post,* the *Smart Set,* and his publisher's own house organ, *Scribner's Magazine.* In slightly more than ninety days, the Princeton University dropout and former U.S. Army lieutenant had become famous, sold three stories to the movies (with a fourth sale imminent), and earned more money than he had ever expected.[1] Amid this rush of life-altering events he even found time to wed the young woman whose spurning the previous year had motivated him to pursue his literary fortunes by quitting a lowly ninety-dollar-per-month job cranking out advertising copy. On 3 April, exactly eight days after his novel went on sale, the not-yet-twenty-year-old southern belle Zelda Sayre officially became Mrs.

F. Scott Fitzgerald. The writer pondered his sudden rise to notoriety that fall in the *Post:* "Then my novel came out. Then I got married. Now I spend my time wondering how it all happened" (*MLC* 5).

For a century now, critics have spent a great deal of time wondering what exactly happened to *The Beautiful and Damned,* the follow-up that finally emerged on 4 March 1922 after nearly two and a half protracted years of writing and revision. Fitzgerald's second novel is one of the most famous examples in American literary history of a sophomore slump. Despite its scope and size—it is twice as long as *Gatsby* but feels far more diffuse—it is widely regarded as an artistic misfire: too transparently autobiographical, too enamored with the past-its-peak naturalism of Frank Norris and Theodore Dreiser, too reliant on preening bursts of prose rather than penetrating insights into the deleterious effect of inherited wealth on moral character. Fitzgerald's most recent biographer, David S. Brown, summarizes its reputation:

> Despite the novel's deft handling of several familiar Fitzgerald themes—
> namely, the struggle between prewar convention and postwar flux—*The
> Beautiful and Damned* has long battled a kind of literary inferiority complex.
> . . . Among critics, the artistically superior duo of *The Great Gatsby* (1925)
> and *Tender Is the Night* (1934) understandably overshadow *This Side of Par-
> adise* (1920) and *The Beautiful and Damned* (1922)—and, of the latter two, it
> is *Paradise's* expressive portrait of youth, its quixotic coming-of-age quest,
> that has struck the more resonant chord among readers. (136–37)

Fitzgerald considered *Damned* a more proficient book than *Paradise.* Yet he also regarded it as a "false lead" (*Correspondence* 139) away from his innate sense of wonder toward a decadent philosophy called "The Meaninglessness of Life" (51), a judgment with which most observers agree. The story of a wealthy couple, Anthony and Gloria Patch, who succumb to dissipation and financial ruin before they turn thirty, the novel seems to lack just about every quality for which the writer is revered. It is arch and sarcastic where his most enduring work is melancholy but idealistic; it almost gloats in its nihilism, posturing in attitude rather than opening itself up to the rapture of emotional vulnerability. It is also notably rife with stylistic faults. In the same pivotal year that modernism produced the rigorously impersonal experimentation of T. S. Eliot's *The Waste Land,* James Joyce's *Ulysses,* and Virginia Woolf's *Jacob's Room* (to name just three), *The Beautiful and Damned* features an omniscient narrator who interrupts to comment on the action with all the digressive chattiness of a Thackeray or a Trollope. Readers who adore the evocative lyricism of *The Great Gatsby* will scratch their heads at passages of windy expatiating that even in 1922 sounded like old-fashioned nattering: "It is in the twenties that the actual momentum of life begins to slacken, and it is a simple soul indeed to whom as many things are significant and meaningful at thirty as at ten years before. At thirty an organ-grinder is a more or less moth-eaten man who grinds an organ—and once he was an organ-grinder! The unmistakable stigma of humanity touches all those impersonal and beautiful things that only youth ever grasps in their impersonal glory" (146).

Finally, speaking of stigmas, the novel suffers one of the most embarrassing gaffes Fitzgerald ever committed, one his own wife gleefully pointed out in the acerbic 2 April 1922 mock review that the *New York Tribune* commissioned (Z. Fitzgerald, *Collected Writings* 288; see also Ullrich, "Mr. Fitzgerald" 105–33). As the author was mortified for a fan letter to point out, he cites three different months for Gloria's birthday: August (164), May (231), and February (326)—a cruel fate for a character repulsed by aging. "God!" Fitzgerald wrote back. "This bugbear of inaccuracy" *(Correspondence* 98–99).

Because of its reputation as confused in conception and sloppy in execution, *The Beautiful and Damned* has received only sporadic critical analyses. To cite one index of its neglect, the MLA International Bibliography database lists a paltry twelve essays on the novel since the 1990 founding of the F. Scott Fitzgerald Society, an organization expressly established to promote appreciation of oft-ignored entries in the author's canon. Compare that to nearly a thousand for *The Great Gatsby* and the point seems obvious enough. Even Fitzgerald's most famous stories garner more interest than his second novel: MLA lists three dozen essays on "Babylon Revisited" (1931; *TAR* 157–79) going back five decades, with "The Curious Case of Benjamin Button" (1922; *TJA* 169–95) inspiring twenty since 1984 alone. (Most of these "Button" pieces appeared in the wake of David Fincher's 2008 in-concept-only movie adaptation, suggesting that the quickest strategy for reviving interest in the Patches' tale might be an Academy Award–nominated showcase for Brad Pitt.)

The present collection is an effort to redress the perception that *The Beautiful and Damned* is unworthy of study. While not excusing the book's faults, the eleven essays gathered here argue it is rich in cultural and historical import. Most obviously, it interrogates the American class system in the first two decades of the twentieth century, finding the scions of the robber-baron generation corrupted by privilege and bereft of intellectual substance. Yet it is also a narrative steeped in a wide variety of ideas au courant in the transition between the Progressive and modern eras of American history. Its characters question the value of work and professionalism, ambition, morality and reform, spirituality, and modernity. Although not as flagrantly as *This Side of Paradise*, *The Beautiful and Damned* can be fairly accused of name-dropping the philosophies and thinkers it references rather than examining them in depth. Gloria Patch is described as a "consistent, practicing Nietzschean" (139), while a pivotal scene is titled "Nietzschean Incident" (172). There are passing mentions of Immanuel Kant (166) and attacks on the Bible (217). One drunken friend of the Patches declares that in fifty years the world will witness a wave of conservatism that will mark "the triumph of Christ over Anatole France" (216), a pretentious nod to the modish popularity in intellectual circles of France's *The Revolt of the Angels* (1914), an atheist novel that imagines the death of humanity's subservience to deities.[2] Fitzgerald even parodies the mystical fad known as theosophy that promoted communing with God, dubbing it Bilphism (69–70).

The Beautiful and Damned is, furthermore, as lacerating an anatomy of marriage as any social novel by Edith Wharton or Leo Tolstoy. It contains at least one scene of domestic violence that delves, chillingly, into the psychology of the patriarchal desire to break the spirit of defiant women (166–71). (In doing so it makes Anthony Patch a clear precursor to the abusive Tom Buchanan in *Gatsby*, who bruises his wife's finger and breaks his mistress's nose [*GG* 15, 45].) *Damned* also includes an adultery subplot and barely concealed references to abortion. The novel takes on finance and the management of household expenses, showing how incomes and inheritances are squandered by living up to a lifestyle that encourages debt over savings. In this regard, the book critiques conspicuous consumption as virulently as Thorstein Veblen's *Theory of the Leisure Class* (1899), cautioning against an emerging ethos of wastage that celebrates the pleasures of using up and throwing away over the productivity of the Protestant work ethic (Curnutt, "Youth Culture" 93–101). *The Beautiful and Damned* is also an addiction narrative: Anthony Patch descends into alcoholism and ends up in several brawls, eventually suffering a breakdown.

In terms of setting, the book is both a metropolitan novel that captures the pulsating energies of New York City *and* a novel of the burgeoning suburbs that exposes the malaise of bedroom communities. The plot even takes an excursion to the South, where Fitzgerald's trademark plot of a northern soldier romancing a small-town southern girl, based on his 1918 courtship of his Alabama wife, is recast in a far darker mode than in either *The Great Gatsby* or "The Last of the Belles" (1929; *TAR* 50–66), where the mood is elegiac and nostalgic. Along the way, the story casts a critical eye on the movie industry, on automobile travel, on Wall Street stock scams and America's relentless culture of snake-oil salesmanship, on immigration and xenophobia. It is difficult to think of an era topic or theme not touched upon.

As the composition history of *The Beautiful and Damned* demonstrates, Fitzgerald placed immense pressure on himself to advance his artistry. His desire to grow helps explain both the broad scope of the book's themes and its shortcomings. The ambitious author did not want to produce a second novel that was a mere retread of his first, yet that desire led him to aesthetic choices that were foreign to his temperament. Additionally, Fitzgerald suffered the basic problem as a newlywed of finding time and energy to work on the book. The final version of *This Side of Paradise* was dashed off in a frenzied two-month spree while living in a quiet room in his parents' three-story rental apartment at 599 Summit Avenue in his hometown of St. Paul, Minnesota.[3] While writing *The Beautiful and Damned*, by contrast, he had a wife to support and a home to maintain—or, rather, homes, since the Fitzgeralds lived a peripatetic existence during the novel's long gestation, moving from New York City to Westport, Connecticut, and back, then to St. Paul, with a European jaunt in between. "The history of my life is the history of the struggle between an overwhelming urge to write and a combination of circumstances bent on keeping me from it," he lamented while laboring over the manuscript (*MLC* 3).

From the outset, the desire not to produce "*Paradise Redux*" led to an enormous amount of wheel-spinning. No sooner did Scribner's accept his debut novel on 19 September 1919 than he circulated several titles and potential plots for his next project. That fall, as he and Zelda worked out their marriage plans, he boasted to Perkins of beginning a "very ambitious novel called 'The Demon Lover' which will probably take a year to write" (Kuehl and Bryer 22). That title would eventually appear in *The Beautiful and Damned* as a fictional example of trashy reading tastes, but no actual discarded drafts survive. At the same time,

Fitzgerald outlined a seemingly different project in a 5 October letter to Robert Bridges, the editor of *Scribner's Magazine,* who had recently accepted two of his more moralistic short stories, "The Cut-Glass Bowl" (*F&P* 87–107) and "The Four Fists" (*F&P* 169–88): "It is a literary forgery purporting to be selections from the note-books of a man who is a complete literary radical from the time he's in college thru two years in New York. . . . It will be in turns cynical, ingenious, life saturated, critical and bitter" *(Correspondence* 46). Whether this effort somehow related to "The Demon Lover" is unclear; he claimed he had already completed a novella-sized twenty thousand words, but little else is known about this untitled work, other than that he envisioned it as a spin on *The Notebooks of Samuel Butler* (1917), one of his favorite books.

Then, in February 1920, Fitzgerald confessed to abandoning a whole other manuscript: "I certainly touched the depths of depression tonight," he wrote Perkins from New Orleans, where he resided for a brief six weeks. "The action on that book *Madeline,* has knocked the hell out of my new novel 'Darling Heart' which turned completely on the seduction of the girl in the second chapter. . . . I don't know what I'll do now—what in the hell is the use of trying to write decent fiction if a bunch of old women refuse to let anyone hear the truth!" (Kuehl and Bryer 27–28). Prompting this outburst was a censorship campaign on the part of the New York Society for the Suppression of Vice against the memoir of a pseudonymous French immigrant prostitute, Madeleine Blair, that had just earned Harper and Brothers publisher Clinton T. Brainard an obscenity conviction. (The conviction was reversed on 9 July, two days after the missive to Perkins in which Fitzgerald promised to finish his book by September.) Despite his advocacy for artistic freedom, Fitzgerald apparently made no more headway on "Darling Heart" than he did on "The Demon Lover." No manuscript of it exists either.

A letter dated 17 July 1920 to his agent, Harold Ober, suggests the novel was barely in its infancy: "I'm *starting* on that novel for the Metropolitan Magazine," he wrote from Westport, where he and Zelda rented a house at 244 Compo Road South (Bruccoli, *As Ever* 17; emphasis added). Ober had recently signed a contract with managing editor Carl Hovey that gave *Metropolitan* the first right of refusal on Fitzgerald's next six stories for nine hundred dollars each. The *Post* was paying only five hundred dollars at the time, and the author felt that the deal would guarantee the magazine's interest in serializing the novel, supplying needed income. But while Fitzgerald promised Ober he would finish the book that fall, just as he had assured Perkins the previous week, life in Westport was a hectic social whirlwind that left precious little time for actual work. Immediately after writing Ober, he and Zelda spontaneously embarked on a three-week, 1,200-mile road trip from Westport to her hometown of Montgomery, Alabama. An account of the jaunt would appear in 1924 as "The Cruise of the Rolling Junk" (*LK* 295–324), published in three installments in *Motor* magazine, where, significantly, there is no mention of the excursion interfering in his productivity.

Another letter upon his return to Connecticut demonstrates that by early August 1920 Fitzgerald had finally committed to a plot and a protagonist. As he wrote Perkins's boss, Charles Scribner II, his second novel "concerns the life of one Anthony Patch between his 25th and 33d years (1913–1921). . . . How he and his beautiful young wife are wrecked on the shoals of dissipation is told in the story." Yet at this point the book went by still another prospective name, "The Flight of the Rocket." Fitzgerald exuded the same cautious optimism about finishing it he had with Perkins and Ober: "I hope it'll be in your hands by November 1st" (*Fitzgerald: A Life in Letters* 41). As November came and went, he dispatched somewhat misleading updates to Hovey, H. L. Mencken, and Edmund Wilson, but the distractions were numerous. Aside from the road trip to Alabama, there were interview requests from celebrity magazines, short stories cranked out for quick cash like "His Russet Witch" (published as "O Russet Witch!" in *TJA* 204–38), and countless benders at the 38 West Fifty-Ninth Street apartment where Scott and Zelda lived from October 1920 to April 1921. Along the way were even more titles, including "The Drunkard's Holiday" and "The Beautiful Lady without Mercy," the latter the translated name of a favorite poem by John Keats.[4] By this point he was also warning his audience not to expect another coming-of-age novel, or even a college novel, in the *Paradise* vein. "It seems to me that the most overworked art-form at present in America is the 'history of a young man,'" he groused in a public declaration, taking a swat at Floyd Dell's derivative *Moon Calf* (1920). "This writing of a young man's novel consists chiefly in dumping all your youthful adventures into the readers' lap with a profound air of importance" (*LK* 271).

When Fitzgerald finally completed a draft shortly after New Year's Day 1921, he felt uncertain enough about its quality to ask his Princeton friend Edmund Wilson, whom he would later call his "intellectual conscience" (*MLC* 148), for editorial advice. Although the critic was busy with his own debut, *The Under-*

taker's Garland (1922; coauthored with John Peale Bishop), he agreed to the favor. As Amy J. Elias observes, "Wilson was a good editor for Fitzgerald, one who kept him from confusing allusions, writing illogical sentences, penning purple prose, or employing a pompous narrative voice" (255–56). While Wilson found the manuscript a marked improvement over *This Side of Paradise*, his recommendations were numerous and took deep into April to incorporate. When Fitzgerald submitted the manuscript to Hovey to prepare for its serialization that spring, his relief was palpable: "After the ten months I have been working on it it has turned out as I expected—and rather dreaded—a bitter and insolent book that I fear will undoubtedly offend a lot of people" (*Correspondence* 82).

Although Fitzgerald finally hit upon a title he was happy with, the book now known as *The Beautiful and Damned* was far from finished. Scott and Zelda embarked upon their first trip abroad in late spring 1921 as a reward for his exhausting labor, yet he came home two months later to another round of rewriting. Fitting the novel into seven installments required *Metropolitan* to excise nearly a third of the text, playing havoc with its character development and amputating passages of intellectual debate that Fitzgerald felt essential to a novel of ideas, the genre in which he wanted readers to interpret it (Elias 256–63). News filtered back to him that the literary cognoscenti he wanted to impress found the story line overheated, implausible, and at points (thanks to Hovey's surgery) incoherent. When Scribner's sent proofs of the unexpurgated version in September 1921, he attacked what he saw as its lingering weaknesses with renewed intensity, polishing for clarity and adding passages as connective tissue. "Its a changed book from the serialized version," Fitzgerald assured Ober in late November. "I've almost rewritten parts of it since I came home [from Europe] this summer" (*Correspondence* 31).

Indicative of the struggle to complete the novel was the ending. Early in his career, Fitzgerald was prone to climaxing his plots with emotional ruminations on a central theme, such as lost love. These exclamatory rhapsodies frequently blur the line between the euphoric and the florid. This propensity works to marvelous effect in *Paradise*, for as Amory Blaine contemplates his generation's fate of having "grown up to find all Gods dead, all wars fought, all faiths in man shaken," he realizes he has only his intense self-awareness to guide him: "I know myself . . . but that is all—" (*TSOP* 260). The lack of resolution, symbolized by the em dash, captures the anxiety of Fitzgerald's generation that the road to adulthood might be a dead end.[5] The first attempt at an ending for *The Beautiful and Damned,* however, was far from stirring. It revived the novel's most dubious gambit, a regrettable supernatural interlude called "A Flash-Back in Paradise" in which a deity known as "THE VOICE" incarnates "BEAUTY" in the earthly form of Gloria Gilbert, dispatching the spirit to Earth to experience the "melancholy spectacle" of vulgar modernity (30–32). In the original conclusion, the Patches' long, slow decline inexorably tarnishes "BEAUTY." "How remote you are," observes "THE VOICE." "You seem to have no heart." Such a scene would have ended the novel with a whimper, not a bang.[6]

For the serial version, Fitzgerald replaced this tepid denouement with an oration that even for him was overwrought. "That exquisite heavenly irony which has tabulated the demise of many generations of sparrows seems to us to be content with the moral judgments of man upon fellow man," it begins—and grows no less portentous from there. Gloria "yielded up her gift of beauty," Fitzgerald declares, piling words upon words, for the "tinsel joys" of money and the "exquisite perfection of . . . boredom." Somehow the tone manages to be both preachy and precious. At both Perkins's and Zelda's urging, Fitzgerald cut this meandering, maundering summation in favor of a bitterly ironic final scene. After a long legal battle, Anthony wins his inheritance from his grandfather's thirty-million-dollar estate, saving the Patches from poverty (367). "I showed them," Anthony declares after the verdict. "It was a hard fight, but I didn't give up and I came through!" (369). Yet he and Gloria hardly "come through" unscathed: Anthony is bundled in a wheelchair and the once radiant Gloria now looks "dyed and *unclean*" (368). The Patches may have money, but they are social pariahs, pathetically broken, bitter, and alone. Such may be the punishment readers wish upon the amoral rich, but as drama, the ending feels as subtle as a hammer blow. To the *Harvard Crimson* the conclusion suggested that "Mr. Fitzgerald has joined the ranks of the 'HaHa' school of ironists. He has made every effort, sometimes it seems through a natural perversity, to mock every one of the aspirations of his characters. . . . Compared to the Fates of Mr. Fitzgerald, those conceived by Thomas Hardy are a trio of well-intentioned, kindly old ladies taking afternoon tea" (M.P.B.). Whether *The Beautiful and Damned* is as bleak as *Tess of the d'Urbervilles* (1891) or *Jude the Obscure* (1895) is debatable. Anthony and Gloria do not go to the gallows or hang themselves, and the author's own preoccupation with youth sometimes results in unintentionally comic assessments of the couple's decline, such as when the wife observes of her husband, "He was thirty-three—he looked forty" (365). Even so, the sour ending seems to betray the "beauty and tenderness" that Gertrude Stein identified as the main tenor of Fitzgerald's sensibility, assuring him his sensitivity was "a comfort" to readers (qtd. in Wilson, *Crack-up* 308).

By the time *The Beautiful and Damned* hit bookshelves, Fitzgerald was prepared for a negative response. *Flappers and Philosophers* had received mixed reviews in September 1920, with many critics claiming his writing was slick but shallow. That attitude still lingered a year and a half later; as Jackson R. Bryer's essay in this collection demonstrates, some reviewers deemed Fitzgerald overrated and decided cutting him down to size was their personal duty. Many others objected to the alcoholism and adultery and condemned it on moral grounds. Most did not go as far as the Madison, Wisconsin, *Capital Times*, which declared, "If one is a regular reader of the Police Gazette one will get a most profound kick out of F. Scott Fitzgerald's latest literary gusher" (Seaman 7). The newspaper's headline is even more over-the-top: "Indecency Seethes in Latest Spasm from Petting Apostle." Overall, the book's reception in 1922 reinforced stereotypes of Fitzgerald that not even the perfection of *The Great Gatsby* could overcome in his lifetime.

In the absence of critical acclaim, Fitzgerald could at least console himself with the novel's commercial success. Often forgotten is the fact that *The Beautiful and Damned* actually outsold *This Side of Paradise* by a few thousand copies. In addition to appearing in *Metropolitan* (where serial rights earned $7,000), the novel was popular in the "second serials" marketplace, appearing in newspapers from Washington, DC, to New Jersey to Georgia, advertised as "a vivid picture of the ultimate Gehenna of flappers—a work that will make the sauciest bobbed head wag aghast" ("I'm Being True to Me" 5).[7] A film adaptation that netted the author $2,500 in rights kept its name alive throughout 1923, earning $350,000 in box-office receipts worldwide. Once Scribner's hardback sales petered out, the reprint publisher A. L. Burt produced an edition that was sold in nontraditional literary retail outlets, such as tobacco shops and pharmacies (West, "Introduction" xxiii). Measured strictly on these grounds, *The Beautiful and Damned* was the biggest hit of Fitzgerald's career. Even after flappers fell out of fashion and Fitzgerald's popularity nose-dived, the book retained its cultural notoriety. The title entered the popular vernacular, borrowed for headlines and captions in countless newspapers and magazines throughout the 1930s. Occasionally the next generation even paid it literary

William E. Hill's jacket cover for *The Beautiful and Damned*, which
Fitzgerald disliked because he felt the representation of Anthony and Gloria Patch
too closely resembled him and his wife, Zelda Sayre.

due: in her 1946 novel *Delta Wedding*, Eudora Welty describes an adolescent heroine sneaking a copy to bed to read in secret (83). Even so, as Fitzgerald was posthumously rehabilitated into a classroom staple and his biography from the 1940s on became an enduring pop-culture fascination, the book was usually glossed over. Commentators remembered *This Side of Paradise* for the youth culture it popularized and celebrated *The Great Gatsby* as his masterpiece, but they often had to remind each other, as *Esquire* editor Arnold Gingrich did in his memorial to Fitzgerald, that this second novel was *not* called "The Beautiful and *the* Damned" (478).

Throughout its critical history then, the kindest thing most biographers and scholars have said about *The Beautiful and Damned* is that it was a necessary stepping-stone to the polished jewel of *The Great Gatsby*. But two concluding observations, one about genre and the other about characterization, dramatize the importance of rereading the novel for its merits rather than its flaws.

One can argue that a major reason *The Beautiful and Damned* suffers in esteem is the lack of a proper literary context for appreciating its aims. Too frequently it is read as a foray into naturalism, as Fitzgerald's effort to curry favor with Mencken by writing in the vein of Dreiser and of both Norrises, Frank and Charles. Such was Fitzgerald's own postmortem when in 1924 he called the book a "concession" to the editor of the *Smart Set* (*Correspondence* 139). Yet as Michael Nowlin has argued, neither Mencken nor his momentary acolyte was wholly committed to the defining principles of the school: "Neither . . . was committed to literary naturalism's first article of faith, that human behavior was radically determined by the forces of heredity and environment, nor to its social Darwinist premise that civilized human beings were but thinly veiled beasts" ("Naturalism and High Modernism" 181). While *The Beautiful and Damned* may rip the veneer of cultural sophistication from Anthony and Gloria, neither of these explanations really accounts for their downfall: their own fatal flaws defeat them more than their environment (despite occasional suggestions that it does), and no matter how debased they become, they do not devolve into McTeague-like animals.

A narrower but more congenial genre for understanding the novel is what might be called, for lack of a better name, the "bright young things" (BYT) school of fiction. A twentieth-century phenomenon, BYT novels synthesize *fin de siècle* decadence with the generational consciousness that had been so-

An advertisement from the 26 June 1922 Washington Herald,
promoting the novel's serialization in the newspaper.

lidifying among literary movements from the Romantics on through the pre-Raphaelites into the Great War generation. As its name suggests, the genre may be more recognizable in the British rather than the American tradition. In 1924 London's *Daily Mail* coined the phrase "bright young people" to describe the antics of a coterie of socialites and fringe aristocrats hatching pranks, throwing parties, and generally running wild throughout the city (D. J. Taylor 15). The group was at once pilloried and publicized until immortalized in Evelyn Waugh's satirical *Vile Bodies* (1930), which might be considered the closest transatlantic cousin of *The Beautiful and Damned*. Novelists soon turned from fictionalizing specific members of this circle such as Cecil Beaton, Brian Howard, and Diana Mitford to using the related term "bright young things" to critique any twentysomething clique pouring their restlessness into frivolity and debauchery. Works as different as George Orwell's *Keep the Aspidistra Flying* (1936) and Cyril Connolly's *The Rock Pool* (1936) are early examples, while *Bad News* (1992) and *Some Hope* (1994), the second and third installments of Edward St. Aubyn's Patrick Melrose quintet, adapt elements of the genre in recent decades. In American literature, a short list of Fitzgerald-inspired BYT narratives might note James G. Dunton's appropriately named *Wild Asses* (1925), a Harvard novel, and Carl Van Vechten's *Parties* (1930), which includes a fictional treatment of Scott and Zelda. More recent entries would include a pair whose continued popularity remains rather baffling, Jay McInerney's *Bright Lights, Big City* (1984) and Bret Easton Ellis's *Less Than Zero* (1985). As unreadable as it is, Ellis's even more notorious *American Psycho* (1991) is a grotesque satire of the genre. (And as with many satires, the point of *American Psycho*—that materialism is soul-sapping—is reiterated with the same bludgeoning desperation with which its yuppie serial killer, Patrick Bateman, dispatches victim after victim.) Not all BYT novels become instant period pieces: Donna Tartt's *The Secret History* (1992) remains a critical favorite for its patina of intellectualism (its BYTs are Greek scholars), while Claire Messud's much-praised *The Emperor's Children* (2006) demonstrates what a mature version of the form can accomplish in the hands of a veteran writer. Recent young-adult fiction seems particularly enamored with BYT characters. Cicely von Ziegesar's thirteen-installment *Gossip Girls* series (2002–9) and Anna Godbersen's aptly named *Bright Young Things* trilogy (2010–12) are just two recent examples. (The latter series is even set in 1929.) All of these works testify to the endurance of a genre that seems to persevere in the face of critical derision. Indicative of Fitzgerald's link to them is the fact that newspapers and magazines often headline their reviews of such works "The Beautiful and Damned."

These are works that do not quite fit the coming-of-age genre to which *This Side of Paradise* belongs; the main characters in a BYT novel are more likely in their twenties and perhaps even thirties than in their adolescence. Although

14

they may have conflicts with authority figures (such as Anthony Patch's Comstockian grandfather, Adam), the "bright young things" themselves struggle less with the pressures of maturation than the pleasures of consumerism. The dramatis personae are typically wealthy (or at least upper-middle-class), materialistic, narcissistic, and therefore exceedingly unsympathetic. Usually depicted as dilettantes, bacchantes, and/or wastrels, they seem created to appease the middle-class desire to believe that the rich are indeed different from you and me—they deserve whatever schadenfreude they rile in us plebes. The engine propelling their plot poses a basic moral question: *how low can one go?* A BYT descends into either alcohol or drug abuse (or both), indulges in sex that is more seamy than steamy, fritters away a livelihood, and demonstrates a lack of purpose in life. Perhaps most intriguingly, these novels blame the protagonists' amorality not on BYTs themselves, but on the preceding generation. *If only our elders had given us something we could have truly cared about,* these characters insist, *we would not have ruined ourselves.* Their inability to accept responsibility for their degradation is responsible for the major complaint most critics level against such books: BYTs almost always appear whiny and childish. Gloria certainly does throughout the early portion of *The Beautiful and Damned,* and her establishment of the BYT prototype early on helps cloud our ability to recognize her development later in the story.

The focus in BYT fiction on "damned" characters points to a contemporary controversy that also helps explain why Fitzgerald's second novel generates so little interest. In a *Publishers Weekly* article promoting her 2013 novel, *The Woman Upstairs,* Messud snapped at interviewer Annasue McCleave Wilson for asking whether the author would be friends with her main character: "For heaven's sake, what kind of question is that? Would you want to be friends with Humbert Humbert? . . . Hamlet? . . . Oedipus? . . . Antigone? Raskolnikov? . . . If you're reading to find friends, you're in deep trouble. We read to find life, in all its possibilities. The relevant question isn't 'is this a potential friend for me?' but 'is this character alive?'" (qtd. in A. Wilson). The response sparked a long but fruitful debate about why readers prefer "likable" characters and how writers can challenge expectations for them without losing their audience. Somewhat overlooked in the conversation was the way that the parallel demand for character development often influences perceptions of likability—and vice versa. For obvious reasons, readers are most apt to identify with fictional people who change positively by overcoming plot obstacles: not only are "round" characters more dynamic than "flat" ones, but their growth feeds our yearning as audiences to believe that we, too, can evolve limitlessly through our life experiences. Likable characters who reach an optimistic if hard-won outcome provide models for our personal self-improvement: they are inspirational. Yet no narrative logic precludes an unsympathetic figure from also changing. That is, a character is not obliged to evolve in ways that makes us regard them as congenial souls. The danger is that we may overlook their development if it does not affect us as emotionally as that of a sympathetic character does.

This distinction is important because critics of the novel often accuse Fitzgerald of inconsistency in his stance toward the Patches. One the one hand, he condemns; on the other, he glorifies. This contradiction is most evident in Gloria, a heroine who elicits less sympathy than even Daisy Buchanan, the golden girl whom critics of previous generations once commonly referred to as a "bitch goddess" (Fahey 146).[8] For so much of the narrative, this baby vamp lacks the appeal of contemporaneous heroines such as Ardita Farnam in "The Offshore Pirate" or Marcia Meadow of "Head and Shoulders" (both 1920; *F&P* 5–35 and 61–86, respectively). Whereas those women are by turns flirty and sentimental, Gloria appears merely spoiled and self-infatuated, despite her propensity for coquetry and poignancy.

Yet something curious happens in chapter 3 of book 2, in a subsection called "Retrospect" of a larger chapter dubbed "The Broken Lute." In this expository section, Fitzgerald summarizes the character changes in Gloria that his dramatic skills were not yet quite developed enough to depict:

> Things had been slipping perceptibly. There was the money question, increasingly annoying, increasingly ominous; there was the realization that liquor had become a practical necessity to their amusement. . . . Moreover, [the Patches] seemed vaguely weaker in fibre, not so much in what they did as in their subtle reactions to the civilization about them. In Gloria had been born something that she had hitherto never needed—the skeleton, incomplete but nevertheless unmistakable, of her ancient abhorrence, a conscience. (233)

From this point on, Gloria *should* become far more sympathetic for readers who might discern the change. While Anthony declines, she shows backbone. She resists an affair with Captain Collins, "the lure of promiscuity, colorful, various, labyrinthe, and ever a little odious and stale . . . hav[ing] no call or promise" for her (305). Later, she assumes management of the couple's dwindling finances and maintains their ever-downsizing household. Granted, Fitzgerald wants to portray these actions as a devolution; in what may be the book's most overt nod to naturalism, Gloria is described as "bent by her environment into a grotesque similitude of a housewife" (349). Some readers, on the other hand, will call this transformation growing up. Yet it remains easy to overlook Gloria's steady maturation, for Fitzgerald emphasizes at all times her dread of growing old in a language that is often melodramatic, emphasizing her vanity. This is especially true in the scene in which Gloria's worst fears are confirmed when movie executive Joseph Black (formerly Bloeckman) informs her that at twenty-nine she appears too old on-screen to portray anything other than "a small character part supposed to be a very haughty rich widow" (333). But the breakdown she suffers upon discovering her eyes wrinkled and cheeks thin is not entirely a product of her vanity. It reflects the interiorizing of the cultural judgment that likes "to predict a somber end for [a woman] in the loss of [her] 'looks,'" as Fitzgerald editorializes (248). By the end of the book, while Anthony regresses into a petulant child, Gloria, although worn and faded, has become a full-fledged adult, nursing her husband (368). Yet critics rarely give her credit for this change, in a large part because Fitzgerald makes little effort to make her likable. Gloria inspires none of the sympathy that readers feel for Amory Blaine's uncertain direction in life, Gatsby's pursuit of Daisy Buchanan, Daisy's own entrapment in her abusive marriage, or even Dick Diver's fall into mediocrity and Nicole Warren Diver's mental illness in *Tender Is the Night*. Because so few readers would want her for a friend, most remain indifferent to her growth and dismiss her as a stagnant character.

A close reading like this reveals how much nuance remains in *The Beautiful and Damned* to untangle. Such is the goal of each essay gathered here. In the opening contribution, Jackson R. Bryer, the president of the Fitzgerald Society since its founding, surveys the critical response to the novel from its earliest reviews to its most recent exegeses. Bryer notes how, over the decades, patterns in these initial reactions have calcified into misperceptions. Bonnie Shannon McMullen's essay on the "sombre pattern" of the story line, meanwhile, explores how Fitzgerald developed its core themes and narrative structure in tandem with the twenty short stories published during the novel's two-and-a-half-year gestation. As is the case with much of Fitzgerald's short fiction, few of these stories, whether "Dalyrimple Goes Wrong" and "The Smilers" (*F&P* 151–68, 254–62) or "Porcelain and Pink" and "The Camel's Back" (*TJA* 61–114, 33–60), have generated significant critical interest. McMullen demonstrates that within them readers can trace the Conradian notion of the "shadow-line," the growth from youthful insouciance to somber maturity, that helps explain why in substance and form *The Beautiful and Damned* diverges so distinctly from *This Side of Paradise*.

Kirk Curnutt subsequently explores anxieties over the cultural value of books and magazines prevalent throughout the novel. As his essay suggests, Fitzgerald struggled to reconcile his dual identity as a purveyor of popular fiction and a "serious" literary writer by dramatizing the disposability of textual material in the 1910s and 1920s. At the tail end of this Great Age of Print, commentators complained that the industrial output of reading matter had created near neurotic consumer habits that diminished the importance of reflection in favor of pure sensation. Yet reading the serialized version of *The Beautiful and Damned* alongside advertisements and stories *Metropolitan Magazine* featured from September 1921 to March 1922 suggests the popular periodical industry insisted that print had ceded none of its authority as an arbitrator of knowledge. The essay makes a case for studying the serial text in its original context, a task that has proved prohibitive given the relative scarcity of surviving copies of *Metropolitan*.

Walter Raubicheck then tackles the thorniest issue surrounding *The Beautiful and Damned*—namely, its affinities with naturalism. Reading the novel alongside the work of H. L. Mencken and George Jean Nathan, who as editors of the *Smart Set* published Fitzgerald stories too tarty for the *Post,* Raubicheck clarifies just how literary naturalism had evolved twenty years after Dreiser's *Sister Carrie* (1900). As he argues, while Fitzgerald may have flirted with elements of this school, his residual Romanticism and Catholicism, along with key modernist influences, prevented him from fully absorbing its aesthetics. Like McMullen, he, too, examines the Patches' decline alongside contemporaneous short stories, in particular "May Day" (*TJA* 61–114), whose own Menckenian tenor has also perpetuated naturalist truisms that require deconstructing.

Although *The Beautiful and Damned* is set in landscapes familiar to Fitzgerald fans—most notably, New York City and the Deep South—a significant portion of it takes place in Westport, Connecticut. Inspired by the Fitzgeralds' five-month honeymoon in 1920 in the blossoming suburb, this section of the novel has inspired none of the fascination with locale that *The Great Gatsby* does with Great Neck, Long Island, or that *Tender Is the Night* does with Paris and the French Riviera. As Richard Webb Jr. notes, some devotees may not even realize that the residence in which Scott and Zelda lived still stands on Compo Road South, as recognizable today as it was in 1922 from the novel's descriptions of the "grey house" that Anthony and Gloria rent for three summers. Asking why Fitzgerald did not dramatize the thriving conflux of wealth, art, and Prohibition crime that characterized Westport in 1920, Webb suggests that the novel is more concerned with themes that in subsequent decades would grow synonymous with suburban fiction, including domestic disaffection and the malaise of leisure culture. To dramatize the Patches' alienation from New York City and its many metropolitan temptations, *The Beautiful and Damned* even draws upon its author's occasional Gothic tendencies to add an aura of the supernatural to its depiction of the grey house and other still-standing sites in Westport. In the end, Webb's essay offers not only a vivid introduction to Westport itself but a reminder of how much interpretation remains to be done to understand Fitzgerald's treatment of place.

Following Webb, David W. Ullrich explores the influence of reformer Anthony Comstock on the novel. Not simply an inspiration for Anthony's stern, moralistic grandfather, Adam J. Patch, Comstock represents "a death-like force of fatherly repression" that contrasts with the ethos of the book's most overlooked character, the Patches' Japanese house servant, Tanalahaka, or "Tana." Typically dismissed as a racist caricature of the Fitzgeralds' own butler during their Westport months, Tana instead represents "Eros, the creative force, professionalism, and a distinctively romantic representation of the artist struggling to express himself—a moral and aesthetic imperative to which Fitzgerald is steadfastly committed." Ullrich's research into the "railroad song," or "testudo shoka," that Tana performs (221) is a reminder of just how much forgotten cultural history is buried in the book. Tana's presence also demonstrates how many models Anthony and Gloria possess that offer "alternative modes of existence, other potential life choices" that could prevent their decline were they mature enough to take advantage of them.

In the next contribution, Gail D. Sinclair explores the dynamic between romance and economy in the Patches' courtship and marriage. Dramatizing the stages of Anthony and Gloria's relationship by analogy to the pas de deux, the "step of two," or duet dance, that is a feature of classical ballet, Sinclair demonstrates that the couple's marriage has its own logic of repulsion and attraction that may not be apparent amid the larger distractions of its various subplots. *The Beautiful and the Damned* does not, unlike Zelda Fitzgerald's lone novel, *Save Me the Waltz* (1932; *Collected Writings* 1–196), specifically dramatize dance as a corollary of narrative form. Yet Sinclair rightly argues that Zelda's lifelong passion for the medium makes the pas de deux's five distinct sections appropriate conceptual vehicles for categorizing the flux and flow of the Patches' love, providing a model that can be extended as to *The Great Gatsby* and *Tender Is the Night* to appreciate how domestic tensions in this second novel evolved in subsequent efforts.

Like Sinclair, Meredith Goldsmith is interested in marital waxing and waning, but her approach is historical instead of formalistic. Specifically, her essay examines how the Great War affects the Patch home, focusing on the relationship between militarism and masculinity to assess the wider cultural changes the cataclysm brought to the American scene. In doing so, Goldsmith draws attention to the predicament of another overlooked secondary character, Dorothy "Dot" Raycroft, the working-class southern woman who becomes Anthony's mistress as he trains in South Carolina and later Mississippi. At the same time, the essay points out the extended contrast Fitzgerald draws between the 1914–18 conflict and the Civil War, the conflagration from which Adam Patch emerges to build his fortune. Along the way, Goldsmith explores related issues of anti-immigrant xenophobia (in the representation of Tana) and regionalism (in the depiction of Zelda's territory of the Deep South), providing, like Ullrich, a thorough contextualization long-ignored points of plot tension.

Like Raubicheck, James L. W. West III tackles one of the rare issues to prompt much debate in *The Beautiful and Damned*: Fitzgerald's treatment of anti-Semitism. As West points out, both the main Jewish character, the aforementioned movie-industry executive Joseph Bloeckman (later Joseph Black) and several minor players like Gloria's friend Muriel Kane epitomize the emergence of this minority in twentieth-century New York, when its population surged from 80,000 in 1880 to 1.6 million in 1920, comprising a quarter of the city's citizenry. Fitzgerald's regard for Jews as they emerged as leaders in the entertainment industry was ambivalent: on the one hand he admired their intelligence and ambition, but what he perceived as their clannishness and arrogance peeved him. While these mixed feelings are evident in the treatment of Bloeckman, Fitzgerald's narrative strategy complicates their attribution. By mingling an omniscient narrator with free indirect discourse (which conflates authorial and character thoughts), the novel makes it difficult to decide whether the writer voices his own prejudice or satirizes Anthony Patch's. West attempts to sort the confusion by reading *The Beautiful and Damned* alongside both later Fitzgerald stories such as "Two Wrongs" and "The Hotel Child" (*TAR* 24–44 and 288–309, respectively) as well as additional era novels, including Edith Wharton's *The House of Mirth* (1905) and *The Custom of the Country* (1913), which are equally complex. In the end, though, the book offers no easy answers. As West concludes, *The Beautiful and Damned* is an unreliable if not outright frustrating index of American racial animus.

Following West, Joseph K. Stitt explores what Fitzgerald regarded as "the problem of overcivilization," the belief that cultural progress was exhausted and that the world was in precipitous decline as decadence and nihilism superannuated traditional aspirational values. Carefully parsing divergent strands of Fitzgerald's sensibility, from his innate Romanticism to his intellectual interest in the medievalism of Henry Adams and the cyclical history of Oswald Spengler, Stitt demonstrates how different characters in *The Beautiful and Damned* represent different responses to the drift and defeatism of the modern age. The essay is especially useful in explicating the cynicism of the Patches' friend Maury Noble, a pseudophilosopher, and the reactionary puritanism of Adam J. Patch. Stitt also offers a valuable assessment of why Anthony's mistress, Dorothy "Dot" Raycroft, reappears without warning at the novel's end, sparking her former lover's collapse. As Stitt notes, Fitzgerald has always been handicapped by the perception that he dealt more in emotion than in ideas; the essay's exploration of different strands of early twentieth-century intellectualism proves that assumption wrong.

In the final essay, "'No Matter!': Work and the Empty Spaces of *The Beautiful and Damned*," William Blazek argues that Fitzgerald's theme of nihilism manifests doubly: Anthony and Gloria's inability to find a meaningful purpose in life results in an emptiness of spirit that is in turn inscribed in the novel's spatiality. From stuffy Manhattan apartments to oppressive and seemingly haunted suburban rental homes to increasingly dingy living quarters, *The Beautiful and Damned* squeezes the couple's lack of ambition and, later, economic options into tighter and tighter confines, conveying a surprising amount of claustrophobia for a metropolitan novel of ideas. The smaller and ever-more-constricting rooms Anthony and Gloria inhabit embody their narrowing expectations both of each other and their future. In the end, these restrictive spaces suggest Fitzgerald's struggle to break the bounds of his own theatrical decadent posturing to embrace the wide horizons of his belief in productivity and labor.

The range of themes and issues dissected in these essays establishes once and for all that F. Scott Fitzgerald's second novel is more than a misstep or a stumble on the path toward *The Great Gatsby*. As we mark its centennial, *The Beautiful and Damned* deserves to be read for the breadth and force of its critique of American culture. Anthony and Gloria's story may lack the emotional warmth and cathartic pining of the writer's most beloved work, but its brash cynicism and irony need not doom it to dismissal. In advocating for its reassessment, this collection seeks to prove the obverse of its sarcastic title: just as modernity likes to insist that "beautiful people" are damned, critics ought to ensure that even the ugly stepchild in a celebrated oeuvre receives some love.

NOTES

1. Those sales include "Head and Shoulders" (released in 1920 as *The Chorus Girl's Romance*), "Myra Meets His Family" (released as well in 1920 as *The Husband Hunter*), "The Offshore Pirate" (released under the same name in 1921), and soon "The Camel's Back" (released in 1924 in virtually unrecognizable form as *Conductor 1492*). As noted, *The Beautiful and Damned* itself was adapted in 1922. For a discussion of these and other adaptations, see Grissom; and Mastandrea.

2. Fitzgerald mentions *The Revolt of the Angels* by title in "The Offshore Pirate" (*F&P* 7).

3. In August and then October 1918 Scribner's rejected two early attempts at the novel then titled "The Romantic Egotist."

4. As Elias notes, Fitzgerald scribbled other potential titles on his holograph manuscript's cover page, including "The House of Pain," "Misfortune Street," "O Beautiful," "The Broken Lute," "The Corruption of Anthony," "A Love Affair," and "Corruption" (248).

5. As West notes in his introduction to *This Side of Paradise,* the dash appears in the manuscript but was changed by some unknown editorial hand into a standard period in the first edition. The Cambridge Edition that West edited in 1995 restores the more open-ended punctuation (xxx).

6. These endings are discussed in detail both in Bruccoli (*Some Sort* 182–84) and West's introduction in the Cambridge Edition of *Damned* (xxi–xxii).

7. For a discussion of this forgotten reprint market, see West's "The Second Serials of *This Side of Paradise* and *The Beautiful and Damned.*"

8. For a rare sympathetic reading of Gloria, see Tangedal.

THE CRITICAL RECEPTION
OF *THE BEAUTIFUL AND DAMNED,*
1922–2022

Jackson R. Bryer

In terms of its critical reception and reputation among scholars and general readers, *The Beautiful and Damned* is indisputably the ugly stepchild of F. Scott Fitzgerald's full-length fictional offspring. This fact is made graphically apparent when one notes how often the title of Fitzgerald's second novel has been incorrectly cited as "*The Beautiful and the Damned.*" Aside from its inherent aesthetic limitations, at least two extraliterary reasons can be offered for this negativity and neglect. Viewed from our present vantage of being able to see the full span of its author's career, *The Beautiful and Damned* is in the unfortunate position of following the sensational critical and popular success of *This Side of Paradise* (1920) and preceding its author's two most highly regarded novels, *The Great Gatsby* (1925), often considered among the twentieth century's best works of fiction, and *Tender Is the Night* (1934), increasingly in recent years valued as Fitzgerald's finest fictional achievement. A second reason can be found in Fitzgerald's own comments about the novel; just as his frequent disparagements of his short stories have undoubtedly led later critics to undervalue them, so too have his oft-quoted doubts and criticisms of *The Beautiful and Damned* taken a toll. Writing to Carl Hovey, the editor of *Metropolitan Magazine,* who was about to begin publishing *The Beautiful and Damned* in serial form ahead of its book publication, Fitzgerald, only slightly tongue-in-cheek, called it "a bitter and insolent book that I fear will never be popular and that will undoubtedly offend a lot of people" (*Correspondence* 82);

and two years later, in a letter to Carl Van Vechten, he admitted, "I'm always glad when anyone likes *The Beautiful and Damned*—most people prefer *This Side of Paradise* and while I do myself I hate to see one child preferred above another" (*Letters* 476–77).

Given its later reception, it is difficult now to realize that, in the spring of 1922, Fitzgerald's publisher had very high expectations for *The Beautiful and Damned* because of the great success of *This Side of Paradise*. Although the first printing of *This Side of Paradise* had been only 3,000 copies, it had gone through nine printings in its first year, had sold over 49,000 copies in its first two years (Bruccoli, *Fitzgerald: A Descriptive Bibliography* 16, 18–21), and had reached "well over a million" additional readers when it was serialized after book publication in the *Chicago Herald and Examiner* and the *Atlanta Georgian* (West, "Second Serials" 73). With this precedent in mind, the first printing of *The Beautiful and Damned*, on 4 March 1922, was 20,600 copies; a second printing of 19,750 copies and a third printing of 10,000 copies appeared within the next month, and two other printings followed almost immediately (Bruccoli, *Fitzgerald: A Descriptive Bibliography* 15, 43–44). This positive anticipation was mirrored in the expectations of critics and reviewers who had eagerly awaited Fitzgerald's second novel after the enthusiasm with which many of them had greeted his first.

The first indication that the critical response to *The Beautiful and Damned* might not be positive actually came before the official publication date, when Edmund Wilson, Fitzgerald's friend at Princeton, spoke of it in a March 1922 piece in the *Bookman*. In that article, he referred rather vaguely to a "first version" of *The Beautiful and Damned*, which he asserted "ended in a carnival of disaster for which the reader was imperfectly prepared" ("Literary Spotlight" 24). What Wilson neglected to mention was that Fitzgerald had sent him this version of the novel in early 1921, inviting Wilson to make any suggestions he wished (*Correspondence* 81), that Wilson had done so—marking up the manuscript with marginal comments—and that Fitzgerald, according to James L. W. West III, "took nearly all of Wilson's advice, revising and cutting as he suggested," with the result that Fitzgerald got "rid of illogicalities and pomposities and of a good deal of overcooked writing" (West, introduction, *Beautiful and Damned* xv). To be fair to Wilson, in his *Bookman* essay he also praised his friend's new novel, calling it "an advance over 'This Side of Paradise': the style is more nearly mature and the subject more solidly unified and certain scenes in it are probably the most real he has ever done"; and, furthermore, granting that Fitzgerald "has his intellectual importance" ("Literary Spotlight" 24–25).

Because of the eagerness with which it was anticipated, upon its publication *The Beautiful and Damned* received more reviews than any Fitzgerald book during its author's lifetime. It was also received more negatively than any of his books (Bryer, *Fitzgerald: The Critical Reception* xv); but, echoing Wilson's advance assessment, the response was decidedly mixed. Many reviewers seemed surprised that the author of a book like *This Side of Paradise* could, two years later, produce so different a work as *The Beautiful and Damned;* and they reacted either with praise or displeasure—and in some instances with both. Among the loudest naysayers were Thomas Caldecot Chubb, who called it "a tedious dull book with hardly an illuminating flash in all of its 400 odd pages"; Louise Maunsell Field, who observed that "not one of the book's many characters . . . even rises to the level of ordinary decent humanity"; Carl Van Doren, who faulted it for its "deliberate seriousness—or rather, a seriousness not deliberated quite enough"; the reviewer for the *Columbus (OH) Dispatch,* who called it "unconvincing, uninspired, preaching an unwholesome contempt for beautiful things"; and Burton Rascoe, who described it as "banal and commonplace" (Bryer, *Fitzgerald: The Critical Reception* 62, 76, 93, 97, 121).

Those who felt positively were equally vehement: John V. A. Weaver praised it as "a novel to read which is a duty and a privilege that you owe to yourself"; Harry Hansen said that "it shows Fitzgerald well on his way to become one of the major novelists of our own time"; John S. Cohen Jr. deemed it "the best American novel in several years"; Catherine Myers found that it "reveals a fund of imagination and ability to set forth Fitzgerald's ideas in a series of scenes and episodes in brilliant and colorful language"; and William Curtis felt that it was "something that the most literary of readers can enjoy as engrossingly as the most avid of sensationalists" (Bryer, *Fitzgerald: The Critical Reception* 70, 91, 101, 115, 117).

Many reviewers, however, expressed ambivalence; representative of these, and significant because later scholars, taking their cues from Fitzgerald's letters, were to credit him with having been a great influence on *The Beautiful and Damned,* was H. L. Mencken. While he criticized the author for "navigating, at times, rather cautiously and ineptly," and for botching the end of the novel "by the introduction of a god from the machine," Mencken also asserted that "Fitzgerald . . . discharges his unaccustomed and difficult business with ingenuity and dignity" and that, with this novel, he "ceases to be a *Wunderkind*, and begins to come into his maturity" (Bryer, *Fitzgerald: The Critical Reception* 107). Several other reviewers agreed: Henry Seidel Canby confessed that the book left him "a little disgusted, a little touched, and profoundly interested"; John Clair Minot said that "it is so uneven that you are alternately exasperated and filled with enthusiasm while reading a single page"; Phil A. Kinsley felt that, in *The Beautiful and Damned*, "Mr. Fitzgerald is at his best—and his worst"; Robert F. Rogan found Fitzgerald "the greatest spoofer among American contemporary writers or the biggest rotter—we don't know which"; Gilbert Seldes lamented the "carelessness about structure and effect which one who has so much to gain from the novel ought to find displeasing," while calling the novel "important because it presents a definite American *milieu* and because it has pretentions as a work of art"; and Mary M. Colum found Fitzgerald's "character-drawing" "somewhat amateurish" and took him to task for using "his characters indifferently to express opinions quite unrelated to their characters," but she also found the book "an achievement for so young a writer" (Bryer, *Fitzgerald: The Critical Reception* 64, 83, 88, 100, 108, 120–21).

Of course, the most famous review the novel received appeared in the *New York Tribune* on 2 April 1922. Headlined "Friend Husband's Latest," it was written by Zelda Sayre, who began by explaining that she had been asked to "analyze" *The Beautiful and Damned* "in the light of my brilliant critical insight, my tremendous erudition and my vast impressive partiality," and who revealed, in the course of her nonreview review, that, "on one page" of the novel, "I recognized a portion of an old diary of mine which mysteriously disappeared shortly after my marriage, and also scraps of letters which, though considerably edited, sound to me vaguely familiar" (Bryer, *Fitzgerald: The Critical Reception* 110, 111; see also Z. Fitzgerald, *Collected Writings* 387–89).

It is worth mentioning here that one of the striking aspects of the contemporary reviews of the American edition of *The Beautiful and Damned* is how many reviewers showed extraordinary prescience in assessing Fitzgerald's career: Canby—"When Mr. Fitzgerald himself grows up, in art as well as in philosophy, he may tell us more, and more wisely"; E. W. Osborn—"Some day Mr. Fitzgerald is going to write a book that will be warm, human and precious"; Kinsley—"Some day . . . Fitzgerald will have become a creator, and interpreter, a real philosopher, to whom the outpourings of today will be but prentice musings"; William Huse—"He still has his equipment for doing good, decisive work; but the accomplishment must wait until a third novel"; the *Minneapolis Sunday Tribune*—"If Fitzgerald is wise, he will concentrate more and more on the sheer matter of fictional architecture"; and *Literary Digest*—"it is likely that he will turn to a wider field and dig up matter of more moment in some book to come" (Bryer, *Fitzgerald: The Critical Reception* 64–65, 79, 87, 88, 95, 128, 133).

When *The Beautiful and Damned* was published in England by W. Collins on 28 September 1922, it sold poorly—"899 Home and 335 Export" (Bruccoli, *Fitzgerald: A Descriptive Bibliography* 47)—but British reviewers, much like their American counterparts, were hardly unanimous in their assessments. On the negative side, the critic of the *Sheffield Daily Telegraph* asked chauvinistically, "Why should a country, in which the original settlers were of English stock and which is within a week's journey, seem so strange in its moral and social aspects?," and the *London Observer* described it as "a poor specimen of a very poor class of fiction." More positive were the *Glasgow Herald*—"a long, unsparing, and brilliantly written study"; the *Nottingham Guardian*—Fitzgerald "is a shrewd observer, and his pen-pictures of his observations are of finished excellence"; and the *Johannesburg Star*—Fitzgerald "shows a very notable insight and can write as convincingly of the mental state of his characters . . . as he can of the purely material things of which he is such a wonderfully close observer and chronicler." Several others were more ambivalent: the *Times Literary Supplement*—it is "cleverly written, sometimes witty, often pungent, but the good effect which it momentarily leaves is swamped by the general impression of futility and waste, both in human life and in the delineation of such worthless characters"; Silas Wegg—Fitzgerald "has a clever pen, but there is a hard, cold brilliance about his work that . . . is repellent"; and H. C. Harwood—"The humour is admirable, and something of the author's gay delight in extremes is communicated to the reader, but it lacks solid stuff" (Bryer, *Critical Reputation* 38, 39, 38, 39, 38, 40).

In the years between 1922 and Fitzgerald's death in 1940, *The Beautiful and Damned* received virtually no attention; the numerous newspaper editorials that appeared when he died focused on him as the bard of the Jazz Age and excluded mention even of *The Great Gatsby* in favor of *This Side of Paradise*. Typically, the *Philadelphia Record* considered the latter Fitzgerald's "best book" and praised him for doing "a bang-up job of recording his own generation. But the flappers grew up. And that seems so very long ago" (Bryer, *Critical Reputation* 204). As posthumous editions of Fitzgerald's work began to be published during the 1940s and reviewers of those volumes wrote extended analyses of his work, *The Beautiful and Damned* was hardly mentioned, the one exception being William Troy's brief and oft-quoted observation, in a 1945 piece in *Accent,* which dismissed it as a "frayed and pretentious museum-piece and the muddiest in conception of all the longer books," noting that "[i]t is not so much a study in failure as in the *atmosphere* of failure—that is to say, of a world in which no moral decisions can be made because there are no values in terms of which they may be measured." It is not, Troy concluded, "a world suited to the purposes of the novelist, and the characters float around in it as in some aquamarine region comfortably shot through with the soft colors of self-pity and romantic irony" (188).

As the Fitzgerald Revival began in earnest in the 1950s and, especially in the 1960s, with a profusion of book-length critical studies and biographies, most mentions of *The Beautiful and Damned* were brief, dismissive, and largely negative. The one exception, not surprisingly, is the earliest, Arthur Mizener's extended and balanced analysis in *The Far Side of Paradise: A Biography of F. Scott Fitzgerald* (1951), still, after seventy years of Fitzgerald research and commentary, among the most astute and nuanced work on Fitzgerald that we have. In many respects, Mizener's critique set the parameters for the future directions of criticism of *The Beautiful and Damned* when he cited "a confusion of the novel's form [that] is increased by Fitzgerald's disregard for form," which allowed the author "to go haring off in any direction which promised a little smart satire or talk about the meaninglessness of it all" (139), and when the critic pointed out that while "[t]he story of Anthony and Gloria is full of precisely observed life, and Fitzgerald makes us feel the grief they suffer . . . he is able to provide neither an adequate cause for their suffering nor adequate grounds in their characters for the importance he gives it" (143). In the end, Mizener asserted, Fitzgerald aimed for the "tragic" but achieved only the "merely pathetic" (141). Many of the later considerations of Fitzgerald's second novel would grapple with the issues Mizener raised.

Other mentions in biographies and critical books, while they were far briefer and more cursory than Mizener's, resembled his in that they could view *The Beautiful and Damned* within the context of Fitzgerald's full career, a luxury that reviewers in 1922, preoccupied with how different it was from *This Side of Paradise,* did not have. The result was that later commentators, while generally critical, also were able to view his second novel as an advance over its predecessor because they could also see how it led from Fitzgerald's first novel to his third. Thus, Andrew Turnbull, in his 1962 biography/memoir *Scott Fitzgerald*, called *The Beautiful and Damned* "more consciously wrought and constructed than *This Side of Paradise*" but nonetheless labeled it "in some ways a weaker book" because "for all its wealth of irony and satire, [it] seems a bit labored" (131–32). In his *F. Scott Fitzgerald and His Contemporaries* (1963), William Goldhurst stressed Fitzgerald's debts to Mencken in the novel, another focus of future criticism, but he also saw a "confusion": "Anthony is supposed to represent a satirical thrust at an American type defined by Mencken; but Anthony is also the embodiment of Fitzgerald's yearning after sophistication" (103). Nonetheless, Goldhurst felt that *The Beautiful and Damned* was not "an artistic failure": rather it was "in many respects a solid achievement [because] . . . it defines for us the painful experience of an individual at odds with the prevailing mores of his time and place; and more important, it exhibits those social mores in something approaching the fullness of life" (104).

James E. Miller, Jr., in *F. Scott Fitzgerald: His Art and His Technique* (1964), also concentrated heavily on Mencken's influence, but, bringing up another criticism that was to reappear, he complained that "[t]here seem to be . . . two themes" in the novel, "one concerned with the revolt of youth and the other with the meaninglessness of life, both developed side by side but never quite merging into a unified view" (63). Miller established still another strand of future criticism when he contended that, at the time he was writing *The Beautiful and Damned*, Fitzgerald was "still too close to his material to see it clearly" (64). Similarly, Kenneth Eble stressed the novel's autobiographical aspects in his *F. Scott Fitzgerald* (1963), like Miller, faulting its author's "inability to keep Anthony Patch and Gloria at a distance after the first third of the book" (72); they "only feebly enlist the reader's interest or sympathy" (71). But he also saw it as "a better novel than *This Side of Paradise*" because "in a technical way" it was "orderly" (71). Miller agreed here, too, finding the second novel "technically an advance over" the first because it "contains a central and unifying action"; it was, for its author, "a novel of transition" (77). Calling *The Beautiful and Damned* Fitzgerald's "longest, least successful book" (34), K. G. W. Cross, in *F. Scott Fitzgerald* (1964), also recognized it as an essential stepping-stone; in it, Fitzgerald "had found his major theme—the need for illusion, and the tragedy that springs from its inevitable failure" (37).

In the second major Fitzgerald biography, *F. Scott Fitzgerald: A Critical*

Portrait (1965), Henry Dan Piper introduced Frank Norris as another influence, "the kind of literary model" for its author's second novel that "Compton Mackenzie had been" (89) for his first. Piper also reiterated the novel's autobiographical components, "the extent to which Gloria and Anthony and their companions were exaggerated portraits of the Fitzgeralds themselves and their friends," seeing that as the source of "private jokes" that most readers could not appreciate (87). While he praised the "power" that was derived "from the accumulative effect of many excellent separate episodes" (93) in the novel, like several previous commentators and numerous later ones, he faulted Fitzgerald for the confusion caused by "trying to write two stories": "One was a tragedy of modern married life" inspired by Mencken and Norris, and the other "a brittle comedy of ideas in the manner of Shaw or Wilde" (87).

Far harsher was Sergio Perosa's critique in *The Art of F. Scott Fitzgerald* (1965). While he recognized, as had Miller and Cross, its thematic importance in Fitzgerald's career—it "is a parable on the deceptiveness of dreams, on the impossibility of evading reality through illusions, and on the painful destructiveness of time" (43)—he also decried "the poor quality of the language," how the sentences are "long and twisted, elaborate and overloaded with images, full of round-about expressions and far from fluent" (50), and how its major flaw, the sort of confusion cited by earlier critics, is reflected in its title: "the . . . inescapable result of the action is that Anthony and Gloria are 'damned'; and they cannot be, therefore, as 'beautiful' as the author tries to make them" (46). Richard Lehan, in *F. Scott Fitzgerald and the Craft of Fiction* (1966), using almost the same words as Miller, also discerned "two separate themes" in the novel—"Meaning opposed to the meaninglessness of life, and youth opposed to the ravages of time"—but Fitzgerald "treats them as one, unable to see that they are distinct, and unable to dramatize them convincingly" (90). But he too felt it represented "an advance over" *This Side of Paradise* because "Fitzgerald is developing a sense of irony, of self-mockery" (81).

In *F. Scott Fitzgerald: The Last Laocoön* (1967), Robert Sklar reiterated the Mencken and Norris influences and was quite harsh in his judgment: "Universal language pervades the novel as if it were a medieval fantasy, and ultimately social observation becomes irrelevant, for Anthony and Gloria are playballs of the gods, not responsible for their own conduct, and surely not to be considered as judgments on their place and time." *The Beautiful and Damned,* Sklar concluded, "might as well be about the Stone Age as the Jazz Age" (99).

Milton Hindus's assessment, in his *F. Scott Fitzgerald: An Introduction and Interpretation* (1968), was equally harsh: "From the point of view of literary form, *The Beautiful and Damned* is probably the weakest of Fitzgerald's novels": it is "a ponderous case history which seems to aim at factual truth rather than at aesthetic beauty and to prove that the two are mercilessly at odds with each other" (27). But Hindus singled out Gloria as "one of [Fitzgerald's] most interesting feminine creations" (30).

The first two scholarly articles on *The Beautiful and Damned* also appeared in the 1960s. Although neither broke new critical ground, both were detailed and careful studies that were in conversation with earlier analyses. Barry Gross's "'The Dark Side of Twenty-Five': Fitzgerald and *The Beautiful and Damned*," like Hindus, praised Fitzgerald's depiction of Gloria, his "best female characterization, his most detailed and most developed golden girl" (47), but he echoed earlier critics in asserting that, "[a]t twenty-five Scott Fitzgerald . . . is too young and too close to his subjects to see them completely whole" (51). In *"Vandover and the Brute* and *The Beautiful and Damned*: A Search for Thematic and Stylistic Reinterpretation,"* Richard Astro expanded on the suggestion of influence made by Piper and Sklar with a close reading of both novels that revealed, in response to Mizener and others who saw Fitzgerald's novel as failing to achieve its aim to be a tragedy, that "Anthony and Gloria are not tragic figures . . . because Fitzgerald never intended them to be. . . . [It] is a successfully conceived moralistic tract against self-indulgence, not an imperfectly drawn tragedy of the twentieth-century intellectual" (405).

Three full-length critical studies of Fitzgerald in the 1970s devoted substantial sections to *The Beautiful and Damned,* and each in its own way viewed it as a transitional text necessary to move its author on to the better novels that followed. Chief among these was Milton R. Stern's fifty-two-page chapter, *"The Beautiful and Damned*: The Ironical-Pessimistic,"* in *The Golden Moment: The Novels of F. Scott Fitzgerald* (1970), which stands as not only the most extensive and detailed but also the best explication/analysis of the novel to date. Stern agreed with Hindus and Gross that Gloria "offers the fullest development of the golden girl as an independent character" (137), but he also found it Fitzgerald's "dullest" novel, whose "essential fault" is that "the density is that of the imagination not yet ripened by experience" (156). Nonetheless, it was "an absolutely necessary book, for only from the consolidation of both aspects of his materials, the anticipation as well as the failure, and from the artistic control the consolidation gave him, could he move forward to his high creations" (158). Thomas J. Stavola agreed with Stern, observing in his *Scott Fitzgerald: Crisis in an American Identity* (1979) that *The Beautiful and Damned* "is Fitzgerald's first full-length study of the theme of loss and failure" and that Anthony's "major fault is the inability to distinguish clearly between reality and illusion, the spiritual and the material" (108). In *The Achieving of "The Great Gatsby": F. Scott Fitzgerald, 1920–1925* (1979), Robert Emmet Long saw it as both "the most seriously flawed novel Fitzgerald wrote" and "a step forward in some important respects" (38) in that "it reveals a great deal about Fitzgerald's development and the large literary background from which he drew and attempted to assimilate. It is a transitional work" (60). Brian Way, in his *F. Scott Fitzgerald and the Art of Social Fiction* (1980), disagreed vehemently with Stern, Stavola, and Long, sounding an entirely negative note: "It is an extremely bad novel by any standard, but what makes it especially disturbing is that it seems to cancel out all the gains Fitzgerald had made so far. It carried him clear out of the path that appeared to be leading directly to the creative climax of 1924–26" (64).

In the 1970s and early 1980s there was a smattering of scholarly essays on *The Beautiful and Damned*. Leonard A. Podis's "*The Beautiful and Damned*: Fitzgerald's Test of Youth" (1973) described it as Fitzgerald's "first major attempt . . . to reconcile his romantic faith in the magic of youth with his morally ingrained suspicions that life wasn't 'the reckless business' for which he and his young creatures had been taking it" (142); and Robert Roulston, stressing the autobiographical elements of what he called "the least loved of F. Scott Fitzgerald's novels" in "*The Beautiful and Damned*: The Alcoholic's Revenge" (1977), argued that, "despite its defects, [it] is an engrossing and at times moving work" (156) in which Fitzgerald "defiles his own adolescent years by imposing upon them many of his own most recent and still rankling tribulations" (158). In "The Symbolic Function of Food and Eating in F. Scott Fitzgerald's *The Beautiful and Damned*" (1981), George J. Searles contended that, in the novel, "repeatedly, Fitzgerald underlines his characters' lack of substance by drawing attention to their poor eating habits, or by otherwise alluding negatively to food" (15); and Ronald J. Gervais, in "'Sleepy Hollow's Gone': Pastoral Myth and Artifice in Fitzgerald's *The Beautiful and Damned*" (1981), saw it as "a reworking of the pastoral for people who have lost the American pastoral vision as public myth but want it back again as private fantasy" (75).

The Fitzgerald biographies and full-length critical studies of the 1980s remained divided in their opinions of *The Beautiful and Damned*. Matthew J. Bruccoli, considered the preeminent Fitzgerald scholar of his generation, dismissed it as "intellectually pretentious" (165), "flawed by sideshows as well as by inconsistencies in tone and style" (155), in *Some Sort of Epic Grandeur: The Life of F. Scott Fitzgerald* (1981, rev. 1991 and 2002); and André Le Vot, in *F. Scott Fitzgerald: A Biography* (1983), felt that it was a book in which the author "had resorted to dishing up his leftovers" because he "was not yet artistically mature enough to conceive of a novel as anything but a series of incidents, of episodes juxtaposed without artfully machined interlocking" (98). John B. Chambers's good close reading in *The Novels of F. Scott Fitzgerald* (1989) was much more positive than Bruccoli's and Le Vot's; he studied Fitzgerald's first two novels together, concluding that doing so "reveals not only a careful organization based upon a coherent ironic point of view but also evidence that these early works should be viewed as being much closer to *The Great Gatsby* and *Tender Is the Night* than any double vision theory has so far allowed" (90). The two other critical studies of the decade were revised doctoral dissertations that each considered Fitzgerald's second novel within the narrow frame they were pursuing: Dan Seiters's *Image Patterns in the Novels of F. Scott Fitzgerald* (1986) examined transportation imagery, communication imagery, light-dark imagery (at some length), and water imagery (also at length); and Sarah Beebe Fryer, in *Fitzgerald's New Women: Harbingers of Change* (1988) assessed Gloria Gilbert in detail, declaring that she "distinguishes herself from other Fitzgerald women by her impressive degree of self-knowledge, dignity, and fortitude" (29).

If there is a turning point in the direction of the critical reception of *The Beautiful and Damned*, it might well be Andrew Hook's appropriately titled essay "Cases for Reconsideration: Fitzgerald's *This Side of Paradise* and *The Beautiful and Damned*" (1989), which made a compelling case that the two novels were "eminently readable, written with verve, and containing substantial amounts of often self-contradictory emotional honesty and power" (23). Hook reiterated and deepened his appreciation of Fitzgerald's second novel in *F. Scott Fitzgerald* (1992) with statements that are much more emphatic and unambivalent than those of any previous critic: "What is now not in question is that *The Beautiful and Damned* in no way merits neglect. It is a remarkable book" (32), a "novel of manners" in which "[e]very detail seems to count and pretentiousness is replaced by a hard honesty and authenticity that make the analysis wholly convincing" (39). Hook's positive estimate was not shared by

Robert Roulston and Helen H. Roulston in *The Winding Road to West Egg: The Artistic Development of F. Scott Fitzgerald* (1995), which emphasized Mencken's influence in an extended chapter on *The Beautiful and Damned* but also labeled it "Fitzgerald's most negative book" (95) and "sour" (106). Yet Hook's essay and book do seem to have been factors in attracting new serious scrutiny of this hitherto relatively neglected book. One manifestation of this is that, in 1998, three paperback reprintings of *The Beautiful and Damned* appeared, each prefaced with a thoughtful introduction by a major scholar/critic of modern American literature. The most substantial of these was by respected Fitzgerald scholar Alan Margolies for Oxford University Press's prestigious Oxford World's Classics series. Margolies emphasized the novel's recurrent motifs—"the sights, sounds, and smells of New York" (xviii), its portrayal of alcoholics, the "making of movies," and "the mistrust of the upper classes" (xxv)—and praised its "freshness and sense of originality" (xvii). Jay Parini's introduction to the Signet reprinting made a virtue out of what previous critics had cited as one of the novel's defects when he lauded its "collection of brilliant sketches with markedly different tones" (viii), and he rejected another commonplace of earlier criticism when he asserted: "To call *The Beautiful and Damned* transitional is to belittle its achievement. . . . It is the first comment on the American dream in its most illusory aspects" (xiv). Kermit Vanderbilt's introduction to the Penguin edition was useful mostly for its account of the composition of the novel and for its lengthy excerpts from contemporary reviews (vii–xxv).

Accompanying this increased positive critical attention to *The Beautiful and Damned* was an interest in the novel's complex textual history. Two early articles, Matthew J. Bruccoli's "Bibliographical Notes on F. Scott Fitzgerald's *The Beautiful and Damned*" (1960) and James L. W. West III's "The Second Serials of *This Side of Paradise* and *The Beautiful and Damned*" (1979), dealt, respectively, with the two impressions of the 1922 first edition and the seventy-eight corrections made when the novel was republished in 1978 and with the newspaper serializations of Fitzgerald's first two novels that greatly increased their readerships. But the most important textual contributions were the publication in 1990 of the two-volume edition, *The Beautiful and Damned: The Manuscript,* edited by Alan Margolies, volume 2, parts 1 and 2 in the *F. Scott Fitzgerald Manuscripts* multivolume series under Bruccoli's editorship, and Amy J. Elias's "The Composition and Revision of Fitzgerald's *The Beautiful and Damned"* (1990), a very valuable and detailed examination of the substantial differences between Fitzgerald's holograph manuscript of *The Beautiful and Damned* (housed at Princeton and available in facsimile in Margolies's *Manuscripts* edition), the serialized version in *Metropolitan Magazine,* and the published first edition. The culmination of this textual research was West's 2008 definitive edition of *The Beautiful and Damned* in The Cambridge Edition of the Works of F. Scott Fitzgerald, which contains in its introduction a concise description of the novel's gestation and publication history, a carefully researched text with explanatory notes, and an appendix that publishes "The Far-Seeing Skeptics" (421–22), a section of the novel that Fitzgerald extensively revised in proof (introduction, *Beautiful and Damned* xiii–xxix).

The founding of the F. Scott Fitzgerald Society in 1990; the first international conference it sponsored in 1992 (one has been held every two years since then), and the inauguration in 2002 of an annual scholarly journal, the *F. Scott Fitzgerald Review,* have greatly stimulated further study of *The Beautiful and Damned.* The effects of the conferences and journal were twofold: they increased the amount of scholarship and criticism produced on Fitzgerald, and they widened the focus to the full range of his writings. When papers delivered at the conferences were revised and published either in the journal or in books based on conference presentations, scholarship on *The Beautiful and Damned* benefited, both with respect to aspects of the novel covered as well as depth of analysis. Further, these essays were either written by established Fitzgerald scholar/critics and/or had been vetted by them.

The book derived from selected papers at the First International F. Scott Fitzgerald Conference in 1992 at Hofstra University, *F. Scott Fitzgerald: New Perspectives* (2000), included two thoughtful and highly original essays on *The Beautiful and Damned.* Catherine B. Burrough's "Keats's Lamian Legacy: Romance and the Performance of Gender in *The Beautiful and Damned"* focused on how Keats's narrator in *Lamia* "influences the narrative voice" of Fitzgerald's novel and "reveals the narrative's ambivalent presentation of romantic love and the romance genre" (52); and Steven Frye's "Fitzgerald's Catholicism Revisited: The Eucharistic Element in *The Beautiful and Damned"* suggested that "[t]he characters in *The Beautiful and Damned* seek a kind of communion through material glitter that must be doomed to failure, particularly from a Catholic viewpoint, since it is a fatal error to invest mystical significance in just any physical object, particularly those of the secular world" (74).

A second book, drawn from the 1996 Fitzgerald Centennial Conference at Princeton University, *F. Scott Fitzgerald in the Twenty-First Century* (2003), likewise included two essays on *The Beautiful and Damned*. Kirk Curnutt provided an informed examination of the novel's depiction of young people in "Youth Culture and the Spectacle of Waste: *This Side of Paradise* and *The Beautiful and Damned*," asserting that Fitzgerald's first two novels "not only . . . critique outmoded Victorian ideals of maturation . . . they explore the ambiguous power that flagrant displays of youth styles afford people" and "reflect the anxiety of a burgeoning age-consciousness that encouraged the young to maximize their youth before losing it to middle age" (82). Michael Nowlin's "Mencken's Defense of Women and the Marriage Plot of *The Beautiful and Damned*" similarly was more detailed and sophisticated than previous analyses of Mencken's influence, focusing on "the ways in which Mencken may have helped Fitzgerald articulate the radically unsentimental views of heterosexual relations" in the novel (105).

The centrality of New York City in *The Beautiful and Damned*, previously noted by Margolies and others, has been the subject of three recent essays. Both articles on the novel published in the *F. Scott Fitzgerald Review* focus on this topic. Nathalie Cochoy's "New York as a 'Passing Stranger' in *The Beautiful and Damned*" (2005) looked at the depiction of the city "in the light of" Fitzgerald's 1935 essay "My Lost City" (*MLC* 106–15), declaring that the novel "interlaces the melancholic expression of amorous desire and the vocation of the modern city" (69). Pascale Antolin, in "New York in *The Beautiful and Damned*: 'A City of Words'" (2009), went even further into the topic, finding that the city plays three roles: "It provides the novel with a fundamental referential background and . . . the necessary verisimilitude"; it demonstrates the "damaging influence" of "the modern urban world" on "the individual and community"; and while Fitzgerald is "aware of the dangers of progress," he "also appears to be fascinated by its power" (114). The chapter on *The Beautiful and Damned* in Lauraleigh O'Meara's *Lost City: Fitzgerald's New York* (2002) stressed the diversity of the New York neighborhoods depicted and closely read how they each function thematically, noting that Fitzgerald "understood that New York City was near-mythic in stature, complex, contradictory, vast, and dynamic" (47).

In general, the increased attention *The Beautiful and Damned* has received in recent years has been characterized by a tendency to consider it seriously rather than as a work to be mocked or trivialized and to be more positive about it, both in terms of its position in Fitzgerald's career and as an individual literary achievement. Typically, James L. W. West III, in "The Question of Vocation in *This Side of Paradise* and *The Beautiful and Damned*" (2002), asserted that Fitzgerald's second novel "marks the end of [his] literary apprenticeship" and "signals his beginnings as a professional" (50); both it and its predecessor are "considerable achievements" and "searching examinations of the importance of vocation in American life, where ease and riches have always been the material of our dreams" (56). And Michael K. Glenday's chapter on the novel in *F. Scott Fitzgerald* (2012) called it "a real advance" in that it incorporated "within its drama clear signs of what has been regarded as the core theme of [Fitzgerald's] art, 'the need for illusion, and the tragedy that springs from its inevitable failure'" (39).

Other essays on *The Beautiful and Damned* in the past two decades have suggested new ways of approaching the novel. Craig Monk, in "The Political F. Scott Fitzgerald: Liberal Illusion and Disillusion in *This Side of Paradise* and *The Beautiful and Damned*" (1995), viewed it in the context of "the role played by" the Great War in "transforming society," seeing that the war "is the root of the social illusion in the novel" (66). Ross Tangedal's "'At Last Everyone Had Something to Talk About': Gloria's War in Fitzgerald's *The Beautiful and Damned*" (2016) focused more narrowly on "Gloria Patch and her role in Fitzgerald's treatment of war," concluding that "Fitzgerald offers a fascinating and timely portrait of a young wife dealing with war and remembrance from multiple perspectives, from her Midwestern roots to her ascendency within the nouveau riche of New York." She "represents a complex identity indicative of World War I" and "as a conduit for domestic fears, anxieties, and exasperations, all results of the war that changed the world forever" (70).

Jonathan Enfield's very original "As the Fashion in Books Shifted: *The Beautiful and Damned* as Arc-Light Fiction" (2007) dealt with "film's surprisingly complex and pervasive contributions to the novel's plots and themes"; film "is a crucial and overdetermined nexus in the novel's growing anxiety about social change" (671). Enfield looked specifically at such filmic techniques as dissolves, close-ups, flashbacks, and fade-outs as integral in shaping the novel. Madeleine Glaser's brief but intriguing note on "Fitzgerald's *The Beautiful and Damned*" (1993) gets its point of departure from the novel's epigraph, "The victor belongs to the spoils," contending that such plays on words that feature "inverted semantic elements" and that recur three times in the novel are used intentionally to "correlate plot and theme in the text" (238, 239).

Anthony J. Berret and Jonathan Schiff each devoted a chapter to *The Beautiful and Damned* in their recent books about Fitzgerald. In *Music in the Works of F. Scott Fitzgerald: Unheard Melodies* (2013), Berret detailed the presence of popular music in the novel and its contributions to its "poetic structure" (99); and Schiff, in *Ashes to Ashes: Mourning and Social Difference in F. Scott Fitzgerald's Fiction* (2001), suggested new autobiographical elements: Fitzgerald's "parents' half-buried grief and [Fitzgerald's] resultant experience with parental deprivation as an infant" and "Fitzgerald's relationship with Zelda's family [which] informs his portrayal of Gloria and her familial background" (81). In *Fitzgerald and Hemingway on Film: A Critical Study of the Adaptations, 1924–2013* (2014), Candace Ursula Grissom devotes ten pages to a consideration of what she calls "Richard Wolstencroft's independent, revisionist [film] adaptation" of *The Beautiful and Damned* (2008), concluding, somewhat generously in the view of those of us who saw it screened at the 2009 International Fitzgerald Conference in Baltimore, that Wolstencroft's version "focuses on his own philosophical commentary on the state of youth culture in the 21st century, rather than to interpret Fitzgerald's 20th-century views on the subject for a new generation" (81, 82).

The most recent critical biography of Fitzgerald, David S. Brown's fine *Paradise Lost: A Life of F. Scott Fitzgerald* (2017), continues the trend of taking *The Beautiful and Damned* seriously by devoting an extended and thoughtful chapter to it, offering such original observations as, "As a kind of sweeping civilizational commentary, it might plausibly be paired with the politically tinted poetry of contemporaries T. S. Eliot and Allen Tate or the slightly more distant observations of Henrys James and Adams" (135), and "As a social history, *The Beautiful and Damned* offered caustic appraisals of many American institutions, none more so than higher education" (143). Looking forward, J. Bret Maney's essay "Going South: Disaster beneath the Mason-Dixon Line in *The Beautiful and Damned*," which is forthcoming in a collection edited by Kirk Curnutt and Sara A. Kosiba on the Fitzgeralds and the South, dramatizes just how much remains to be said about the novel. Focusing on Anthony Patch's failed military training in camps in South Carolina and Mississippi, Maney plays off the dual meaning of "going south" as both a travel direction and slang for deterioration to explore how *The Beautiful and Damned* demonizes the poverty and ruination of the Deep South. In this regard, the novel departs decisively from the approach of stories such as "The Ice Palace" (*F&P* 36–60), the first of Fitzgerald's three Tarleton stories, in which he generally depicts Zelda Sayre's hometown of Montgomery, Alabama, as genteel and picturesque.

Brown's and Maney's provocative analyses reinforce the current critical status of Fitzgerald's second novel. Still the most understudied of his full-length fictions, it has begun to attract serious critical attention and is no longer simply derided and dismissed as unworthy of exegesis. We are a long way from the dismayed responses of some reviewers in 1922 as well as from Sergio Perosa's description of it as a "pathetic struggle" (37) in 1965, Milton Hindus's calling it "a ponderous case history" (27) in 1968, and Brian Way's "a truly bad novel by any standard" (64) assessment in 1980. One can only hope it will continue to secure its place in Fitzgerald's career by attracting thoughtful and informed commentary.

CROSSING THE "SHADOW-LINE"
TOWARD THE "SOMBRE PATTERN" OF
THE BEAUTIFUL AND DAMNED

Bonnie Shannon McMullen

Had *The Beautiful and Damned* (1922) been published anonymously, few who had enjoyed *This Side of Paradise* (1920) might have recognized Fitzgerald's second novel as the same author's work. Only two years had passed between Scribner's acceptance of the twenty-two-year-old writer's debut novel and the start of the serialization in *Metropolitan Magazine* of his second, and yet, from September 1919 to September 1921, an epochal change in mood and narrative sophistication had occurred. The outward events that followed in rapid succession as Fitzgerald was transformed from an obscure, impoverished Princeton dropout to a best-selling author do little to account for Fitzgerald's accelerating artistic maturity. The 26 March 1920 publication of *This Side of Paradise* made possible his marriage to Zelda Sayre one week later on 3 April. Then came their much-chronicled celebrity lifestyle in New York City and Westport, Connecticut, a first trip to Europe, and Zelda's pregnancy. In the midst of this resounding "success," the couple's only child, Frances "Scottie" Fitzgerald, arrived on 26 October 1921 almost simultaneously with proofs for the book publication of her father's most relentlessly pessimistic novel.

Joseph Conrad, in the 1920 "Author's Note" to *The Shadow-Line* (1917), dedicates his book to his son and the young men of his generation who had just experienced "the change from youth, care-free and fervent, to the more self-conscious and more poignant period of maturer life" (viii).[1] What Conrad addresses is the transition from insouciance to an apprehension of mortality, something that was driven home with unforgettable violence by the Great War.

Although Fitzgerald, to his embarrassment, just missed active service, from 1919 on he would assimilate the war's effects and seek to reflect its meaning in his writing. The energy that might have been expended in combat went into a struggle to hone his art as a means of expressing truths that can only be conveyed through literature. The result of this struggle was a movement in his artistic vision from a world of youthful uncertainty and hope to the "sombre pattern" (258) of maturity dramatized in *The Beautiful and Damned*.

During the two-year period under discussion, this effort is reflected in the short stories that Fitzgerald produced at an impressive pace. At first, with no reason to anticipate the rapturous reception of, and consequent earnings from, *This Side of Paradise,* Fitzgerald wrote out of financial necessity as much as for any other motive. The stories also show how he was trying to work out, in his fiction, the balancing act of pleasing magazine editors in order to sell his stories, whetting the appetite of readers to buy these magazines, and keeping intact his integrity as an artist, something that Anthony attempts, but fails to achieve, in *The Beautiful and Damned* (251–53). Some stories brilliantly demonstrate how he was often able to bury a parable concerning artistic form within a seemingly light story of youthful romance or a conventionally moralistic story of retribution. The stories, considered as a group, appear heterogeneous, as Fitzgerald tried his hand at different approaches, subjects, and genres. Nevertheless, considered chronologically, in spite of overlap, certain groupings are discernible, as his attitudes toward literary form and toward the country about which and for which he was writing developed in subtlety and scope.

COURAGE AT A CROSSROADS

In subject matter, the first four stories appear to range between the sublime and the ridiculous. Nevertheless, just as Fitzgerald himself was daily making artistic choices that would determine his future, these stories all concern characters who face decisions. "Dalyrimple Goes Wrong" (*F&P* 151–68) was written in the late summer of 1919, immediately after Fitzgerald had, for the third time, dispatched *This Side of Paradise* to Scribner's for consideration. It depicts a decorated war hero who finds, once his acclaimed homecoming recedes, that he is broke, with no qualifications to do much about it. Stuck in a menial dead-end job, he concludes that "happiness . . . could be bought with money" and turns to a life of street mugging and burglary (*F&P* 160). Robert Merrill has drawn attention to allusions in the text to that other great warrior turned criminal, Macbeth, allusions that lend a minor-key accompaniment to a largely comic narrative (32–33).[2] Dalyrimple's deliberate decision to abandon conventional morality is rewarded when his employer and the local political power broker decide to put him in the state senate, a gateway to a career in the U.S. Senate. He must sell his soul, however; the sponsorship is conditional on his not having "too many ideas . . . about how things ought to be run" (*F&P* 167).

The story could also be read as a self-reflexive narrative, revealing much about Fitzgerald's state of mind at the time. With very uncertain prospects, like his protagonist, Fitzgerald also believes that money is necessary for the "gratifications of the normal appetites" (*F&P* 160). The completion of *This Side of Paradise,* the painstaking marshaling of the right words in the right sequence, might have seemed to him comparable to Dalyrimple's heroic feats "between the lines" (*F&P* 162). Dalyrimple steals from his fellow citizens, just as Fitzgerald appropriates material wherever he finds it.[3] Even the dead are not safe from a grave-robbing writer, as witness the references in the story's opening salvo: "In the millennium an educational genius will write a book to be given to every young man on the date of his disillusion. This work will have the flavor of Montaigne's essays and Samuel Butler's notebooks—and a little of Tolstoi and Marcus Aurelius" (*F&P* 151). Comparably explicit allusions appear later as Dalyrimple's rebellion gains momentum: "He was more than Byronic now: not the spiritual rebel, Don Juan; not the philosophical rebel, Faust; but a new psychological rebel of his own century—defying the sentimental a priori forms of his own mind—" (*F&P* 160).

Dalyrimple's state of mind as he executes his first burglary might also provide an insight into Fitzgerald's approach to writing. He knows his strengths—"lucrative in intelligence, intuition and lightning decision"—and that "a method preconceived" is less useful than "the skeleton of a campaign" (*F&P* 162). The story also has a proleptic dimension. Having moved from hectic involvement to oblivion (Fitzgerald's seclusion while rewriting *This Side of Paradise* in his parents' top floor room at 599 Summit Avenue in St. Paul, Minnesota, in July and August 1919 must also have seemed like relegation after his years at Princeton and in the U.S. Army), Dalyrimple's reputation will be resurrected by the press. "Linotype is a resuscitator of reputations," he is assured by his patron (*F&P* 167). The hot metal of the machine gun first brought Dalyrimple public acclaim, and hot metal would be Fitzgerald's salvation.

Linotype, literally, "line of type," enabled Fitzgerald's career. Invented in 1884, just twelve years before Fitzgerald's birth, the technology was nearly as revolutionary as Gutenberg and moveable type had been. Linotype made possible newspapers of more than eight pages and caused the proliferation of magazine publishing, crucially important to Fitzgerald's career. It also facilitated the popular reputation of celebrity authors (Douglas and McDonnell 77–78). The parts of a linotype machine correspond, in some respects, not just to a Lewis gun, with which Dalyrimple performed his battlefield heroics, but to the creative writing process. The matrices (matrix from the Old French for "pregnant animal," in turn from the Latin matrix for "dam" or "womb," and mater, "mother") contain the letter forms. These, like bullets in a gun, are stored in a magazine and released by escapements when keys are pressed on a keyboard. For Fitzgerald, escapements brought to the world his stored creative potential, enabling escape from St. Paul bachelorhood and obscurity.

In *The Beautiful and Damned*, Anthony and Gloria, like Dalyrimple, have an unwavering belief in the connection between money and happiness. Their expectation of an inheritance, however, depletes their physical and moral energy to such an extent that when it finally arrives, they are unable to appreciate it. Anthony, bound by the attitudes of his class and education, is incapable of making a Faustian pact such as Dalyrimple's, but he also lacks Dalyrimple's energy and courage to do anything. One sells his soul through too much ambition, the other through too little.

"The Smilers" was also written in September 1919 and, like "Dalyrimple," published in the *Smart Set*. Here, Fitzgerald exchanges a provincial setting for New York, anticipating *The Beautiful and Damned*. "The Smilers" is experimental in style, with the stories of three strangers held together by their association with the figure Fitzgerald refers to as "the plot," Sylvester Stockton (*F&P* 254). Stockton, once a "prize pigeon in the eyes of debutantes," blessed with wealth and leisure, sees not a half-empty glass but one that has never held a drop (*F&P* 256). A former girlfriend, a bond salesman, and a waiter all annoy him by smiling. In his view, these "hollow optimists" smile because "they think they're always going to be happy" (*F&P* 262). All three, in fact, are in personal crisis: the woman is about to leave her husband and children, the bond dealer is ruined by a crash in his investments at the very moment his wife is giving birth, and the waiter's girlfriend has become a dancer in a cheap cabaret because he cannot support her. The tone of the story allows for more than one interpretation. Are these people really too shallow to perceive "the underlying misery" of the world, as Sylvester believes, or should they be commended for presenting a brave face in public, in spite of their private tragedies? (*F&P* 262). Sylvester's pessimism gives him no joy, while darkening the world around him. He can acknowledge no point of view but his own, whereas the others see their place in a wider social fabric. Although Sylvester does not cause the suffering of the other three, his inability to appreciate anything at all makes him a negative social vortex. As an idler with nothing important to do, he foreshadows Anthony Patch in some respects, as well as Tom Buchanan in *The Great Gatsby* (1925) and Anson Hunter in 1926's "The Rich Boy" (*ASYM* 5–42). When Muriel Kane, in *The Beautiful and Damned*, tells Anthony he cannot "park" his "pessimism" in her "sun-parlor" (336), she repeats a phrase from "The Smilers" (*F&P* 255). Privileged but lost characters such as Sylvester, in the end, seem pitiable; Sylvester is mired in misanthropy, while the other three demonstrate grace under pressure. Arguably, however, "The Smilers" highlights a limitation of short-form fiction in the realization of character. We know nothing of the causes of Sylvester's social alienation, while the characterization of Anthony Patch benefits from the way that his outward attitude is shown to be a mask for fear and loneliness, the result of a materially advantaged but emotionally starved childhood.

"Porcelain and Pink," written in October 1919 and published a short three months later in the *Smart Set*, has the subtitle "A One-Act Play." Fitzgerald later included it in *Tales of the Jazz Age* (1922), suggesting that he considered it more of a story in dialogue than a piece for the stage (*TJA* 115–26). Light and witty, the story nevertheless dramatizes psychological complications. It concerns two sisters, the clever but outwardly frivolous Julie, and her physical look-alike Lois, who is serious in dress and demeanor. Julie, from a hidden position in a bath, converses through a window with Lois's suitor, the studious Mr. Calkins. Calkins, believing he is talking to Lois, is aroused to a high pitch of desire and cries, "Lois, I love you . . . I want you" just as Lois herself enters the room, surprising Calkins, who expects to see her in pink (*TJA* 124). She faints from shock, while Julie exits. The sisters are two sides of one person, the repressed, disciplined Lois, reduced to a vulnerable, unconscious body, and the sexually alluring, but evasive, Julie. Through their alternations and juxtapositions, Fitzgerald suggests the contradictions in human motivation and behavior, as both sisters, in opposite ways, manage to avoid a decision with respect to the suitor. The porcelain bath is deeper than expected.

Certain motifs in this story are exploited in *The Beautiful and Damned*. For example, the technically chaste Gloria excites Maury early in the novel by talking to him about her legs, invisible under her dress, and her skin, fashionably tan rather than pink (46–47). Later, when Joseph Bloeckman makes an impromptu visit to the grey house, the Patches' rented home in Marietta, she calls down from a window that she is "in the tub," again tantalizing the imagination of a man she keeps at arm's length (180). The story depicts an uneasiness with female sexuality, and a tendency to divide women between the pure and the sensual. Anthony loves the chaste Gloria but is more relaxed with the lower-class Geraldine (106) or the obliging Dorothy "Dot" Raycroft (286). His alter-ego is the Chevalier O'Keefe and his fanciful story in *The Beautiful and Damned*, who, having retired to monastic seclusion to avoid sexual temptation, falls to his death from a tower when a passing peasant girl stops to adjust her garter (77–83).

"Benediction" (*F&P* 134–50) is a considerably revised version of "The Ordeal," published in the *Nassau Literary Magazine* in 1915 (*S&G* 112–17). Lois, at a turning point in a romantic relationship, visits her brother, Kieth, who is about to take his vows as a priest.[4] Lois embodies in one person the conflicting characteristics of Julie and Lois in "Porcelain and Pink." Kieth, a precursor for the parodic Chevalier O'Keefe, and Lois both face decisions that will bind their futures. Lois, not sharing her brother's faith, pities him for his vocation, thinking, "What a life for a man!" (*F&P* 137). However, like "the smilers," Lois has come to this solemn community determined "to give her very best imitation of undiluted sunshine," in spite of her own preoccupations (*F&P* 137). At the Benediction service, she perceives those around her as "dead men" and Kieth as an "unnatural person," and she faints from the shock of her perception (*F&P* 144–45). Kieth, having cut himself off from the world as a reaction against an early life of dissipation, has projected everything that is missing in his life onto a much younger sister he hardly knows. "I'm awfully in love with my little sister," he declares, referring to her "little white soul," her "white innocence" (*F&P* 143, 148–49). This pressure overwhelms Lois; Kieth's idealization of her makes him unable to understand or guide her. Lois wavers about whether to commit herself to her freethinking lover, and when she finally chooses, it is impossible to know if it will lead to fulfilment or catastrophe. Kieth, meanwhile, kneels for hours before an image of the Virgin, with whom he seems to identify his worldly sister. Kieth's strength is the result of a hard-won discipline, but, in spite of his wayward past, he is naïve about the contemporary world. Lois, courageous in embracing life, needs some firmer principle to anchor her impulses. She shares the beauty and courage of the young Gloria Gilbert, but Kieth, in his commitment to a life of belief and order, represents the opposite of the aimless Anthony. The story is finely balanced, and shows Fitzgerald's breadth of understanding and compassion, as well as demonstrating an evolving attitude toward the Roman Catholicism of his upbringing.

Read self-reflexively, however, the story says more. "Tough-minded" Ignatius Loyola, who founded the Society of Jesus, trained men to "do it and not argue" (F&P 136). Fitzgerald answered an equally exacting call, one that required, not obedience to a hierarchical order but flexibility, imagination, and responsiveness to life in all its permutations. Service to art meant risk-taking and courage, with no organizational support or safety net when things went wrong.

THE HOME FRONT

Three stories that follow deal with family life, dispelling all notions of a "happily ever after." "Benediction" serves as a bridge between Fitzgerald's earliest work and the more narratively complex "The Cut-Glass Bowl," also of October 1919, which appeared in *Scribner's Magazine* the following June (F&P 87–107). Matthew J. Bruccoli describes this supernaturally tinged tale as "moralizing" (*Some Sort* 111), Bryant Mangum as "overly didactic" ("Short Stories" 65). But if that was Fitzgerald's intention, the story sits oddly with the larger body of his work, which depicts a moral universe that includes forgiveness and redemption. True, Fitzgerald had a teacherly, preacherly side to his makeup, but if "The Cut-Glass Bowl" is a moral tale, it is set in a world far harder than the rigid Puritan society that punishes Hester Prynne in Hawthorne's *The Scarlet Letter* (1850). Hester eventually achieves a role on the edge of the community, while her triumphantly beautiful illegitimate daughter marries into the English aristocracy (263). Evylyn Piper, for a much slighter offense of an unconsummated adulterous flirtation with Freddy Gedney, is punished by the estrangement of her husband, Harold, and his business failure, the maiming of her daughter, the death-in-action of her son, and finally, her own premature death. She pays a steep price for what her husband calls "an imprudent friendship" (F&P 91).

The cut-glass bowl, the gift of a vindictive rejected suitor, is a poison chalice supposed to embody Evylyn's qualities: "hard," "beautiful," "empty," and "easy to see through" (*F&P* 88). In maturity, Evylyn has none of those characteristics. As her life darkens, however, she blames herself for the family misfortunes, projecting her misplaced guilt onto the bowl, in a manner similar to the way that Gloria projects her fear of aging and death onto the grey house, which becomes a site of horror to her (197). When Evylyn destroys the bowl, it is, symbolically, an act of suicide (*F&P* 107).

For those determined to find a moral, it might be more rewarding to look at Harold Piper rather than at his wife. Evylyn does all in her power to repair the hurt she has caused her husband, but he rebuffs all her loving overtures with "woodenness" (*F&P* 90). Congratulating himself on his "big way of looking at" Evylyn's indiscretion, he is, "like all men who are preoccupied with their own broadness . . . exceptionally narrow" (*F&P* 90). The "aching silences" that Harold inflicts upon Evylyn dry up "the springs of affection" she felt for him (*F&P* 92–93). His inflexible hardness turns Evylyn old before her time, and it is more Harold's fault than Evylyn's that they eventually come to look "at each other with the toleration they might have felt for broken old chairs" (*F&P* 102), a fate that also befalls the Patches as their marriage deteriorates along with their income (323). The burden of guilt that Evylyn internalizes and projects on her double, the cut-glass bowl, is grossly disproportionate.

Correcting this imbalance in earlier readings, however, leads to an insight into Fitzgerald's larger concern in this story. The Pipers' house, "the nicest smaller house in town," stands in relation to larger houses as a short story stands in relation to the novel (*F&P* 88). Like a well-constructed story, the house gives "the effect of largeness . . . by the open sweep from the spacious music-room, through the library," and from there to the dining room (*F&P* 88). While writing this story, however, Fitzgerald was already meditating the form and theme of his next novel, and a novel, by contrast, like a house of many rooms and passages, has a complexity of construction difficult to apprehend all at once. The cut-glass bowl, in its beauty, transparency, and perfect design, is a microcosm of the smaller house. Bowl and house, however, are empty containers, lacking life. As aesthetic models, they are all form without content.

In "The Birthmark" (1843), Nathaniel Hawthorne dramatized a quest for perfection in the story of how the scientist Aylmer succeeds in removing a small, hand-shaped birthmark from his otherwise flawlessly beautiful wife's cheek but in so doing kills her. Considered a "charm" by earlier admirers, the "hand" is the "bond by which an angelic spirit kept itself in union with a mortal frame" (*Short Stories* 178, 193). Indeed, Georgiana's name connects her to the earth (it comes from Γεωργιος, the Greek word for "farmer"), just as Evylyn's suggests "Eve," from the Hebrew for "life," and life and earth are inextricably connected. Absolute perfection cannot exist in a house, a marriage, a human being, or any work of art that contains life. The cut-glass bowl, in its crystalline completion, is empty, a symbol of death and an aesthetic ideal that is fundamentally anti-art, just as the alcoholic punch it is used for is anti-life. Fitzgerald knew, and demonstrates through this story, that for his highly wrought sentences to breathe, they must also carry the birthmark of human imperfection.

"The Cut-Glass Bowl" is a far cry from the "flapper" stories that surround it in *Flappers and Philosophers,* the author's first short-story collection, published as a follow-up to *This Side of Paradise* in September 1920. For a young, single author at the time of the tale's composition, the insight into a marriage's drift "into a colorless antagonism" and his observations on the once-beautiful Evylyn's passage into middle age are acute, anticipating the extended analysis of the gradual erosion of the Patch marriage. Evylyn "began for the first time to seek women friends, to prefer books she had read before, to sew a little" (*F&P* 93) and "worried about little things" (*F&P* 102). Bravely, she "did her best to be cheerful under the worrying depression of living with a disappointed man" (*F&P* 102). While Evylyn sacrifices herself to domestic duties, Gloria, similarly aging, "has been bent by her environment into a grotesque similitude of a housewife" (349), consoling herself with hectic socializing. Both Harold and Anthony sink into alcoholism.

"Head and Shoulders" (*F&P* 61–86), written in November 1919, marks the beginning of Fitzgerald's long association with the *Saturday Evening Post,* where the story appeared on 19 February 1920. Like "Porcelain and Pink," it derives its energy from the juxtaposition of a flirtatious girl and a scholarly young man. Horace Tarbox, whose name suggests entrapment, is a prodigy who sees the world solely through philosophical abstractions. He is ripe for the picking when the vivacious and very substantial Marcia Meadow, whose name, by contrast, suggests nature and open space, knocks on his study door. Extending the theme beyond "Porcelain and Pink," the infatuated Horace marries Marcia and, to supplement her income as an actress and dancer, takes a job in an export company, reserving his evenings for study. Marcia encourages him, for his health, to exercise at a gymnasium. There, his shoulder-stunts on a trapeze lead to a career at the Hippodrome when Marcia becomes pregnant. Meanwhile, Marcia writes a farcical, modern-day version of Samuel Pepys's diary called *Sandra Pepys, Syncopated*, which becomes an overnight sensation, compared by some to *Huckleberry Finn* (*F&P* 85). To Horace's humiliation, she wins the adulation of the very philosopher, Anton Laurier, whose respect he had long coveted. Once Horace dreamed of returning to Princeton as head of philosophy; now he is invited as head of gymnastics.

This ruefully ambiguous ending to a comic love story seems to foreshadow a later development, when Fitzgerald, by then a married man with a daughter, like Horace, felt that his own authorial standing was threatened by Zelda's writing (Milford 328). The story also offers insight into Fitzgerald's insecurity as an author and fears that he might be compromising his ideals to satisfy a market, a practice Dick Caramel justifies in *The Beautiful and Damned* with arguments that fail to persuade Anthony (160–61).

Marcia and Horace might be seen as representing two sides of Fitzgerald, as he honed his technique to consolidate his authorial identity. His growing mastery of plot, dialogue, narrative structure, and other components of fiction might have seemed to him comparable to Horace's gymnastic stunts. However, if Fitzgerald's intellectual and literary capital was far more extensive than many contemporaries were prepared to acknowledge, that was largely because he had the skill, when it suited him, to hide his sophistication behind a Marcia-like persona. Some of the characteristics of Marcia's manuscript are quite reminiscent of Fitzgerald's own drafts: "sprawly writing," "constant mistakes in spelling and grammar," "weird punctuation" (*F&P* 83). These are easily corrected technical problems, however, and the strengths of Marcia's writing are telling: "a peculiar vividness of phrasing and a haunting undertone of sadness" (*F&P* 84). Only one contemporary author was master of this particular voice. The story also demonstrates Fitzgerald's emphasis on the connections between popular theater and literature, and later, cinema. Anthony's opposition to Gloria's becoming a film actress, and his disdain for Bloeckman, the producer, show him as a man out of step with his time and help explain his own failure to find an audience for his stories (180–81). Written with an engaging lightness of touch, "Head and Shoulders" delivers a sardonic assessment of the difficult balancing act that is marriage, a central theme in *The Beautiful and Damned*.

"Mr. Icky," a parody written as a one-act play, is another product of November 1919. A few exchanges contain memorable one-liners, such as Mr. Icky's interview with his prospective son-in-law:

MR. ICKY: "Is your mind in good shape?"
DIVINE: (Gloomily) "Fair. After all what is brilliance? Merely the tact to sow when no one is looking and reap when everyone is."
MR. ICKY: "Be careful. . . . I will not marry my daughter to an epigram. . . ."
DIVINE: (More gloomily) "I assure you I'm a mere platitude. I often descend to the level of an innate idea." (*TJA* 264–65)

Seen along with "Porcelain and Pink" as an experiment in form, the story has relevance to Fitzgerald's narrative technique in *The Beautiful and Damned*, where a number of pivotal scenes are set apart from the main narrative by being written as a play script, emphasizing the performative aspect of social interchange.[5] The most significant of these is the "Broken Lute" section (227–31), an account of a drunken party at the grey house into which Adam J. Patch walks and, appalled, disinherits his grandson. Three other chapters employ the device as well: "The Three Men" (24–26), a colloquy between Anthony and his friends Maury Noble and Richard Caramel; "A Flash-Back in Paradise" (30–32), a supernatural interlude in which Beauty's spirit of defiance is incarnated in Gloria; and "The Ushers" (131–33), in which Anthony's drunken groomsmen gossip while waiting for the Patches' wedding ceremony to begin.

A NATION DIVIDED

Two stories that follow address divisions of class, gender, and geography in society and in the nation, demonstrating Fitzgerald's move toward a broader canvas. In December 1919's "Myra Meets His Family" (*F&P* 229–53), Fitzgerald, like Dalyrimple, performs heroic feats "between the lines." "Myra," while superficially an entertainment for casual readers, contains buried subject matter that, if overt, would have been unacceptable in a family publication such as the *Saturday Evening Post* (where it appeared on 20 March 1920). In a world where females reach their "prime" at nineteen, Myra is both a type and an individual. Known as "the famous coast-to-coast Myra" (*F&P* 229), she directly prefigures "Coast-to-Coast Gloria" in her celebrity (56). However, at twenty-one, Myra feels "ancient" (*F&P* 231). Her married friend Lilah, suggesting "Delilah," advises her to choose a man and "go after him hammer and tongs" (*F&P* 231). The metaphor has its origins in blacksmithing; and smiths, in European mythology and folklore, have long been associated with black magic. Once held to the fire and hammered on an anvil, a man would lose his former identity, just as Samson lost his strength at the hand of Delilah. If the Ivy League men Myra meets at dances have benefited from their elite educations, they should know that Myra, from the Greek "Moira," means "fate, destiny, or doom."

Although "Myra" is, on the surface, a flapper story with a twist at the end, it concerns a world of subtle class and gender differences resulting in cruelty and violence. Before the story even begins, two of Myra's earlier suitors have died as a result of the war. Knowleton Whitney, whose name suggests he knows the town, has "fought shy" of Myra but soon succumbs to her "fascinating" ways, becoming so "enmeshed in the toils that it was hard to say which was toils and which was he" (*F&P* 231–32).

To escape the "snare," Knowleton sets a humiliating trap for Myra (*F&P* 232). He invites her to his family estate, having hired actors to play his absent family and servants in such a way as to frighten her off. The coup de théâtre is the unveiling of a borrowed "family" portrait of a Chinese woman, indicating a mixed bloodline contradicting the associations of "Whitney."

Myra, whose prejudices Knowleton has correctly guessed, faints "dead away," and at this point in the battle of the sexes Knowleton, holding her unconscious body, appears victorious (*F&P* 246). When the narrative cuts to the next scene, Myra is in bed. She supposes a maid has undressed her, although the last person she saw was Knowleton. Hearing a cry in the next room, she is horrified by the thought of "a Chinese child brought up there in the half-dark" (*F&P* 246). Realizing she has been violated and remembering "ghastly tales she had heard of reversions to type," she weeps from "an intense sense of shame," "her tangled hair spreading like a dark aura round her head" (*F&P* 245, 249). In the Middle Ages, texts in Latin were interlineated in the vernacular for the benefit of less educated readers. Fitzgerald's "writing between the lines," however, presents an accessible main text, with a subtext available only to very careful readers. The novel allowed Fitzgerald more linguistic freedom than popular magazines did, which helps to explain Fitzgerald's occasional impatience with short-story writing.

Dark passions motivate the characters, but they are never allowed expression through speech. Knowleton, too cowardly to confront Myra, instead frightens her with an elaborate charade. Part of the charade involves a demand for "Silence!" and imprecations to "Hush that racket!" (F&P 240, 238). A supposed child's cries are stifled "by the placing of a hand over its mouth" (F&P 241). Myra herself, when trapped into performing before an audience of strangers, instead of expressing indignation, slips into the character of Al Jolson, crossing gender boundaries to impersonate an even greater crosser of boundaries, the Lithuanian-born Jewish entertainer who specialized in appearing in blackface. Myra, realizing the degree to which she has been abused by the now repentant Knowleton, enacts her outrage through a masquerade of her own, a fake marriage ceremony. She outdoes Knowleton at his own game. Silence, where meaning is conveyed by performance, suggests that Fitzgerald is addressing the essence of fictional narrative, where unspeakable truths are delivered in the form of drama and masquerade. By the last chapter of *The Beautiful and Damned*, Anthony and Gloria, increasingly unable to communicate, have "become like players who have lost their costumes" (334), no longer able to perform on the social stage that has been their previous existence.

Myra appears to win this battle, ending up with the girl's best friend, a diamond. However, the Knowleton episode takes place when she is twenty-one. In the introduction, she is twenty-four, a girl who has "given her youth," and although "she does the best she can," she sees little future for herself (F&P 229). Gloria, like Myra, has staked her happiness on her beauty, depreciating as rapidly as the income from Anthony's bond fund. Fitzgerald's preoccupation with the fading beauty of some of his female protagonists—Evylyn, Myra, Gloria, and others—could be connected to a fear that his own power to please through written performance could be limited by time and fashion, and that his store of talent might be expended without any lasting reward.

"The Ice Palace," written in 1919 and published in the *Post* on 22 May 1920, is memorable for the contrast it draws between the North and South. These differences were an inevitable preoccupation for Fitzgerald while courting Zelda. The story also marks the beginning of an examination of the question of American identity and unity in a regionally diverse country, an increasingly important theme in much of Fitzgerald's subsequent work, including *The Beautiful and Damned*, where Gloria has a midwestern background that complicates her adjustment to eastern life (121), and Anthony, losing his bearings in the unfamiliar South, has an irresponsible, arguably exploitative, adulterous affair with a southern girl (270–91). The contrasts of climate, culture, and hence, character, are so vividly drawn that it becomes a question of where to find common ground or a unifying way of being. The picturesque South in "The Ice Palace" is a scene of defeat, decay, and death, death of the will above all. It is a place of "dusty road-street[s]," "dust ruts," "dusty air," "opiate" residential streets, and shops with "yawning doors . . . retiring into a state of utter and finite coma" inhabited by "youths who were always just about to do something" and "gracious soft-voiced girls, who were brought up on memories instead of money" (F&P 36–38). This "languid" scene may be as close to Eden as possible "this side of paradise," but its latter-day Eve, presented "eatin' 'n apple," has rejected what seems like, in Keats's phrase "easeful death" (191), for a future in the North where she hopes to express the side of herself "that makes me do wild things" (F&P 40).

The cold and darkness of the North soon oppress Sally Carrol Happer, culminating in her getting lost in the dark labyrinth of the ice palace. This terrifying experience is a playing out of her inarticulate fears. The North is not just cold, but hard, "a man's country" (F&P 47). Sally Carrol is the center of her social circle at home; however, at a northern dinner party "the men seemed to do most of the talking while the girls sat in haughty and expensive aloofness," exhibiting "spiritless conventionality" (F&P 47, 51). At stake is her very existence as a fully realized, balanced human being, as the climate and people of the North would curtail her development and freeze her expressiveness until she became as "listless" as society demanded (F&P 44). Annihilation of the self, as for Evylyn in "The Cut-Glass Bowl," would be the cost of marriage to Harry and life in the North.

As a model for art, the ice palace, frozen and dangerous, shares the defects of the cut-glass bowl, with the additional feature that one can be lost and trapped in its labyrinthine passageways. The narrative structure of *The Beautiful and Damned*, while moving inexorably forward toward what seems like an inevitable conclusion, consists of episodes and subplots that also dramatize the main characters' entrapment in dark and dangerous patterns that rob them of agency.

Sally Carrol is last seen back in Tarleton eating, not an apple, that hardy fruit of the North, but one that flourishes in mild winters and hot summers, a Georgia peach. The South has reclaimed its daughter, but serpent imagery hints that all may not be well. Her friend Clark Darrow, arriving as before to take her swimming, has appeared "tortuously" from his "very ancient Ford" and "twisted himself a last impossible notch to get a view of her face" (*F&P* 60). As in its "very ancient" prototype, this Eden has its tempter. Clark's invitation to swim in a pool "warm as a kettla steam" may well turn Sally Carrol's joke, "Spect to die any minute," into reality (*F&P* 60). In Robert Frost's "Fire and Ice," published later in the same year as the story, the poet, having considered the superior destructive power of fire, concludes that "for destruction ice / Is also great, and would suffice" (*Collected Poems* 220). In like manner, Fitzgerald envisions two diametrically opposed destructive forces, each answering to different aspects of human nature, and each sufficient to destroy the world. Just as "Myra" dramatizes unresolvable differences of class and gender, so, too, "The Ice Palace" suggests that the cultural and geographical diversity within the United States has the power to destroy the individual who tries to bridge the gap and is a major challenge for the artist writing about and for America.

With its vivid contrasts between northern and southern settings and cultures and its insight into Sally Carrol's state of mind, "The Ice Palace" is the most ambitious in scope of Fitzgerald's stories to date. In *The Beautiful and Damned*, Fitzgerald achieved an even wider national view, with characters moving from New York to California and back through the agrarian heartland, and then to suburban Connecticut, the South, and finally, newly enriched but personally diminished, sailing to a Europe they can no longer enjoy (368–69). The effect is of a restless quest; the structure is multifocal, reflecting unstable characters in an unstable world.

DANGEROUS LIAISONS

Three stories that follow raise issues of social disguise and trust, while showcasing Fitzgerald's brilliance as a literary impresario. In "The Camel's Back" (*TJA* 33–60), serpent imagery employed in "Myra Meets His Family" and "The Ice Palace" is even more conspicuous. Perry Parkhurst is mocked as a "parlor snake," suggesting one whose outward gentility masks threatening intentions (*TJA* 36). His erstwhile fiancée, Betty Medill, appears at a circus ball as a snake charmer.[6] This story, inspired by a real event in St. Paul on 29 December 1919 and, according to the annotated table of contents included in *Tales of the Jazz Age*, written in twenty-two hours just a few weeks later (*TJA* 5), has an impressive richness of allusion that unobtrusively demonstrates the breadth and depth of the author's immersion in several different literary traditions. Apart from the biblical tradition, Fitzgerald's most direct source was probably Keats's "Lamia" (1820; *Selected Poems and Letters* 199–240), which had its source in Burton's *Anatomy of Melancholy* (1621–28), based, in turn on *De vita Apollonii* of Philostratus.[7] Betty's effect on the other guests seems drawn from an unexpected source, namely, Gwendolyn Harleth's appearance in the gambling casino in George Eliot's *Daniel Deronda* (1876). Betty displays writhing snakes on her arms, legs, and back, with "eyes of venomous green," while "wound about her neck was a glittering cobra" (*TJA* 48). Gwendolyn is observed as:

> "A striking girl—that Miss Harleth—unlike others."
> "Yes, she has got herself up as a sort of serpent now, all green and silver, and winds her neck about a little more than usual." (13)

Just as Gwendolen's "Lamia beauty . . . much observed by the seated groups," attracts comments such as "it is wonderful what unpleasant girls get into vogue" (14), so Betty causes "the more nervous among the older women to shrink away from her . . . and the more troublesome ones to make great talk about 'shouldn't be allowed' and 'perfectly disgraceful'" (*TJA* 48–49).

Another text, more familiar to American readers, also lies buried in Fitzgerald's narrative, one that involves a masquerade and an uninvited guest.[8] In Poe's "The Masque of the Red Death" (1842), Prince Prospero has gathered masked revelers in his abbey to escape the plague outside. The Townsends have also assembled "a shouting, laughing medley" of masked figures (*TJA* 48). When the last guest appears, Poe's narrator observes that "in an assembly of phantasms such as I have painted, it may well be supposed that no ordinary appearance could have excited such sensation" (*Tales and Sketches* 674). Similarly, "even amid the luxury of costume and high spirits represented there, the entrance of the camel [Perry and a cab driver] created something of a stir," the crowd "attempting to penetrate the identity of this beast" (*TJA* 48). Prospero's guest is "shrouded from head to foot" (*Tales and Sketches* 675) while, perspicaciously, the camel costume has been taken for a shroud by Perry's other half. The shroud/camel costume marks not only the death of dignity for the man who initially hoped to appear as Julius Caesar but might also have implications for the future of the accidental newlyweds. Significantly, Betty is an Egyptian snake charmer whose repeatedly noted "tawny eyes and hair" recall the "tawny front" of Shakespeare's Cleopatra, Caesar's onetime lover who died from the bite of an asp (*TJA* 48–49, 56, 60; Shakespeare, *Antony and Cleopatra* 269).

Indeed, when Betty proceeds to the altar with her camel to Mendelsohn's Wedding March from *A Midsummer Night's Dream*, she is as deluded as Titania in her infatuation with Bottom wearing the head of an ass, a figure Perry resembles. While Bottom declares that "good hay, sweet hay hath no fellow" (Shakespeare, *Midsummer* 123), the camel would like to eat the woman disguised as a bale of hay, because, he declares, "you're so sweet" (*TJA* 52). Titania wishes to "coy," that is, caress, the ass's "amiable cheeks" (Shakespeare, *Midsummer* 121), just as Betty rests her "brown hand . . . lightly on [the camel's] shoulder, defiantly symbolizing her complete adoption of him" and strokes his "cardboard muzzle" (*TJA* 51, 55). "You're going to belong to the nice snake-charmer ever afterwards," she tells him (*TJA* 54); Titania would possess Bottom as "the female ivy so / Enrings the barky fingers of the elm" (Shakespeare, *Midsummer* 124).

Wherever there is mask and delusion, danger lurks. When the "beast" arrives at the Tates' party, his "muffled steps" and "dark brown form . . . looking down . . . hungrily" cause the dancers to "shriek" in terror (*TJA* 45). Tate, suspecting "an ingenious burglar" (recall Dalyrimple's nocturnal intrusions into neighbors' houses) or "an escaped lunatic," grabs his revolver and locks the library door (*TJA* 46). He, himself, however, will soon be donning a clown costume, and corresponds to Shakespeare's clown Stephano in *The Tempest*. Upon discovering that the four-legged "monster" with two voices is, with respect to one-half, part of his own circle, he responds by offering drink, only to find that the back half requires similar refreshment. This episode drives home the truth of what Mrs. Nolak, the owner of the costume shop, has repeatedly said, "it needs two people," "you have to have two people," "you got to have two people" (*TJA* 38–39). The camel's very form symbolizes the doubleness of Perry, who, again, like the "monster" Trinculo finds in *The Tempest*, can "speak well" with his "forward voice," while "his backward voice is to utter foul speeches and to detract" (Shakespeare, *Tempest* 82–83). When Betty marries the camel, she marries two men, one with the license and the other with the ring, and, significantly, it is Perry's collaboration with his back end that wins her when his earlier unaided efforts failed. The story dramatizes the need to acknowledge the animal side of human nature, something with which Anthony Patch struggles.

The night before his wedding, he is "shaken" by the "animal quality" in the laughter of a woman under his window, reacting with "aversion and horror" (129–30). "Life was that sound out there," and Anthony longs "to live serene and detached back in the corners of his mind" (130). Gloria, when thoughts of childbearing intrude, recalls that "motherhood was also the privilege of the female baboon" (324).

"Bernice Bobs Her Hair" underwent several revisions before its final form in January 1920; originally the manuscript ran much longer and the heroine was named "Barbara" (*Correspondence* 8–9). Much of the story's popularity depends on its insight into the complicated rivalries between teenaged girls. The initially unpopular Bernice is coached and fed lines by her cousin Marjorie, and soon eclipses Marjorie in her own circle. One particularly shocking line is her pretended intention to cut her abundant hair, "a dark-brown glory," and Marjorie vindictively traps her into carrying out this bluff (*F&P* 129). Having done so, Bernice realizes that her opportunity to shine in a small-town arena is over, but at the same time she gains a new strength and confidence. Her last act is severing Marjorie's own blonde braids, "restive snakes" in Bernice's eyes, and throwing them on the porch of her cousin's erstwhile beau on her way to the train station (*F&P* 131). Swinging her grip "like a shopping-bag," she is headed for a new life in New York, where her former "Madonna-like simplicity" would be out of place (*F&P* 133, 129). There, it is implied she will fill her "bag" with more satisfying experiences. In New York, bobbed hair is the coming fashion, a sign of the modern woman. Bernice, potentially, will find herself in the vanguard of a growing movement of social and intellectual freedom. Where bobbed hair is merely a fashion choice, however, as for Gloria Patch, no such satisfactions are likely to follow.

The many revisions that "Bernice" underwent also tell a tale, as each revision resulted in a shortening from the original ten-thousand-word version. Bernice's cropped hair reflects Fitzgerald's writing process, a realization that less is more, a step off the family porch "feeling oddly happy and exuberant" into a challenging but rewarding postwar cosmopolitanism (*F&P* 133). The story's implications are positive, but in *The Beautiful and Damned* Fitzgerald explores the dangers, as well as the attractions, of such cosmopolitanism.

Stories of performance and masquerade demonstrate Fitzgerald's understanding of how all social interaction involves playing a part. In "The Offshore Pirate," Toby Moreland, disguised as the pirate Curtis Carlyle, is supported in his act by his menacing-looking Six Black Buddies, who play a "death dance from the Congo's heart" (*F&P* 29). These unpredictable men lend stature to Curtis as their leader, as well as giving the situation an element of danger and an underlying sexual frisson, working in a similar way to win the lady as the compound nature of the camel.[9]

"The Offshore Pirate" is a maritime version of *The Taming of the Shrew*, although Fitzgerald's reading of this problematical play was arguably ahead of his time. Like Katharina, Ardita is unbiddable. She is violent when crossed, hurling a book and a lemon at her match-making uncle, just as Katharina breaks a lute on Hortensio's head and strikes Petruchio (Shakespeare, *Taming* 85). Toby Moreland, alias Curtis Carlyle, tames, or seems to tame, Ardita by hijacking her uncle's yacht and kidnapping her. Both characters, like Shakespeare's Katharina and Petruchio, are assuming roles. While Petruchio has carefully thought through his courting strategy, refusing to succumb to taunts and insults, so Toby plays the strongman. Petruchio shows great insight when he observes of Katharina, "If she be curst, it is for policy" (Shakespeare, *Taming* 97), for Katharina can only accept a man who can stand up to her apparent bad temper. After the marriage, Katharina turns the tables on Petruchio, pretending compliance when he is unreasonable. Their compatibility is founded on a mutual appreciation of each other's performance. In like manner, Toby sees through Ardita's bad temper, while she perceives that under his "pirate's" disguise "this man was somehow completely pregnable and quite defenseless" (*F&P* 14). She falls for his performance, while recognizing that it is a show, just as Katharina succumbs to Petruchio's assumed brashness. "Set a crank to catch a crank," says Colonel Moreland (*F&P* 34), words that would apply equally to Petruchio's courtship of Katharina. The overriding irony, however, is that, while the women believe they are exercising free will, in fact both matches have been engineered by parents or guardians. There is a lot of money at stake. Petruchio announces from the start, "I come to wive it wealthily in Padua" (Shakespeare, *Taming* 54), while Toby frankly admits, "I've always wanted to be rich—and buy all this beauty" (*F&P* 15).

Another common feature of *The Taming of the Shrew* and "The Offshore Pirate" is the explicit foregrounding of artifice. *The Taming of the Shrew* is a play within a play, performed by hired actors for a drunk who is duped into believing that he is a lord. The role-playing and disguise of the characters parallels the fluidity of identity of the spectators within the play and, by implication, those in the wider audience. In "The Offshore Pirate," there is a similarly focused unreality. The sea is a "blue dream," calling attention to the artificiality of everything that follows (*F&P* 5). The dreamers, however, are not the fictional characters, but the readers. When Toby confesses to Ardita that the entire Florida plot was "invented," he is echoing Prospero's revelation in *The Tempest* that "'These our actors / As I foretold you, were all spirits, and / Are melted into air, into thin air" (Shakespeare, *Tempest* 133). Delighted by the artifice, Ardita, like Fitzgerald's readers then and now, declares, "I want you to lie to me just as sweetly as you know how for the rest of my life" (*F&P* 35). Fitzgerald here seems to be questioning the very premises of realist fiction. The "truth" of the story is Toby's love and bags of "Florida mud" (*F&P* 35). Anthony and Gloria are also in love, but their inability to sustain their performance makes Anthony's inheritance, on which their dream of happiness is based, in the end, little more than Florida mud.

Ardita, in her peevishness, courage, and confidence in her beauty, prefigures Gloria. In a darker note in the story, however, the narrator confesses, "To me the interesting thing about Ardita is the courage that will tarnish with her beauty and youth" (*F&P* 27), a process documented in Gloria's growing disillusionment. In fact, the mood of the story is recapitulated in book 2, chapter 1, "The Radiant Hour," of *The Beautiful and Damned* (115–62). Just as Ardita imagines herself "dancing with a ghost in a land created by her own fancy" (*F&P* 30), so Anthony and Gloria are both "walking alone in a dispassionate garden with a ghost found in a dream" (120).

HONORABLE DEFEAT

The last two pieces return to the question of war and its aftermath, asking, in different ways, if victory is ever possible. "May Day" (*TJA* 61–114), a story written in March 1920, is interesting for its contrast in style and subject with the work that preceded it. Much longer than the *Post* stories, it interweaves several strands of narrative that cohere according to the Aristotelian unities of time, place, and action. All the events take place during about twenty-four hours from 1 May 1919. Characters range from an impoverished commercial artist, his lavishly spending former Yale roommate, a debutante old flame of the artist, recently demobbed soldiers, and socialist agitators and publishers. The confrontation between the socialite and socialist, the silk-stockinged Edith and her brother, Henry, is reminiscent of "Benediction," where two people who love each other inhabit separate, even antagonistic, worlds (*TJA* 96–100). Moreover, they are almost the only characters, apart from waiters and taxi drivers, who are not drunk. Alcohol saturates the rest of the diverse assembly, two drunken soldiers, Carrol Key and Gus Rose, forming a counterpoint pattern to two drunken Yale men, Philip Dean and Peter Himmel, who make their last incoherent appearance as Mr. In and Mr. Out (*TJA* 107–13). All of the truly violent clashes take place between the narrowly nationalistic soldiers and the internationally orientated socialists, accused of supporting Germany in the war. The Yale graduates and debutantes, meanwhile, dance and drink at Delmonico's, oblivious to the turmoil outside and its social and economic implications. Fitzgerald's skillful narrative orchestration, where events involving different characters take place simultaneously, creates a picture of chaos and division as destructive, possibly, as the war that has just ended.

As the opening section makes clear, New York is a huge commercial emporium, where "spenders" come "to buy . . . furs . . . and bags of golden mesh and varicolored slippers" (*TJA* 61). Girls covet "platinum wrist watches" in shop windows (*TJA* 69), just as Gloria, unaware that time is her enemy, hopes to replace her gold watch with "one made in a platinum oblong and incrusted with diamonds" if she gets a movie role (332). The real divide in the story is between those who can buy these things, such as Philip Dean, who amid his spending spree laments that the clothier "Rivers [a fictional Brooks Brothers] couldn't get any more Welch Margetson collars," and his "shabby suit[ed]" former roommate (*TJA* 70, 62). In this world, wealth clings to wealth. Edith feels "revulsion" for Gordon Sterrett when she finds him broken financially and emotionally (*TJA* 86). Poverty, in the eyes of the rich, carries a moral taint; Philip Dean sees an "aura about" Gordon that is "a sort of evil," while Edith tells him he looks "like the devil" (*TJA* 66, 85). The demobbed soldiers and others, unable to participate in the spending carnival, vent their resentment on the socialists who wish to raise their consciousness of social injustice. These two groups have no understanding of each other, and meanwhile, in Delmonico's, the band plays on.

Gordon, a demobbed soldier and a Yale graduate, feels alienated from all. Succumbing to Jewel—who boasts of her wide acquaintance among the "college fellas," an acquaintanceship shared by Edith, and who watches Gordon "with the alertness of a hawk"—Gordon exhibits the same weakness as the crowd who are seduced by the wares on offer in this great emporium (*TJA* 93, 103). When he awakens to find himself "irrevocably married" to Jewel, he commits suicide with a bullet to the head (*TJA* 114).

Both in its setting and in a number of incidents, "May Day" anticipates much of *The Beautiful and Damned*. Gordon's decline into drunken self-pitying poverty parallels Anthony's, just as his affair with Jewel parallels Anthony's affair with Dot. Both men fail to take responsibility for their own actions, let alone for the women they involve in their lives, Anthony reflecting, somewhat preposterously, that "all the distress that he had ever known, the sorrow and the pain, had been because of women" (365). Philip Dean, approached by Gordon for a loan, declines to help (*TJA* 64–68), as does Anthony's former friend Maury when asked for money (355–56). In both works, the physical and social geography of New York is vividly evoked, a labyrinth as inviting and life-threatening as the ice palace.

"The Jelly-Bean" (written May 1920 and published in *Metropolitan Magazine* that October) is the first story that Fitzgerald wrote after his marriage, and both its content and setting, particularly the crap-shooting episode (*TJA* 25–27), show Zelda's influence. In a country where the Horatio Alger or Lincolnian "log cabin to White House" paradigms were prevalent, Fitzgerald preferred to chronicle failure and decline. In "May Day," the "chinless" Carrol Key, who shares part of Fitzgerald's proud family name, has blood "diluted by generations of degeneration" (*TJA* 72). Jim Powell, a contemporary of Sally Carrol Happer in Tarleton, Georgia, has descended through the social hierarchy from a pillared white house on extensive grounds to a room above a garage where he does odd jobs. The energy and willpower, or possibly ruthlessness, that enriched his ancestors has dissipated over the generations, and is symbolized in "The Jelly-Bean" by Jim's "blue eyes faded like a piece of very good old cloth long exposed to the sun" (*TJA* 14). Jim's pathos lies in his consciousness of this decline: "I had a family once . . . and I'm the last of 'em . . . and I ain't worth shucks. . . . People who weren't worth nothin' when my folks was a lot turn up their noses when they pass me on the street" (*TJA* 30). It is hinted that Jim's family has declined as a result of the Civil War, the same war that gave Anthony's grandfather, Adam J. Patch, his start in life. His uncle cannot work his farm in the northern part of the state properly because there are "not enough niggers around" (*TJA* 17). Jim is a man in decline from a family in decline in a region in decline, unable, in this story at least, to find a remedy. Jim retains one quality lacking in the others, however, a capacity for shame. He has used "a dingy subterfuge" to save Nancy when she is losing in the crap game and retains enough pride to regret it (*TJA* 29).

Both Gordon and Jim stand as figures for the artist, albeit artists with tragic flaws of character. Gordon lacks the ability to develop and market his talent, while Jim, with more insight and skill than he knows, has no idea how to use it effectively. He despises the ease with which he makes a winning through a cheap trick, just as Horace Tarbox loses self-regard in performing his gymnastic stunts, because the Hippodrome is not his chosen arena (*F&P* 81–82). Fitzgerald, too, had a facility for story writing that could have, if allowed, degenerated into narrative tricks, enough to win editors and readers but not to satisfy his own high standards. Unlike Dalyrimple, who sells himself to the highest bidder to achieve worldly advancement, Gordon and Jim, who measure themselves against a stricter standard, lack the strength to change the self-destructive patterns they have fallen into. Anthony Patch, his mind focused on future wealth, never seizes the present and wastes it in a maze of dissipation.

SUMMARY AND CONCLUSION

It is impossible to say exactly when the seed that grew into *The Beautiful and Damned* first began to germinate. Fitzgerald's correspondence shows that he made a few false starts, but by July 1920, living in Westport, Connecticut, he was deeply committed to his next novel. His *Ledger* for June records that he was beginning the novel (174), and he wrote to Maxwell Perkins on 7 July that he hoped to finish by 15 September (Kuehl and Bryer 31). Almost inevitably, Fitzgerald missed this self-imposed deadline and took until the following spring to complete the novel. Nevertheless, stories that Fitzgerald wrote after June 1920 cannot be considered to be part of the creative development that culminated in *The Beautiful and Damned,* for by that time the novel was assuming its mature shape.

What then can be learned from a survey of Fitzgerald's stories between "Dalyrimple Goes Wrong" and "The Jelly-Bean"? One of the first things to note is the sheer diversity of subject and style. A common theme in a number of stories is the legacy of the war, from the effects on war hero Dalyrimple to Jim Powell, who never got over. Evylyn Piper loses a son in the war, leading directly to her own death. Myra, somewhat nonchalantly, loses her first two lovers through enemy action and a flying accident. An allusion to Serbia (where the assassination occurred that triggered the Great War) in "The Ice Palace" suggests an irreconcilable difference between Sally Carrol and Harry, between South and North, but the tragedy of war is more strongly suggested by depictions of the defeated Confederacy and "a thousand greyish-white crosses stretching in endless ordered rows" (*F&P* 42). "Bernice Bobs Her Hair" demonstrates how a warlike frame of mind infects even the social activities of provincial adolescents, whereas "May Day" is centrally concerned with the position of recently returned veterans, two of whom do not survive reentry into society. In *The Beautiful and Damned,* the war interrupts the narrative, sending Anthony to a military camp in an unfamiliar region and social milieu where the dislocations he experiences cause moral turmoil and mental instability. Anthony's casual affair with a southern woman, Dot, comes back to haunt him, just as Gordon Sterrett's affair and marriage to Jewel are destructive to him.

Although Fitzgerald is often thought of as the chronicler of courtship and young love, there is little of the latter in these stories. "The Smilers" has a married woman who leaves her husband and children, while Sylvester Stockton, who holds the narrative together, is incapable of affection. "Porcelain and Pink," a comedy of mistaken identity, suggests that love can easily be redirected from one object to another, having more to do with imaginative projection than actual people. "Benediction" presents a celibate priest and his sister who is wavering over whether to embark upon an affair; it is hinted that for both their choices may result in unhappiness. "The Cut-Glass Bowl" dramatizes the first "till death do us part" relationship; tragically, it takes a death to end the double misery. "Head and Shoulders" depicts a genuine, if unlikely, love match that goes wrong when the wife outshines her husband as a writer. Myra plays the courtship game for social position and financial security more than love, which explains her resilience after setbacks. Sally Carrol Happer's initial choice of a northern man has more to do with her fear of southern stagnation than with the particular man. When she discovers that the North can kill her, it is easy to discard the man. Perry Parkhurst wins the elusive Betty by subterfuge, as Toby, the "pirate," wins Ardita. Bernice realizes she has no allies of either sex in the provincial popularity war and leaves for another arena. Edith, in "May Day," sees love as transitory and transferable: "The new love words, the tendernesses learned, are treasured up for the next lover" (*TJA* 87). The "jellybean" gets only a broken heart when he sacrifices his honor for the inconstant

Nancy Lamar. Not one story shows a truly successful relationship. Further-more, although Fitzgerald's women usually fail to find fulfilment in marriage, they are never shown to find happiness outside of marriage either. Marriages are often ill-considered or the result of drunkenness, such as Gordon's in "May Day" or Nancy's in "The Jelly-Bean." In *The Beautiful and Damned*, Fitzgerald, in almost forensic detail, dissects the emotional complexities of a marriage, the fluctuations of feeling and eventual disillusion that evolve as Gloria and Anthony attempt to capture the happiness that their seemingly auspicious union initially promised.

Fighting for his place in the publishing world was, in many respects, Fitzgerald's substitute for active duty. While Dalyrimple performed his heroic feats "between the lines," Fitzgerald did the same, employing the camouflaged heavy artillery of a rich literary heritage, much as Dick Caramel advises Anthony to do, unless his stories are "exceptionally brilliant" (251). Like Divine, Mr. Icky's prospective son-in-law, Fitzgerald understood how to "sow when no one is looking and reap when everyone is" (*TJA* 264).

Many of the stories mirror Shakespeare's plots and are peppered with numerous Shakespearean allusions. As Shakespeare himself usually took his plots from other sources, if Fitzgerald is a thief he is stealing in an honorable tradition.[10] These echoes and allusions give a vertical dimension to contemporary subject matter, stretching far back and down to ancient storytelling traditions and creating resonances and ripples more likely to be felt than consciously recognized by readers. In *The Beautiful and Damned*, where Anthony and Gloria desire Adam Patch's death, and arguably help hasten it when the old man walks in on one of their raucous parties, ferociously disappointing him, one can find a parallel with *Macbeth*.

In addition to Shakespeare, however, many later writers contributed to a style that Fitzgerald made so distinctively his own. The influence of Keats has been widely recognized. Fitzgerald also was alive to contemporary writing, and his affinity with James Joyce, particularly the Joyce of *Dubliners* (1914), has been noted by John Kuehl (*F. Scott Fitzgerald* 10, 57, 63). Internal evidence in some of the stories suggests that Fitzgerald's first encounter with Joyce may have been with the 1914 edition, and not the 1922 edition, which Kuehl notes Fitzgerald owned (*F. Scott Fitzgerald* 36). Shane Leslie, an early mentor, could have introduced Fitzgerald to Joyce's writing, or he could have encountered Joyce's work through Princeton friends such as Edmund Wilson and John Biggs. The emotional dialectic that informs *Dubliners* is the longing to escape a restrictive environment, which is balanced by a deep attachment to a specific locale, a home. Fitzgerald lived through this tension in his own life, and in most of the stories of this period one sees characters who either effect an escape, but at a cost, or fail to make that break, also at a cost. In Joyce's "A Little Cloud," Chandler reflects that "if you wanted to succeed you had to go away" (58). Most of Joyce's characters fail to do so, however. In "Eveline," a girl rejects "escape" and the promise of "life," committed by a vow to her dying mother "to keep the home together," in spite of this "home" being dominated by a violent father (40), just as Evylyn in "The Cut-Glass Bowl" is unable to escape her miserable marriage. The demobbed soldiers, Key and Rose, resemble Joyce's "Two Gallants" (49–60) as do their upper-class counterparts, Mr. In and Mr. Out.

These stories demonstrate that Fitzgerald was immersed in a deep and developing literary tradition, comprising many forms from the told-tale, liturgy, drama, and prose fiction in all its variations. His originality and genius lay in his ability to use his deep imaginative communion with this tradition to create stories and novels both popular and enduring. Unlike Gloria, who comes to feel oppressed by the ghosts of previous occupants of the grey house, messengers of the fate that would ultimately befall her, Fitzgerald allowed his ghosts to inhabit and enrich his small and large houses of fiction. Anthony fails by trying to write down to a popular audience, but Fitzgerald, with a lightness of touch that belies its difficulty, found a way to use, rather than discard, the tradition he was part of to entertain and move generations of readers.

In the stories between *This Side of Paradise* and *The Beautiful and Damned*, starting with "Dalyrimple," there is often a sense that life is happening somewhere else, usually in the East. "May Day," where all the main characters except Jewel Hudson have roots elsewhere, is a vivid depiction of the false attractions, confusions, and dangers of the city, a central theme in *The Beautiful and Damned*. Even Anthony, based in the East, is only two generations from the farm in Tarrytown, and lacks the qualities required for success in an urban setting, as his abortive attempts to find paid work demonstrate. Just as Joyce left Ireland *for* his writing but never left Ireland *in* his writing, Fitzgerald based his values in his provincial background. His troubled characters, looking for some solid ground that they had left along the way, were received by a cosmopolitan audience whose deep but unacknowledged roots were often no farther removed from the American heartland than Fitzgerald's. Like Joyce, Fitzgerald rejected the crystal perfection of the cut-glass bowl for a messier organic expression of life. Compared to the exuberance of *This Side of Paradise,* these stories show a range of characters confronting maturity and assuming, or, more often, failing to assume, adult roles. Fitzgerald's increasing technical mastery, demonstrating his artistic maturity, culminates in the tour de force of narrative construction that is "May Day" and leads to the darker vision that informs *The Beautiful and Damned.* Fitzgerald had crossed "the shadow-line" that defined the formative experience of his generation.

NOTES

1. Fitzgerald's first known mention of Conrad was in February 1920 where, in a letter to Maxwell Perkins, he wrote, "I'm not so cocksure about things as I was last summer—this fellow Conrad seems to be pretty good after all" (Kuehl and Bryer 28).

2. Throughout his life and writing Fitzgerald demonstrated an easy familiarity with Shakespeare's plays and poems. One of his earliest stories, "Tarquin of Cheapside" (1917; *TAR* 196–203), concerns the composition of Shakespeare's "Rape of Lucrece." Shakespeare, in this period, would have been a standard part of the curriculum at the elite educational institutions that Fitzgerald attended.

3. See my discussion of "Dalyrimple Goes Wrong" in "Architecture and Design" 353–62.

4. There has never been an adequate explanation for why Fitzgerald spelled the name with *i* before *e* instead of the standard "Keith," other than he was a habitually poor speller.

5. Fitzgerald also uses the script format in *This Side of Paradise* when dramatizing Amory Blaine's romance with the Zelda-inspired Rosalind Connage (*TSOP* 157–81). The section was originally published in *the Nassau Literary Magazine* as "The Debutante" (*S&G* 144–54).

6. Betty takes her name from the powerful Medill family, founders of the *Chicago Tribune,* which published Fitzgerald's story "The Lees of Happiness" in 1920 (*TJA* 239–60).

7. Another source for the snake imagery in a number of Fitzgerald's stories is possibly John Singer Sargent's well-known 1889 painting of Ellen Terry as Lady Macbeth, wearing a shimmering gown covered in green beetle wings that resembled the scales of a serpent.

8. Fitzgerald was introduced to Poe in childhood by his father, and his life and writing had many parallels with those of Poe. In a letter of February 1920 Fitzgerald mentions both Poe and Shakespeare in a list of writers who were not respected while alive but whose importance outlived that of the businessmen and politicians of their day (*Correspondence* 80).

9. See also Petry 77.

10. In *Shakespeare's Originality,* Kerrigan explores not only Shakespeare's daunting range of sources but the daunting ways in which Shakespeare adapted them, demonstrating that borrowing can result in a higher originality. The same might be said of Fitzgerald.

THE PERIODICAL WORLD OF *THE BEAUTIFUL AND DAMNED*

Kirk Curnutt

Like many F. Scott Fitzgerald fans my age, I experienced *The Beautiful and Damned* in the form neither of a hardback nor a mass-market softcover but in that liminal hybrid of the two, the trade paperback.[1] To be specific, I was introduced to Anthony and Gloria Patch's story through the 1995 Scribner Paperback Fiction edition, a name that sounds almost as fancy as the cover appears. Adorned with a J. C. Leyendecker portrait of the Arrow Collar Man and art-nouveau typography framed by decorative curlicues and borders, the book radiated the glamour one expects of a Roaring Twenties author associated with tuxedos, spats, and gold cuff links. At the same time, my trade paperback was lighter and more flexible than a hardback, far easier to squeeze into the backpack that I still toted in my early years as an assistant professor. Most importantly, my copy was budget friendly: twelve dollars, cheaper than a compact disc of music back then.

Had I entered literary studies a generation earlier, I might not have had the luxury of purchasing an edition so prepossessing and yet affordable. In all likelihood I would have cracked the spine of the Scribner Library paperback. Like other entries in this series that began in 1960 (*The Beautiful and Damned* was no. 90, while *The Great Gatsby* was no. 1), this 1966 edition featured text superimposed over an abstract background of longitudinal grooves that to this day reminds me of the texture of the wood paneling in my parents' basement.

Had I waited longer to acquire the novel, I might have been overwhelmed by options. In 1998, Fitzgerald's pre-1923 work entered the public domain, flooding the market with discount editions of the Patches' cautionary tale. Some were reputable mass-market paperbacks designed for classroom use, such as the Signet Classics edition that featured an introduction by the prolific biographer Jay Parini. (Signet reprints after 2007 added a valuable afterword by Fitzgerald Society cofounder Ruth Prigozy, who passed away in 2017.) Most were cheap knockoffs by fleeting imprimaturs. The e-book revolution that followed circa 2010 only encouraged more publishers to churn out versions riddled with typos because they cut-and-pasted the text straight from Project Gutenberg, the self-proclaimed "world's oldest digital library." The profusion of corrupt editions has perpetuated the perception that *The Beautiful and Damned* is the weakest of Fitzgerald's novels.

Because my Scribner Paperback Fiction edition has served me so well these near thirty years, I own fewer copies of *The Beautiful and Damned* than any other Fitzgerald book. I routinely log into eBay to scour for copies of, say, the Bantam tie-in paperback to the 1949 movie version of *The Great Gatsby,* whose cover features a shirtless Alan Ladd underneath the legend "The Great Novel of the Sinful Twenties." I also collect Bantam's 1950 paperback of *Tender Is the Night,* on which a pensive Dick Diver stares at a naked Nicole Warren high above the Riviera ("The famous novel of a strong, strange love *and a man who risked destruction*"). Yet I have never felt much inclination to scoop up the 1951 PermaBooks edition of *Damned* ("A Searing Tender Story of the Passion and Heartbreak of Youth"), mostly because Robert Stanley's rendering of a baggy-eyed, bemused Anthony seems the antithesis of the kitschy sexiness that post–World War II pulp paperbacks are supposed to radiate. Of the two other copies in my home library, one I consult for copyediting—James L. W. West III's Cambridge Edition (2008)—and one I display in my living room. I will admit to having opened only a handful of times my 2010 Penguin hardback that the celebrated designer Coralie Bickford-Smith created to commemorate the seventieth anniversary of Fitzgerald's death; it is an objet d'art.[2] I like to stare at the metallic spine because it reminds me of holding a first edition at the Scott and Zelda Fitzgerald Museum in Montgomery, Alabama, in 2014—the lone time I ever held a first edition. The perfectly preserved dust jacket made me feel as if I cradled a holy relic. Knowing I could never afford my own first printing, I grew suddenly aware of just how substantial a book in all its 449-page glory *The Beautiful and Damned* is.

THE WORLD OF BOOKS

I spend so much time talking about editions of the novel because an unacknowledged concern of *The Beautiful and Damned* is the status of books in the modern age. The theme is not as obvious as moral and fiscal wastage, but anxieties about the place of print in characters' daily lives reverberate throughout the plot. Most obviously, one foil of Anthony's, Gloria's older cousin, Richard Caramel, writes a best-selling novel, *The Demon Lover,* whose success tempts him into churning out seven subsequent works that are "execrably awful, without sincerity or grace," making his name "almost a byword of contempt" (347).

As critics have suggested, Fitzgerald used Caramel to channel his unease over his uncertain literary standing as his succès de scandale debut, *This Side of Paradise,* was alternately hailed and ridiculed in 1920–21.[3] In mocking this "prosperous, fattening" Harvard man for "writing trash" (344, 347), the twenty-four/five-year-old writer warned himself against pursuing money and fame over art. Lambasting Caramel for sensationalizing "the preposterous actions of a class of sawdust effigies who, one was assured, were New York society people" and for hackneyed plots that "turned . . . upon questions of the heroine's technical purity, with mock-sociological overtones about the 'mad antics of the four hundred'" (252), Fitzgerald allusively educates readers on what type of novel *The Beautiful and Damned* is not: his New York story is not to be confused for the work of Robert W. Chambers (1865–1933), the prolific, multigenre author to whom he was frequently compared before *The Great Gatsby.* The grounds for comparison are tenuous, arising from the popular romances Chambers cranked out that dealt, in a discreet fashion, with the sexual mores of "the younger set" (to quote the title of his 1907 novel). Two metatextual moments link Fitzgerald to Caramel for the express purpose of distancing himself from this Chambersesque hack.[4] At one point, Anthony ridicules Dick for proffering pretentious quotes to reporters, including the line, "the wise writer [writes] for the youth of his generation, the critic of the next, and the schoolmaster of ever afterwards" (161). This declaration, as readers familiar with the biography know, paraphrases a motto Fitzgerald crafted for the 1920

American Booksellers Association conference (*LK* 379). More directly, Caramel late in the novel denounces Fitzgerald's first novel by name: "Everywhere I go some silly girl asks me if I've read *This Side of Paradise*," he complains. "Are our girls really like that? If it's true to life, which I don't believe, the next generation is going to the dogs" (347). The first self-reference seems Fitzgerald's precaution against his glib habit of posturing in interviews, which prejudiced critics against taking him seriously. The second makes clear that Caramel, forty-three by the novel's end, is already too old to appreciate the accomplishment that *Paradise* represents. Both allusions are self-protective strategies for Fitzgerald to deny accusations that he was callow and to promote his literary standards.

The Beautiful and Damned is not just concerned with authorial values, though. Readers' regard for books is as much a subtheme as that of writers. Fitzgerald's second novel is not, as he described *Paradise*, a "romance and reading list" (*Notebooks* 158): it does not name-drop formative books as initiation rites that advance protagonists' intellectual journey. Far from it. Both Anthony and Gloria are dilatory readers, lacking focus and concentration, and their inability to find meaning in literary tradition or the world of ideas is a sign of their superficiality. Anthony's bathtub may come equipped with "an ingenious book-holder," but when he sinks into the "soothing steamings of hot water," he is more apt to stare at the framed photos of "four celebrated thespian beauties of the day," musing "warmly and sensuously" on their pulchritude—a fairly unsubtle suggestion of masturbation (17–18). And although the spoiled heir likes to read in bed, often falling asleep with the lights on, he does so less to expand his mind than to stave off his "hypochondriacal imagination," his fear that "life was a struggle against death" (14).

When it comes to ideas, like his friend Maury Noble, Anthony is "not particularly technical" but, rather, "in love with generalities" (46). Not surprisingly, his attention wanders while reading: "He had been sitting in his apartment trying to read 'L'Éducation sentimentale,' and something in the book had sent his thoughts racing in the direction that, set free, they always took, like horses racing for a home stable" (108). Despite an affinity for Edith Wharton's *Ethan Frome* (1911), Booth Tarkington's *Penrod* (1914), and "some novels of [John] Galsworthy's" (178, 308), Gloria, too, flits from book to book, unreflective and ping-ponging between boredom and tears, never gaining any larger perspective that might forestall the pair's downward spiral. (As if to take another swat at the pompous Caramel, Fitzgerald makes a point of announcing both in the beginning and ending that Gloria refuses to read *The Demon Lover* [124, 364].)

Clearly, the Patches' lackadaisical attitude toward books as fonts of knowledge is symptomatic of their entitled aimlessness and squandered privilege. Fitzgerald's controversial deus ex machina of restoring Anthony's inheritance in the final pages may save them from destitution (367), but the pair learns nothing from their travails. Indicative of their incurable solipsism is the fact that the last book mentioned in *The Beautiful and Damned* is not a historical, sociological, or literary work that might serve as a correlative to their redemption. Rather, the final text is Anthony's childhood stamp book, which he regressively rifles through during his crack-up, his favorite volume symbolizing his ultimate childishness (367–68). For her part, the book that most engages Gloria is her own diary, which she pores over on the eve of her wedding, signaling her self-absorption (125–30).[5]

Throughout the novel then, the couple's intellectual shallowness underscores a deeper fear that texts have become tokens of affluence and conspicuous consumption. Books are mentioned everywhere in the plot, but never as arbiters of culture, only as decor: they are shelved in opulent home libraries and piled up on desks and nightstands, but they are never transformative. During his Harvard years, Anthony spends a portion of his seven-thousand-dollar yearly allowance on a book collection: "He laid the foundations for a library by purchasing from a wandering bibliophile first editions of Swinburne, Meredith, and Hardy, and a yellowed illegible autograph letter of Keats's, finding later that he had been amazingly overcharged" (14–15)—a clear indication that his interest is in the conspicuous display of these symbols of elevated culture, not edification. Later in the plot, when Anthony briefly becomes a stock broker at the "imposing offices of Wilson, Hiemer and Hardy," he gazes contemptuously upon the portrait of a vice president: "In vain did Anthony try to open his mind to the romance of finance; he could think of Mr. Ellinger only as one of the buyers of the handsome leather sets of Thackeray, Balzac, Hugo, and Gibbon that lined the walls of the big bookstores" (193). Despite his snobbery, Anthony is no different from Ellinger, at least when it comes to his personal library: the point of a book collection is for books to be collected, not studied. In this way, Fitzgerald voices his concern that the medium in which he hopes to realize his intellectual capital is merely ornamental, an accoutrement for small imaginations and cheap minds.

THE WORLD OF NEWSPAPERS AND MAGAZINES

Books are hardly the lone textual form *The Beautiful and Damned* evokes. Newspapers also play a role, with the Patches becoming gossip items in the metropolitan dailies after they file their lawsuit to reinstate Anthony's inheritance (248). Long before that plot twist, Anthony expresses disdain for the proletariat nature of the medium's rotogravure sections while enjoying the funnies page, even though his limited attention span causes him immense impatience when he has to explain the humor to his Japanese butler, Tana (166). Just as his mind races while delving into Flaubert, he is too stimulated to comprehend his reading, scouring "down a column of the 'Sun' three times in succession without understanding a single sentence" (106). Fitzgerald also complains that big-city papers stoke narcissistic fantasies so national audiences see only reflections of their own desires, not news or information. As Anthony and Gloria promenade along Broadway, the narrator comments, "The gay habitats of the very rich and the very poor, the very dashing and the very criminal, not to mention the lately exploited very Bohemian, are made known to the awed high-school girls of Augusta, Georgia, and Redwing, Minnesota, not only through the bepictured and entrancing spreads of the Sunday theatrical supplements but through the shocked and alarmful eyes of [columnist] Mr. Rupert Hughes and other chroniclers of the mad pace of America" (63).[6] As Fitzgerald implies, newspapers are one engine of this "mad pace." He even impugns the accuracy of the medium. Before *The Demon Lover*'s runaway success, Richard Caramel works briefly as a reporter for the *New York Sun* but is fired when he produces an account of a military parade he has slept through. Only after submitting his fabrication to his editor does Dick learn the event was canceled due to a snowstorm (69).

At the other circulation extreme, *The Beautiful and Damned* also touches upon the erudite world of academic journals. In a rare burst of productivity, Anthony publishes an essay in the *Florentine,* though for little money and zero response from readers. "Why don't you go over and write about these Germans?," his grandfather demands on the eve of the Great War when Anthony brags of this modest achievement. "Write something real, something about what's going on, something people can read" (174). In the old man's eyes, scholarship—and, by extension, literary criticism—is irrelevant.

More prominent in the novel than either newspapers or academic journals, though, are periodicals. As Anthony seduces his wartime mistress, Dorothy "Dot" Raycroft, she warns they must be quiet: "Mother sits up reading *Snappy Stories*," she whispers (273), referring to the saucy 1912–30 romance pulp whose provocative covers featured scantily clad pinups. When old Adam Patch intrudes upon a drunken revelry at the "grey house" that Anthony and Gloria rent in the village of Marietta (a fictionalized Westport, Connecticut), a New York gossip rag called *Town Tattle* reports on the party's fallout (248). News that the Patches' "brilliant" friend Maury Noble intends to marry a rich Philadelphia woman, implying he is a kept man, is likewise announced in this scandal sheet (337). The name *Town Tattle* should ring a bell to fans of *The Great Gatsby*. In his 1925 classic, Fitzgerald memorably reinvokes this fictional forerunner to *the National Enquirer* when Myrtle Wilson buys a newsstand copy on her way to a Manhattan assignation with Tom Buchanan (*GG* 31). As both Sharon Hamilton and Sarah Churchwell have examined, *Town Tattle* is a barely concealed allusion to the real-life *Town Topics,* a notorious Gilded Age purveyor of high-society rumor that blackmailed the haut monde to keep its names out of its tawdry pages (Hamilton, "New York Gossip Magazine" 34–56; Churchwell, "Scandal Detectives" 1–47).

Notably, Fitzgerald does not mention the magazines in which his own short stories were appearing, whether the *Saturday Evening Post,* the *Smart Set,* or *Scribner's Magazine.*[7] Yet much as he consoles concerns over the status of book culture in American life, he also soothes apprehensions over his dependency on the periodical market to support his novel writing. In an unlikely plot twist, Anthony tries to earn a fast buck writing popular fiction. Not surprisingly, Richard Caramel is the character who encourages him, warning Anthony not to deviate from the formula of commercial short stories if he is serious about cracking the market: "Unless they're exceptionally brilliant, [stories] have to be cheerful and on the side of the heaviest artillery to make you any money" (251). Anthony dutifully "investigat[es] the files of a popular magazine" at the public library to learn what editors want (252). None of the "six wretched and pitiable efforts" he completes sells, however; none contains any "spark of vitality," and "their total yield of grace and felicity" is "less than that of an average newspaper column" (253). Plot summaries of the two titles Fitzgerald cites,

"The Dictaphone of Fate" and "The Little Open Doors," resemble the story lines of didactic efforts Fitzgerald himself produced to finance the writing of *The Beautiful and Damned,* including "The Cut-Glass Bowl" (*F&P* 87–107), "The Four Fists" (*F&P* 169–88), "The Smilers" (*F&P* 254–62), and "The Lees of Happiness" (*TJA* 239–60). As Fitzgerald derisively describes "The Dictaphone of Fate": "It purported to be the sunny tale of an office boy who, quite by accident, hummed a wonderful melody into the dictaphone. The cylinder was discovered by the boss's brother, a well-known producer of musical comedy—and then immediately lost. The body of the story was concerned with the pursuit of the missing cylinder and the eventual marriage of the noble office boy (now a successful composer) to Miss Rooney, the virtuous stenographer, who was half Joan of Arc and half Florence Nightingale" (252). "The Little Open Doors," meanwhile, "concerned the occult: an estranged couple were brought together by a medium in a vaudeville show" (253). In both cases, Anthony blatantly panders to magazine readers: "He offered, in his protagonists, the customary denizens of the pink-and-blue literary world, immersing them in a saccharine plot that would offend not a single stomach in Marietta. . . . After reading it to a bored Gloria [he coaxed] from her the immemorial remark that it was 'better than a lot of stuff that gets published'" (252–53).

Anthony's pathetic efforts hint at the frustration and shame Fitzgerald felt writing for the market. "I am rather discouraged that a cheap story like *The Popular Girl* [*F&P* 263–303] written in one week while the baby was being born brings $1500," he complained to his agent, Harold Ober, just two months before *The Beautiful and Damned* was published, "+ a genuinely imaginative thing into which I put three weeks of real enthusiasm like *The Diamond in the Sky* ["The Diamond as Big as the Ritz," *TJA* 127–68] brings not a thing" (Bruccoli, *As Ever* 36).

As if to distance himself from dismissing his commercial stories as "cheap," he ridicules his protagonist as the true hack, such an amateur that Anthony consults a booklet called *Success as a Writer Made Easy* for tips. Its author, R. Meggs Widdlestein, supplies the all-important artistic advice that submissions should be double-spaced (252). Because the pamphlet cannot teach Anthony creativity or craft, he proves just another "ambitious plumber of the futility of perspiration." As with Richard Caramel, two intertextual "Easter eggs" are planted to distinguish character from creator. Fitzgerald notes that Anthony abandons fiction writing after a mere "thirty-one rejection slips" (253). This number is significantly fewer than the "one hundred and twenty-two rejection slips" Fitzgerald claimed in a 1920 *Saturday Evening Post* personality profile to have pinned "in a frieze about [his] room" as he attempted to become a professional writer just a year earlier (*MLC* 5). Significantly, that apartment was on Claremont Avenue (*MLC* 108), the same street to which Anthony and Gloria relocate at their lowest (334). Fitzgerald implicitly credits his persistence to his rise from these lowly environs, whereas Anthony's dilettantism lands him there.

THE SERIAL VERSION OF *THE BEAUTIFUL AND DAMNED*

The prevalence of references to periodicals throughout the novel underscores a reality that audiences today may overlook: hundreds of thousands more readers consumed the Patches' story through a twenty-five-cent monthly than the fifty thousand or so who purchased the original two-dollar hardback. Enthusiasts recall that the novel was serialized from September 1921 to March 1922 in *Metropolitan Magazine,* with a circulation of 302,202 at the time. Most discussions of Fitzgerald's relationship with the periodical—it also published four short stories, including, most notably, 1920's "The Jelly-Bean" (*TJA* 13–32) and 1922's "Winter Dreams" (*ASYM* 43–65)—focus on the forty thousand words managing editor Carl Hovey chopped from the manuscript. As Amy J. Elias notes, Hovey "pruned incidentals" (descriptive passages irrelevant to the plot) and cut references to premarital sex, abortion, and unpatriotic sentiments (257–58).[8] Due to the excisions, the periodical version has long been considered a lightweight version of the Patches' downfall, generating little critical interest.

There is a more basic reason that the serial version garners paltry attention, though: installments of *Metropolitan* are not easy to come by. On eBay and used-book sites Fitzgerald collectors can purchase original issues of the *Post, Esquire, McCall's, Scribner's, Red Book,* and *Liberty* for as little as fifty dollars; most of these publications are also archived online. Copies of *Metropolitan* from 1921 to 1922, by contrast, are seemingly as rare as a 1909 Honus Wagner baseball card or a Gutenberg Bible. In all my three-plus decades of searching for the seven issues featuring *Damned,* only once has even one popped up for sale on the Internet, in May 2018, and the price quickly shot to four figures. Fitzgerald collections at Princeton and the University of South Carolina house tear sheets of the installments but not complete issues. By my count, in World-

Cat, the OCLC global database of publicly accessible collections, fewer than a half-dozen hard copies of *Metropolitan*'s 1921–22 run are shelved in university holdings.[9] Although they have been out of copyright since 1998, only one issue as of this writing has been digitally scanned for online access—and it did not appear in Google Books, unannounced, until November 2019.[10] Only the Library of Congress offers volumes 54 and 55 for interlibrary loan . . . but only on microfilm. What the Library of Congress cannot readily lend borrowers is a microfilm reader—the machines have been obsolete since the beginning of the millennium, when digital scanning and PDFs became the norm.

The major consequence of *Metropolitan*'s scarcity is that it prevents periodical-studies approaches akin to Jennifer Nolan's excellent work on Fitzgerald stories like "Bernice Bobs Her Hair" (*F&P* 108–33), "The Rich Boy" (*ASYM* 5–42), and "Babylon Revisited" (*TAR* 157–77; see "May Wilson Preston and the Birth of Fitzgerald's Flapper: Illustrating Social Transformation in 'Bernice Bobs Her Hair'" 56–80; "Reading 'Babylon Revisited' as a *Post* Text: F. Scott Fitzgerald, George Horace Lorimer, and the *Saturday Evening Post* Audience" 351–73; and "Visualizing 'The Rich Boy': F. Scott Fitzgerald, F. R. Gruger, and *Red Book Magazine*" 17–33). That is, contextualizing the serial version (and Leslie L. Benton's accompanying illustrations) alongside other *Metropolitan* content is impossible for all but the most industrious of scholars. This situation may be slowly changing: in 2018 Liberty University's digital repository posted an impressive master's thesis exploring how the magazine's advertising complements themes in the installments. But while Anna Sweeney focuses on the juxtaposition of beauty-product ads and Gloria's fixation on her pulchritude (25–28), she does not address the theme of textuality itself—that is, on the cultural standing of books and magazines in Fitzgerald's day. Which is unfortunate, because, as we shall see, printed matter is as celebrated in the ads and stories that surround *The Beautiful and Damned* in *Metropolitan* as the novel itself decries textuality's loss of cultural authority.

This theme is significant because it points to pervasive anxieties over print's status throughout the 1910s and 1920s. Much of this concern blamed the accelerating rate and volume with which texts could be manufactured for enabling their disposability. *The Beautiful and Damned* appeared at the end of what is often called "The Golden Age of Print," the era between 1880 and 1930 when technological innovations—most notably, the linotype machine, which sped up the typesetting process fivefold—made the mass manufacture of print cheaper and speedier. The result was a glut of textual matter. The number of U.S. newspapers peaked in 1914 (the year Anthony and Gloria marry) with 2,042 different titles circulating, up from 850 in 1880. Although this number declined from 1916 to 1922 (in which the latter half of *The Beautiful and Damned* is set), settling at a pre-Depression annual average of 1,942, the number of individual copies nearly doubled from 22 to 39 million (Kaestle and Radway 11). Meanwhile, the number of different magazine titles grew from fewer than 1,000 at the start of the postbellum era to nearly 6,000 by 1920 (Hinnant and Hudson 113).

As the variety of reading options expanded, commentators complained that technology transformed interpretive habits, replacing contemplative reflection with the sensational stoking of excitement. Magazines and popular fiction—the very type of "saccharine" formula stories Anthony half-heartedly attempts (252–53)—were singled out as major agents of this change. Typical was Herbert Ellsworth Cory's 1917 complaint in the *Dial* that the "demand for the short-story" was "artificially stimulated":

> We do not want the short story. We *think* we want it. In our healthier moments we condemn our modern speed mania. In our healthier moments we desire the literature of cool reflection. The very technique of the short story is pathological, and titillates our nerves in our pathological moments. The short story is the blood kinsmen of the quick-lunch, the vaudeville, and the joy-ride. It is the supreme art-form of those who believe in the philosophy of quick results. . . . The incessant readers of the short-story are sufferers from that same nervous irritability which marks alike the capitalist and the labor-agitator when they cry, "For God's sake let's *do* something." (380)

On the one hand, such grumbling simply reiterated condemnations of American fiction dating back to the Revolutionary era, when ministers and educators denounced popular literature for ratcheting emotions.[11] Nor is Cory's complaint much different from contemporary versions of this concern, such as Sven Birkerts's many protests against the Internet's fracturing of attention spans, how "what had once been a singular entity"—concentration—"is now subject to near-constant fragmentation by the turbulent dynamic of life as we live it" ("Reading in a Digital Age"). But while concerns about the "nervous irritability" of reading habits will no doubt continue with whatever "platform" replaces the cybersphere as the next crucible of human consciousness, Cory's warning that the cultural pace precluded "the literature of cool reflection" offers an apt an explanation for why Anthony and Gloria's thoughts race like "horses . . . for a home stable" when they read (108).

The novel even extends this criticism to the cinema, which is blamed for backhandedly influencing fiction. During a night on the town, Richard Caramel quizzes Anthony's rival for Gloria's affection, the movie-industry flak Joseph Bloeckman, on what literary properties are likeliest to be adapted for the screen:

> "I hear all the new novels are sold to the moving pictures as soon as they come out."
> "That's true. Of course the main thing in a moving picture is a strong story."
> "Yes, I suppose so."
> "So many novels are all full of talk and psychology. Of course those aren't as valuable to us. It's impossible to make much of that interesting on the screen."
> "You want plots first," said Richard brilliantly.
> "Of course. Plots first—" (86)

Later on, when Caramel is accused of "writing trash"—he must crank out short stories for steady income because his publisher only pays book royalties quarterly—he admits that the cultural pace negatively affects his art: "I'm certainly writing faster and I don't seem to be thinking as much as I used to" (160). Dick suffers from "sentence-fever," a "sort of intense literary self-consciousness that comes" from "forcing" himself to write on deadline to pay his bills, leading him to "wonder whether any writing is worth while at all—I mean whether I'm not a sort of glorified buffoon" (161).

Caramel's susceptibility to the "modern speed mania" Cory attacks is only one consequence of the ever-expanding industrial capacity for print. The accelerating pace also lent new valence to the metaphor of "trash reading": by the early 1920s, as observers noted, garbage dumps and landfills overflowed with paper rubbish.[12] Maxwell Bodenheim captured the jarring omnipresence of throwaway reading material in his elliptical verse fragment "Garbage Heap" (1922). This poem, which appeared in the New Orleans–based journal the *Double Dealer,* juxtaposes a "woman's garter wast[ing] its faded frills / Upon a newspaper argument" (202), blaming emotional stultification on modern dis-posability. Two decades later, Wallace Stevens surveyed a similar wasteland in "The Man on the Dump" (1942), which features even more references to paper trash: "The dump is full / Of images. Days pass like papers from a press. / The bouquets come here in the papers" (*Collected Poems* 214). More typical if not quite as imagistic was a 1916 editorial in the *Los Angeles Times* that lamented the Golden State's polluted landscape: "Visit our beaches any Monday morn-ing, after a summer-life Sunday. Every get-at-able foot of clean sand has been turned into a garbage dump. Newspapers, greasy popcorn bags, orange peel and egg shells—all the refuse of careless, lazy, unthinking pleasure-seeking throngs is left to defile—not even the cleansing might of the ocean can remove all the contamination" ("Where Only Man Is Vile" 16). While periodicals and papers ended up in incinerators as often as dumps, the sight of them in trash bins suggested the short lifespan of most printed material.

In *The Beautiful and Damned* it is indicative of the utter disposability of texts that the one character who conserves printed matter is the most anti-quated: during the Great War old Adam J. Patch is so obsessed with news from the front he religiously stuffs away reports of casualty counts. "The old man attacked each paper with untiring fury," writes Fitzgerald, "tearing out those columns which appeared to him of sufficient pregnancy for preserva-tion and thrusting them into one of his already bulging files" (174). As I have written elsewhere, one underappreciated theme in the novel is the "spectacle of waste" that results from conspicuous consumption: Anthony and Gloria end up misspending not only their financial capital but their psychological and (admittedly modest) moral reserves until the resource they most squander is their youth (Curnutt, "Youth Culture"). In metaphorical terms, the Patches trash their own lives: they treat their potential like they treat their books—as resources to use up, quickly and dramatically.

Fitzgerald does not extend the theme of wastage to anything resembling an ecological novel—no image is as environmentally arresting as the Valley of Ashes in *The Great Gatsby* (*GG* 27–28). Yet occasional scenes do convey how printed matter was discarded while consumed. Whenever Anthony is agitated, he does not simply read a newspaper—he strews it across his library floor: "The Sunday 'Times,' scattered about his feet, proclaimed by rotogra-vure and editorial, by social revelation and sporting sheet, that the world had been tremendously engrossed during the past week in the business of moving toward some splendid if somewhat indeterminate goal" (92). Similar imagery surrounds Gloria. Late in the book, Anthony returns from the war to discover a strange new addition to the couple's decor: "'Gloria!' His voice was trembling. No answer. A faint string of smoke was rising from a cigarette-tray—a number of 'Vanity Fair' sat astraddle on the table" (296). This reference to the glamorous Frank Crowninshield–edited monthly is curious given Gloria's previously noted fondness for her "beloved moving-picture magazines" (164), a far cry from the literary gilt of Conde Nast's celebrated publication. Perhaps Fitzgerald was cracking an inside joke on Edmund Wilson, who served as managing editor of the periodical in 1920–21, or perhaps the reference dramatizes Gloria's nostalgia for her own extinct chic. In the absence of firm clues, what seems most significant is how the issues' "astraddle" position dramatizes the agitated voracity of Gloria's reading: the magazines are stretched apart and left in disarray before, presumably, their eventual pitching.

Periodical editors rarely responded to accusations that the magazines were literal "garbage." In December 1924, however, *Saturday Evening Post* editor George Horace Lorimer grew infuriated when former contributor Sinclair Lewis took satirical shots at America's most popular magazine in the *Nation*. Lorimer's rebuttal, "The Unpopular Editor of the Popular Magazine," published in the *Bookman*, redresses charges levied against commercial fiction: that it favored "mush and happy endings"; that editors dictated plots; that readers preferred mediocrities from "big names" over innovative unknowns—basically, all of Fitzgerald's indictments of Richard Caramel's and Anthony's efforts to write for market. Lorimer replies with the fairly predictable riposte that critics of popular-magazine writing lacked the skills to produce popular-magazine writing and that their animadversions arose mostly from jealousy. More surprising is his insistence that Lewis's points of attack do not "distinguish between the place of the popular magazine and that of the book" (396). In a printed volume "the author accepts full responsibility for what he says," but "in a magazine his editor shares it with him." And whereas a "book is bought or left on the stalls on the strength of printed or oral criticism," a magazine has the ability to reach "all classes, ages, and conditions. The editor must be their reviewer," ensuring their contents are consistent in quality. The key criterion for a successful issue is "good workmanship," a uniform quality of parts so the overall product is part and parcel of the lifestyle and values of "our popular audience," reflecting its "good sense, good judgment, and good taste" (397). To Lorimer, every issue of the *Post* was constructed with the same standard of craftsmanship as the automobiles, home furnishings, and other goods he advertised. And although "The Unpopular Editor" does not make the point, he also conceived of the *Post* as just as durable as these consumer items. With its gorgeous cover art by Leyendecker, Norman Rockwell, and other leading commercial artists, as well as its interior illustrations, type design, and layout, the *Post* was not designed to be read once and discarded. Subscribers were encouraged to collect and display issues around the house, making the magazine not just a vehicle for selling decor but an essential part of it (Bigelow 30). In other words, the *Post* was as essential a part of a home library as any book.

Unlike Lorimer, Carl Hovey never defended *Metropolitan* from accusations that it was "trash reading." He did, though, like the *Post,* advertise special slip-cases for readers to store their monthly issues, suggesting the magazine did not consider itself refuse. In content terms, the progressive agenda *Metropolitan* advocated overtly in its nonfiction and more obliquely in its fiction promoted the idea that books and magazines were complementary media for audiences to attain culture and knowledge. In doing so, the publication inherently countered the insistence of critics of popular reading that textuality was disposable.

THE TEXTUAL WORLD OF *METROPOLITAN MAGAZINE*

For the first fifteen years after its 1895 founding, *Metropolitan* was the equivalent of a circa 2000 "lads' magazine" such as *Maxim, Stuff,* or *Loaded.* As Frank Luther Mott writes in his magisterial history of American magazines, it had the reputation of a "naughty picture" publication selling "sex sensationalism" (4:47; 5:145)—although what accounted for a salacious photo in the early twentieth century was far from Jazz Age pinups. Despite its reputation, *Metropolitan* even in its early years promoted literacy through the acquisition of books. A typical 1906 advertisement offered readers a promotional tie-in with the Tabard Inn Library of Philadelphia. For the low price of $1.80 per year, a new *Metropolitan* subscriber could select one bound volume shipped in a special Tabard Inn case from a list of twenty literary options, including Wharton's *The House of Mirth,* Jack London's *The Call of the Wild* (1903), Owen Wister's *The Virginian* (1902), and *The Man on the Box* (1902) and *Hearts and Masks* (1905), two popular novels by Harold MacGrath, a prolific contemporary of Robert W. Chambers to whom Fitzgerald was also frequently compared (see note 4 of this essay). Thanks to the collectors' item case, this special edition of contemporary fiction allowed *Metropolitan* readers a fancy but affordable addition to their home library. In other period advertisements, the Tabard Inn Library also offered readers a handsome revolving cabinet that could store as many as one hundred books ("Why Not Operate" 718).[13]

Opportunities in *Metropolitan* to obtain such special editions became even more common after 1912, when the Gilded Age scion Harry Payne Whitney underwrote the purchase of the magazine by an editorial collective coheaded by Hovey. In his 1948 memoir, *Enjoyment of Living,* Max Eastman, who oversaw the short-lived socialist journal *The Masses,* noted the rather bitter irony of a rich man funding a mass-market magazine advocating for a classless society: "The socialist idea flourished to its highest bloom in America in that exciting year," Eastman wrote of 1912. "Harry Payne Whitney, the polo-playing millionaire, rather took the wind out of [*the Masses'*] sails by buying the already popular *Metropolitan Magazine* and installing as its editor a British Fabian socialist named H. J. Whigham" (390). In fact, Henry James Whigham's precise title was president and secretary because his day job was editing *Town and Country,* where he worked until 1935, a decade after *Metropolitan* folded; it was Hovey who oversaw day-to-day operations under the title "managing editor." In practice, the duo worked in tandem, collaborating on editorials, recruiting former president Theodore Roosevelt as a columnist, and soliciting short fiction from a range of major writers across the political spectrum, from Joseph Conrad to the more avant-garde D. H. Lawrence and from the politically conservative Booth Tarkington to his ideological opposite, John Reed. Laura L. Davis explains how the duo's politics shaped the editorial vision of what they humbly dubbed "The Livest Magazine in America":

> As Whigham had noted, stories were to be the draw for popular readers, who, once inside the covers, might be won to agreement with his Progressive views. Readers were offered about six or seven stories per issue, which were not in themselves political, but by featuring female and male protagonists, the working class and the middle and wealthy classes, the fiction suited the magazine's Progressive temper. While not aiming at social edification, the stories depicted complications that might be ethical as well as romantic—and they did not always end happily. As such, they marked some literary progress. (257)

By the time Fitzgerald began appearing in *Metropolitan,* Whitney was losing interest in funding the magazine, and it began to suffer a cash-flow crunch that delayed contributor payments; Fitzgerald's correspondence with Ober in 1921 and 1922 expresses repeated frustration that checks were not arriving in a timelier fashion (Bruccoli, *As Ever* 26–27, 33, 35, 47). Nevertheless, both in content and advertising *Metropolitan* promoted print culture as a stable medium for "social edification" and self-advancement. The seven issues in which *The Beautiful and Damned* was serialized feature a myriad of ads for encyclopedias, self-help guides, and money management. Offers for books, in fact, far outnumber ads for beauty and home products. A significant portion of them promote leather-bound book sets far fancier than even the Tabard Inn editions. Whether collecting the works of famous authors (Shakespeare) or more obscure ones (the journalist William Cowper Brann, known as Brann the Iconoclast), these products are exactly the type of multivolume collections from which Anthony snobbishly and dismissively imagines Mr. Ellinger, the first vice president of Wilson, Hiemer and Hardy, deriving his so-called "fine education" (193).

The insistence on books as tools both *for* and status symbols *of* self-improvement is most evident in a "valuable little book" called *Fifteen Minutes a Day* that the publisher P. F. Collier & Son offered for free to promote Dr. Eliot's Five-Foot Shelf of Books. This fifty-volume set of canonical texts, subsequently known as the Harvard Classics, was first published in 1909–10 and remained in print in various editions until 1973. As 1921–22 ads in *Metropolitan* noted, Dr. Eliot was Charles W. Eliot, the president of Harvard University for forty years (1869–1909), who had distilled the essence of liberal education down to 418 essential selections of poetry, history, science, and biography. Offered as a "guide book to good reading," the sixty-four-page *Fifteen Minutes a Day* was designed to sell recipients on the benefits of a hefty investment that, depending on the specific edition of Eliot's project a reader purchased—and Collier printed several different editions—cost anywhere from $100 to $345, the equivalent in today's dollars of $2,000 to $5,000. "The pleasantest, easiest way to learn to think clearly and talk interestingly," insists the promotional text for the pamphlet. Particularly relevant is the way the sales pitch employs Abraham Lincoln to convince audiences to allow the eminent Dr. Eliot (who died in 1926) to curate their reading: "You, yourself, have probably read as many books as Lincoln read in the first thirty years of his life," the ad proposes, before warning that most audiences' reading habits gained them "only a smattering of knowledge . . . while [Lincoln] gained a liberal education from his." The reason for that mere "smattering" was the wasted effort that went into consuming indiscriminate texts (such as, perhaps, contemporary periodicals): "Why not decide right now—today—that you will stop wasting your reading? Why not say to yourself: 'In my own small way I am going to do what Lincoln did. I will read in such a way that six months from now I will be a bigger, more effective, more interesting man or woman than I am today'" ("Just a Few Great Books" 39). The appeal was wildly successful: by the time of its twentieth anniversary at the decade's end, Dr. Eliot's Five-Foot Shelf of Books had sold some 350,000 sets—not 350,000 individual volumes but 350,000 *complete sets* (Kirsch).

Late in *The Beautiful and Damned* Fitzgerald takes a fairly pointed poke at this type of canon-creating collection. A drunken Anthony encounters Richard Caramel, who invites his fallen friend to his apartment on Forty-Ninth Street, where "four walls [are] lined with books" (346). As Anthony pontificates on the death of poetry, Caramel interrupts him to insist that he has created his own library of essential works—in effect, his own version of Dr. Eliot's five feet of shelves: "I've made an exhaustive collection of good American stuff, old and new," Caramel brags. "I don't mean the usual Longfellow-Whittier thing—in fact, most of it's modern." When Anthony steps forward to peruse this section of the library, he discovers that under a "printed tag" that reads "*Americana*" the once-famous, now-derided writer displays "six long rows of books, beautifully bound and, obviously, carefully chosen." The joke is that between Mark Twain and Theodore Dreiser Caramel has "wedged" in his own eight novels, at least seven of which are "execrably awful" (347). The presumptuousness embarrasses even the author himself, who defensively insists his publishers are promoting him as "The Thackeray of America." Fitzgerald specifically invokes the metaphor of disposable textuality as his intrusive narrator contrasts the dissolute Anthony and Caramel, who is at least working diligently at his profession, even if his books are garbage:

> —And that night while Richard Caramel was hard at toil, with great hittings of the wrong keys and screwings up of his weary, unmatched eyes, laboring over his *trash* far into those cheerless hours when the fire dies down, and the head is swimming from the effect of prolonged concentration—Anthony, abominably drunk, was sprawled across the back seat of a taxi on his way to the flat on Claremont Avenue. (348; emphasis added)

Here Fitzgerald seems conflicted about his literary antithesis: he implies that, however awful a writer Caramel has become, at least he works, unlike the plastered, unemployable grandson of Adam Patch. Yet the disgust for Anthony's alcoholism should not overshadow the Cory-like contempt for the writer's misguided frenzy of pace. With his "great hittings" and "screwings up," Caramel devalues the cultural authority of books by cranking out junk that no one but he will ever collect. Although this specific paragraph appears in the serial version, Caramel's book collection does not. No evidence exists that Hovey cut the satire to shore up the authority of Dr. Eliot's reading guide, yet its absence in *Metropolitan* has just that effect: the final installment of the novel does not question the power of the texts advertised in the adjacent pages to instill culture.

The pamphlet format of Dr. Eliot's *Fifteen Minutes a Day* also points to a significant type of textuality promoted in *Metropolitan*. Such booklets constitute a major proportion of ads in the magazine's early 1922 issues, perhaps a sign of its need to generate new income streams as Whitney's growing disinterest hurtled it toward receivership. In terms of cultural status, a pamphlet, as the suffix "-let" implies, sits somewhere between a book and a periodical: while a stand-alone text like a printed volume, it also resembles a magazine in that it is designed to be disposable. The promotional pamphlets *Metropolitan* offered readers included etiquette guides, diet and weight-loss advice, and nerve treatments. But by far the most intriguing content in an era in which Charles Ponzi's name became synonymous with pyramid schemes came from investment firms offering free tutorials on stocks, bonds, and foreign currency markets. "Scientific Methods of Investing and Trading in Stocks" reads a representative headline of one such booklet that promised expertise in "income building" through strategies from "averaging" to "using stop loss orders" (111). Of course, the pamphlet was not performing a public service; it was a covert sales pitch, aimed at recruiting investors to the firm of Rogers and Sullivan.

As with multivolume book sets, *The Beautiful and Damned* satirizes pamphlets as ephemeral reading. We have already noted an earlier parody of this format when Fitzgerald mocks Anthony for consulting R. Meggs Widdlestein's *Success as a Writer Made Easy* in his desultory attempt at writing commercial short fiction (252). A more developed satire occurs when Anthony returns from the war and finds that amid the 1919 recession jobs are scarce. One morning he happens upon an ad in the newspaper that insists "YOU

CAN SELL!!!": "Why not earn while you learn? Our salesmen make $50–$200 weekly" (312). Gloria encourages him to attend the Madison Avenue seminar the ad promotes, despite his intuition that "it's one of [those] crazy schemes" (312). As one might expect, the meeting turns out to be a marketing pitch: a shady entrepreneur named Sammy Carleton is looking to recruit salesmen to hawk stock in his company, which publishes a series of pamphlets called "Heart Talks" that outline "the principal reasons for a man's failure and the principal reasons for a man's success" (314). Anthony half-heartedly attempts to sell shares in Carleton's dubious publishing company, allowing Fitzgerald to eviscerate the aspirational rhetoric of salesmanship: "Of the chosen few who, in the words of Mr. Carleton, 'were determined to get those deserts that rightly and truly belonged to them,'" Anthony observes of his fellow "Heart Talk" recruits, "less than half a dozen combined even a modicum of personal appearance with that great gift of being a 'pusher.' But they were told that they were all natural pushers—it was merely necessary that they should believe with a sort of savage passion in what they were selling. [Carleton] even urged each one to buy some stock himself, if possible, in order to increase his own sincerity" (317). After multiple rejections, a desperate Anthony gets drunk and harangues employees in a delicatessen:

> "Af'ernoon," he began in a loud thick voice. "Ga l'il prop'sition."
>
> If he had wanted silence he obtained it. A sort of awe descended upon the half-dozen women marketing and upon the grey-haired ancient who in cap and apron was slicing chicken.
>
> Anthony pulled a batch of papers from his flapping brief case and waved them cheerfully.
>
> "Buy a bon," he suggested, "good as liberty bon'!" The phrase pleased him and he elaborated upon it. "Better'n liberty bon.'" . . . His mind made a hiatus and skipped to his peroration, which he delivered with appropriate gestures, these being somewhat marred by the necessity of clinging to the counter with one or both hands. "Now see here. You taken up my time. I don't want know *why* you won't buy. I just want you say *why*. Want you say *how many!*" (319–20)

Intriguingly, Hovey did *not* cut this particular scene when he trimmed the novel for serialization. One thus reads the February 1922 issue aware of a tension between the specious platitudes of "Heart Talks" and the supposed sincerity of the free pamphlets firms like Rogers and Sullivan offered readers. In this case, the passage calls into question the reliability of such booklets to reveal the secrets of success, skewering them as fronts for frauds.

As intriguing as the clash between Fitzgerald's critique of junk reading and these ads' devout promotion of printed matter is, the installments of *The Beautiful and Damned* generate even greater friction when one reads the short stories that accompany them. In keeping with Whigham and Hovey's progressive agenda, references to books, magazines, home libraries, and newspapers depict textuality as an ameliorating social force, completely avoiding the novel's sardonic portrayal of it as devolved. None of these tales is particularly memorable; with the exception of efforts from Stephen Vincent Benét, Noel Coward, and the British mystery writer Henry P. Holt, none of the contributors' names is likely to ring a bell, either. Although positive depictions of texts are plentiful, I will offer a single representative example of how the stories promote print culture and periodicals like *Metropolitan* in particular.

At first glance, October 1921's "Sentimental Solon" may seem a rather disposable goof on the formula romances that were popular magazines' bread and butter. That is, until one recalls that the author's byline, Nancy Boyd, was the pseudonym of Edna St. Vincent Millay, who cowrote the fabulist tale with her younger sister Norma. A few months after the story appeared in *Metropolitan,* Millay supplied, albeit under the anonymous guise of a "celebrated person," the unflattering lede of Edmund Wilson's March 1922 *Bookman* review of *The Beautiful and Damned,* which compares Fitzgerald to a "a stupid old woman" gifted with a diamond (a metaphor for talent) that "she is extremely proud of" but who "in nothing does she appear so inept as in the remarks she makes" about her prized jewel ("Literary Spotlight" 20). The opening paragraphs of Millay's farce might mislead one to expect she employs her piquant intellect in a similar vein to skewer in magazine fiction the same "lack of discipline and poverty of aesthetic ideas" Wilson singles out in Fitzgerald's work ("Literary Spotlight" 22). Yet far from mocking popular fiction, "Sentimental Solon" suggests stories can invigorate readers' lives by providing imaginative models of adventure and passion. In this way, the story's humor is more affectionate than satirical, as far as imaginable from Fitzgerald's caustic depiction of Anthony's "The Dictaphone of Fate" and "The Little Open Doors" or Caramel's *The Demon Lover* and subsequent Robert W. Chambers–styled output.

Millay's hero, Solon P. Bliss, Jr. is a talented storywriter who refuses to allow his father to publish his fiction in the family's mass-market magazine, *Good Stories*. A devotee of art for art's sake, Solon rejects the stock characters and plot twists Old Man Bliss happily perpetuates in the periodical. Informed he will be fired if he does not soon submit a story that fits the publication's target market, Solon scouts Manhattan for inspiration. He quickly begins flirting with a beautiful young woman who dazzles him by acting out a dizzying array of roles and gestures from the types of heartwarming romances *Good Stories* publishes. Norman A. Britton correctly calls these roles "literary stereotypes": as they romp through Manhattan, the girl becomes "the Wonderful Person, Princess, Queen . . . Heroine of the Story, Adventuress, Sultan's Favorite . . . Woman-Who-Just-Loved-Boys," while Solon "is by turns Page, Astrologer, Lord of the Manor, Tired Business Man, Villain, Man of Mystery . . . Her Captor, Boy-She-Had-Known-from-Childhood." But while the story feels like a burlesque, it never denounces or renounces these clichés as *The Beautiful and Damned* does when it chides Anthony's efforts to regurgitate "the customary denizens of the pink-and-blue literary world . . . in a saccharine plot that would offend not a single stomach" (252). Instead, after an accidental separation, Solon and The Girl are reunited in the offices of *Good Stories* when each submits a version of the encounter, and they suddenly realize they have discovered their soulmates. In Britton's words, what starts off as a "spoof of trite literary situations" ends "as a kind of modern fairy tale—self-consciously done—that might have been written by a more literary O. Henry" (36).

Millay and her sister may have intended "Sentimental Solon" as an inside joke on popular fiction, or they may have simply dashed it off for quick cash. (Notably, the tale was not included in *Distressing Dialogues*, Millay's 1924 collection of poetry and fiction published under the Boyd pen name.) Motive is irrelevant, at least when reading the text in *Metropolitan;* alongside other romances and adventure tales in the same issue, "Solon" suggests that popular fiction dramatizes fantasies that readers can enjoy in their own lives with just a little imagination and a simpatico partner. If Solon and The Girl can have such fun, the tale implies, audiences can, too. The story reinforces popular reading rather than repudiating it as trash, as Fitzgerald does: Anthony has none of the imagination of Solon because he sees no connection between print and real life. Coincidentally, the subplot of Anthony's attempts at writing commercial short stories is nowhere to be found in the serial version.

To put it bluntly then, *The Beautiful and Damned* sticks out like a sore thumb in *Metropolitan.* The novel's dour dissection of wealth and marriage seems fundamentally at odds with the generally upbeat story lines of other contents. More importantly, Hovey and Whigham's progressivism encouraged their insistence both in content and ads that books, magazines, and other print media enabled self-improvement and upward mobility. Fitzgerald's critique of junk reading, on the other hand, led him to view the authority of textuality as decaying. Not all of the novel's references to print culture's devolution appear in the serial version, although many do—Hovey cut some, while other passages were added during the final round of revision leading up to book publication. Yet reading the novel alongside the seven issues that feature the installments in their entirety reveals significant friction between text and context. That this endeavor is complicated by the scarcity of surviving copies of the magazine only undermines further the claims of editors in the Golden Age of Print that periodicals were not disposable. At the same time, the possibility that one day an enterprising scholar may scan and post online volumes 54 and 55 of *Metropolitan* suggests texts are only "lost" or unavailable until someone recasts them in a new, widely accessible medium. Until that hope is realized we can only say that Fitzgerald's anxieties about the value of printed works is a central theme that proves *The Beautiful and Damned* is far from trash.

NOTES

1. The invention of the trade paperback is credited to Jason Epstein who, at twenty-two in 1953, founded Anchor Books to publish softcover editions that provided an "upscale" but still-affordable alternative to the mass-market "pocket-sized" paperback market. Epstein was inspired in part by the Armed Services Editions of the World War II era that made available more "quality" fare (such as *The Great Gatsby*) to general readers. Trade paperbacks were largely aimed at collegiate readers until the 1980s, when they became an alternative less to mass-market editions than to expensive hardbacks whose retail prices were breaking the twenty-dollar mark. See the chapter "Young Man from the Provinces" in Epstein's 2011 memoir, *Book Business* (39–68).

2. For a layman's assessment of Bickford-Smith's much-lauded covers, which a decade later remain fixtures on social media and design blogs, see LaBarre.

3. See, for example, Johnson, who (in an essay written in French) calls Caramel "une sorte d'alter ego caricaturé" (42). For a dissenting opinion, see Gillin, who argues, provocatively, that Caramel is a refracted version of Mark Twain as depicted in Van Wyck Brooks's *The Ordeal of Mark Twain*: "Fitzgerald obviously wished to engage Brooks's theme of the great strains that American society places on its talented sons." When Caramel defends his pursuit of popularity by comparing himself to both Twain and Shakespeare, Anthony and Maury "can only nod their

heads in sad disapproval; they presumably have a proper Brooksian sensitivity toward the tragic pitfalls that underlie [Dick's] reefs of thought" (261).

4. Fitzgerald had already sought to distance himself far more overtly from Chambers in a collegiate parody published in *the Nassau Literary Magazine* called "The Usual Thing by Robert W. Shameless" (*S&G* 131–36). By the time *Damned* was published, Fitzgerald had already dismissed Chambers and his ilk as "cheapjacks" in interviews (Bruccoli and Baughman, *Conversations* 43). Even so, the connection persisted: when H. L. Mencken reviewed *Flappers and Philosophers*, he asked rhetorically whether Fitzgerald would "proceed via the first part of *This Side of Paradise* to the cold groves of beautiful letters, or will he proceed via [his short story] 'Head and Shoulders' into the sunshine that warms Robert W. Chambers and Harold MacGrath?" (Bryer, *Fitzgerald: The Critical Reception* 48). MacGrath, like Chambers, was a purveyor of popular fiction.

5. This section is one of the most controversial in the novel inasmuch as Fitzgerald liberally borrowed from Zelda's own diaries for it. Zelda playfully mentions the appropriation in her mock *New York Tribune* review of *The Beautiful and Damned*, suggesting that for her husband, "plagiarism begins at home" (*Collected Writings* 387).

6. Rupert Hughes (1872–1954) was a prolific journalist, novelist, composer, and columnist. His novels, such as *Excuse Me!* (1911), tend to make farcical hay of technological change and the accelerating pace of American life.

7. *The Great Gatsby,* however, does make reference to at least one of Fitzgerald's own bread-and-butter outlets: in the opening chapter, Jordan Baker reads the *Saturday Evening Post* aloud to Tom Buchanan while his wife, Daisy, and narrator Nick Carraway look on (*GG* 22).

8. Hovey (1875–1956) is portrayed rather derogatorily in most Fitzgerald scholarship, which does a disservice to a man who was something of a Zelig figure, thanks in part to his marriage to his former secretary Sonya Levien, who became a major Hollywood screenwriter in the mid-1920s until her death in 1960. (She cowrote the film version of *Oklahoma!* nearing seventy, for example.) For the congenial relationship in the early 1920s between the Fitzgeralds and the Hoveys, see Trower. Despite the friendship, the novel apparently tested Hovey's patience: the January issue labeled installment five as "Part IV," which was the December installment. Hovey did not correct the error in the February or March issues.

9. Earlier issues from 1897 to 1918 are available online, however, at the Hathi Trust through a link to the University of Virginia at https://catalog.hathitrust.org/Record/009793643.

10. The digitized copy comes from the University of Texas at Austin library. The library possesses only volume 56, however.

11. For a survey of these early responses to American fiction, see Baym.

12. See the rather preachy editorials "Trash Reading Matter" and "Don't Read Trash" (both 1916) as examples of this metaphor in action.

13. The Tabard Inn Library also operated as a for-profit version of the "little free libraries" that have been popular in recent decades: store owners could buy the cabinet and an assortment of titles that consumers could trade out for five cents a book.

FITZGERALD AMONG
THE SMART SET

Walter Raubicheck

The differences in form and theme between *This Side of Paradise* (1920), F. Scott Fitzgerald's first novel, and his second, *The Beautiful and Damned* (1922), were partially the result of the author's personal and professional relationships with H. L. Mencken and George Jean Nathan, the editors of the *Smart Set*, the journal that published a number of Fitzgerald's stories between 1919 and 1924.[1] Although paying its authors far less than more popular magazines such as the *Saturday Evening Post*, the *Smart Set* provided a literary cachet that was just as valuable to the young Fitzgerald as the higher paycheck. Mencken, the renowned journalist, editor, essayist, and literary critic, and Nathan, the most respected drama critic in the country, both espoused a satirical, often cynical view of a mainstream America that they regarded as still crippled by a nineteenth-century Puritanism and an early twentieth-century mob mentality. When Fitzgerald began *The Beautiful and Damned* in July 1920 (*Fitzgerald's Ledger* 174), he was definitely responding to the ideas of these two men, but a close study of the book reveals that, in the end, he remained true to his own conceptions of character and destiny and never fully adopted their ideas about the requirements of serious fiction. Identifying those aspects of the novel that do derive from Mencken and Nathan and those that do not reveals much about Fitzgerald's view of both life and literary culture as he and his country entered the Jazz Age.

Mencken spent his entire career working for Baltimore newspapers—first the *Herald* and eventually the *Sun*, where he was employed from 1906 until 1948 as editor, editorial writer, and columnist. He started as a literary critic at the *Smart Set* in 1908 and then became coeditor with Nathan in 1914. Until 1924, when they started the *American Mercury,* which would be more of a cultural review than a literary one, the *Smart Set* was the most sophisticated and progressive literary magazine in the United States, publishing fiction, poems, and plays by such promising writers as Eugene O'Neill, Dashiell Hammett, Edna St. Vincent Millay, Theodore Dreiser, Willa Cather, and even James Joyce. Thus, when the magazine printed Fitzgerald's "Babes in the Woods" in September 1919 (*S&P* 187–95), "Porcelain and Pink" in January 1920 (*TJA* 115–26), "Benediction" (*F&P* 134–50) and "Dalyrimple Goes Wrong" (*F&P* 151–68) in February, and "Mr. Icky" (*TJA* 261–68) in March, his appearances in its pages signified that he was becoming recognized as an important new writer even before his first novel, *This Side of Paradise,* was published on 26 March 1920.

Mencken's reputation by 1920 as a central American cultural figure was due not only to his skills as an editor but also to *The American Language,* a multi-volume work he wrote that first appeared in 1919 and was immensely popular.[2] This study explored and defended how English is actually spoken in the United States, as opposed to the mother country. Mencken also published several collections of essays entitled *Prejudices,* consisting mostly of expanded versions of his magazine pieces. The installment published in 1920, *Prejudices: Second Series,* contained the influential, multipart essay "The National Letters" (9–101) that defined Mencken's own version of what the canon of American literature of the preceding hundred years should actually consist. Mark Twain and Theodore Dreiser emerge as his more recent heroes, Edgar Allan Poe and Walt Whitman as earlier ones. The "Sage of Baltimore" was also the first American to write a book on George Bernard Shaw (1905) and another one on Friedrich Nietzsche (1907), accomplishments that were remarkable for many reasons, not least of which is the fact that Mencken was largely an autodidact, his formal schooling having ended when he graduated in 1896 from the Baltimore Polytechnic Institute. Nevertheless, by the time he published the first series of *Prejudices* in October 1919, he seems to have read extraordinarily widely in American, English, and Continental literature and to have formed definite and highly original critical opinions about everything and everyone he read.

Nathan, in addition to serving as coeditor of the *Smart Set,* was in charge of the theater reviews and essays, and by 1920, he had come to prominence as America's foremost drama critic. He worked tirelessly to bring attention to Eugene O'Neill, whom he recognized as the first American playwright to produce work on a par with European dramatists such as Anton Chekhov, Henrik

Ibsen, and August Strindberg. He befriended and encouraged the playwright while striving in his own work to create an audience that could appreciate O'Neill's experiments. At the same time, he encouraged and befriended the young author of short fiction and one completed novel, F. Scott Fitzgerald. Although as a writer Nathan primarily produced drama reviews and criticism all his life, as a coeditor of the *Smart Set* he proved himself to be a knowledgeable and perspicacious reader of all kinds of fiction and poetry as well.

The *Smart Set* appealed to a sophisticated readership that was suspicious of mainstream American platitudes about democratic ideals—which were indistinguishable from what *The American Credo,* a volume composed by both Mencken and Nathan in 1921, calls "the Presbyterian code of ethics": "We are both opposed to moral enthusiasm, and never drink with a moral man if it can be avoided" (xxii).[3] Considering Fitzgerald's Catholic background and the occasional Puritan attitudes towards sex that characterize *This Side of Paradise,* it is somewhat surprising that he responded so wholeheartedly to the two editors' consistent attack on traditional values.[4] Nevertheless, he clearly relished the chance to associate himself with such literary luminaries as his professional career began.

Of the two editors of the *Smart Set,* Mencken had the strongest influence on Fitzgerald's craft. In 1920, the year that saw the publication of his first novel as well as his marriage to Zelda, Fitzgerald began a correspondence with Mencken and met with him occasionally when the latter came to New York from Baltimore. Yet between 1920 and 1922 Nathan was closer personally to both the Fitzgeralds, who began socializing regularly with Nathan in New York and Westport, Connecticut. As biographers note, he enjoyed a fairly bold flirtation with Zelda during this period that seemed to fire up the competition at the heart of the couple's often fractious relationship.[5] During this same time, Fitzgerald also began writing *The Beautiful and Damned* and creating the character of Anthony Patch. The novel features a major character, Maury Noble, who is largely based on Nathan and who espouses many of the cynical ideas that characterize *The American Credo.* So while it might be accurate to say that Mencken was an intellectual influence and Nathan a more personal one, the character of Maury Noble indicates that the novelist believed that his portrait of young contemporary New York writers and intellectuals needed to foreground a character with Nathan's distinctly ironic wit and cultural sophistication.

Mencken particularly championed the work of Theodore Dreiser, believing that serious American novelists should realistically portray the decline of individuals whose abilities are thwarted by the narrowness of their culture. The term "naturalism" began to be applied by academic critics to Dreiser's work and that of the Norris brothers, Frank and Charles, largely because of the perceived influence of the French naturalist writer Émile Zola. However, to understand how Mencken influenced the creation of *The Beautiful and Damned* we need to look past assumptions about Mencken and naturalist writers as well as the confusing historical relationship between naturalism and realism as literary terms. As Michael Nowlin points out, "Mencken's tastes were in fact far more catholic than the popular association of him with naturalism would suggest, and his impact on *The Beautiful and Damned* is far more manifest in its irreverent, cynical attitude toward contemporary American pieties" ("Naturalism and High Modernism" 181). Although Mencken championed the group of American novelists who were becoming known as naturalists, Mencken himself never applied the term "naturalist" to Dreiser. In fact, he all but dismissed any influence of Zola on Dreiser: "Dreiser, in point of fact, is scarcely more the realist or the naturalist, in any true sense, than H. G. Wells or the later George Moore, nor has he ever announced himself in either the one character or the other—if there be, in fact, any difference between them that any one save a pigeon-holing pedagogue can discern" (*American Scene* 149). As usual with the Baltimore Sage, the fact that the American authors considered to be "naturalists" often adopted a skeptical attitude toward Puritan and Victorian values is what he admired in their works rather than their emphasis on heredity and environment as shapers of character. For him the only meaningful fiction is that which discards the moral absolutes of America's Protestant past and, instead, as he says in "The National Letters," presents "the significant conflict between a salient individual and the harsh and meaningless fiats of destiny, the unintelligible mandates and vagaries of God. . . . [W]e see him sliding downhill, his character in decay. Character in decay is thus the theme of the great bulk of superior fiction" (*Prejudices: Second Series* 40–41).

In a well-known inscription in the copy of *Paradise* that Fitzgerald sent to Mencken in 1920, he wrote, "As a matter of fact Mr. Mencken, I stuck your name in on page 224 of the last proof [of *This Side of Paradise*]—partly I suppose as a vague bootlick and partly because I have since adapted a great many of your views" (*Correspondence* 57), an admission that alerts us to the fact that Mencken's influence began as early as 1919. Amory Blaine, the protagonist of *This Side of Paradise*, specifically mentions Frank Norris's *Vandover and the Brute* (1914), Dreiser's *Jennie Gerhardt* (1911), and Harold Frederic's *The Damnation of Theron Ware* (1896) as "excellent American novels" discovered "through a critic named Mencken" (*TSOP* 195), an opinion shaped by Fitzgerald's recent reading of the critic. In February 1920 Fitzgerald wrote to Perkins that "[a]nother of my discoveries is H. L. Mencken who is a factor in present day literature. In fact I'm not so cocksure about things as I was last summer—this fellow Conrad seems to be pretty good after all" (Kuehl and Bryer 28).

What had Fitzgerald read before he came under Mencken's influence? In *This Side of Paradise* Amory's reading at Princeton, both in and out of the classroom, is a fairly accurate description of Fitzgerald's own during the years 1913–18 (Kuehl, "Scott Fitzgerald's Reading" 58–89). The texts include the standard Romantic, Victorian, and Edwardian English authors; a representative sampling of early twentieth-century Catholic writers such as G. K. Chesterton, Robert Hugh Benson, and Compton Mackenzie; and contemporary middlebrow American authors such as Booth Tarkington. Significantly, there is no mention of the American naturalists Frank Norris and Stephen Crane, nor of novelists of manners such as Henry James and Edith Wharton. Fitzgerald was, of course, exposed to literature as it was taught in school, prep school, and the university in early twentieth-century America: English literature was the real thing, after the Greek and Latin classics. For example, when Burne Holiday mentions Walt Whitman to Amory, both he and Tom D'Invilliers acknowledge that they have not read him. Burne refers to Whitman as a "definite ethical force . . . he's tremendous—like Tolstoi. They both look things in the face, and somehow, different as they are, stand for some of the same things" (*TSOP* 118). Fitzgerald's formal education preceded by at least a decade the codifying of the nineteenth-century American canon of Poe, Emerson, Thoreau, Hawthorne, Melville, Whitman, Dickinson, and Twain. It was Mencken more than anyone else, especially in *Prejudices: Second Series,* who introduced Fitzgerald to these giants of the American nineteenth century. As always, Mencken championed writers striving to rise above their Puritan environment—by which Mencken even meant the worldview of the most popular nineteenth-century American authors, such as the liberal Christians Longfellow, Bryant, and Holmes, just as much as more conservative Congregationalists or Presbyterians.

Fitzgerald first read a "naturalistic" novel in 1919, Charles Norris's *Salt.* In 1921 he wrote:

In the dawn I wrote him [Norris] an excited letter of praise. To me it was utterly new. I had never read Zola or Frank Norris or Dreiser—in fact the realism that now walks Fifth Avenue was then hiding in Tenth Street basements. No one of my English professors in college ever suggested to his class that books were being written in America. Poor souls, they were as ignorant as I—possibly more so. But since then Brigadier General Mencken has marshaled the critics in [an] acquiescent column of squads for the campaign against "Philistia." (*LK* 143)

Note Fitzgerald's use of the term "realism," as opposed to "naturalism," a designation that was clearly more significant for him, inasmuch as it represented a rejection of nineteenth-century genteel assumptions about literature. For Fitzgerald, 1919 was a turning point. Under Mencken's guidance, he rejected Victorian and Edwardian models of the novel and instead embraced more contemporary templates; he intended *The Beautiful and Damned* to be classed with the modern "realists," not with the earlier fiction that had led to *This Side of Paradise*.

Significantly, Mencken associates Dreiser with Joseph Conrad instead of Zola. As he writes in "Theodore Dreiser": "Of the general ideas which lie at the bottom of all of Dreiser's work . . . [i]n their main outlines they are not unlike the fundamental assumptions of Joseph Conrad. Both novelists see human existence as a seeking without a finding; both reject the prevailing interpretations of its meaning and mechanism; both take refuge in 'I do not know'" (*American Scene* 123). Here lies the crux of Mencken's impact on Fitzgerald: as he developed his second novel, the novelist made "character in decay" the keynote to the story of Anthony Patch and his wife, Gloria, who both take refuge from their own weaknesses in the skeptical view that their lives can only be a "seeking without a finding." But their decay is not the result of heredity and environment, of atavistic impulses overwhelming conscious intentions, as it is in Zola and to some extent in Frank Norris and Stephen Crane. Nor is it the direct result of social pressures. Instead, Anthony, unlike his predecessor Amory Blaine, is unable to "do the next thing," as Monsignor Darcy had urged Amory to do in order to become a "personage" rather than merely a "personality," an attractive but ineffectual individual who, like Anthony, can never attain the discipline to perform any meaningful work (*TSOP* 101). The result was a protagonist whose conflict represents a necessary step toward the author's creation of Jay Gatsby, he of the "gorgeous" personality (*GG* 2).

While the "personality/personage" dichotomy can be pushed too far as a critical assessment of the characterization in Fitzgerald's early fiction—who is a "personality" and who is a "personage" in "May Day" (1920; *TJA* 61–114) or "The Diamond as Big as the Ritz" (1922; *TJA* 127–68), for example?—it does point to a recurring moral concern in the totality of Fitzgerald's work, attaining its strongest expression in Charlie Wales's recognition in "Babylon Revisited" (1931) that "character" is the basis for human relationships (*TAR* 161). Fitzgerald replaced the earlier titles "La Belle Dame sans Merci," the title of one of Keats's most well-known poems (*Selected Poems and Letters* 171–74), and "The Flight of the Rocket" with *The Beautiful and Damned* because he wanted to stress the novel's ethical theme, not its secondary elements of Romantic self-fulfillment.[6]

The strongest connection between *The Beautiful and Damned* and naturalism, then, is not determinism but precisely what Mencken valued in Dreiser: a skeptical view of human possibilities. It is also, like most naturalist novels, a long book, at 449 pages Fitzgerald's longest. The first third, to use Henry James's terms from "The Art of Fiction" (1884, rev. 1888), does move toward the novel of "selection" as opposed to the novel of "saturation" in that it focuses on a concentrated period of the protagonist's life—the year of his courtship of Gloria and the beginning of their married life—and on crucial incidents within that concentrated period (53–162; see James, *Art of Criticism* 177).[7] However, the remainder of the novel, and especially book 3, covers several years of Anthony and Gloria's deterioration, as well as a long section detailing Anthony's experience as a recruit and his affair with Dorothy "Dot" Raycroft, the young girl he meets while in army camp (270). In constructing Anthony's character, Fitzgerald follows the model of *Sister Carrie* (1900), describing each step in the gradual but steady process of his decay, just as Dreiser does with George Hurstwood, who, after he meets Carrie, gradually declines from a prosperous bar manager to a beggar on the street. Thus, although *The Beautiful and Damned* should not simply be classified as a naturalist novel, it shares some of the typical characteristics of the genre, particularly in the American (as opposed to the French) mode. Bryant Mangum summarizes its status best when he claims that several of the early stories and *The Beautiful and Damned* represent Fitzgerald's "flirtation with naturalism" ("Short Stories" 65).

The first Fitzgerald fiction that reveals that he has been thinking seriously about Mencken's mandate to reshape American literature is "May Day," published in the *Smart Set* in July 1920. Mencken liked to talk about the American "mob-man, a savage set amid civilization," as he wrote in "On Being an American" (*American Scene* 17), and in this text Fitzgerald dramatizes the mob mentality in action during the attack on the office of the socialist newspaper the *New York Trumpet* (based on the real-life daily the *New York Call*) (*TJA* 99–102). The suicide of the once-promising Gordon Sterrett at the story's end (*TJA* 114) demonstrates that Fitzgerald now agrees with some of Mencken's convictions about what constitutes serious fiction, particular his preference for "character in decay." However, Ronald Berman has convincingly argued that the characters in the novelette have "no *internal* connection to Mencken's ideas about life in America": "This beginning work has a powerful and accomplished understanding of the mind's variousness. . . . [Mencken] assumed that character was static, predictable, and socially determined; [Fitzgerald believed] that it was governed—as Edith Bradin [the major female character in the story] realizes—by 'the twist of her imagination'" (56–57). Edith's sudden decision to leave the Delmonico's dance by herself and seek out her socialist brother is an action that belies her age, social class, and breeding (*TJA* 92).

What Berman says about characterization in "May Day" is likewise true of *The Beautiful and Damned*. Anthony must confront varied social forces, including the all-controlling factor of money represented by Adam J. Patch, his plutocrat grandfather; the commercial imperatives of the advertising industry and the motion picture industry that he experiences; and, for the first half of the novel, the expectations and demands of the Ivy League postcollege environment of hotel cocktail lounges, university clubs, and weekend parties, a world fueled largely by alcohol. He fails to convince his grandfather that he is worthy of the promised inheritance, he fails to conform to or understand the worlds of business, and he succumbs to the excesses of his postcollege leisure class.

But in Fitzgerald's world, social behavior is a direct outcome of his protagonists' self-image or philosophy of life, such as Gatsby's "Platonic conception of himself" (*GG* 118), attitudes of which they are more or less conscious as they encounter their social challenges and interpersonal conflicts. Anthony Patch is markedly different from Amory Blaine in their fundamental attitudes. Amory concludes at the end of Fitzgerald's first novel that "I know myself . . . but that is all" but also that "he could not tell why the struggle was worth while, why he had determined to use to the utmost himself and his heritage from the personalities he had passed" (*TSOP* 260, 60). By contrast, Anthony Patch, six years older than Amory is when we last see him, has moved decidedly toward nihilism. The omniscient narrator, commenting on Anthony's indolence, claims: "In justification of his manner of living there was first, of course, The Meaninglessness of Life. As aides and ministers, pages and squires, butlers and lackeys to this great Khan there were a thousand books glowing on his shelves, there was his apartment and all the money that was to be his when the old man up the river should choke on his last morality" (51). As for his occasional lapses into guilt for not doing the writing that he has claimed to his grandfather will be his life's work, normally "the notion of sitting down and conjuring up, not only words in which to clothe thoughts but thoughts worthy of being clothed—the whole thing was absurdly beyond his desires" (22). It is this basic conviction of the uselessness of all work, especially intellectual and creative work, that is most responsible for his precipitous decline as he approaches thirty. His cynicism is matched by Gloria's: "From her conversation it might be assumed that all her energy and vitality went into a violent affirmation of the negative principle 'Never give a damn'" (172). It can be argued that their intellectual "environment"—the early twentieth-century atheistic *Weltanschauung* derived from the thought of Darwin, Freud, and Nietzsche—has shaped their attitude toward life. Yet Maury Noble, the character based on Nathan whose darkly ironic speech about the cynical nonbelievers who created the Bible is the novel's most rhetorically effective outburst of cynicism—"Let's join together and make a great book that will last forever to mock the credulity of man" (217)—never fully succumbs to Anthony and Gloria's hedonism.

At the close of Fitzgerald's first novel, we believe that Amory will achieve something significant as he moves on in life from Princeton and his military experiences—as Fitzgerald wants us to believe. However, he wants us to judge Anthony and Gloria completely differently, as the title of the second novel implies. This is not another bildungsroman; it is a tragedy in which Anthony Patch succumbs not to Mencken's "harsh and meaningless fiats of destiny" but to his own inner weaknesses, more evidence that Fitzgerald wanted to follow Mencken's dictum about "character in decay" as the hallmark of serious fiction but do it according to his own particular psychological insights.

In more superficial matters Mencken's influence can be felt throughout the novel: Anthony's scorn for "Bilphism," or theosophy (46, 69, 115), matches Mencken's own ("the so-called philosophy of India['s] ... only coherent contribution to Western thought has been theosophy—and theosophy is as idiotic as Christian Science" [*Minority Report* 37]). "The Voice" in the "A Flash-Back in

Paradise" section tells the platonic Beauty that she will now enter a "land whose wisest are but little wiser than its dullest; a land where the rulers have minds like little children and the law-givers believe in Santa Claus" (30), a passage that closely resembles many comments in any number of Mencken's writings, such as, in "On Being an American," "Third-rate men, of course, exist in all countries, but it is only here that they are in full control of the state, and with it of all the national standards" (*American Scene* 14). The fatuousness of the "social reforming" of Anthony's puritanical grandfather is an embodiment of what Mencken, in "On Being an American," calls the American "savage," who is "the most meticulously moral of men; there is scarcely an act of his daily life that is not conditioned by unyielding prohibitions and obligations, most of them logically unintelligible" (*American Scene* 17). And here is the summation of a minor character, one of Anthony's drinking companions in the latter part of the story: "He was nine out of ten people that one passes on a city street—and he was a hairless ape with two dozen tricks. He was the hero of a thousand romances of life and art—and he was a virtual moron, performing staidly yet absurdly a series of complicated and infinitely astounding epics over a span of threescore years" (342). At these times the nameless narrator seems to be the voice of Mencken, the great debunker, himself, decrying the ubiquity of his favorite target, the "booboisie" (*American Language* 506).

Fitzgerald the moralist clearly intends Anthony and Gloria to be responsible for their own declines, yet the narration can give the impression that they are both victims of impersonal forces, some social and some metaphysical, that cannot be resisted. Consider this passage from late in the novel:

> She wondered if they were tears of self-pity, and tried resolutely not to cry, but this existence without hope, without happiness, oppressed her, and she kept shaking her head from side to side, her mouth drawn down tremulously in the corners, as though she were denying an assertion made by someone, somewhere. She did not know that this gesture of hers was years older than history, that, for a hundred generations of men, intolerable and persistent grief has offered that gesture, of denial, of protest, of bewilderment, to something more profound, more powerful than the God made in the image of man, and before which that God, did he exist, would be equally impotent. It is a truth set at the heart of tragedy that this force never explains, never answers—this force intangible as air, more definite than death. (341)

Here we have a fictional approximation of Mencken's view, cited earlier, that life consists of "the significant conflict between a salient individual and the harsh and meaningless fiats of destiny." Twenty years later this philosophy would have been labeled "existential," implying, as it does, the absurdity of existence. But in the early 1920s, it is a Nietzschean idea filtered through Mencken and utilized by Fitzgerald in his attempt to inject a modern conception of tragedy into his novel.

The perspective of the novel's ostensibly objective narrator is actually as pervasive as that of Nick Carraway in *The Great Gatsby*. As Matthew J. Bruccoli points out, "The authorial voice is intrusive and usurps the qualities of a first-person narrator; it analyzes, soliloquizes, and engages in discourses with the reader" (*Some Sort* 156). Where this technique becomes particularly problematic is in the narrator's use of figurative language. In *The Great Gatsby* the first-person, retrospective perspective makes it obvious that Nick supplies most of the imagery about "the incomparable milk of wonder" (*GG* 134) and the "count of enchanted objects" (*GG* 113) in his attempt to interpret Gatsby's behavior and history. But Anthony has had the education and has the potential talent to poeticize his own reactions, so when the narrator claims that "[w]hen Anthony spoke it was with the surety that his words came from something breathless and desirous that the night had conceived in their two hearts" (90), are we to assume that it is Anthony whose mind has devised the trope of conception? Or is the narrator supplying the figure to convey the character's inchoate emotion? If we read the language as Anthony's, and I believe that we are meant to assume it is, then throughout the section of the novel in which he courts Gloria, Anthony's Romantic sensibility is quite appealing, so much so that he is hard to reconcile with the Anthony of the second half of the novel and in general with the narrator's ironic tone. This disparity contributes to the common response of readers since the novel's publication that the book is uneven and lacks coherence, and these criticisms are a direct result of the tension between Fitzgerald's innate temperament and the cynicism he imbibed from his relationships with Mencken and Nathan.

We are finally left with an ambivalence about the cause of Anthony's and Gloria's decline, an ambivalence that stems from the author's own. Richard Caramel sees Anthony's nihilism as the main cause. In their final conversation he says: "I used to listen to you and Maury when we were young, and I used to be impressed because you were so consistently cynical, but now—well, after all, by God, which of us three has taken to the—to the intellectual life? I don't want to sound vainglorious, but—it's me, and I've always believed that moral values existed, and I always will" (345). This claim that Anthony is ruined by his lack of "moral values" can be borne out by several episodes in the novel—in particular the drunken revel that is interrupted by his grandfather's impromptu visit to the Patches' rented grey house in Marietta (230–31), causing Anthony's disinheritance. Notably, this assessment comes from Richard Caramel, a writer whose first novel was a critical and popular success but who has continued to write less and less acclaimed and successful books, though his ego will not permit him to see how his talents have faded. Is this self-deluded character a reliable judge of Anthony? Here the narrator's irony leaves the reader with no barometer by which to measure Anthony and Gloria's dissipation or their ulti- mate "victory" at the end of the book, when the courts settle his grandfather's contested will in their favor, but too late to save Anthony's mental equilibrium.

Certainly, irony is the novel's most prevalent tone. From its epigraph ("The victor belongs to the spoils") through its opening sentence ("In 1913, when Anthony Patch was twenty-five, two years were already gone since irony, the Holy Ghost of this later day, had, theoretically at least, descended upon him" [11]), to Anthony's final self-deluded comment, "It was a hard fight, but I didn't give up and I came through!" (369), *The Beautiful and Damned* is a testament to that very Holy Ghost. Fitzgerald wanted his second novel to be a "modern" novel in the sense that would please Mencken, and he found the ideas at hand in his reading of his mentor's essays and the novels Mencken led him to read. But these ideas ran counter to his own idealism and his deeply felt instincts about the centrality of moral character and self-discipline that would reassert itself in *The Great Gatsby*. After he had begun his new novel in 1924, he wrote to the editor of *Adventure* magazine: "The B & D was a better book than the first but it was a false lead . . . a concession to Mencken. . . . The business of creating illusion is much more to my taste and talent" (*Correspondence* 139). Indeed, he had come to realize that instead of stressing the Meaninglessness of Life, his real theme was meant to be a tragic Platonism, his deep sense of our continual beating against the current in pursuit of an ideal. In *The Beautiful and Damned* the characters' nihilism and the cynicism of the nameless narra- tor were "concessions to Mencken," but not the beautiful prose that describes the meeting of Anthony and Gloria and their passionate courtship and early months of marriage, nor the analysis of the consequences of the failure to "do the next thing" that had been "told" but not "shown" in *This Side of Paradise*. But all "illusions," and particularly the Keatsian illusion so central to Fitzgerald that "truth and beauty were in some way entwined" (344), are undercut by the novel's ironic tone and plot.

In addition to Fitzgerald's innate Romantic temperament, another feature working against the irony of the novel is his lingering Catholicism. For example, despite his intellectual milieu, Anthony is considering writing about the Middle Ages and the Renaissance popes, and he even begins "a Chestertonian essay on the twelfth century" (161), a surprising remnant of the Catholicism of Amory Blaine and the influence of Fitzgerald's adolescent mentor, Monsignor Cyril Sigourney Fay (1875-1919), who died during the influenza epidemic. Chesterton is mentioned several times in *This Side of Paradise* (*TSOP* 55, 119, 153, 195) and was clearly an author the young Fitzgerald read either at the Newman School or at Princeton or both; in 1918 he referred to his "Romantic Chestertonian orthodoxy" (*Fitzgerald: A Life in Letters* 18). In addition to "Benediction" (1919) and "Absolution" (1924; *ASYM* 78–93), the several references to Chesterton indicate that throughout the late teens and well into the twenties, Fitzgerald was still sensitive to the Catholic milieu of Fay and the Newman School. Indeed, the novel is dedicated to Nathan, Perkins, *and* Shane Leslie, the Catholic writer introduced to Fitzgerald by Fay, who originally recommended Fitzgerald to Scribner's.

In addition to Catholic medievalism, another influence on the novel that he did not derive from Mencken is the *élan vital* of Henri Bergson, whom Fitzgerald read in 1917 during his last year at Princeton (Bruccoli, *Some Sort* 77), as he did William James and Arthur Schopenhauer. At first Anthony flippantly couples Bergson with Bilphism together with the "one-step" as faddish topics of light conversation (46) in an ironic manner that is reminiscent of Mencken. As for Fitzgerald himself, the evidence in his fiction up to and including *Gatsby* points to a more serious response to the French thinker. Although we do not know exactly how much of Bergson's thought appealed to Fitzgerald, the idea of "vitality" begins to take on an astonishing prevalence in Fitzgerald's early work. Bergson's *élan vital* refers to a life force that is not reducible to chemistry or biology but that can be intuited as a primary determinant of personality and behavior (*Creative Evolution* 5–6). Early twentieth-century writers such as T. S.

Eliot and Gertrude Stein responded positively to this neo-Romantic, unscientific concept, for it is an energy field that required the imagination, not reason or science, to detect and understand its power, and it defied the prevailing worldview of a mechanistic universe. Tom Quirk's *Bergson & American Culture* (1990) examines how Bergson affected Willa Cather and Wallace Stevens, in particular, quite profoundly. Bergson's theory gave Fitzgerald a new vocabulary with which to describe the presence (or its lack) of an otherwise indefinable characteristic of the impact of particular personalities, especially women. I have pointed out elsewhere (Raubicheck and Goldleaf 303) that *The Beautiful and Damned* uses the word "energy" nine times and the words "intensity" and "vitality" eight times each: "Gloria appeared, fresh in starched yellow, bringing atmosphere and an increase of vitality" (180).

Mencken does not seem to have taken much notice of Bergson; for him, Nietzsche's analysis of the will explained sufficiently the unconscious forces that drive each individual. In addition, he subscribed wholeheartedly to a materialist explanation of man and nature, so the ideas of such thinkers as Bergson or Carl Jung held little interest for him. Here is one more instance of how Fitzgerald's own preoccupations differed from those of his editor and mentor, even while he allowed his second novel to accord with Mencken's general ideas about the concerns and structure of a serious modern American novel.

The novel's study of a gradual personal dissolution accords with Mencken's preference for "character in decay" (*Prejudices: Second Series* 41). In its broad outlines the downward spiral of Anthony Patch's life is characteristic of naturalist fiction, yet, as we have seen, the effect on the reader of his steady decline is modified by Fitzgerald's inherent idealism, evidenced by the bursts of Romantic imagery, the remnants of his Catholic inheritance, and his developing interest in vitalist philosophy. The result is a book of conflicting themes, it is true, but also one of considerable complexity. In his next novel Fitzgerald would reconcile all his competing influences, including new ones such as James Joyce's *Ulysses* (1922), T. S. Eliot's *The Waste Land* (1922), and the novels of Joseph Conrad. From the "realism" of *The Beautiful and Damned* Fitzgerald moved toward adopting what might be called a Romantic modernism, combining his own Keatsian lyricism and idealism with the narrative strategies he learned from Conrad and the use of symbolism that impressed him in Eliot and Joyce. The result of Fitzgerald's continuing search for literary models and this reassertion of his own vision of life was, of course, *The Great Gatsby*.

NOTES

1. Both Mencken and Nathan wrote about their personal acquaintance with the Fitzgeralds after the couple's death, although factual inaccuracies mar their accounts. See Nathan's "Memories of Fitzgerald, Lewis and Dreiser" (1958) and select passages from Mencken's posthumously published *My Life as Author and Editor* (1993), most significantly 274–84.

2. Fitzgerald gives a fictional tip of the hat to Mencken in the first story he published in the *Saturday Evening Post*, "Head and Shoulders" (20 February 1920), by portraying him as the columnist Peter Boyce Wendell, who has the power to create literary reputations with a single mention in print (*F&P* 71, 82–84).

3. For an analysis of why Fitzgerald's early work fit so well with the tone and taste of the *Smart Set*, see Hamilton, "Mencken and Nathan's 'Smart Set' and the Story behind Fitzgerald's Early Success."

4. *This Side of Paradise* includes a widely ridiculed scene in which Amory Blaine flees a sexually available woman, Axia Marlowe, after a vision of the Devil appears in the apartment of her friend Phoebe Column (*TSOP* 106–14).

5. For a discussion of Zelda and Nathan's flirtatious relationship, see Milford 71–72; and Wagner-Martin, *Zelda Sayre Fitzgerald* 50–51.

6. For the evolution of the novel between 1920 and 1922, see Elias.

7. For an analysis of Fitzgerald's career that views his art as evolving from "the novel of saturation" (*Paradise* and *Beautiful*) to the Jamesian "novel of selection" (*Gatsby*), see J. Miller, *Fitzgerald: His Art* xiii.

"THAT DAMNED BEAUTIFUL SUMMER"
THE FITZGERALDS IN WESTPORT

Richard Webb Jr.

F. Scott Fitzgerald, a writer, has leased the
Wakeman Cottage near Compo Beach.

—*Westporter-Herald*, 4 June 1920

The sun . . . pounded suddenly on my eyes with broad,
hot hammers. . . . I awoke into Connecticut.

—F. Scott Fitzgerald, "The Cruise of the Rolling Junk"

During the summer of 1920 Scott and Zelda Fitzgerald honeymooned in Westport, Connecticut. Due to the relative brevity of their five-month residency,
critics have understandably—albeit wildly—underestimated how the town
contributed to their collective literary output, providing material for their fiction as significant as other, better-known sites where they lived and worked.
Unlike St. Paul, Minnesota; Montgomery, Alabama; Paris and the French Riviera; Baltimore, Maryland; Asheville, North Carolina; Hollywood; New York
City, or even Long Island's Gold Coast, Westport has been virtually ignored.
Yet this small but fashionable enclave remained imprinted in their imaginations. Westport is name-checked in short stories such as "The Diamond as
Big as the Ritz" (*TJA* 152), and Zelda would wrongly remember the couple
writing "Dice, Brassknuckles and Guitar" (*TJA* 277–97) there while she was
hospitalized a decade later (Bryer and Barks 67). The city influenced many

other works, including the nonfiction travelogue "The Cruise of the Rolling Junk" (*LK* 295–342), *The Great Gatsby*, and several Zelda efforts, including "A Millionaire's Girl," "Show Mr. And Mrs. Fitzgerald to Number —," her lone play, *Scandalabra*, and her only published novel, *Save Me the Waltz* (*Collected Writings* 327–36, 419–32, 197–268, 1–196, respectively). Most significantly, Westport inspired the depiction of the fictional village of Marietta in *The Beautiful and Damned*, where nearly a third of the novel's action unfolds.

Why Westport has been ignored by critics is a bit of mystery. Great writers have always made New York City's most famous suburb their home. In 1930 Sinclair Lewis received the phone call in his Westport living room informing him that he had won the Nobel Prize. Two decades later J. D. Salinger finished *The Catcher in the Rye* (1951) in town, its iconic first-edition jacket art drawn by his neighbor E. Michael Mitchell. Resident writers throughout the twentieth century include Sherwood Anderson, Peter De Vries, John Hersey, Shirley Jackson, Rod Serling, Max Shulman, Max Wilk, and Sloan Wilson, all of whose works feature suburban themes into which Fitzgerald tiptoes in *The Beautiful and Damned*, one of the earliest novels to presage the literary critique of what Robert Beuka calls "SuburbiaNation" (1).

I grew up only a half mile away from the house at 224 South Compo Road that Scott and Zelda rented in 1920. When I first read *The Beautiful and Damned*, I instantly recognized both what in the book is called "the grey house" and the geography of Westport, which reads like a road map—and a detailed and precise one at that. As Walter Raubicheck has pointed out, "No other Fitzgerald novel contains 200 pages that are placed in an autobiographical setting that remains largely unchanged" (qtd. in Webb, *Boats* 8). The lack of any detailed exploration of the setting inspired me and a fellow resident, Robert Steven Williams, to produce a full-length documentary on the subject, *Gatsby in Connecticut: The Untold Story*, a labor of love that occupied us from 2013 to 2020. I also published my research into their stay in a coffee-table book, *Boats against the Current: The Honeymoon Summer of Scott and Zelda: Westport, Connecticut 1920* (2018; 2nd ed. 2020), which is designed as a counterpart to similar photography-rich books celebrating other major sites in their lives, such as Dave Page and Jeff Kruger's *F. Scott Fitzgerald in St. Paul: The Writer and His Friends at Home* (2017). Additionally, Robert and I have conducted numerous talks and tours in Connecticut and New York, sometimes sparking controversy (Barron).[1] At the very least, Fitzgerald's use of Westport in *The Beautiful and Damned* demonstrates that setting and place in general were essential to his imagination. More provocatively, my collaborator and I argue that while the town's eclectic mix of millionaires, artists, writers, bootleggers, and show business personalities may not be present in the author's second novel, they are a subtext of *The Great Gatsby*.

A MOVE TO A "CRADLE OF GENIUS"

In May 1920 the Fitzgeralds, tired of hotel life in their second month of marriage, purchased a secondhand roadster and drove to Westport for the first time. A letter to Ruth Sturtevant from Scott explains why: "In acute agony and despair we at last forcibly left the Commodore [Hotel], bought a car, threw our bags in the back seat and set out. . . . [I]f Zelda can't swim she's miserable. . . . So we bore East, arrived here at nine o'clock this morning and found the slickest little cottage on the Sound." He also described the setting in detail: "There's a beach here and loads of seclusion and just about what we were looking for. We'd just about given up hope so now we're in the most jovial mood imaginable" (*Letters* 461). The couple rented the William Wakeman House in the Compo Beach area, a New England colonial built in 1780. Fitzgerald specifically evokes its New England past in *The Beautiful and Damned* when he describes it as a "house [that] had been there when women who kept cats were probably witches, when Paul Revere made false teeth in Boston" (152). He refers to the home as "the grey house" both in reference to its color (which remains the same to this day) and to its builder, William Gray. (This allusion is somewhat dampened in James L. W. West III's Cambridge Edition of the novel, which changes the spelling to "grey.")

A mile or so from the house sits Compo Beach, where Scott and Zelda frequently swam. The beach had a saucy reputation even before their stay: "Compo Beach Pavilion Scene of Midnight Orgies," reported the *Westporter-Herald* on 22 August 1919 (1). "More Nude Bathers at Compo Beach," the *Herald* announced the following year (1). Zelda would later reminisce to Scott: "We swam in the depth of the night . . . parties . . . The beach, and dozens of men" while recalling "mad rides along the Post Road and trips to New York" (Bryer and Barks 67). Edmund Wilson would claim the couple reveled "nude in the orgies of Westport" (*Letters on Literature and Politics* 82), although, like the *Herald*, he was not referring to literal orgies (or so one assumes). Whether in or out of their clothes, the Fitzgeralds also sunned and swam at the private beach of their millionaire next-door neighbor, Frederick E. Lewis. The Lewis estate was the Fitzgeralds' first prolonged exposure to the beach and the sea, a leisure landscape that would become integral to *Gatsby*. When narrator Nick Carraway in its final scene describes how he "wandered down to the beach and sprawled out on the sand" to contemplate the significance of his mysterious millionaire-neighbor's quest to reclaim Daisy Buchanan (*GG* 217), Fitzgerald is more likely drawing on memories of Compo Beach than on the Sound's New York coast: the couple spent far more time seaside in 1920 than they did during their 1922–24 stay in Great Neck. Indeed, one frequently reprinted photo of the couple was taken at Compo Beach. It shows Scott and Zelda in their swimsuits, sitting on a bench leaning against the clubhouse.

During the Fitzgeralds' time in Westport, numerous celebrities were likewise relocating to the suburb. On 23 July 1920—while the couple were on a 1,200-mile road trip to Montgomery that is the subject of "The Cruise of the Rolling Junk"—the *Herald* commemorated the arrival of two sibling cinema stars, Owen Moore (the first husband of Mary Pickford) and his younger brother, Tom:

WESTPORT NOW HOME OF FAMOUS MOVIE ACTORS
OWEN AND TOM MOORE SELECT HOME IN STONY BROOK
WOODS—ENJOY COMPO BEACH

Westport contains many people who are prominent in all walks of life. The most noted authors and illustrators of the country are proud to have Westport as their homes. Writers whose stories appear in the leading magazines and periodicals of the country are also coming here and quite a number of late popular stories have a tinge of Westport atmosphere about them. (1)

The Moores were Irish immigrants, and Owen in particular faintly resembled Scott, though there is no record of them ever encountering each other at Compo Beach. The brothers were hardly alone. There is no indication either that the Fitzgeralds met another denizen the *Herald* embraced as a local:

OOH, SKINNAY! BILL HART MAY BE OUR NEIGHBOR SOON

> William S. Hart, the movie star . . . has just added 65 acres to his large realty holdings in Westport, purchasing from Willard S. Adams. Westport folks are wondering whether he'll entertain them someday soon by filming one of his wild west pictures in their little town. ("Ooh, Skinnay!" 1)

Hart, who turned fifty-six in 1920, was a contemporary of Dustin Farnum, whose matinees Ruth Prigozy reminds us Fitzgerald religiously attended during his childhood decade in Buffalo, New York, before his family returned to St. Paul in 1912 ("Fitzgerald's Flappers" 129). Hart was beloved in Westport; an unpublished memoir by artist Lee Townsend recalls how the bartender in one local hotel "liked to show where Bill stood at the end of the bar with his English bulldog, Mac, at his feet" and then show off a telegram from the star asking to charter a boat for a day's fishing (n.p.). Yet Fitzgerald appears never to have visited Hart's "realty holdings" over the summer.

Westport was also home to a number of artists in addition to Townsend. Sculptor Berthold Nebel moved to town in 1913. His neighbor and colleague was James Earle Fraser, one of the most foremost portrait sculptors and the designer of the Indian Head nickel. Fraser also created the famous Native American tribute *The End of the Trail*, first displayed in plaster in 1915 and cast in bronze thirteen years later in Waupun, Wisconsin.[2] Other artists in residence included John Steuart Curry, one of the three top regionalists in the country, and Everett Shinn, an American Academy of Arts and Letters inductee known as a member of "The Eight" whose work in 1908 challenged the reigning conservatism of the National Academy of Design. Henry Longan Stuart was a reviewer and critic in the *New York Times* and author of *Weeping Cross: An Unworldly Story* (1908). Westport also claimed the British Great War veteran Hugh Lofting, whose first installment of *Dr. Doolittle* was published in 1920, just like Fitzgerald's *This Side of Paradise*. Lee Simonson, meanwhile, was a pioneering architect, painter, and stage designer.

Two important intellectuals—one established, one emerging—likewise resided in the city. When Fitzgerald moved to Westport, his Scribner's editor, Maxwell Perkins, sent him a copy of Van Wyck Brooks's hot-off-the-press *The Ordeal of Mark Twain* (1920), a study of the alienation that the artist in American society is doomed to suffer. Perkins felt Brooks's thesis was simpatico with many of Fitzgerald's views. The young author agreed: "Its [*sic*] one of the most inspirational books I've read and has seemed to put the breath of life back in me," Fitzgerald replied on 7 July (Kuehl and Bryer 31). Perkins and Brooks were childhood friends, and the editor presumably thought the critic, who commuted from Westport to New York, where he edited the literary section of *the Freeman*, might be a maturing influence. Yet despite his admiration of *Ordeal*, Fitzgerald never dropped by the older author's house just north of town. After Scott and Zelda relocated to Long Island, the missed opportunity inspired Edmund Wilson to write "The Delegate from Great Neck" (*Shores of Light* 140–55), a mock conversation grounded in the irony that while the Fitzgerald reveled in all those Compo Beach "orgies," Brooks "while in the same town, probably without ever knowing they were there," was "grinding out his sober plaint against the sterile sobriety of the country" (*Letters on Literature and Politics* 82). For his part, Brooks in his memoir of the 1920s, *Days of the Phoenix* (1967), remembered meeting Scott and Zelda in New York City, not in Westport. The couple arrived at a party late, he wrote, and fell asleep over soup, exhausted from partying (109).

Also in Westport at the time was Brooks's eventual protégée Paul Rosenfeld, who took an early perceptive measure of Fitzgerald's strengths and weaknesses in *Men Seen: Twenty-Four Modern Authors*, published in 1925 just as *The Great Gatsby* tumbled off the printing press (215–26). Rosenfeld mailed Fitzgerald an abashed letter of admiration for the novel, wishing he had read it before forming his judgment in his study (*Correspondence* 171). Despite the essay's ambivalence toward his work, Fitzgerald admired the critic's own *Port of New York* (1924), an assessment of fourteen artists, writers, and educators, many of whom, like Brooks, had Westport ties, including Arthur G. Dove, Alfred Stieglitz, and Georgia O'Keeffe. Had the pair met in 1920, the critic may have influenced Fitzgerald away from the faults he perceived in *The Beautiful and Damned*, while Fitzgerald might have tempered what he saw as Rosenfeld's "nervous critical entheusiasm [*sic*]" (*Correspondence* 141).

There were still more intriguing denizens of Westport in 1920. Just up the road from Scott and Zelda's grey house lived Edward T. Bedford, one of the many millionaires who made the city their home. Bedford was a director of Standard Oil and helped develop the petroleum by-product Vaseline. He was one of the richest men in America; *Fortune Magazine* said of him in 1923,

"Fundamentally the thing he does and always has done is make money" (qtd. in Klein 163). His Greens Farms Estate was several thousand acres in size, and his extensive gardens pulled tourists from all over the East Coast, including the frequently motoring Fitzgeralds. Most significantly, Frederick E. Lewis—race car driver, rancher, and yachtsman who inherited the equivalent today of $240 million while in his early twenties—owned 175 acres that compromised a significant portion of the Compo area. The grey house sat on a corner of Lewis's estate.

Thanks to a series of agricultural disasters, Westport became home, too, to a different breed of robber baron. In 1919, a blight wiped out the major onion-producing fields of the county. Local wheat farmers like Stephen Wakeman also lost their entire crop the summer before the Fitzgeralds arrived, and excessive rain destroyed roughly 50 percent of the state potato crop. Unrecoverable losses led farmers to turn to drastic extremes for survival: they could either sell failed farms to wealthy urbanites, sparking the city's transition from an agricultural village to residential suburb, or they could turn to bootlegging (Mangan). No sooner did the Eighteenth Amendment go into effect in January 1920 than empty onion storehouses along Long Island Sound became repositories for booze shipped down the coast. Rumrunners often hung up on rocks off Compo Beach; one nearly drowned bootlegger was rescued by a neighbor of the Fitzgeralds (Solomon 82).

Controlling most bootlegging in Westport was Jacob Rosenzweig, who grew up in neighboring Norwalk. Rosenzweig was a key member of the "Kosher Nostra," as Jewish organized crime circles in New York City were known (La Sorte). Nicknamed "Bald Jack Rose," he served as the critical witness in the prosecution of corrupt NYPD lieutenant Charles Becker for the 1912 murder of Herman "Rosy" Rosenthal at the Metropole, an event that the Jewish gangster Meyer Wolfshiem in *The Great Gatsby* recalls to Nick Carraway (*GG* 84–85). Rosenzweig likely played a central role in the Rosenthal hit but soon after reinvented himself as a speaker on the Christian reform circuit while Becker and three other men went to the electric chair in 1915. Ostensibly, the alopecia-stricken gambler, sometimes known as "Billiard Ball Jack" for his completely hairless face and pate, retired to Norwalk. Yet in the fall of 1920, shortly after Scott and Zelda moved back to New York City, his name reappeared in papers in connection with his brother-in law, Jacob Levy, who owned the Compo Inn, a notorious speakeasy frequented by local personalities. Fight promoter Joseph

Mulvihill publicly named Levy as the face of an illegal liquor operation earning a half-million dollars, claiming one of Levy's henchmen threatened his life at the Bridgestone rail station for reporting the gang to the federal authorities ("Charges Levy Heads Bootleggers' Ring" 1). Scott and Zelda knew Levy and his wife, Marion; he was most likely their source of alcohol. According to local legend, Zelda once careened down the steep road of the Compo Inn on a car hanging on to the hood ornament. Another time she supposedly drove to a nearby river steering with her feet.[3] Such tales of Prohibition and intoxication circulated freely in Westport: the *Herald* reported that sixteen stills were rumored to operate in the city, although one "Deputy Sheriff Perry" failed to find any confirmation ("Sixteen Stills" 1). The minuscule local police force rarely enforced the law and often blocked efforts by federal agents to do so. A truck once overturned in town spilling booze in the street. Two New York men of Jewish heritage, most likely in the employ of Rose, were arrested ("Truck Carrying $17,000 Worth of Booze" 1). Shortly afterward, a taxi was stopped carrying tens of thousands of dollars' worth of alcohol hidden in false compartments ("Thousands of Dollars" 1).

As this colorful history suggests, Westport offered an intriguing sociological mix of the staid and the brash, the elite and the criminal, from which Fitzgerald could have drawn in writing *The Beautiful and Damned*. Criticism galore has analyzed how he did so when writing *The Great Gatsby*, transforming Great Neck and Sands Point, Long Island, into West and East Egg respectively, capturing the conflux of new and old money between them. Much of this analysis has focused on the real-life figures and events who may have inspired Fitzgerald's cast of characters. Sarah Churchwell, for example, argues that the legendary parties of newspaperman Herbert Bayard Swope inspired Gatsby's ostentatious fetes (*Careless People* 93–94), while Horst H. Kruse details the background of Thomas "Tommy" Hitchcock Jr., the polo player remembered today as a partial model for Tom Buchanan and later Tommy Barban in *Tender Is the Night* (83–85). Other critics note the presence of Allan Dwan and Gloria Swanson in the cameo of "the moving picture director" who kisses "his Star" under a "white plum tree" at Gatsby's final party, prompting an envious comment from Daisy: "I think she's lovely" (*GG* 129; see Kim). Countless news reports, meanwhile, have attempted to identify this or that lavish estate—some still standing, but most torn down long ago—as the models for Gatsby's gaudy mansion in West Egg and the Buchanans' more tasteful abode to the east.

In a 1996 *New Yorker* article, Barbara Probst Solomon argued that the "cultural mix" of Westport, the city's mingling of "Jews and Christians, the arts, old money and the brash new kind" (82) inspired East Egg and West Egg as much as Great Neck and Sands Point. *Gatsby in Connecticut: The Untold Story* is an effort to both revive and extend the parallels she drew between the opulence of Lewis and Bedford and Jay Gatsby's mansion and parties and between Wolfshiem and Bald Jack Rose (83–84)—parallels that were largely ignored or discounted by Fitzgerald scholars at the time (also a theme of both our documentary and of my book). While we hope *Gatsby* fans will at least remain receptive to the argument, what remains undebatable is that in *The Beautiful and Damned* Fitzgerald was simply not interested in the "lush beach parties, bootlegging, and movie activity" that "were all happening within a two-mile radius of his cottage" on South Compo Road in 1920 (Solomon 84). He had other intentions for his fictional Marietta.

SUBURBAN BLUES:
MATRIMONY, MASCULINITY, AND BOREDOM

Throughout the novel, Anthony and Gloria Patch are contemptuous of New York City's bedroom communities, dismissing them as a "wide murky district which alternated cheerless blue-green wastes with suburbs of tremendous and sordid activity" (150). They view the village of Marietta where they rent the grey house as a "cluster of dull roofs around a white tall steeple" with a "somnolent and dilapidated" inn that is "too broken for even chance immoralities and consequent gaieties of a country roadhouse" (152). The real-life steeple belonged to the Saugatuck Congregational Church. Constructed in 1832, it sat across from the boardinghouse where Scott and Zelda initially stayed in Westport. Steeple imagery is rich in Fitzgerald, reflecting his fascination with medieval literature. From the "Spires and Gargoyles" section in *This Side of Paradise* in which the Princeton architecture symbolizes intellectual ambitions of Amory Blaine that the postwar world thwarts (*TSOP* 42–89, 259–60) to the reference in *The Great Gatsby* to Nick Carraway staring at his neighbor's mansion like "Kant at his church steeple" (*GG* 106), such Old World constructions represent human aspiration. Yet the Patches find no such possibilities for wonder in their new adopted home:

Marietta itself offered little social life. Half a dozen farm-estates formed a hexagon around [the steeple], but these belonged to ancient men who displayed themselves only as inert, gray-thatched lumps in the back of limousines on their way to the station, whither they were sometimes accompanied by equally ancient and doubly massive wives. The townspeople were a particularly uninteresting type—unmarried females were predominant for the most part—with school-festival horizons and souls bleak as the forbidding white architecture of the three churches. The only native with whom they came into close contact was the broad-hipped, broad-shouldered Swedish girl who came every day to do their work. (159)

Other residents are either farmers or "yokels, red-eyed, cheerless as scarecrows" (166). Gloria tries to stave off boredom by visiting former friends from her school and debutante days in nearby towns such as "Rye, Port Chester, and Greenwich," but she finds the women tediously domesticated, all seeming "to be in different stages of having babies" (158). She and Anthony attempt to socialize with Eric and Constance (Shaw) Merriam, but Gloria dismisses the husband as too conventional in his expectation that wives will be obedient and retiring: "[Eric's] idea of respecting Constance," complains Gloria, "is to leave her at home with her sewing and her baby and her book, and such innocuous amusements, whenever he's going on a party that promises to be anything but deathly dull" (192). Such passages define American wives' first basic discontent with the suburbs, a disgruntlement that contemporaries of Gloria's such as Myra Babbitt in Sinclair Lewis's *Babbitt* (1922) shared: for all the "'splendid' privileges of the suburb," women felt isolated in the home more than they had in larger cities where communities existed in closer proximity. Very quickly they expressed "a rightful boredom with the limited [domestic] role permitted them" and sought ways of "revolting against the dull, uncultured life" (Jurca 59). No symbol better captures the monotony of life in Marietta than the grey house's prized piece of "furniture," the hammock. Although this leisure symbol begins for the Patches as a cradle for "a host of new dreams" birthed "in tune to its imagined rhythm" (153), it quickly becomes a straitjacket that constantly reminds them of their indolence (177).

Gloria's revolt against Marietta's "voluptuous" lethargy is perhaps the most shocking among these early fictional female suburbanites, although by no means uncommon: when confronted by the possibility that she is pregnant, she decides with Anthony's passive consent that she does not want children, and she plans a visit to Constance for what numerous critics like Tanfer Emin Tunc interpret as an abortion (173; see Tunc 195–97). Gloria makes it clear she will not conform to the suburban expectation of motherhood: "I'm being true to me, you know," she insists to her husband when she seeks reproductive relief in what the novel labels a "Nietzschean Incident" (172).

Although in Marietta the Patches do dine out at "various country clubs," they have little interest in local entertainment or leisure activity. Anthony loathes golf (158), and the couple's excessive drinking and odd sexual dynamic offend established residents: when "cute little freshmen" at a dinner party "violent[ly] rush" Gloria, the husband is vaguely thrilled. To underscore the dowdy morality of the area, Fitzgerald gives one miffed hostess the name of "Mrs. Granby"—a Connecticut variation on "Grundy," the rising generation's stock name in 1920 for disapproving grumps.[4] But why did he portray Westport as this *Babbitt*-esque landscape of bleak souls instead of depicting it as the syndicated columnist O. O. McIntyre would a few years later when he described it as a "cradle of genius"? (26).[5]

One answer is that at this period of his career Fitzgerald was so reliant on autobiographical material that he simply failed to register the artistic possibilities of including the city's intellectual coterie in his story line. Many of the incidents that occur in the Patches' marriage in Marietta have some genesis in Scott and Zelda's personal experience in Westport. For starters, there are the almost constant automobile problems the Fitzgeralds suffered while living on South Compo Road. On 25 June 1920 the *Herald* took note when Scott lost control of his car:

AUTHOR ON THE ROCKS
TRIED TO TAKE A COUNTRY ROAD AND
HE LOST A WHEEL

Author Fitzgerald, who rents the Burritt Wakeman place at Compo, went onto the rocks when he attempted to drive up old Spicer Road, just off State Street, last evening. As a result he lost a wheel and the occupants of the car were more or less shook up. The party was on its way to Miramar Inn. (1)

The Spicer Road accident was nothing compared to an earlier incident that set the tone for the couple's stay in Westport. "We have a house and a room for you," Zelda wrote their drinking companion Ludlow Fowler on 19 May, "and a ruined automobile because I drove it over a fire-plug and completely deintestined it" (qtd. in Milford 70).[6] In *The Beautiful and Damned*, the accident is played for laughs to dramatize Gloria Patch's complete unsuitability for marriage. Like the dirty laundry she lets collect in piles in the couple's closet and her fussiness with food (she has a perpetual upset stomach), her driving is "one of the trinity of contention" that drives Anthony to exasperation. Thus, as they roll into Marietta for the first time, Gloria hesitates "between two approaches, and making her choice too late," drives "over a fire-hydrant and rip[s] the transmission violently from the car" (152).

The scene is one of several automobile collisions in Fitzgerald's fiction that capture the era's fascination with the damage that could be inflicted both on this revolutionary marvel of technology and on the human body.[7] In *This Side of Paradise*, Amory Blaine happens upon a wreck that claims the life of his Princeton classmate Dick Humbird (*TSOP* 85), while in *Gatsby* a guest at a lavish West Egg party tears a wheel off a coupe, only to insist, drunkenly, that he can still drive away on three wheels (*GG* 67–68). Gloria's glib description of gutting the transmission—"I drove over a fire-hydrant and we had ourselves towed to the garage and then we saw your sign," she explains when a real-estate agent asks how they decided to rent in Marietta (152)—anticipates the recklessness of other female characters. Jordan Baker is a famously haphazard driver in *Gatsby*, nearly clipping pedestrians who she expects will get out of her way (*GG* 71). Nicole Diver, meanwhile, hysterically veers off a steep Swiss hillside in a car carrying her husband and children (*TITN* 218–19).

But perhaps the most illuminating connection between the bad driving motif, legends of the Fitzgeralds' marriage, and this scene in *The Beautiful and Damned* is Zelda's revision of it in her *Save Me the Waltz* (1932). When she reclaimed the couple's Westport memories a dozen years after their Connecticut summer for her only novel, she attributed the accident not to her autobiographical heroine, Alabama Beggs, but to two drunken friends of Alabama's husband, the painter David Knight. David's buddies fail to register the consequences of their recklessness: "There were people in automobiles all along the Boston Post Road thinking everything was going to be all right while they got drunk and ran into fireplugs and trucks and old stone walls. Policemen were too busy thinking everything was going to be all right to arrest them" (*Collected Writings* 54). At least in the first half of *The Beautiful and Damned,* Fitzgerald seized upon examples of Zelda's theatrical immaturity in marriage—Mrs. Fitzgerald turned all of twenty during their Westport summer—to underscore the conflict between Anthony's infatuation with Gloria's flagrant incaution and his impatience with it. Eventually, the couple's dynamic changes as the husband succumbs to alcoholism and the wife evolves into the more responsible partner. Yet no such shift of roles occurs in *Save Me the Waltz.* From the outset Alabama is the steadier, more responsible spouse, and that revision of the couple's history changes how Westport is portrayed. If Gloria is bored in Marietta, Alabama Beggs Knight wants "the green hills of Connecticut" to preach a "sedative sermon" on home and family, stabilizing forces that David in his alcoholic selfishness cannot provide (*Collected Writings* 51). Significantly, the first scene set in Westport in *Save Me the Waltz* takes place in the Knights' bedroom, where their massive bed ("the biggest bed that both of them could imagine") symbolizes the domestic coziness and unity that will prove elusive for Alabama.

Not every wild moment from Scott and Zelda's stay in Westport found its way into *The Beautiful and Damned.* That summer the *Herald* featured an unamused headline:

FALSE ALARM SENT FROM COMPO DISTRICT
FIREMEN MAKE QUICK RUN TO MINUTEMAN—
ALARM CAME FROM FITZGERALDS—THEY DENY IT

A follow-up article reported in its subhead that the couple

SAY THEY WERE OUT OF THE HOUSE, BUT WILL PAY COSTS

Zelda pasted both *Herald* articles in her scrapbook (87). Few biographers can resist recounting this incident, noting that Zelda reportedly pointed to her breast and announced that "the fire is here" (Cline 92). The absence of this particular event in *The Beautiful and Damned* underscores an important point. Although the novel was accused of glorifying drinking, Fitzgerald, at least in the Marietta section—and with two important exceptions, noted below—tends to summarize the couple's parties rather than dramatize their antics.

Thus, when the Patches return to the grey house for their third (and disastrous) summer in 1916, the novel passes quickly over their "muddled" moments, either deemphasizing the intoxication or focusing on its aftereffects:

> More from their fear of solitude than from any desire to go through the fuss and bother of entertaining, they filled the house with guests every week-end, and often on through the week. The week-end parties were much the same. When the three or four men invited had arrived, drinking was more or less in order. . . . Sunday afternoon meant good-bye to the one or two guests who must return to the city, and a great revival of drinking among the one or two who remained until next day, concluding in a convivial if not hilarious evening. (198–99)

Doing so allows Fitzgerald to place a proportionate amount of blame for the couple's decay on the competition for power in the relationship, for control over each other's behavior. In this way, the novel dramatizes another core theme of suburban fiction, the idea that marriage turns ever more unsatisfactory as notions of togetherness idealized in these supposedly perfect communities give way to resentment, recrimination, and, in some cases, violence (Donaldson, *Suburban Myth* 187–88).

Here, too, in dramatizing this theme Fitzgerald relied on autobiographical inspiration, although *The Beautiful and Damned* is far from a roman à clef in which fictional characters are thinly veiled real-life public figures. Twice in close succession, Anthony's former rival for Gloria's affection, the movie executive Joseph Bloeckman, visits Marietta from his residence in nearby Cos Cob, sparking Anthony's jealousy. The first time, Bloeckman offers Gloria an opportunity to audition for a role in one of his productions, a possibility that agitates the husband's insecurities over his half-hearted, dilettantish attempts to write for a living (182–83). During the second visit Bloeckman squires Gloria on a "jaunt" through the countryside in his roadster, which he even rather bravely allows Gloria to drive (183–84). Fitzgerald channels through Gloria's friendship with this onetime suitor his ambivalence toward the flirtation Zelda struck up with *Smart Set* coeditor George Jean Nathan during their Westport summer. As Linda Wagner-Martin writes, "While Scott was pleased when *Smart Set* took his first story ["Babes in the Woods," *S&P* 187–95], and he admired both [H. L.] Mencken and Nathan as intellectuals, he was surprised that a man such as Nathan would be interested in Zelda—or would pretend an interest in Zelda" (*Zelda Sayre Fitzgerald* 50).

In a controversial decision, Scott declined Nathan's offer to publish Zelda's diary in the *Smart Set,* which the critic enthusiastically read during a visit to South Compo Road; Fitzgerald insisted he needed his wife's quips and idiosyncratic insights for his own fiction (Nathan 148–49; Curtiss 162–63). Like Bloeckman, Nathan was Jewish, though the movie executive exudes none of the urbanity and "sexual sophistication" for which the editor and theater critic was known (Wagner-Martin, *Zelda Sayre Fitzgerald* 50). Far from it: Bloeckman is caricatured whenever he appears as dull and conventional, no matter his success in the film industry; in this regard he seems the quintessential resident of the suburbs. Yet even though Gloria exhibits no adulterous interest in the man, Anthony experiences both panic and fury when Tana, their houseboy, informs him that she and her spurned suitor are off galivanting. "So this was Gloria's idea of excitement, by God!" the husband rages. Fitzgerald seems to overstate his ire to the point of parody: "His fists were clenched; within a moment he had worked himself up to a tremendous pitch of indignation. . . . Anthony neither laughed nor seemed absurd to himself. To his frantic imagination it was already six—seven—eight, and she was never coming! Bloeckman finding her bored and unhappy had persuaded her to go to California with him" (183–84). Yet as soon as Gloria returns she unknowingly snuffs out his indignation with an innocent, "I know you wouldn't mind"—her assumption that her husband trusts her. Anthony promptly sinks "listlessly" in a chair, exhausted both by his own impulse to dominate his wife and the cultural obligation he feels as a man to control happenings in his home, a "weight he had never chosen to bear" (184). While Anthony wants to feel he is beyond the staid traditional morality his grandfather espouses, his status as the head of the household leaves him resentful of the "reasonable privileges" a twentieth-century wife expects, and it "wearie[s] him that he fail[s] to understand" his desire to dominate Gloria. Anthony seems to suffer the same unease that Princeton friend Alexander McKaig diagnosed in Scott when he wrote in his own diary that "Fitz should let Zelda go & not run after her. Like all husbands he is afraid of what she may do in a moment of caprice" (qtd. in Milford 75).

Yet another autobiographical episode suggests that Fitzgerald did not simply transcribe scenes from his Westport honeymoon into the novel without some fictional alchemy. Since Nancy Milford's 1970 biography *Zelda,* critics have drawn from McKaig's 15 September entry to describe "an incident [that] provided material for a chapter in *The Beautiful and Damned*" (Le Vot 89; see also Wagner-Martin, *Zelda Sayre Fitzgerald* 53). As McKaig recorded: "In the evening Zelda—drunk—having decided to leave Fitz & having nearly been killed walking down R. R. track, blew in. Fitz came shortly after. He had caught same train with no money or ticket. They threatened to put him off but finally let him stay on—Zelda refusing to give him any money" (qtd. in Milford 75).

In fact, *The Beautiful and Damned* contains no such scene in which a penniless Anthony pursues a fleeing Gloria onto a train into New York City, where she refuses to pay his fare. Rather, Fitzgerald splits the incident in half. The first vignette occurs during the Patches' second summer (1915) in the grey house and—significantly—precedes Anthony's jealousy over Bloeckman's visits. During a hot day at the beach with the Merriams, Gloria suddenly decides she wants to return home. Irritated, Anthony determines he must exert his "mastery" lest he forever be subjected to her mood swings: "This was the occasion of all occasions," Fitzgerald writes, "since for a whim she had deprived him of a pleasure. His determination solidified, approached momentarily a dull and sullen hate" (168).

The conflict leads to an argument in the Redgate railroad station in which Anthony refuses to buy tickets for the train home to Marietta, demanding instead they visit other friends to continue their drinking. When Gloria attempts to purchase the fare with her own money, her husband grabs her hard enough that other passengers turn and stare. "Oh, if there was one *man* here you couldn't do this!" Gloria screams. Anthony releases her only after the train departs, gloating in patriarchal authority: "The test was done and he had sustained his will with violence. Let leniency walk in the wake of victory" (170). Not even when Gloria angrily bites his thumb, drawing blood, does Anthony relax his certainty that "he must be right." Instead, he revels in the sight of her "broken and dispirited, humiliated beyond the lot of her measure to bear" (171).

Fitzgerald's clinical description of the husband's desire to "triumph" is fascinating to read against McKaig's account of the railroad episode. First, it suggests Scott's resentment at Zelda's refusal to pay his fare (with money he had earned for the family) upon chasing after her that 15 September. In this fantasy revision of their argument, he imagines both refusing to pay *her* way and stopping her from boarding the train. Yet the episode also suggests why later, after Gloria's joyride with Bloeckman, Anthony (thankfully) does not force an argument that turns violent as this one does. On the taxi ride to Marietta from the Redgate station he regrets reducing Gloria to tears, though not because of the physical force he exerted: "While he did not believe she would cease to love him—this, of course, was unthinkable—it was yet problematical whether Gloria without her arrogance, her independence, her virginal confidence and courage, would be the girl of his glory, the radiant woman who was precious and charming because she was ineffably, triumphantly herself" (171). In other words, Anthony regrets crushing the very qualities he finds most attractive in his wife and wonders if he will still love her if she were *not* willful and impetuous. This dynamic sets the novel apart from later suburban novels that depict domestic violence. In them husbands usually abuse their wives to exert the power that their white-collar occupations stymie as labor is corporatized (Jurca 167). Fitzgerald's drama is unique in that the Patches' domestic conflicts arise from their clash of personalities; the suburb is merely the backdrop against which their purposelessness explodes, not the claustrophobic cauldron that causes it.

The second half of the scene based on the argument McKaig recorded centers on the part about Zelda "having nearly been killed walking down R. R. track." During one of the two parties at the Patches' that Fitzgerald depicts in detail, Joe Hull, a guest of their friends Maury Noble and Richard Caramel, so disturbs Gloria that she flees the grey house. Supposedly based on Scott's Princeton roommate John Biggs (K. Taylor, *Gatsby Affair* 33), Hull is a physically menacing man with a "yellow beard continually fighting through his skin" who drunkenly grabs Gloria for a dance and leers at her drowsing body after she calls it a night (200, 204). Terrified of the stranger, Gloria tries to escape by rushing to the Marietta train station. Visitors to contemporary Westport can walk the exact path she takes: past the grey house on South Compo Road "probably half a mile" to a "single deserted barn" that still stands today on the corner of East Ferry Lane, which leads to a railroad bridge. An eighth of a mile farther are the electrical towers and wires that Fitzgerald describes as a "great cascade" rising "high above the river . . . and ran with the railroad Bridge in the direction of the station" (206–7). As Gloria crosses the Saugatuck River on a thin, yard-wide plank that parallels the elevated train tracks, hearing Anthony call after her, her thoughts echo a letter of Zelda's that some biographers suggest references the incident: "Let him come now—she no longer feared that, only she must first reach the station, because that was part of the game" (208).[8] When she reaches the station, however, she does not board a train without her husband—at least not immediately. Rather, in one of the novel's tenderest moments, Anthony soothes her fears before Noble and Caramel arrive, and the conversation shifts abruptly to a long monologue by Maury on his intellectual education that gives the chapter its title ("Symposium"). Only after their friend's lecture on "the unreality of ideas," as the sun comes up, does Gloria board for New York. The reason is unclear, though. Presumably, Gloria refuses to return home until Hull has departed, but the narrator mentions only a "quick controversy" and "another clamor" over whether Anthony should accompany her—which he does not do (219). The scene suggests again how Fitzgerald adapted his Westport material using actual locations. In this version, he allows Zelda/Gloria to go her own way without giving chase, sparing himself and his alter ego the humiliation of lacking money for his fare. He may not imagine himself as Anthony exerting as much mastery as he does in the Redgate scene, but at least by remaining in Marietta with his friends the husband retains some dignity of control over the situation.

The second fully developed Marietta drinking scene, even more crucial to the plot, likewise demonstrates how Fitzgerald reshaped autobiographical events in Westport to formulate the novel's themes and plot. Employing the same theater-script format as the earlier, ill-advised "Flash-Back in Paradise" episode in which God incarnates Beauty in the form of Gloria Gilbert (30–32), he dramatizes a rollicking party in the grey house in which Anthony's Harvard acquaintance Fred Paramore succumbs to the temptation of alcohol. Paramore no sooner downs a few cocktails than he transforms from a priggish charity worker into a "rip-roaring tippler" (228) by leaping onto the Patches' improvised living-room dance floor and imitating Gloria as she performs a "swan dance." Spinning around "more and more dizzily," he topples into an unexpected guest, Anthony's Prohibition-supporting grandfather, Adam J. Patch, "whose approach has been rendered inaudible by the pandemonium in the room" (230). The old man's disgust at the inebriated revelry (including the sight of Paramore crawling around on his hands and knees) leads him to disinherit Anthony, thereby igniting the Patches' humiliating descent into poverty in the novel's final quarter.

Biographers suggest that Adam Patch's dismay at Anthony and Gloria's lifestyle was partly inspired by a visit to Westport from Zelda's parents, Anthony and Minnie Sayre, in mid-August 1920, shortly after the "Cruise of the

Rolling Junk" misadventure. As Milford writes: "One can imagine the Judge's glacial attitude toward the life Scott and Zelda were leading. The Sayres' visit was not a success and they left a full week earlier than they had anticipated" (74). *Save Me the Waltz* depicts a scene that at least one other biographer argues is barely fictionalized: when Alabama's parents visit, the two same drunken friends of David's responsible for the wrecked car stagger from the couple's hammock and cause "a not very edifying scene" that leads to the mortified heroine breaking her nose on a swinging door.[9] Judge and Mrs. Beggs quickly excuse themselves from the chaos to shelter with Alabama's older, staider sister, wounding Zelda's alter ego: "You just disapprove, so you're not going to stand it," a dejected Alabama tells her parents. "If I don't accept your way of think-ing, you'll leave me to myself" (*Collected Writings* 56). If some version of this scenario actually occurred in Westport, dramatic necessity required Fitzgerald to shift the disapproval from Gloria's family to Anthony's: by this point in the narrative, Mrs. Gilbert is already dead (161), with her henpecked husband soon to follow (253). Lording his money over the young couple, Grandfather Patch is a far more fearsome presence than either of those elders, whom the novel satirizes as frivolous and fatuous. More importantly, the disinheritance also helps shape the proto-critique-of-suburbia theme. Amid fears for their suddenly insecure financial future, Gloria and Anthony leave the grey house for good, hoping against hope to economize by downsizing to one residence. On the train ride back to New York City Anthony realizes how unfulfilling suburban life in Marietta has been, and how his unhappiness there has cost him his romantic innocence, leading to the Patches' marital misery:

> The drab visions of train-side Mamaroneck, Larchmont, Rye, Pelham Manor, succeeded each other with intervals of bleak and shoddy wastes posing ineffectually as country. He found himself remembering how on one summer morning they two had started from New York in search of hap-piness. They had never expected to find it, perhaps, yet in itself that quest had been happier than anything he expected forevermore. Life, it seemed, must be a setting up of props around one—otherwise it was disaster. There was no rest, no quiet. He had been futile in longing to drift and dream; no one drifted except to maelstroms, no one dreamed, without his dreams becoming fantastic nightmares of indecision and regret. (236)

Once the train pulls into the Bronx, however, Anthony's spirits suddenly lighten as he sees in New York a source of authenticity and vibrancy. He may view the borough's tenement dwellers and upwardly mobile Jewish storekeepers solipsistically, imagining they exist to inspire and entertain him, but his vision of the metropolis as a "vigorous colorful revelation" invigorates him—at least until Gloria punctures his balloon by reminding him of his Jewish rival from Cos Cob:

> "I like these streets," observed Anthony aloud. "I always feel as though it's a performance being staged for me; as though the second I've passed they'll all stop leaping and laughing and, instead, grow very sad, remembering how poor they are, and retreat with bowed heads into their houses. You often get that effect abroad, but seldom in this country." . . .
> [The city] was impressive—in perspective it was tremendous. . . .
> Gloria's voice broke in with strange appropriateness upon his thoughts.
> "I wonder where Bloeckman's been this summer." (237)

As Pascale Antolin has argued, such moments are indicative of how Fitzgerald portrays New York in *The Beautiful and Damned* as a "city of words": he "never tries to reconstruct or represent New York realistically or even explicitly to his readers. On the contrary, though omnipresent, the city turns out to be mostly absent, a descriptive ellipsis, a missing object—in other words, an object of desire" (120). The treatment of the urban setting is neither realistic nor naturalistic (in which the setting would dominate the individual will) but, rather, modernistic: New York appears as a fragmented, cinematic dream whose subjective perception is far more akin to John Dos Passos's *Manhattan Transfer* (1925) than, say, to Stephen Crane's *Maggie: A Girl of the Streets* (1893), in which the Bowery slums, Antolin notes, are rendered in objective, documentary detail (113, 120). As she argues, New York is a linguistic mirror, reflecting in the text's first half the fantasies Anthony and Gloria project onto the cityscape. As an example, "Fifth and Sixth Avenues" early on are pictured in Anthony's mind as "the uprights of a gigantic ladder stretching from Washington Square to Central Park" (16). (In the second half, New York turns darker, reflecting the couple's nightmares.)

Marietta, by contrast, inspires no such grandiose metaphors. Both it and the bedroom communities that separate it from New York are just plain dull and uninspiring, full of "houses at a hundred a month which closely adjoined other houses at a hundred a month" with "interiors furnished either 'commercially' with slab-like chairs and unyielding settees, or 'home-like' with the melancholy bric-à-brac of other summers—crossed tennis rackets, fit-form couches, and depressing Gibson girls" (148–49)—the type of "boxes" that future generations would ridicule as "ticky tacky." The suburbs constitute a world as grey as the Patches' grey house; indeed, the word "grey" is repeated more frequently in the Marietta section to contrast the suburbs' monochromatic blandness to New York's multicolored whirl (232). But the color scheme is only one cue to this monotony; the figurative language likewise dramatizes the emotional drought of these "drab" communities. As Anthony realizes the morning after the debacle with his grandfather, Marietta has turned him and Gloria into "two goldfish in a bowl from which all the water had been drawn; they could not even swim across to each other" (231).

This is not to say, however, that Fitzgerald depicts Marietta in a realist style (and certainly not in a naturalistic one). Rather, in dramatizing Gloria's feelings toward the suburb and the grey house, he experiments with a mode that will later become its own subgenre of suburban fiction, the Suburban Gothic. As Bernice M. Murphy notes, this type of fiction applies the conventions of Gothic literature (spectral figures, haunted houses, etc.) to dramatize the artificiality of suburbia as otherworldly, confirming "the niggling suspicion that something dark lurks below suburbia's peaceful façade" (1). Fitzgerald was already predisposed toward critiquing marriage and domesticity through such supernatural means, having shortly before he began *The Beautiful and Damned* published "The Cut-Glass Bowl," a proto–Stephen King short story about a housewife who believes the titular kitchen accoutrement is inflicting harm on her family (*F&P* 87–107). In the novel he provides a rationale for why Gloria believes in spirits: like her mother, she is a Bilphist (253), a term Fitzgerald invented to parody theosophy, or the "practice" of communing with spirits (Tate 33). Significantly, however, it is only while in Marietta that Gloria is haunted; her "penchant for premonitions and . . . bursts of vague supernaturalism" do not emerge until after they move to Connecticut, surprising her husband, and they abruptly end after the return to New York. The grey house in particular excites her "hypersensitiveness" toward ghosts: "The desperate squeakings about the old house on windy nights that to Anthony were burglars with revolvers ready in hand represented to Gloria the auras, evil and restive, of dead generations, expiating the inexpiable upon the ancient and romantic hearth" (159). By the Patches' third summer of marriage, Marietta becomes such a phantasmic projection of their discontent and disappointment that Fitzgerald titles a chapter "The Sinister Summer" and adopts a Poe-like tenor to describe its atmosphere: "There was a horror in the house that summer. It came with them and settled itself over the place like a sombre pall, pervasive through the lower rooms, gradually spreading and climbing up the narrow stairs until it oppressed their very sleep" (197).

The major Gothic scene set in Marietta is the party that Joe Hull attends, the one from which Gloria flees on foot to the train station. Here Fitzgerald pulls out all the horror-story stops: thunder and lightning, a storm, the spooky "scrape" of "tall bushes against the house" (203), along with unnervingly hypnotic onomatopoeia ("Drip! Drip! Drip!" [204]).[10] Gloria is even possessed by a vision worthy of Charles Brockden Brown. In a passage that recalls the much-ridiculed moment in *This Side of Paradise* in which Amory Blaine imagines the devil staring at him as he visits the apartment of a pair of sexually available showgirls (*TSOP* 106–11), Gloria spies a "figure, swaying, swaying in the doorway, an indiscernible and subtly menacing terror, a personality filthy under its varnish, like smallpox spots under a layer of powder" (204). This demonic presence—which proves to be Hull peeking in her bedroom—sends Gloria bolting into the night, her frightful dash to the train station staged like a Walpole or Radcliffe heroine fleeing a castle. A passing train draws her into a "trance-like torpor" as its lights glare toward her like "a sputtering flame in a lamp beside a corpse": "The light was tepid, the temperature of warm blood. . . . The clicking [wheels] blended suddenly with itself in a rush of even sound, and then, elongating in sombre elasticity, the thing roared blindly by her and thundered onto the bridge, racing the lurid shaft of fire it cast into the solemn river alongside. Then it contracted swiftly, sucking in its sound until it left only a reverberant echo, which died upon the farther bank" (207).

Fitzgerald lays on the eeriness so thick here the scene really has nowhere to go: as previously noted, shortly after Anthony catches up to Gloria, Maury Noble and Richard Caramel join them, and the quartet spends the rest of the night listening to Maury boast of his skeptical philosophy of life (212–19). This does not mean the Suburban Gothic style simply peters out. Rather, Fitzgerald offers a clear transition out of the supernatural mood. It occurs when Gloria scales the bridge over the river and spots the train station in the distance—

literally, her way out of Marietta: "Not two hundred yards away at the end of the bridge squatted the station, marked by a sullen lantern. The oppression was lifted now—the tree-tops below her were rocking the young starlight to a haunted doze. She stretched out her arms with a gesture of freedom" (208). When Anthony finally reaches her, Gloria is blunt about her desire: "I want—I want to go away. . . . anywhere" (209). It takes only one more party—the far more disastrous one that Adam Patch wanders into—for her to get her wish. And once she and Anthony abandon the grey house and Marietta, she is never again bothered by phantoms, thus confirming that the suburban setting is what excites her paranormal superstitions.

The Patches are far from their nadir when they depart the suburbs to return to the city: more than 150 pages of improvident spending, adultery, alcoholism, and relocating to ever-grubbier living quarters remain before Fitzgerald ironically reverses their fortunes and awards them Anthony's inheritance. But while the metropolis may overshadow the village in the sections covering 1917–22, Marietta plays an important role in the couple's disaffection from 1914 to 1916, its bland environs bringing into relief the "meaninglessness of life" theme to which the newlyweds succumb. In depicting Westport as tedious and lethargic, Fitzgerald anticipated a tradition of American literature in which—fairly or not—my hometown becomes the prime target for lamenting the artificiality of middle-class life in the latter half of the twentieth century. When the narrator notes that the Patches "were weary of the place" before their final summer in Marietta, and that "they had built themselves a prison" (196–97) in the grey house, the novel anticipates the commonplace criticism that suburbia is boring. As Max Shulman would say in *Rally Round the Flag, Boys!* (1957), a fictional Westport is "a town whose founder was scalped . . . the last interesting thing that happened there" (1). And when *The Beautiful and Damned* describes Gloria shaking "her fist defiantly at the four walls" and declaring, "Oh, my God, how I hate this house!" (236), Fitzgerald anticipates the similar feelings of imprisonment that Tom and Betsy Rath express in Sloan Wilson's *The Man in the Gray Flannel Suit* (1955): the Raths think of their house as "a trap . . . they no more enjoyed refurbishing it than a prisoner would delight in shining up the bars of his cell" (5). Wilson's novel begins, in fact, with one of the bluntest denunciations of the city where I have spent my life: "By the time they had lived seven years . . . in Westport . . . they both detested it" (3).

Would Westport have fared better in *The Beautiful and Damned* if Fitzgerald had dramatized the city's mix of millionaires, gangsters, intellectuals, and artists as *The Great Gatsby* would three years later? Undoubtedly. In a letter written only six months before his 21 December 1940 death, Fitzgerald assured his daughter, Scottie, that his second novel did not denigrate her mother: "Gloria was a much more trivial and vulgar person than your mother. I can't really say there was any resemblance except in the beauty and certain terms of expression she used, and also I naturally used many circumstantial events of our early married life. However the emphases were entirely different. We had a much better time than Anthony and Gloria had" (*Fitzgerald: A Life in Letters* 453). The same might be said of Westport: it has always been far less trivial and "vulgar" than fiction has depicted it, and far more complex politically and socially than *The Beautiful and Damned* portrays it. Lifelong residents typically chuckle at our literary notoriety: we have a better time here, too, than Anthony and Gloria did.

NOTES

1. For more information on our documentary, please visit www.gatsbyinct.com.

2. The statue is also notably featured on the cover of the Beach Boys' 1971 LP *Surf's Up*.

3. Two Westport sources cite legends of the Fitzgeralds and the Compo Inn. The first is an interview Robert Steven Williams and I conducted with local historian Eve Potts, who remembers hearing the tales from a neighbor shortly after moving to the town in 1956: "I met a wonderful woman named Mary Wilson whose husband was a Pulitzer Prize winner—he had written the biography of Harriet Beecher Stowe. And she used to regale us with tales about what Westport was like in the early days. And although I am not sure she participated in any of the shenanigans that went on I remember her telling me the story of the Fitzgeralds driving their car down the hill from the Compo Inn which was on the Post Road at that time on a hill across from Kings Highway School. And that Zelda would be riding off of the front fender nude—which I love—and I remember going back up and the Compo Inn was still here when I first was in town and I remember going out just to see what the place was like—it was up on a hill and it used to attract apparently all the New Yorkers because at that time the only way you could get from New York to Boston or anywhere else was on the Post Road and so everybody went right by there and that's why they stopped there for dinner" (Webb, Eve Potts interview).

The second source is an interview Robert and I conducted with Lou White, the then-ninety-year-old granddaughter of famed sculptor Berchtold Nebel. She also shared the Compo Inn story with us, although not the part about Zelda's nudity. White recalled being cautioned never to go to the inn as a child due to its unsavory reputation. "My father attended a 'key party' with the Fitzgeralds," she informed us. "The couples present threw their keys in a hat, which the wives then picked at random and went home with whatever husband's keys they retrieved" (Webb, Lou

White interview). She also cautioned us that her parents did not participate but only observed. Just how reliable such tales are remains anyone's guess.

4. For the popularity of the Grundy name, see John F. Carter Jr.'s "These Wild Young People," perhaps the most famous of the postwar generational declarations not written by Fitzgerald. Carter's widely quoted essay is a response to a previous *Atlantic* essay called "Polite Society" by one "Mr. Grundy" (606–12).

5. Writing in 1926, McIntyre claims that the Fitzgeralds reside in Westport "when they are not in France" (26). In reality, they had not lived there for a half decade; the columnist confused Westport for Great Neck, Long Island—even though Scott and Zelda had left there for good a year and a half earlier, too.

6. Fowler was the friend, as Zelda would note, who recommended the Fitzgeralds try Westport (*Collected Writings* 451).

7. For a fascinating analysis of why car wrecks haunted Fitzgerald, see Workman, who explores the lingering trauma the writer experienced by witnessing his St. Paul neighbor Stuart Beebe Shotwell Jr. mowed down by a car in 1910 and later by the fatalities of two Princeton classmates, Robert E. Sniffin and Charles O. Wiegand, in two separate incidents on 27 and 28 April 1917. *This Side of Paradise* references both tragedies (*TSOP* 17, 84–85).

8. According to Milford, "Shortly after the incident McKaig refers to, Zelda wrote Scott a letter, a fragment of which exists, in which she tries to express her dependence on him" (76). The letter reads as follows: "I look down the tracks and see you coming—and out of every haze + mist your darling rumpled trousers are hurrying toward me—Without you, dearest dearest I couldn't see or hear or feel or think—or live." The editors of the Fitzgeralds' letters to each other, *Dear Scott, Dearest Zelda* (2002), however, date the missive March 1920 and cite its origin as Montgomery, sent before the Fitzgeralds married, much less before they moved to Westport. Although they do not comment on Milford, the implication is that Zelda's biographer reads the opening line too literally and assumes it refers to the 15 September incident (see Bryer and Barks 45).

9. See K. Taylor, *Sometimes Madness Is Wisdom* 86; see also her *Gatsby Affair* 37.

10. *The Herald* noted several remarkable thunderstorms during the summer of 1920, the most important of which occurred on 2 July: "The hardest part of the shower came about 8:30 when there was several very heavy blasts of thunder, followed by many crashes, which shook houses from attic to cellar. . . . One of the bolts of lightning struck the house of Lawrence Mazzanovitch, the well-known artist, located on the west side of the river. The bolt entered the house by following the leader pipe into the cellar, where it ripped the electrical fuse box open, taking off the lid and blowing out all of the fuses" ("Lightning Tears" 1).

FATHERLY DESIGNS
AND CHILDISH BEHAVIORS,
OR ANTHONY COMSTOCK VS. TANALAHAKA
IN *THE BEAUTIFUL AND DAMNED*

David W. Ullrich

Mister Comstock's indignation
Gives a picture reputation
And doubles its sales as Art.

—F. Scott Fitzgerald, "Is It Art" (1916)

As the essay's epigraph from *Safety First!* suggests, even as an undergraduate, F. Scott Fitzgerald was keenly, pragmatically, aware of the complex relationship between artistic self-expression, censorship, notoriety, and the fluctuating value of a given work of art.[1] Fitzgerald's quip refers, explicitly, to one of Anthony Comstock's most celebrated, and infamous, instances of artistic censorship: his much-documented public indignation over a reproduction of Paul Émile Chabas's painting *September Morn* (1911). In May 1913, the art dealers Braun and Company had placed "a copy of the picture" in "the window of their shop at 13 West Forty-sixth Street" in New York (Broun and Leech 239). According to the *New York Times*, Mr. Comstock ordered "Mr. James Kelley, a salesman," to "'Take her out at once. . . . The picture of the girl without any clothes on.'" Mr. James Kelly obliged ("Comstock Dooms").[2] However, Mr. M. Philippe Ortiz, the establishment's manager, replaced the reproduction "out of sheer defiance" and kept the picture in the window, even past its accustomed period of showcasing (Broun and Leech 238–39; see also Bates 181 and Boese for differing accounts of these controversial events).[3] Fitzgerald's lyric for *Safety First!*—"a satire set in 'a Futuristic art community'" (qtd. in Bruccoli, *Some Sort* 66)—draws attention to the ironic, unintended consequences of "Comstock's indignation": "the *September Morn* image became an iconic part of American popular culture during the early twentieth century" (Boese); "the value of the original painting increased from thirty-five dollars to ten thousand dollars," and "the sensation caused the sale value of the prints to soar" as "art dealers across the country sold seven million copies of the picture" (Bates 181).

Paul Émile Chabas's *Matinée de Septembre,* or *September Morn* (1911), which outraged anti-vice crusader Anthony Comstock and ignited a censorship battle.

Fitzgerald revives Anthony Comstock (1844–1915) in *The Beautiful and Damned* (1922) by (*a*) modeling Anthony Patch's grandfather, Adam J. Patch, after Comstock and having him "emulat[e] the magnificent efforts of Anthony Comstock" (12); (*b*) having the elder Patch "request" that Anthony be "christened Anthony Comstock Patch" (13); and as a result, (*c*) tethering Anthony's attempts at self-expression and empowerment to the legacy of Comstock, as embodied in Adam Patch, and also to Anthony's indefinitely postponed, but perpetually anticipated, inheritance of the Patch fortune. Anthony Comstock and his fictional counterparts in *The Beautiful and Damned* loom over Anthony and Gloria Patch as a death-like force of fatherly repression. Through the allusion to Anthony Comstock and buttressed by Fitzgerald's many descriptions, the crusader "more familiarly known as 'Cross Patch'" (12) comes to signify a host of pernicious characteristics. Fitzgerald crafts Adam Patch's "moral righteousness" (18), "profound cynicism" (120), and "pious browbeating" (121) as so prevailing and authoritative that Anthony and Gloria cannot overcome his oppressive presence hovering over their financial hopes and personal aspirations—even after his death. To further complicate this unhealthy dynamic, Anthony and Gloria reflect what Fitzgerald remarked about himself and Zelda at the time he wrote the novel: "We felt like small children" (*MLC* 110). They remain childlike throughout the text, never developing into adulthood, autonomous prosperity, or self-actualization. Despite their protests to the contrary, Anthony and Gloria need guidance in their life choices and validation that meaning and fulfillment exist in the world, rather than "The Meaninglessness of Life" (51). However, each potential father figure helps destroy their nascent, ineffectual gestures toward adulthood, creativity, and self-realization. Fitzgerald uses Anthony Comstock as his prototype for these various father figures. Anthony and Gloria are stymied in their attempts to enter into a professional vocation and, finally, to procreate, in either the literal or figurative sense of the word. As a result, and by design, they implode. As will be discussed, only one character serves as a counterforce to Anthony Comstock and Adam Patch, and Fitzgerald makes sure to undercut this source of Romantic, spirited creativity by presenting him in a disparaging, comedic portrait.

ANTHONY COMSTOCK >>> ADAM PATCH
"Weeder in the Garden of the Lord"

Anthony Comstock's influence on the American cultural landscape began in earnest with his appointment as special agent of the United States Post Office in 1873 and continued well after his death in 1915. As Amy Werbel's recent study makes abundantly clear, he remains a powerful force of censorship down to this very day.[4] The Comstock Law was passed on 3 March 1873, "during the last minutes of the forty-second Congressional session . . . at 2:00 in the morning" and "out of consecutive order with the other bills under consideration" (Bates

90). The bill was passed by "a dysfunctional legislature" and was bolstered by Congressman Clinton Merriam "moving to suspend the rules and vote on the law without debate" (Werbel 77). The formal title of the law is the Act for the Suppression of Trade in, and Circulation of, Obscene Literature and Articles of Immoral Use. The act prohibited, in part, anyone who

> shall sell, or offer to sell, or shall give away, or offer to give away, or shall have in his or her possession with intent to sell or give away, any obscene or inde-cent book, pamphlet, paper, advertisement, drawing, lithograph, engraving, wood-cut, daguerreotype, photograph, stereoscopic picture, model, cast, in-strument, or other article for indecent or immoral nature, or any article or medicine for the prevention of conception, or for causing abortion except on a prescription of a physician in good standing." (qtd. in Bates "Appendix")

Although Comstock had but a "scanty education," having enlisted in the Civil War while in high school (Broun and Leech 18), he personally authored much of the law, which came about because he was frustrated that the existing federal laws did not "cover sex related writing in newspapers" and did not provide sufficient legal authority to arrest and prosecute potential offenders (Bates 78, 84). When the law passed, Comstock received a commission as spe-cial agent of the United States Post Office, which provided him with "the legal tools and the appropriate powerful position to launch his anti-vice crusade" (90), although he still lacked the authority to arrest an individual.

Powerful politicians and industrialists, among them J. Pierpont Morgan, Samuel Colgate, and Morris Ketchum Jesup—described as "an army of like-minded Soldiers of the Cross, equipped with an arsenal of money and political clout" (Werbel 57)—regarded Comstock as "a valuable policeman who would enforce a moral code conducive to their own prosperity" and "would make an excellent fighter on the front line of their antivice offensive" (Bates 99). Comstock gained entrance into the New York elite through Jesup, and after meeting at Jesup's mansion on Madison Avenue, the "'warfare against obscene books' moved extremely quickly" (Werbel 55–57). Jesup and other New York power brokers formed the infamous New York Society for the Suppression of Vice (NYSSV), whose objective was "the suppression of the trade in and circulation of obscene literature and illustrations, advertisements, and articles of indecent and immoral use." Comstock received an additional appointment as the NYSSV's "Secretary and Special Agent" (Bates 99–100). Significantly, section 5 of the Society's *Act of Incorporation* "justified Society members acting as police officers" (Bates 99). Armed with these powers, possessed by an overzealous and, at times, ruthless determination to "do something for Jesus every day" (qtd. in Bates 105), Comstock waged war against perceived and real sinners for the next forty years.[5] Comstock "believed he was above the law," as he thought he "answered to a higher authority" (Bates 101).[6]

Comstock "attacked literature [i.e., publications] . . . that defended free speech and the right to challenge Christian institutions. Freethinkers, said Comstock, 'ruthlessly trample underfoot the most sacred things, break down the altars of religion'" (Bates 125). He defined morality according to his own strict, puritanical, and patriarchal beliefs and enforced his morality with strong-arm tactics and relentless efforts, as his monikers suggest: "Weeder in the Garden of the Lord" and "Roundsman of the Lord."[7] Bates, one of two reputable Comstock biographers, summarizes his legacy as follows: "Comstock goes down in history as a repressive individual who . . . did more than any other individual to restrict free speech in the United States. The long list of people whose lives he ruined evidences his power" (210).[8] Werbel—whose recent study provides the most informed and in-depth analysis of Comstock, the Comstock Laws, and their combined effects on everything from art to advertisements to reputed pornography—states, "At the time of his death, Comstock served in the public imagination not only as the embodiment of government censorship, but also as the greatest representative of a 'Puritan'" (299).

Much of Comstock's overzealous attention was focused against women: women's access to basic health and medical information, such as "sexual anatomy" (Bates 79), and women's reproductive rights, but also images of women's bodies, and the money spent purchasing those images in quite disparate media, such as pornographic postcards, representations of artistic masterpieces, classical sculpture, and the emerging industry of moving pictures. His lifelong and systematic bullying of women whose moral values clashed with his own began with his early and contentious conflicts in 1872–73 with Tennessee Claflin and Victoria Claflin Woodhull, whose *Woodhull and Claflin Weekly* "supported socialist theories, pantarchy, free love, women's rights, and labor reform" (Bates 71; see also Broun and Leech 93–127; and Werbel 60–64). It extended to his "1902 arrest of [the spiritualist and eroticist] Ida Craddock and her subsequent suicide[, which] caused public outrage" and was deemed "obsessed" (190) and "sadist[ic]" (Bates, 189, 191; see also Broun and Leech 211–14). The ever-vigilant Comstock raided the prominent and well-respected Knoedler Art Gallery on Fifth Avenue (Bates 178; Werbel 190–95) and confiscated New York's famous Art Students' League publication, which he thought "was obscene because it contained drawings of nude human figures" (Bates 178; see also Werbel 271–74). Toward the end of his life, Comstock took action to confiscate the publications of William and Margaret Sanger and repeatedly attempted to suppress a woman's right to have access to medical and health-related information when such pamphlets contained anatomical illustrations of a woman's body or were distributed through federal mail. As one might expect, "one of his longest-running nemeses" in the debate over women's rights was Emma Goldman (Werbel 295). Comstock is also remembered as the self-appointed censor of George Bernard Shaw's *Mrs. Warren's Profession,* which he had barred from the stage in 1905, calling Shaw "this Irish smut dealer" (Broun and Leech 18). Shaw, in turn, coined the expression "comstockery" to suggest excessive or inordinate opposition to alleged immorality in the arts. However, as Werbel points out, "In the course of these events, Comstock learned a valuable lesson about the power of the media: targeting high-profile defendants implicated in spicy crimes was the quickest way for him to build his name as America's pre-eminent vice suppressor" (63).

Fitzgerald's portrait of Adam Patch captures many of Comstock's specific qualities, including his moralizing, physical intimidation and bullying, quick temper, and zealotry. Although Anthony Comstock died 21 September 1915, his influence was, as the *New York Times* attests, still pervasive in 1922, the year *The Beautiful and Damned* was published.[9] Fitzgerald characterizes Adam J. Patch as "a reformer among reformers" (12), and Anthony Comstock's biographer describes him as "no ordinary reformer" (Bates 16). Comstock's biographers speak of his "nearly boundless" energy and that he "vigorously pursued" his targets "at a furious pace" (Werbel 59). Fitzgerald reproduces these specific traits in his depiction of Adam Patch's "untiring fury," "pious rage," and "righteous indignation" (174). Comstock is characterized as "authoritarian," "repressive," and "a fanatic" (Bates 56, 201, and 13, respectively). Fitzgerald captures well these characteristics in his many descriptions of the old man: "He was . . . [a] regular religious maniac," who "attacked each [news]paper" and who exudes a "hellish portentousness" (246, 174, and 231 respectively). As to Comstock's

oft-noted "bellicose" nature (Werbel 4) and his willingness to "fight upon occasion" (Trumbull 20), Fitzgerald describes Patch early in his campaigns as follows: "he levelled a varied assortment of upper-cuts and body-blows at liquor,
literature, vice, art, patent medicines, and Sunday theatres" (12). Fitzgerald is
not being hyperbolic in these passages; he is joining other satirists in mocking
Comstock's pugnacious, vitriolic temperament by emphasizing Adam Patch
as being a "rabid monomaniac" (12). Fitzgerald translates Comstock's irasci-
ble temper, puritanical ambition, and even his partisan, public support into
Adam Patch's "fuss, fume, applause, and ill will" in accumulating seventy-five
million dollars on Wall Street (12). Of course, Fitzgerald redraws Comstock's
"vindictive" personality (Bates 79) in Adam Patch's disinheriting Anthony.[10]

The novel's initial, brief summary of Adam Patch's life suggests that Fitzgerald acquired a detailed knowledge of Comstock's life, which was readily
available in biographical and newspaper format, and used this information in
his fictive construction of Adam Patch's history. Adam Patch lives in Tarrytown, Connecticut, and Comstock is born and lives much of his life in New
Canaan, Connecticut—towns twenty-eight miles apart. Patch enlists "in sixty-
one" in "a New York cavalry regiment" during the Civil War; Comstock "joined
Company H of the Connecticut Seventeenth Infantry" on 23 July 1862 (Bates
39; Werbel 38–41). Adam Patch "had married an anaemic lady of thirty" who
becomes "completely devitalized" in the act of giving birth (12). Comstock
married Margaret Hamilton, "a shy, eighty-two-pound woman" (Bates 54), who
is described as "worn out" and "not strong" (Broun and Leech 62) and characterized by "retiring inertia" (Werbel 50). Significantly, Anthony Comstock
"collected postage stamps down to the day of his death" (Broun and Leech 12;
see also Bates 56). A collection of postage stamps plays a pivotal role in the
dramatic climax of *The Beautiful and Damned* (367).

By modeling Anthony's grandfather on Anthony Comstock, Fitzgerald
extends the contested, claustrophobic relationship between grandfather and
grandson to a broader cultural and political landscape. Fitzgerald dramatizes
how moneyed, repressive puritanism can overpower a young person's inchoate
struggle to discover a means of creative self-expression, a successful vocation,
and a professional livelihood. Thus, *The Beautiful and Damned* can be appre-
ciated in context with other Fitzgerald works at this time of a more obviously
political nature and employing an ambiguous "fatherly" figure, such as Brad-

dock Tarleton Washington in "The Diamond as Big as the Ritz" (1922, *TJA* 127–68), and, assuredly, the father/son relationship (and cultural criticisms implied within) between Horatio ("Dada") Frost and his son, Jerry Frost, in *The Vegetable* (1923).[11]

ADAM PATCH >>> ANTHONY COMSTOCK PATCH

. . . a demand for expression with no outlet. (83)

By requiring the newborn Patch to be "christened Anthony Comstock" (13), Fitzgerald bequeaths Anthony a kind of inherited character flaw, an original sin, much as he does when introducing Amory Blaine on the first page of *This Side of Paradise* (1920) by listing his parents' deficiencies (*TSOP* 11). In similar fashion, Fitzgerald hamstrings Dick Diver from the outset of *Tender Is the Night* when he has the Fairy Blackstick metaphorically christen the Dr. Diver of 1917 by saying, "The best I can wish you, my child . . . is a little misfortune" (*TITN* 117). Thus, to a greater or lesser degree, all three novels center on a family's fortune, or to be more accurate, "misfortune," and its debilitating effects on the protagonist. Once we recognize that Daisy Fay is doomed from the moment she chooses (also in 1917) Tom Buchanan's "three hundred and fifty thousand dollars" worth of pearls over Jay Gatsby's letter (*GG* 91–92), it becomes clear how intentionally—even compulsively—Fitzgerald damns his beautiful central characters. Even Thalia Taylor (later Kathleen Moore) in *The Last Tycoon* does not escape Fitzgerald's predestined, ill-fated plan (*LLT* xxxii).

Early in *The Beautiful and Damned*, we learn that Anthony's mother dies when he is five (13), and that after that Anthony "lived up at Grampa's in Tarrytown" with his father, Adam Ulysses Patch. When Anthony is eleven, his father dies, and he experiences "a panic of despair and terror" and develops "a horror of death" (13, 14). Anthony's arrival at and departure from his grandfather's house is punctuated by his parents' deaths, and so "to Anthony life was a struggle against death, that waited at every corner" (14). By 1913, Anthony is twenty-five years old and living in his "Reproachless Apartment." Initially, the physical details of the apartment seem an extension of Anthony having been "an exquisite dandy" at Harvard, where he "amassed a rather pathetic collection of silk pajamas" and "in this secret finery he would parade before the mirror" (15). Admittedly, Fitzgerald includes these attributes to convey Anthony's decadence and even a kind of weakness. However, Anthony's furnishings and his actions also represent his defiant response to having lived for seven years with his grandfather, Adam J. Patch.

Fitzgerald carefully constructs Anthony's resistance to his grandfather's "power" and "obsessions" (20) and, simultaneously, illustrates Anthony's efforts to renounce the "Comstock" within his given name through (*a*) the descriptions of "The Reproachless Apartment," (*b*) Anthony's actions and attitudes therein, and (*c*) the narrative elements of early chapters, such as "Afternoon" (22–27). Anthony has "framed around the walls" of his bathroom "photographs of four celebrated thespian beauties of the day"—four Gibson Girls who starred in various movies (17).[12] Anthony singles out one of these women, Hazel Dawn, and "put an imaginary violin to his shoulder and softly caressed it with a phantom bow" (22). The image serves as a metaphor for serenading the actress and for Anthony's onanistic self-pleasuring. Fitzgerald clarifies Anthony's masculinized innuendo by an aside, "a print representing a great stretch of snow . . . symbolized the cold shower" (17).

Anthony's bathroom and bedroom provide him with a safe place to revel in a sort of narcissistic eroticism. In it, Anthony surrounds himself with what amounts to a collection of pinup photographs of four idealized, static women. Here, he can express his desires privately and tentatively. His bathroom is "a room to conjure with" but nothing more (17). Like Anthony, the apartment is merely "a magnificent potentiality" (17), a luxurious place of self-indulgence. Fitzgerald expresses Anthony's existential situation through his choice of the conditional pluperfect: "he felt that if he had a love he would have hung her picture just facing the tub, so that, lost in the soothing steamings of the hot water, he might lie and look up at her and muse warmly and sensuously on her beauty" (17–18).

Through the motif of photographs, Fitzgerald demonstrates the marked differences between Anthony's inchoate and immature efforts toward Eros, sexuality, and creativity, and his grandfather's commitment to Thanatos, violence, and destruction in *his* choice of photographic pinups. In contrast to Anthony's pinups of the Gibson Girls, Adam Patch has "plastered his walls" with "[p]in maps" of the Great War (174). In addition, the old man "subsisted on the war news"—that is, he lived for and was sustained by—news of unimaginable violence and the death of, literally, millions of young soldiers. His grandfather's photographs consist of "Photographic Histories of the War," which surely must contain images of embattled soldiers, the misery and filth of trench warfare, and gruesome images of carnage. Adam Patch has also amassed volumes of "'Personal Impressions' of war correspondents and of Privates X, Y, and Z" and "atlases . . . piled deep on tables convenient to his hand" (174). In vampire-like fashion, old Cross Patch feeds on ("subsists on") photographs, autobiographical accounts, "[p]in maps," and "atlases" of the world war. The grandfather has substituted the grandson's undifferentiated, youthful erotica with an overde-termined, fetishistic fascination with death. Fitzgerald underscores the sexual implications of Adam Patch's preoccupation with the death of young soldiers in his choice of diction: "The old man attacked each paper with untiring fury, tearing out those columns which appeared to him of sufficient pregnancy . . . and thrusting them into one of his already bulging files" (174). In this odd and convoluted metaphor, war casualty statistics provide Adam Patch with a continuous supply of data to sustain his fetish for the death of the young, and he entombs them within his engorged folders (174).

A second, early vignette, "Afternoon," arrests the reader's attention with its provocatively voyeuristic scenario and sexually charged details of Anthony un-dressing to take a bath. Fitzgerald selects "[s]tripped," rather than, for example, "undressed," to describe Anthony taking off his clothes, and describes Anthony "adopting an athletic posture like the tiger-skinned man [i.e., Tarzan] in the advertisement" as he "regarded himself with some satisfaction in the mirror" (22).[13] Anthony stands naked, poised, and facing the mirror in a full-frontal, intimate self-evaluation and frank assessment of his body. In this moment, he is narcissistic, confident, and provocative. The scene continues as Anthony "polished himself with the meticulous attention of a bootblack"—a curious simile implying a blemish or stain that needs to be rubbed out—and "enjoy[ed] the warmth of the thick carpet in his feet" (22, 23).

In *Paradise,* Fitzgerald associated three specific words—"feet," "alley," and "window" (*TSOP* 108–14)—with Amory Blaine's sexual conflicts, as portrayed in the so-called "Devil passage," which includes subchapters entitled "In the Alley" and "At the Window" (*TSOP* 110–12 and 112–14, respectively). In "The Reproachless Apartment," Anthony's feet function as metonyms for his entire bodily pleasures: his "exotic rug of crimson velvet was soft as fleece on his bare feet," and another "rich rug . . . [was] a miracle of softness, that seemed almost to massage the wet foot emerging from the tub" (17). In "Afternoon," Fitzgerald reprises these same three images to convey another highly sexualized vision imagined by his protagonist. Anthony has just "emerg[ed] from his bath" (22), "wandered into his bedroom," and looked out the window, where his eyes "focused upon a spot of brilliant color on the roof of a house farther down the alley" (23). The narrator continues: "It was a girl in a red negligée, silk surely, drying her hair by the still hot sun of late afternoon." Amid "the stiff air in the room," Anthony "walked cautiously another step nearer the window with a sudden impression that she was beautiful" (23). The narrator intensifies the scene, noting: "He watched her for several minutes. Something was stirred in him, something not accounted for by the warm smell of the afternoon or the triumphant vividness of red. He felt persistently that the girl was beautiful" (23). Not only does Anthony project his own desire onto the unnamed woman, but he cultivates, even revels in, his projections: "his emotion had been nearer to adoration than in the deepest kiss he had ever known" (23). The narrative unambiguously describes Anthony's intense, but undifferentiated, emotional responses to the scene: "something was stirred in him," "he felt persistently that the girl was beautiful," and "his emotion had been nearer to adoration" (23).

The two vignettes portray Anthony's tentative attempts to develop a sense of self and to reject the damning "christening" of the puritanical "Comstock." However, as a metafictional commentary, they also function as Fitzgerald refuting Comstockian morality and its legislative authority—an issue that will resurface in the litigious complications of Adam Patch's will. Anthony's pinups of the Gibson Girls; his sumptuously furnished apartment; the sexualized manner in which he parades himself, naked, in front of the mirror (twice) in his bathroom; his private, sexual fantasies about the woman in the negligée drying her hair—these intimate events inform Anthony's everyday life, and they conflict with and oppose his grandfather's moral code. Fitzgerald's description of Anthony posed as the Tarzan-like he-man "in the advertisement" (22) is a direct affront to the kinds of paraphernalia Anthony Comstock routinely prosecuted.[14] Fitzgerald constructs these two opening scenes to challenge directly Anthony Comstock's (and Adam Patch's) views as to what constitutes "obscenity" in literature, art, public discourse, and individual public, even private, comportment. Moreover, the narrator is careful to specify what Anthony's apartment has avoided: "it escaped stiffness, stuffiness, barrenness, and decadence" (17). It has escaped his grandfather; it has escaped Anthony Comstock. The apartment is also, significantly, if defensively, given Adam Patch's "sanctimonious browbeating," beyond reproach (21).

Thus, Fitzgerald's opening narrative decisions in *The Beautiful and Damned* consist of a series of not-so-hypothetical test cases for the censors to consider. Fitzgerald constructs both "The Reproachless Apartment" and "Afternoon" as voyeuristic vignettes, as if the reader is watching, unseen, and through a key-hole, so to speak, as Anthony strips and stands naked in the mirror, bathes— and with the suggestion of masturbation—muses "warmly and sensuously on her beauty" (18). Readers are invited to imagine the naked Anthony, detailed in a graphic way through a specific pose, "an athletic posture" of a public figure, "the tiger-skin man in the advertisement" (22), rather than a generic descrip- tion. We must imagine what constitutes "an athletic posture," and in so doing, visualize Anthony as naked. In "Afternoon" the reader is placed in what then would have been considered a "pornographic" perspective: watching Anthony watch a woman in a private, intimate situation—one, in fact, quite similar to that depicted in Chabas's *September Morn*. Fitzgerald adds a clichéd "red neg- ligée" of "silk surely" (23) to ground the scene, visually and tactilely, in order to intensify the reader's imaginative participation in observing these events. The reader is encouraged to participate in Anthony's sexual fantasies by means of several rhetorical devices, such as Anthony's (and the reader's) hidden per- spective, the window as a portal, the aestheticized distance of the woman, her unawareness of being observed, and the hypothetical "silk surely" (23). In constructing this scene—which in its essential elements echoes David watching Bathsheba bathing (2 Samuel 11)—Fitzgerald parodies Comstockian attempts to define what is obscene or pornographic and satirizes corresponding legal efforts to censor artistic expression. Whether or not Fitzgerald intended it, "Afternoon," as written, could not have been photographed or filmed without it being considered pornographic in its day.

From a very different perspective, Anthony's apartment is also described as a "safe place": "he was safe in here from all the threat of life" for "there was the door and the long hall and his guardian bedroom—safe, safe!" (30). Anthony's apartment is a retreat from familial tragedy and from the "clamor" (15) of a teeming New York City that both captivates and bedazzles him. It is a place where Anthony can luxuriate in autoerotic fantasies without consequences or commitments. However, the opening chapters also teach Anthony a harsh les- son, one he will be forced to confront over and over: his amorphous fantasies are not to be trusted, and they will crash against the outside world in startling and debilitating ways. The potential dangers that exist outside of his apartment are foreshadowed in the parable of the "Deplorable End of the Chevalier O'Keefe" (77–83), which is Anthony's "one creation," a "creature of [his] splendid mind" (80). Anthony's story concludes with a sexually motivated suicide; the Chevalier O'Keefe becomes so enraptured with his solitary fantasy that he literally loses his balance and falls to his death. As the final, Catholic, verdict surmises, his death is a kind of suicide—it is self-willed and self-inflicted. No one kills the Chevalier O'Keefe; he kills himself, victim of the very desires from which he seeks to both escape and indulge. This episode should, but does not, forewarn Anthony against his "deep delight in being with [Gloria] that colored the banality of his words . . . and made . . . the posturing seem wise" (99). The episode should caution Anthony that the Gloria he will fall in love with is partly made up by himself—a reflection of his own infantile narcissism.

Finally, then, Anthony is alone and passive in the world. As a simple measure of his apathetic self-absorption, book 1, which is devoted to his life before his marriage (11–112), runs more than one hundred pages, more than a quarter of the novel. Yet halfway through Fitzgerald constructs a not-too-subtle juxtaposing between his protagonist's arrested emotional state and "Announcing Miss Gloria Gilbert." Anthony has "no record of achievement" and is "a pretentious fool, making careers out of cocktails and meanwhile regretting, weakly and secretly, the collapse of an insufficient and wretched idealism." The narrator concludes, "He was empty, it seemed, empty as an old bottle—" (53). Anthony does not need just any woman, a Geraldine. He needs a woman who can stimulate his imagination beyond passive fantasy and into action in the real world, into realizing his dreams. His apartment is "safe," Geraldine is a safe, almost palliative, partner. Only dimly does Anthony realize these things about himself. When he tells Geraldine the story of the Chevalier, it is she, not Anthony, who understands that the story reveals his loneliness and commitment to the pursuit of an idealized woman. Accordingly, Geraldine wisely predicts that Anthony will marry within a year (83). But alone, Anthony is powerless to move out of the world of dreams and into the world of reality. He needs a woman sufficiently glorious to captivate him, to enliven him, to help him transform himself. But, tragically, Gloria, despite her beauty and through no fault of her own, is simply incapable of guiding Anthony in his life's endeavors. She frankly and candidly states, "I've told you I don't know what anybody ought to do" (98). Anthony had hoped that in his relationship with Gloria he would find "the quintessence of self-expression" (116) and he would discover "a hope that would be brawn and sinew to his self-respect" (104). Instead, "Gloria had lulled Anthony's mind to sleep" (163). Anthony needs something more than the beauty of "A Lady's Legs" (42) to counteract his "despair," "melancholy," and commitment to "The Meaninglessness of Life" (13, 14, 51). He never finds it.

JUDGE ANTHONY SAYRE >>> ADAM PATCH >>> ANTHONY COMSTOCK

Family life became a ritual passed through the sieve of Austin's strong conviction.

—ZELDA FITZGERALD,

ON JUDGE AUSTIN BEGGS, IN *SAVE ME THE WALTZ*

Although the timeframe of Adam Patch's unexpected visit to the grey house "of an August evening" occurs in 1916, Fitzgerald's audience in 1922 would have no trouble recognizing Adam Patch's "arriv[al] without any warning" amid "a rather gay party" (246) as Fitzgerald's comic burlesque of a Comstock-like raid on any number of establishments deemed of intemperate or immoral character, either before (1916) or after (1922) Prohibition. Although Comstock died in 1915, his legacy and the Comstock Laws continued to be enforced, especially after Prohibition went into effect in January 1920. The infamous party at Anthony and Gloria's incudes all of the paraphernalia of a saloon or a dance hall. The scene incorporates an impromptu dance floor; mixed couples dancing drunkenly; extramarital flirtation and intrigue; suggestive, contemporary music; and of course, alcohol galore, as Anthony was "asking everyone to have a drink" (225). As the narrator states, "Bedlam creeps screaming out of the bottles," and "pandemonium" drowns out Adam Patch's approach (230). Fitzgerald links the two chronologies—1916 and 1922—in a remark that concludes the episode: "Adam Patch has that morning made a contribution of fifty thousand dollars to the cause of national prohibition" (230).

The entire debauch is hilarious and hilariously delivered, but the consequences are dire. Adam Patch's presence is described in terms of death, censorship, and sexual repression. A "monstrous pall" descends on the room, "the phonograph gags," and suggestively, "the notes of the Japanese train song dribble from the end of Tana's flute" (230). The silence is "weighted with intolerably contagious apprehension" (230), as Anthony says an ineffective "something to

Adam Patch; then this, too, dies away" (231). The immediate effects on Anthony and Gloria are devastating: "Anthony is the color of chalk," and "Gloria's lips are parted and her level gaze at the old man is tense and frightened" (231). Fitzgerald gives the entire vignette special rhetorical treatment, presenting it in dramatic, rather than expositional, format, in order to accentuate the emotional impact on the reader and to achieve a distinctive narrative prominence.

Fitzgerald modeled this episode on an actual occurrence: Judge Anthony and Minnie Sayre's visit to Scott and Zelda's rented Westport home, the Wakeman House, in August 1920. As Sally Cline, Zelda's biographer, recounts, Judge and Minnie Sayre "discovered two drunken friends of Scott's asleep in the hammock who arose and danced drunkenly at the dinner table." These same two men "returned at 3am, whereupon Scott began drinking gin and tomato juice with them" (95). To make matters worse, Zelda, conscious of her parents' presence in the house, "tried to remove the gin bottle from Scott," who "fended her off," and Zelda's "face caught in the swinging door" so that "her nose bled and her eyes swelled up" and blackened (95–96). In the morning, "the Judge was stony with disapproval" (96). Another biographer, Nancy Milford, also remarks on "the Judge's glacial attitude" over these events and toward the life Scott and Zelda were leading (74), and Bruccoli reports that "the visit was uncomfortable" and "the Judge did not conceal his disapproval of the way the Fitzgeralds lived" (*Some Sort* 143). The Sayres quit the Fitzgerald's house "a week earlier than planned, to visit their 'good' daughter," Clothilde, "who lived nearby in Tarrytown" (Cline 96)—which, not coincidentally, is Fitzgerald's pointed choice for the fictive home of Adam Patch. One suspects that Gloria's "level gaze at the old man" and her "tense and frightened" response to Adam Patch approximate Zelda's own reactions to her father Judge Sayre's manifest disapproval of that August night's alcoholic romp.

Fitzgerald transposed this incident into a pivotal episode in *The Beautiful and Damned*. Under Fitzgerald's fictive re-creations, the abstemious and "austere" Judge Anthony Sayre, and especially, the Judge's "devotion to the law" (Bruccoli, *Some Sort* 89) morph onto the intemperate and "hellish portentousness" of Adam Patch (231), and through him, the equally aloof Anthony Comstock and his devotion to *his* Laws. Thus, when Fitzgerald dooms Anthony and Gloria to spend the rest of their lives in various states of neurosis and despair over the legalities of Anthony's presumed inheritance, Fitzgerald is suggesting the long-lasting and debilitating power Judge Anthony Sayre had over Zelda, himself, and their relationship—a nefarious inheritance of sorts. Judge Sayre—as Adam Patch in the grey house scene, and, years later, as Judge Beggs's "outraged decency" in Zelda's *Save Me the Waltz*—symbolizes "the force of law" (*Complete Writings* 11–12), and its consequences, which shape so much of *The Beautiful and Damned*. Perhaps the inconspicuous "J." in Adam J. Patch suggests Judge.

Anthony and Gloria respond to Adam Patch's severity as children—children who have misbehaved, have disobeyed an overbearing, judgmental father figure. First, they bicker among themselves, as "recrimination had displaced affection" (232), and then they are "capable only of one pervasive emotion—fear" (233). Gloria, who "love[s] gum-drops" and is "always whacking away at one—whenever my daddy's not around" (59), reverts to childish behavior, as "the moment required that she should gnaw at her finger like a nervous child" (234), and again, "nibbling at her finger" and "biting" her finger (233, 234). This description squares well with Cline's biographical account of the aftermath of the Sayres' disastrous visit, when "Zelda resettled into her baby role" (95). Anthony is at his wits' end to reconcile with his grandfather and contemplates a "reformation," "biblical quotations," and playing the prodigal son, admitting "that I had walked too long in the way of unrighteousness" (234). However, when, at Gloria's insistence, he finally works up the courage to go to Tarrytown and visit his grandfather and his "violent animosity" (235), the old man's secretary, Edward Shuttleworth, intervenes and stymies his half-hearted efforts. Crestfallen and cowardly, Anthony with "almost a slink" leaves, "glad to escape, boylike, to the wonder-places of consolation that still rose and glittered in his own mind" (235).

TANALAHAKA

But after all every writer writes because it's his mode of living.
—ANTHONY PATCH

In a novel committed to representing an anatomy of lethargy and self-implosion, readers must look beyond the narrator's insistent negativity and unrelenting irony to discover a counterargument, an opposing force, to entropy, stasis, and if not moral decay, then, surely moral despair. Such a character must represent a clear, determined reprisal to Adam Patch but also must embody an alternative to Anthony's "limitations" (187) and "depression" (190) as well as Gloria's "Nietzschean" (139), brittle "Never give a damn" (172).

The Patches' house servant in Marietta, Tanalahaka, or "Tana," represents a direct challenge to Adam Patch, Anthony Comstock, and the Comstock Laws and, further, suggests an instructional directive for Anthony. Again, readers must look past the narrator's disparaging characterization of this "godless Oriental" (as Anthony's rather dense drinking buddy Ted Paramore misleadingly deems him [221]); the text ridicules the one character who offers a much-needed antidote to the troubled universe of the beautiful and damned. Tana represents Eros, the creative force, professionalism, and a distinctively romantic representation of the artist struggling to express himself—a moral and aesthetic imperative to which Fitzgerald is steadfastly committed. Fitzgerald constructs the characterization of Tana as a facade meant to overdetermine the reader's depreciation of Tana by reducing him to a caricature and effacing his character as an emblem of artistic creativity and professionalism.

"Tanalahaka" cannot be a Japanese name. There is no "1" or "la" sound or spelling in Japanese. However, "Tanaka" is a typical Japanese last name. In his *Ledger* for June 1920, Fitzgerald writes only "Tana"; in *The Beautiful and Damned* Maury quips, "*Tana!* That's not his real name. I understand he constantly gets mail addressed to Lieutenant Emile Tannenbaum" (223). The real Tana's full name remains a mystery.

Fitzgerald introduces Tana with explicit reference to the Comstock Laws, and in particular, possessing pornographic materials and receiving such material through federal mail. The "treasure" in Tana's trunk includes "half a dozen [postcards] of pornographic intent and plainly American in origin, though the makers had modestly omitted both their names and the form for mailing" (165). Tana's postcards are a direct affront, an explicit challenge, to the repressive Anthony Comstock, and behind him, Adam Patch. Tana also counters the ever-present Comstock deep inside Anthony, that portion of him that inhibits or denies his latent will to write and his will to procreate in the literal or figurative sense of the word.

Fitzgerald represents Tana as taking himself seriously, carefully contemplating his ideas, struggling to express himself, and bringing his creative expressions to fruition, even at some personal anguish and "pain" (166). When first introducing Tana, the narrator underscores his inventiveness and creativity: he had brought "some of his own handiwork," including "a pair of American pants, which he had made himself," and, significantly, "a flute; he had made it himself, but it was broken" (165). Fitzgerald's second description of Tana calls into question the disparaging tone of the narrator: "he was conscientious and honorable" (166), and later, "[t]he faithful Tana pedagogue by nature and man of all work by profession" (199). Anthony aspires to these qualities and half-heartedly attempts to follow them, but falls short. However, for Fitzgerald, being a professional is the highest praise a writer can garner: "I am in every sense a professional," Fitzgerald claims in his 1933 essay "One Hundred False Starts" (*MLC* 89). And although the narrator adds that Tana "was unques-tionably a terrific bore [i.e., pedagogue]" who "seemed unable to control his tongue, sometimes continuing from paragraph to paragraph with a look akin to pain in his small brown eyes" (166), Fitzgerald himself was charged with much the same fault when, in searching for verisimilitude, he pestered his friends about their personal lives and intimacies, as Gerald and Sara Murphy, among many others, often complained (Bruccoli, *Some Sort* 251). Moreover, the narrator's choice of configuring Tana's verbal expressions as "continuing from paragraph to paragraph" points to Tana as a metaphor for a writer, not a long-winded orator.

Tana represents the personal struggles of an artist committed to his craft and to the desire to be understood, which is rendered in the text through his frustrations in expressing himself in broken English and through his playing the flute.[15] When speaking, Tana "screwed up his face in a tremendous effort to express himself," and again, "[h]e screwed up his face for action" (183). In preparing to play the flute, the narrator notes, "[h]is brow [was] undergoing preposterous contraction" (221). In trying to express himself in a foreign lan-guage, Tana approximates Fitzgerald's own struggles at artistic self-expression as he strived to transform everyday language out of its pragmatic usage and into another language, into poetic discourse, into the lyricism for which Fitz-gerald is famous.

The text underscores Tana's commitment to professionalism and his quest for artistic perfection by foregrounding his practicing and his performing the flute. When Tana practices, the music is described as "the gnarled strain [pun] breaks off and, after an interval of indistinct mutterings, recommences," and this process continues "[just] prior to the seventh false start" (220). Fitzgerald identifies with Tana's predicament, as seen in "One Hundred False Starts," wherein Fitzgerald claims that to "start over . . . is one of the most difficult decisions that an author must make. . . . [It] is a test of whether or not he is really a professional." Again, Fitzgerald speaks of his many "false starts," his belief that "work is almost everything," and his commitment to "the serious business of my profession" (*MLC* 89–90). He concludes the essay by citing Joseph Conrad to suggest the struggle a writer must endure in his quest to be understood: "My task is by the power of the written word to make you hear, to make you feel—it is, before all, to make you *see*" (qtd. in *MLC* 90). Fitzgerald presents Tana as an artist committed to self-expression and to professionalism, to Fitzgerald's personal imperative to "throw it away and start over" (*MLC* 89), and to progressing from private practice (writing) to public performance (publishing), as when Tana performs "the melody of the Japanese train song—this time not a practice, surely, but a lusty spirited performance" (222).

Fitzgerald makes several other narrative decisions that mitigate against interpreting Tana as a derisively comic character. The "typewutter" passage (182–83) begins with Tana "seated at the kitchen table before a miscellaneous assortment of odds and ends," which include nondescript, throwaway curiosities, such as "cigar boxes" and "the tops of cans" (182). However, interspersed within these items, Fitzgerald makes sure to include "pencils" and "some scraps of paper covered with elaborate figures and diagrams" (182). These items function as Fitzgerald's private, professional self-signifiers. They refer to Fitzgerald's preferred method of writing—he only wrote with pencils and loose-leaf paper, never on a typewriter—and to his method for outlining an extended plotline. As Fitzgerald writes to Zelda when beginning *The Last Tycoon*: "My room is covered with charts like it used to be for 'Tender Is the Night' telling the different movements of the characters and their histories" (*LLT* xxxviii).

Tana's commitment to improving the mechanics of the typewriter in order to make the process of writing less arduous is presented in language typically reserved for the compulsive nature of the writer (or artist) obsessed with his material and his struggles to compose, to move from hypothetical content to realized object: "I think, oh all time I think, lie in bed think 'bout typewutta" (182), and again, "I been think—typewutter" and "I been think—many words" (183). Tana's obsession with his "typewutter" echoes Fitzgerald's description of his own preoccupation in planning *The Last Tycoon*: "I think of nothing else" (*LLT* xxxviii). Moreover, Tana's correcting Anthony's "keys" with "lettah" implies an attention to the craft of language. Tana's "I been think—many words— end same. Like i-n-g" and "Many many many many lettah. Like a-b-c" (183) suggest Fitzgerald's own appreciation for the infinite lexical possibilities offered by language. Tana functions in these scenes as a metaphorical account of the writer's compulsiveness, dedication to professionalism, sense of craft in drafting and revising, and obligation to produce a product for public consumption.

Before proceeding with the next section of the essay, an important preliminary point must be established. Tana's *"railroad* song" (221) (testudo shoka) refers, explicitly, to "Tetsudo Shoka Chiri Kyoika," or "Geography Education Railroad Songs," and, as Traganou and others note, were "written by the scholar Owada Tateki" (24).[16]

According to one Japanese cultural critic, "In 1900, the railway songs (testudo shoka), written by the scholar Owada Takeki, became very popular among young Japanese children.... The songs were widely disseminated, since these songs, which comprised a grammar school textbook, helped children learn historical and geographical facts strengthening their national consciousness" (Traganou 24). Thus, the children's railway songs played an important part in integrating and normalizing the newly constructed railway system into Japanese cultural consciousness by associating the railroad with historical and mythological events. The songs also provided a mnemonic heuristic for educating children to the cultural importance of the railroad through its identification with major geographical and religious sites as the trains traversed the Japanese landscape. Another analysis states: "The famous 'Railway Song' (Tetsudo Shoka) by Owada Takeki was an unprecedented hit after it was released on May 10, 1900. Sung in elementary schools in part to teach children about geography, this tune glorified the view from Japan's modern steam locomotive after it left Shimbashi Station, Tokyo's main terminal" (Freedman 39). Most critics interpret the "Railroad Songs" as intended to strengthen a conservative ideology in children by using the railroad as "social symbols" (Gluck 261) or "popular iconography for 'civilization'" (Gluck 101). In this light, the narrator's seemingly offhanded comment in *The Beautiful and Damned* that "one would have thought [Tana] had acquired his knowledge of his native land from American primary-school geographies" has an authentic ring to it (177). It suggests Fitzgerald, characteristically, had several actual, probing conversations with the real Tana, the Fitzgeralds' real, flesh-and-blood housekeeper in Westport.

The fictionalized Tana's "Japanese train-song" (203) is undoubtedly one of the Japanese children's songs written by Owada Takeki. Tana, the actual housekeeper, must have known these songs and their cultural implications, both because Fitzgerald depicts him as such in the text and because the songs were central to so many Japanese children's early educational instruction and were widely disseminated in Japanese popular culture.

In *The Beautiful and Damned* Fitzgerald uses Tana, the train image, and the train depot as Owada Takeki's *"railroad* song" (221) was originally intended: as educational tools, with Anthony, especially, as the "little boy" (172). Tana makes four appearances in the text: he is introduced in the opening chapter of "Symposium" in the context of his photographs and the master/servant discussion (165–66); then in "The Triumph of Lethargy" and the "typewutta" discussion (182–83); followed by a brief appearance in "In Darkness" (202–3), where, before the meaning of the term is defined, he plays "a weird blend of sound" on his flute "known, cried Anthony, as the Japanese train-song" (203); and finally, in the initial chapter of "The Broken Lute," where Tana has evidently repaired his flute, plays it, and expounds on the origin and intent of the train song: "I play train song. How you call?—*railroad* song. So call in my countree. Like train. It go so-o-o; that mean whistle; train start. Then go so-o-o; that mean train go. Go like that. Vera nice song in my countree. Children song" (221).[17]

In the episodes outlined above, Tana attempts to guide, to instruct, to offer an alternative course of action and behavior: "how we do in my countree" (166). In return, he is ignored, condescended to, or ridiculed: although "Tana ha[d] retired for the night," he is awakened in his pajamas, "flute in hand" and "wrapped in a [kimono-like] comforter and placed in a chair atop one of the tables, where he makes a ludicrous and grotesque spectacle" (229).[18] Nevertheless, immediately following each of Tana's appearances, either Anthony or Gloria or both are characterized as their worst selves, quarreling or childish or angry in defeat. In the "Redgate" episode, Anthony physically attacks Gloria (166–72), and afterward, he "knelt down by her bed and cried like a little boy" (172); in the episode in which Gloria and Bloeckman go for "the best jaunt—all over New York State" (184), Anthony is left with "his fists clenched" and "with furious energy" (183) and feeling like he "seemed to have inherited only the vast tradition of human failure—that, and a sense of death" (184); in the episode in which Gloria runs from the menacing Joe Hull (signifying a dark emptiness within: a ship's hull), she is compared to "a startled child [as] she scurried along the plank" (208) to the train station (204–9); and finally, the disaster at the grey house, where both Anthony and Gloria revert to childishness after Adam Patch's severe reproach (233–34).

Thus, Fitzgerald integrates Tana, train imagery, and the train station as key structural components in the narrative and thematic architecture of *The Beautiful and Damned.* For example, when first introduced in the text, "Tana delivered a long harangue in splintered English on the relation of master and servant" (165). The narrator describes how he and Anthony "became rather irritated with each other over the word 'honest' because Anthony persisted stubbornly that Tana was trying to say 'hornets'" (165). Their discussion immediately precedes and contextualizes one of the novel's most significant scenes: Anthony's physical assault on Gloria at Redgate station. Anthony had "persisted stubbornly" (165) with Tana, and Anthony persisted "stubbornly" (168) with Gloria to visit the Barneses over her legitimate objections. Anthony decides to teach Gloria a lesson: "here and now he asserted himself as her master," and as "[h]is determination solidified, [it] approached momentarily a dull and sullen hate" (168). When Gloria goes to purchase a train ticket, Anthony "looked at her with narrowed and malicious eyes" (169). As he begins to physically manhandle Gloria, the narrator interpolates his thoughts, "Ah, she might hate him now, but afterward she would admire him for his dominance" (169), and "he had sustained his will with violence" (170). The narrator emphasizes Anthony's "brutal" (170) drunkenness—"so drunk he did not even realize his own drunkenness" (171). Anthony's violence leaves an indelible mark on their relationship, and Gloria remarks, "what was left of me would always love you, but never in quite the same way" (172). In his ever-mounting anger and specious rationalizations, Anthony has, indeed, confused "hornet" with "honest." Moreover, and as further evidence of the importance of the train motif, Maury Noble's "story of my education" (212) and his controversial account of the origins of the Bible (216–17)—replete with its own issues of censorship—occur "on" (and "above") a train station platform (210–11).

Fitzgerald interweaves Tana's provocative postcards, his "typewutter" invention, his professionalism, and his making and repairing and playing the flute in order to demonstrate to Anthony and Gloria that there are alternative modes of existence, other potential life choices, each of them might select. Fitzgerald's most poignant use of Tana's railroad song occurs when "Tana plunges into the recondite mazes of the train song, the plaintive 'tootle toot-toot' blending its melancholy cadences with the 'Poor Butter-fly (tink-a-tink), by the blossoms wait-ing' of the phonograph" (230). "Poor Butterfly," as James L. W. West III reminds us in his annotations to the novel, "tells the story of a Japanese maiden who falls in love with an American sailor" (400). Fitzgerald juxtaposes deliberately the reference to a Japanese and an American song; there is no happenstance at play. In conjuring these songs together, Fitzgerald juxtaposes in the "tink-a-tink" the wished-for romance of ideal love central to the "beautiful" of *The Beautiful and Damned* with the "melancholic cadences" of being "damned," and represented at this precise moment in the narrative by Tana's "plaintive" flute as "the notes of the Japanese train song dribble from the end of Tana's flute" before the "hellish portentousness" of Adam Patch (230, 231).

Regardless of his ostensible characterization, Tana represents Eros over Adam Patch's Thanatos, is a "man of all work by profession," an artist committed to his craft and to self-expression, and the one person in the text who by example offers the kind of guidance Gloria and Anthony need. Tana enters the novel at the beginning of "Symposium," where he is, indeed, one of the extemporaneous speakers (165); he represents the antithesis of "The Triumph of Lethargy"; and he repairs his broken flute and plays it in "The Broken Lute" (220). Is it any wonder, then, after Anthony and Gloria almost forfeit his inheritance through drunkenness, but just before Anthony sinks into an affair with Dorothy "Dot" Raycroft and Gloria resumes her life as a debutante—after these ineffectual and self-destructive behaviors—"they had vowed they would have no more Japanese" (242), another unfortunate misjudgment.[19]

JUDGE ANTHONY SAYRE >>> ZELDA/GLORIA <<< MR. BLACK (AKA MR. JOSEPH BLOECKMAN)

He and Father do a lot of business.
—GLORIA ON BLOECKMAN

One should not focus critical attention too exclusively on the masculine, (grand)father/son dramas of *The Beautiful and Damned* and neglect the feminine, father/daughter dynamic that, although less visible, is, nevertheless, as powerful and debilitating as the father/son relationship.

Paul Chabas's *September Morn* offers an unexpected heuristic by which to interpret Gloria's thwarted attempts at self-expression and self-realization. To what extent, if any, Scott and Zelda discussed Chabas's work will remain forever a mystery, open to conjecture and debate. However, Zelda was quite familiar with *September Morn* and used the painting as an important metaphor in *Save Me the Waltz*. Early in that novel, Alabama's older sister, Dixie, plans to escape the cruelty of their father, Judge Austin Beggs, by fleeing the South to New York City. Like Dixie, the other children are "[c]rippled," since "[n]othing is good enough for him" (*Collected Writings* 10, 9, and 19, respectively). Alabama watches with envy and admiration as Dixie prepares to leave. The narrator informs us that "Dixie hoarded her money; the only things she bought in a year were the central figures of the 'Primavera' and a German lithograph of 'September Morn'" (*Collected Writings* 19). In Zelda's literary imagination, *September Morn* represents an art object to be purchased and treasured as a visual emblem, a self-signifying icon, of sexual liberation and artistic creativity. Zelda specifies "a German lithograph," which refers to the specific method of reproduction of Chabas's painting, indicating a particular, not generic, knowledge of the reproduction, and suggesting Zelda's own, independent, rejection of the Comstock Laws, which specify "lithographs, prints, engravings" as subject to federal obscenity laws (Bates 78).

September Morn functions in *Save Me the Waltz* as a symbol of sexualized expression, concealed from and opposed to the authoritarian Judge Beggs's moral code, who, in turn, is based upon another repressive judge: Zelda's father, Judge Anthony Sayre. If *The Beautiful and Damned* is examined with special focus on Gloria Gilbert Patch, it becomes clear that the abstemious and dour Adam Patch of the Marietta episode is modeled on the abstemious and reserved Judge Anthony Sayre. Both fictive and real persons have a marked sense of "outraged decency" (*Collected Writings* 13), which, in turn, finds its origin in Fitzgerald's novel in Anthony Comstock. These collective Anthonys represent, to Gloria as to Zelda, a one-in-the-same repressive father figure and judge—impossible to please, airtight in logic, a supreme and removed "force of law" (*Collected Writings* 11). Neither Gloria nor Alabama can escape the brunt of the fathers' censorship and disapproval.

If Zelda were to oppose such patriarchy, she would have to confront Anthony Comstock, Judge Anthony Sayre, and the fictive Adam J. Patch—each on his own terms. Zelda accomplishes this remarkable feat in the colored pen-and-ink illustration she sketches for the dust jacket of *The Beautiful and Damned*. In this drawing, Zelda reinterprets Chabas's *September Morn*, adapting the model's right-of-center positioning, replicating the hair style and coloration of the lips, replacing Chabas's concentric circles of water surrounding his model with her own striated, concentric circles in the base of the cocktail glass, and echoing the predominate coloration in Chabas's painting with subtle, sand-like pigmentations in the fluid in the glass itself. Zelda redraws the demure innocence of the Chabas model's facial expression with a wry and knowing smile in her self-portrait, and of course, transforms the shallow lakeshore waters of the original into an almost-transparent martini in a cocktail glass. Zelda also accentuates her model's sexuality, whereas Chabas underplays sexuality in his painting. In her careful, playful redrafting of Chabas's *September Morn*, Zelda achieves artistic self-expression and creates her own protest against censorship, and specifically, censorship and legislation governing the artistic creation and representation of a woman's body by a woman artist. Zelda pays homage to Chabas's painting by reimagining it, and at the same time, challenging, directly, the Comstock Laws, the Sayre-like father "outrage[d]" (Cline 20) over her unconventional behavior, and Adam Patch's "sanctimonious browbeating" (21). The dust jacket also serves as Zelda's unapologetic and exhibitionistic visual prolepsis and implied rebuttal of potential public (or private) moralizings and criticisms of Gloria's behavior and attitude. Zelda's illustration is her own not-so-hypothetical test case of the legality of the Comstock Laws.

In *The Beautiful and Damned*, Gloria's singular attempt at creative self-expression occurs when she decides to call Mr. Joseph Bloeckman, now Mr. Black, for a screen test. Gloria had harbored desires for a career as an actress, but "only now when the step had at last been taken did she realize how the possibility of a successful screen career had played in the back on her mind for the past three years" (331). Gloria's decision—"I'm going into the movies at last—if I can" (327)—is a desperate, romantic one, a decision fueled by her dread of aging, of losing her "pretty face" (333), itself a metonymy for her physical beauty.

This subplot develops ("The Movies") and concludes ("The Test") in relatively few pages (326–33). Gloria telephones Bloeckman/Mr. Joseph Black, who kindly assures her that it was "merely a question of when she wanted the trial" (327). He writes her a thoughtful, encouraging letter putting forth an appropriate strategy for Gloria's entrance into stage life and with consideration for her future career: "I would like to see you start with something that would bring you notice," he says, but, being circumspect and avoiding potential jealousy and gossip, he adds, "tongues would very likely wag" if Gloria overshadowed "one of the rather shop-worn stars with which every company is afflicted" (327). When she arrives at "Films Par Excellence," Bloeckman (not "Black") is described as "a dark suave gentleman, gracefully engaged in the middle forties,

Zelda's prospective cover for her husband's second novel.

who greeted her with courteous warmth and told her she had not changed a bit in three years" (328). Everything about their relationship exudes grace, warmth, and courtesy. Gloria is then introduced to "the great Percy B. Debris" (329), who conducts the actual screen test, and who explains its criteria: "how your features photograph and whether you've got natural stage presence and how

156

you respond to coaching" (329). He admits, however, that her actual live performance means little, as "I can't tell anything about it until I have it run off" (331).

Gloria is "desolate" (333) when she receives Bloeckman's letter informing her that "Mr. Debris seemed to think that for the part he had in mind he needed a younger woman" (333). As if this was not sufficiently devastating, Bloeckman continues, "there was a small character part supposed to be a very haughty rich widow that he thought you might—" and that is all Gloria reads, as the letter ends with a dash and before the signature (333).

Gloria takes Debris's opinion and Bloeckman's letter at face value. In despair, she scrutinizes herself in the mirror and "whispered, passionately grieving[,] 'Oh my pretty face! Oh, I don't want to live without my pretty face! Oh, what's *happened?*'" (333). Such is the power of fatherly authority and the unwitting internalizing of the false father—of patriarchy—in *The Beautiful and Damned.* If one interrogates the text ever so slightly, one might pause to wonder why the "suave gentleman," the "Ever Faithful" Bloeckman/Black, delivers Mr. Debris's opinion with such devastating cruelty and mean-spiritedness.[20] If he were actually concerned about Gloria's career as a burgeoning actress, as his first letter implied, then why would he mention Debris's "small character part" as "a very haughty rich widow" at all? He could have softened both the blow of rejection—"needed a younger woman"—and not even mentioned the alternative part Debris offered her. Bloeckman's first letter states, explicitly, that part of his job as a manager of aspiring and established actresses is to couch such judgments in inoffensive and positive language. Yet, in his second letter, he selects the most devastating language an actress could imagine. Moreover, Mr. Debris's (and Bloeckman's) assessment and suggested alternative part are based exclusively on Gloria's age, and not on the criteria Mr. Debris set forth during the screen test. Bloeckman's letter does not mention whether or not Gloria responded well to being coached or her natural screen presence; the only consideration mentioned is her age. Bloeckman/Black represents another iteration of The Judge, of a repressive father figure who seeks to thwart an individual's struggle to find meaningful self-expression and an appropriate vocation. Debris says, ironically, "You needn't be afraid we're going to judge this too severely" (330). In a novel replete with satirical names such as the "Oriental" named "Lt. Emile Tannenbaum" (199) and the priggish, prudish "Paramore" (221), why would anyone believe the assessment of a movie director named "Debris"? Fitzgerald draws Bloeckman/Black, Debris, and Adam Patch with the same pencil. They are representations of Anthony Comstock and Anthony Sayre, fathers of censorship and oppression.

Bloeckman's disingenuous remarks to Muriel Kane at Gloria's party at "the Cascades at the Biltmore" prefigure his insincere attitude toward Gloria. Bloeckman "clapped his hands gallantly" at Muriel's "vamp" affectations and volunteers to her, "You ought to be on the stage" (85). When Muriel cried, "I'd like to be!" and "Will you back me?" Bloeckman replies, "I sure will" (85). Clearly, Bloeckman recognizes a stage presence in Muriel's posing and primping herself. However, his promise amounts to nothing. During this scene, Bloeckman also brings up the subject of Adam Patch in conversation with Anthony, and Fitzgerald links Bloeckman to Anthony Comstock through Bloeckman's addled-headed, patriotic praise for Adam Patch: "'He's a fine man,' pronounced Bloeckman profoundly. 'He's a fine example of an American'" (84). Bloeckman then shifts his gaze from "the three young men" to where "his eyes rest[ed] critically on the ceiling" (84), and the narrator states, "there was no hint of understanding in his manner," and he spent the night "watching the others with the bored tolerance of an elder among children" (86). Bloeckman's character, early and late, joins Cross Patch as a father figure who proffers the possibility of self-advancement through personal intercession for employment without sincerity and who is, in reality, quick to judge.

Fitzgerald links the fatherly and economic aspects of Gloria's relationship with Bloeckman by having Mr. Gilbert and Mr. Bloeckman "do a lot of business" together (77). Given Fitzgerald's derisive construction of Mr. Gilbert's character, it stretches narrative credibility that Mr. Gilbert would have anything to do with something as progressive and modern as being the "supervising manager of the Associated Mid-western Film Materials Company" (40) and being even distantly associated with the manufacturing of film. Fitzgerald contrives to link Mr. Gilbert and Mr. Bloeckman together as early as 1913 and before Anthony and Gloria are married, and he makes sure to have them work as business associates in the motion picture industry. Unless Fitzgerald has, literally, forgotten this plotline, it is all the more unfathomable that the tactful and ever-circumspect Bloeckman would risk alienating his supplier of "Film Material" and their long-standing business relationship by writing such a rude letter to Mr. Gilbert's daughter. Fitzgerald invents their relationship to further strengthen the ostensible "fatherly" powers that loom over and prevent Gloria's self-fulfillment. Bloeckman embodies a more modern and menacingly corporate version of the false father than the traditional patriarchs, Anthony Comstock, Old Cross Patch, Judges Sayre and Beggs. It costs Mr. Debris or Mr. Bloeckman next to nothing to simply give Gloria a bit part in a low-budget, second-rate movie. Such a placement would probably be viewed by Mr. Gilbert (had he the sense) for its face value: a personal favor or gesture of appreciation for past business. Significantly, it is Fitzgerald who refuses such a sanguine plot development. Fitzgerald, not Debris or Bloeckman, writes the letter to Gloria; he chooses to merge economics and family to Gloria's detriment and disadvantage. Why?

CONCLUSION:
FITZGERALD >>> NARRATOR >>> AS AN "ANTHONY"

I wish the Beautiful and Damned had been a more maturely written book because it was all true. We ruined ourselves—I have never honestly thought that we ruined each other.
—SCOTT TO ZELDA, SUMMER 1930

Gloria was a much more trivial and vulgar person than your mother. . . .
We had a much better time than Anthony and Gloria had.
—SCOTT TO HIS DAUGHTER, SCOTTIE, JUNE 14, 1940

Countless implications surface in the excerpt from Fitzgerald's letter to Zelda while she is rehabilitating at Prangins and in his letter to Scottie about her mother and about Scott and Zelda's married life circa 1920–22. Nevertheless, these two letters illustrate Fitzgerald's dilemma—his continued struggle to understand and to find closure—about himself, Zelda, their relationship at that time, and their fictional counterparts in *The Beautiful and Damned*. Fitzgerald says, "We ruined ourselves—I have never honestly thought we ruined each other," as though each were existing independently of the other, but also collectively, in their exhibitionisms and overindulgences. Even the pronominals remain confused—first-person plural, then a self-reflexive intensifier, then first-person singular, first-person plural again, and then the final, mutually inclusive yet separated "each other." What a mystifying, double-helix syntax.

The question remains: why would Fitzgerald write a novel, where, to appropriate a phrase from *Romeo and Juliet*, "all are punish'd"? (Shakespeare

5.3.295). Why does Fitzgerald and his constructed voice, his narrator, condemn Anthony and Gloria to a life of indolence, alcoholism, and degeneration—and in such a ruthless and inexorable fashion?

One way to account for Fitzgerald's and the narrator's maliciousness toward the novel's characters is that Fitzgerald does not trust himself in his newfound literary fame and celebrity status. As a result of this mistrust and self-suspicion, he vilifies his characters; he presents the damned in marked disproportion to the beautiful. Gone is the narrative empathy for Sally Carrol Happer in "The Ice Palace" (*F&P* 36–60), for either Horace Tarbox or Marcia Meadow in "Head and Shoulders" (*F&P* 61–86), for Amory Blaine in *This Side of Paradise*—all texts published in 1920. In *This Side of Paradise* Fitzgerald constructs Amory as an outsider looking in on an established Princeton society. Like Fitzgerald, Amory admits to Kerry: "'Oh it isn't that I mind the glittering caste system. . . . I like having a bunch of hot cats on top, but Gosh, Kerry, I've got to be one of them'" (*TSOP* 50). In part, *This Side of Paradise* is fueled by Fitzgerald's indignation and frustration at not being one of the "hot cats," and these emotions are univocal and consistent with Fitzgerald himself, the construction of Amory Blaine, and the sustained emotional pitch of the novel, despite the heteroglossia of the text as a whole.

However, in the interim between *Paradise*'s publication in March 1920 and Fitzgerald's writing and revising *The Beautiful and Damned* in 1921–22, he achieved the literary fame and pubic notoriety he so desperately coveted. Fitzgerald was unsure how to respond to this sudden, deeply desired rise to fame and celebrity status. As Fitzgerald himself recalls in his nostalgic essay "Early Success" (1937), "With its publication [*This Side of Paradise*] I had reached a stage of manic-depressive insanity. Rage and bliss alternated by the hour" (*MLC* 188). The flight of the rocket had been precipitous, violent, and life-changing. Fitzgerald becomes the kind of person he envied in his debut novel but also the kind of person he vilified: the moneyed, rich, select few who have garnered the laurels Amory Blaine sought and failed to achieve. With the publication of *This Side of Paradise*, Fitzgerald had too jarringly, too abruptly, become that which he had both desired and disparaged. These profound and unresolved ambivalences inform the tensions in the narrative perspective of *The Beautiful and Damned*.

In "My Lost City," written in the mid-1930s but published posthumously a decade later, Fitzgerald recounts the bewildering days following the publication of his first novel while he and Zelda lived in New York City: "We felt like children in a great bright unexplored barn. . . . Finding no nucleus to which we could cling, we became a small nucleus ourselves and gradually fitted our disruptive personalities into the contemporary scene of New York." However, "later," he "realized" that "there were only a lot of lost and lonely people." Scott and Zelda had "no center," and significantly, "it seemed inappropriate to bring a baby into all that glamour and loneliness." Fitzgerald uses the same stuttering pronominal usage in this essay: "I, or rather it was 'we' now, found [New York] rather confusing" and in "our precarious position . . . we began doing the same things over and over and not liking them so much." Fitzgerald summarizes their situation: "We scarcely knew anymore who we were and we hadn't a notion what we were" (*MLC* 110–11).

As a result of the financial, cultural, and interpersonal complications of Fitzgerald's success, his narrative voice loses its previous identification with his characters, and he fails to establish a consistent narrative tonality. The narrative voice in *The Beautiful and Damned* is akin to that of "The Diamond as Big as the Ritz" (1922): edgy, fabulous, confused, and similarly inconclusive in its resolution to the complexities presented in the text. Fitzgerald's narrative tone in 1920 is invested and empathetic, if often ironic; his 1922 tone is removed and antagonistic. This abrupt shift cannot be adequately accounted of by reference to what Matthew J. Bruccoli describes as the author's "temporary interest in the school of naturalistic or deterministic fiction" (Fitzgerald, *Short Stories* 97). Rather, Fitzgerald's change in narrative tone and perspective is a defensive reaction to his sudden and confusing achievement as a writer, celebrity, and spouse.

Another way to account for the narrative's maliciousness toward its characters is that Fitzgerald's conscience was haunted by the nagging suspicion that Monsignor Sigourney Fay (and Monsignor Darcy) would object to the lifestyle he (and Anthony Patch) were living. In "My Lost City," Fitzgerald notes with fond melancholy, "Monsignor Fay had taken me to the Lafayette where there was a spread before us a brilliant flag of food, called an *hors d'oeuvres*, and with it we drank claret" (*MLC* 107). Fitzgerald selects this man and this singular incident from hundreds of possible people and episodes to pay homage to in this personal and nostalgic essay. Fay's importance as a moral guide to the early Fitzgerald is documented by Fitzgerald's dedicating his debut novel to him. In Monsignor Darcy, Fitzgerald put into narrative both Fay's wisdom and Fitzgerald's need for and appreciation of that wisdom. Such a figure is conspicuously absent in *The Beautiful and Damned*. Father Darcy's moral imperative to "do the next thing" (*TSOP* 100) is completely ignored in Fitzgerald's second novel. Neither Anthony nor Gloria has the slightest idea what those words mean, and it seems that Fitzgerald himself has forgotten their significance as well. "The First Appearance of the Term Personage" in *Paradise*—with its affirmation that "we're not personalities, but personages" (*TSOP* 101) and all that distinction implies—reads like a homiletic for Anthony, Gloria, and their individual and collective descent into a devitalized lifestyle and abdication of moral responsibility. Perhaps Fitzgerald was being honest when he has Amory confess, "But Monsignor, I can't do the next thing" (*TSOP* 100)—the difference between knowing and doing what is best for one's self.

Fitzgerald replaces Monsignor Darcy with a series of father figures who directly oppose what Darcy represented in *This Side of Paradise:* they are particularly unwise, ungenerous to the young, and oppressively judgmental and puritanical. Fitzgerald does not permit a father figure to guide Anthony or Gloria through the perils of affluence and high society in part because no such father figure guided Scott and Zelda through the perils of becoming an overnight sensation, of living the rags-to-riches story he always dreamed of, and of celebrating without boundaries or constraint. Fitzgerald's earning increased from $879 in 1919 to $18,850 in 1920, and in those heady days, he had the distinct impression that the figure would continue to grow proportionately and forever, as captured in "How to Live on $36,000 a Year": "I had just received a large paycheck from the movies and I felt a little patronizing toward the millionaires riding down Fifth Avenue in their limousines—because my income had a way of doubling every month. This was actually the case. It had done so for several months . . . and it seemed as if it was going to do so forever" (*MLC* 27–28).

The same phenomenon of actively seeking direction and guidance from a father figure holds true for Zelda and for Gloria. We see this most poignantly in Zelda's fictionalizing her father as Judge Beggs in *Save Me the Waltz*. As Milford states, "When she [Alabama] speaks to him it is again for guidance, for some measure of direction from him for her own life" (245). She continues, "After her father's death, Alabama searches for some token of direction, but she finds nothing" (246): "'He must have forgotten,' said Alabama, 'to leave a message'" (*Collected Writings* 188).

Fitzgerald cannot turn to his friends for advice as he did while attending Princeton and in *This Side of Paradise*. The collective quest for meaning that

Amory shares with his college friends in *This Side of Paradise* gives way to competitive posturing and calculated philosophical diatribes in *The Beautiful and Damned*. Richard Caramel (Edmund Wilson) and Maury Noble (George Jean Nathan) inhabit the same literary and social sphere that Anthony (Fitzgerald) and Gloria (Zelda) do. They are willing culprits and coconspirators in *The Beautiful and Damned*. No character in the text is sufficiently removed from, external to, the characters' dramas, and therefore, able to provide a distanced perspective in the way that the elderly Monsignor was able to do for Amory. The "becoming"—"it was always the becoming [Amory] dreamed of, never the being" (*TSOP* 24)—that informed so much of the emotional substructure of *This Side of Paradise* has suddenly transformed into the responsibilities and consequences implicit in "being" in *The Beautiful and Damned*.

So Fitzgerald punishes all his characters. No one escapes his Cross Patch–like vitriol and scorn. *The Beautiful and Damned* concludes with "the victors belong[ing] to the spoils." Gloria is described as "unclean," a talismanic word for Zelda and a textual signifier indicating Gloria's inevitable promiscuity in her future life married to the incapacitated, wealthy Anthony. For his part, Anthony is victim to his own profound, childlike self-delusions, poignantly reminiscent of his grandfather: "I showed them. . . . It was a hard fight, but I didn't give up and I came through" (369). It is a bitter and ironic conclusion to a bitter and ironic text. Anthony Comstock Patch could not escape his fate of being christened "Comstock," and he was blind to the implications of the "Anthony" lying deep within. For whatever complex reasons, Fitzgerald never allows Anthony or Gloria to rise above being "a mysteriously correlated piece of patchwork" (144–45).

NOTES

I wish to thank Yumi Takamiya, at the University of Alabama at Birmingham, for her invaluable information, translations, and guidance in our several discussions of the "Railroad Songs," their cultural significance in Japan, Tanalahaka's name, and for suggesting the probable origin of Tana's flute: many, many thanks. Also, I want to thank my colleague Mr. Joseph Stitt for his helpful reading of this article in manuscript form. Finally, both Kirk Curnutt and William Blazek provided valuable suggestions for this essay.

1. I have been unable to determine whether or not Fitzgerald knew of Comstock's visit to Princeton in 1888. As Bates reports, "When Comstock addressed the YMCA at Princeton University in 1888, a 'sense of modesty' that was 'truly shocking' developed among the students in anticipation of the crusader's visit" (185).

2. Although Comstock is an overzealous reformer by any standards, his actions are a fairly typical reaction to *September Morn* by communities throughout America. Exhibiting a reproduction of *September Morn* was challenged in Chicago by "'Bath House John' Coughlin" ("Comstock Dooms"). See Boese for a more detailed account of the Chicago incident.

When interpreting *September Morn* with respect to the prevailing artistic censorship of the day, one should consider the groundbreaking *International Exhibition of Modern Art,* also known as the *Armory Show,* in New York from 17 February to 15 March 1913. The exhibition instantly became a lightning rod for discussions as to what constitutes art. The *September Morn* controversy followed the *Armory Show* very closely, just two months afterward, and debate over the painting's "morality" should be understood in light of the *Armory Show* and its controversy.

3. Producing a definitive account of the events surrounding Comstock's objection to Chabas's *September Morn* is a difficult task. Three accounts exist: Broun and Leech rely on Comstock's diaries; Bates emphasizes the alleged machinations of "press agent Harry Reichenbach" in creating the scandal around the painting and alerting Comstock of its being displayed (Bates 181); Boese proves that Reichenbach "could not have played a role in promoting September Morn that he later claimed" ("September Morn Hoax"). Boese's recent account seems the most reasonable and factual of the three. For the *New York Times*'s reporting of these events, see "Comstock Dooms September Morn" (11 May 1913) and "Wearies of Waiting a Comstock Arrest" (15 May 1913).

4. There are four studies of Anthony Comstock: Turnbull's biography, *Anthony Comstock, Fighter* (1913) is an "hagiographic" homage to the man, written with Comstock's assistance and approval (Werbel 3); Broun and Leech's coauthored *Anthony Comstock: Roundsman of the Lord* (1927) is noteworthy in that it makes copious use of Comstock's diaries, which have disappeared; Bates's *Weeder in the Garden of the Lord* is scholarly and reliable but focuses on the question, "Why would any man willingly force such suffering on his fellow human beings?" (vii); Werbel's recent *Lust on Trial* (2018) offers the most informed and authoritative analysis of Comstock, the Comstock Laws, and the many and far-reaching implications of the man and his laws.

5. Comstock's diaries have disappeared. Broun and Leech (1927) were the last to have access to them and quote from them. Therefore, all subsequent attributions to Comstock originate from Broun and Leech's biography.

6. Not surprisingly, the United States Post Office, which at first supported Comstock, "now saw the nature of the beast they had unleashed upon the American public" (Bates 101).

7. "Weeder in the Garden of the Lord" is the title of Bates's monograph, and "Roundsman of the Lord" is the subtitle of Bourn and Leech's biography.

8. To be, perhaps, too generous, some of Comstock's efforts—such as his prosecution of quack medicines, of notoriously corrupt gambling, and of potentially unhealthy, dangerous abortifacients—were justified, even beneficial, to the public trust.

9. See, for example, the 12 February 1922, article, "Finds Indecency Flaunting as Art," in which "the controversy which once was aroused over the innocent 'September Morn,' whose display was fought by the late Anthony Comstock, appears to date back to Puritan times, in comparison with the picture which in December was held in court to be chaste and artistic." See also Diana Rice's "Literary Bootlegging" (6 Aug. 1922): "While moralists wail and the energetic followers of the late Anthony Comstock declare the world, with all on board, is headed straight for perdition" (1).

10. An early victim and strident critic of Comstock, D. M. Bennett, titles his book *Anthony Comstock: His Career of Cruelty and Crime* (1878).

11. Fitzgerald characterizes "Dada" in ways that echo Anthony Comstock and the Adam Patch/ Anthony Patch relationship. "Dada" has fought in the Civil War, "looks down as from a great dim height upon Jerry," "has lately become absorbed in the Old Testament," and is "a small, shriveled man with a great amount of hair on his face" (18). The "two cousins" to whom Adam Patch bequeaths a portion of his estate are "from Idaho" (245). The "State of Idaho" figures prominently, if facetiously, in *The Vegetable* (85).

12. Fitzgerald qualifies "of the day," since, by the time he is composing *The Beautiful and Damned*, the so-called Gibson Girl is out of fashion, having been replaced, of course, by the flapper. Yet in 1913, the Gibson Girl represented a considerable advance over the previous generation of more conservative and "Victorian" women. As captured by their creator, Charles Dana Gibson, and configured in many of his magazine sketches, such as "The Weaker Sex," Gibson Girls are often portrayed as confident, if not dominant, in their relationships with men.

13. Although Tarzan is one possible source and is often seen in tiger-skinned outfits in the 1910s, the reference could also be to Bernarr MacFadden (1886–1955), a bodybuilder, health reformer, fraudulent self-promoter, and forerunner to Charles Atlas. MacFadden was a controversial figure who often appeared in advertisements and posters in semi-clothed attire to accentuate his physical form; he advertised heavily to promote his popular *Physical Culture Exhibition*, held at Madison Square Garden (Werbel 263); he was prosecuted by Comstock ("Comstock Takes Hand in Physical Culture Show").

14. For example, see Comstock's *Traps for the Young*, chap. 2, "Newspapers," 13–19, and chap. 4 "Advertisement Traps," 43–55.

15. The instrument Tana plays is, in all probability, the Ginteki, not the Shakuhachi Japanese Bamboo Flute (Takamiya). The Ginteki is similar to a recorder in that it is played vertically and blown into, as opposed to the Western concert flute, which is played from a horizontal position and blown over.

16. Japanese cultural critics commonly note that railroads were an important symbol in turn-of-the-twentieth-century Japan, an increasingly omnipresent and powerful symbol of Japanese industrialization, and therefore progress, on the domestic front, and in international affairs, as way to forge empire (Levey).

17. To hear what is probably the original, 1900 recording of the railroad song, please go to https://www.youtube.com/watch?v=W8Ign36omiU.

18. Tana does not make a spectacle of himself so much as the group makes a spectacle of him. Also, Gloria owns a "kimona" (*sic*) (326).

19. While it is true that in reference to Tana, Gloria says, "That awful little man!" (211), there is no correspondingly objectionable sentiment voiced by Alabama about "Tanka" (i.e., Tana) in *Save Me the Waltz* (Z. Fitzgerald, *Collected Writings* 51–53).

20. It is possible to argue that Bloeckman's mercilessness is a kind of payback for Gloria jilting him in favor of Anthony. However, such a reading implies the agency to Bloeckman, whereas this essay suggests Fitzgerald himself supplies the agency through his narrative decisions and tonality.

FITZGERALD'S PAS DE DEUX
THE DYNAMICS OF ROMANCE AND ECONOMY
IN *THE BEAUTIFUL AND DAMNED*

Gail D. Sinclair

F. Scott Fitzgerald's most acclaimed works revolve in varying degrees around the interplay between a male protagonist and the female character who captures his attention. *This Side of Paradise* and early magazine stories such as "Bernice Bobs Her Hair" (*F&P* 108–33) feature young flappers and their eager beaux engaging in "petting parties" and enjoying the sexual flirtation that the writer glamorizes as his jazz babies flaunt a conviction that their carefree spree is unending. Fitzgerald uses this youth-conscious milieu embodying the nascent stages of gender relations and the ensuing struggle for supremacy as the base for his maturing aesthetics. Beginning with *The Beautiful and Damned*, his first novel featuring adult relationships, Fitzgerald marks a tonal shift he will cultivate with more finesse in *The Great Gatsby* (1925) and *Tender Is the Night* (1934) as he solidifies a dynamic central to his most powerful fiction. In each work, Fitzgerald chronicles a man and woman negotiating a sense of individuality versus engagement as a couple, and in charting this territory, he will combine two forces that held prodigious sway in his private life and his creative psyche: the desire to win the prized lover and sustain the high ideal of that love, complicated by the relationship money plays in achieving and sustaining that goal. These divergent forces were present in much of his early work, but *The Beautiful and Damned* serves as Fitzgerald's first novel-length foray into the terrain he will revisit time and again in his examination of the dynamics between romance and finance.

Fitzgerald conjoins through Anthony and Gloria Patch these two pivotal forces and the subsequent consequences resulting from such a polemic coupling. Initially, he underscores the romantic ideal drawing these young lovers together and shaping the future they envision, but as the novel progresses, he focuses increasingly on the challenge to love when life interjects pragmatic demands. Both husband and wife feel the weight of accumulated emotional loss, and they engage in a Darwinian struggle for survival of the fittest as their dream collapses around them. Fitzgerald memorializes this tug and pull of the heart's longing and its ultimate vulnerability against day-to-day verities, and he does so by using his propensity to draw directly and often verbatim from his own life. He will not only borrow from personal experiences for *The Beautiful and Damned*, he will repeat this practice again in writing *The Great Gatsby*, and yet again in *Tender Is the Night*, the three novels examining his courtship, marriage, and life with Zelda. Perhaps precisely because he traffics in such personal terrain, Fitzgerald tempers his moral assessments with an underlying tenderness for both partners who are called upon with mounting regularity to slay life's dragons while knowing that with increasingly greater frequency they will fail.

The romance of the quest and its often-brutal consequences against colossal odds deeply intrigues Fitzgerald and is something Zelda implicitly understood. In a tribute to her husband after his death, she aptly summarizes his writing and its central purpose: to tell "sagas of people compelling life into some more commensurate and compassionate measure" (*Collected Writings* 441). Instead of a seeming focus on acrimony, what lies at the heart of his fiction is the glamorization of romance and the pathos of loss Fitzgerald finds in the jarring strife of trying to maintain selfhood. That struggle can become antithetical to successful relationships, but he embraces the totality of the journey, both its beauty and its damnation. *The Beautiful and Damned*'s two main characters are inevitably linked in the effort to save themselves as individuals while paradoxically clinging to the identity that becomes their shared fate.

Fitzgerald makes no overt references to classical ballet as a metaphor in his writing, but the pas de deux offers an appropriate model on which to base a relational analysis of Anthony and Gloria and other subsequent couples throughout his oeuvre.[1] Given Zelda's passion for the art form and the obsessive compulsion to its practice in 1928–30, her husband was certainly well acquainted with the elegance of the pas de deux and its function to elevate the emotion associated with the couple.[2] The dance's structure features in duet a ballerina and a danseur in the central portion of the movement who, through much of its five sections, merge into a majestic integrated tableau. Full visceral ascendency depends on the partners' unified choreographic position, each reliant upon the other to support precarious individual poses. In contrast, but equally important, each dancer's solo moments heighten the duet's virtuosity by emphasizing both the strength and vulnerability of the individual perfor- mance. Finally, the pas de deux momentarily separates the dancers from the ballet troupe, isolating the duet in their sensual sovereignty but also enhancing the vulnerability represented in their remoteness from the ensemble. Fitzgerald appropriates the paradigm of the pas de deux but shifts physical interdepen- dency to an emotion-based dance spotlighting such unified moments. These points in time become transfixed in memory as the centripetal force holds his romantic ideal firmly in place while paradoxically realizing that centrifugal forces will tear it apart. All of Fitzgerald's significant couples in his maturing body of work, as he establishes with Anthony and Gloria Patch, will derive initial power from the strength of their romance and the rhythm of the dance that draws them together. Conversely, they will be enervated by the realities, often financial, that impinge upon their ability to sustain such a high ideal.

Basking in the success of *This Side of Paradise,* which preceded his mar- riage to Zelda Sayre by only eight days, Fitzgerald begins in *The Beautiful and Damned* to chronicle Anthony and Gloria Patch's "eternal romance that was to be the synthesis of all romance," although he no doubt already suspects his hyperbole (126). Four months after his marriage, Fitzgerald writes to his editor, Charles Scribner, to announce the new novel's developing focus. He is ready to leave behind his collegiate characters to establish grown-up protagonists who, as James L. W. West III describes them, become "a blueprint for the character types and moral questions that would preoccupy Fitzgerald for the rest of his writing career" ("Question of Vocation" 48). He envisions a story that will not recount emotional, social, or financial ascendency but, rather, will be a tale in which his central couple "are wrecked on the shoals of dissipation" (*Letters* 41). The Patches will serve as a synecdoche of a "whole race going hedonistic, deciding on pleasure" (*MLC* 132). Zelda helps establish this image through her proposed dust jacket sketch of a naked woman kneeling in a filled martini glass, and she sets the novel's title in a box just to the right of the nude figure and topped by damnation's flames.[3] In a postpublication letter to his friend Edmund Wilson, Fitzgerald writes: "Gloria and Anthony *are* representative. They are two of the great army of the rootless who float around New York" (*Letters* 52). A prospective title for the novel, "The Flight of the Rocket," captures the bursting energy and wayward trajectory of this rootless population. Ultimately, Fitzgerald chose a more literal title emphasizing the central focus on romantic and financial ruin. He could not have known that both titles were prophetic, signaling a prolonged tale not just of passive dissolution but of glamorously propulsive wastage emblematic of his career, his marriage, and his era.[4]

Book 1 of *The Beautiful and Damned*, the pas de deux's *entrée* section, encompasses the preface to Anthony Patch and Gloria Gilbert's marriage, beginning with the twenty-five-year-old Anthony metaphorically putting on "the final polish of the shoe, the ultimate dab of the clothes-brush, and a sort of intellectual 'There!,'" though the narrative voice informs the reader of his still-developing nature by saying, "—yet at the brink of this story he has at yet gone no further than the conscious stage" (11). After providing this sense of adult formation, Fitzgerald also establishes Anthony having been a poor little rich boy for whom a measure of sympathy must be given before we too hastily assess his moral character. Orphaned by the age of eleven, life became for him "a struggle against death, that waited at every corner" (14). Left to be raised by a rigid, blatantly moralistic, and emotionally removed grandfather, Anthony's self-assessment and his ego's axis are unsteady and changeable with the winds of fortune, or more aptly with the gales of misfortune. While evaluating his essential self at times exuding "a shameful and obscene thinness glistening on the surface of the world like oil on a clean pond," these feelings are countered when "he thinks himself rather an exceptional young man, thoroughly sophisticated, well adjusted to his environment, and somewhat more significant than anyone else he knows" (11). He finds himself caught between reliance upon the past, represented by his grandfather's wealth, and a future about to be built on unsubstantiated ground he has yet to possess and that with one deterministic blow can be taken from him.

Anthony has developed in his adulthood the confident if premature superiority of the financial power he expects his grandfather's legacy eventually to provide. He has also acquired an arrogance resting squarely on the prowess bestowed by the presence of "the big trust company building," whose vaults shelter his fortune and stoke a belief that he is "adequately chaperoned by the hierarchy of finance" (18). Fitzgerald further portrays Anthony's developing sense of self as "brilliant, magnetic, the heir of many years and many men" (52), and he builds upon the use of "heir" to solidify the concept that money is the power base Anthony accesses in his crusade to win a worthy woman of high social esteem. As sole remaining beneficiary to one of New York's considerable fortunes, one he expects will shortly become his without the necessity to work for it except by currying his grandfather's favor, "he saw himself a power upon the earth; with his grandfather's money he might build his own pedestal" from which to proclaim his dominance and win his girl (52). Anthony feels confidently armored by his economic circumstances and what Fitzgerald projected upon him as one of the most important tools for successful romantic conquest—the greatest bank account actively exploited to win the hand and heart of the most beautiful princess in the highest white castle, a phrase he was fond of using as a marker establishing the valued prize, or more to the point, the value of the prize.[5]

Fitzgerald felt his own experience bore witness to financial capital's potential sway in a battle for the object of love's desire. The success he achieved with *This Side of Paradise* was paramount in strengthening his artistic swagger, but it also enhanced his ability to employ the power of the bank. His earnings for 1920, $18,850 in total, were not based solely on the novel's sales of $6,200. They were significantly augmented by rapidly increasing short-story acquisition prices totaling $4,475, the rising film industry's interest in procuring new script possibilities earning $7,425, and a category listed as "Other writing" with an income of $75 (*Fitzgerald's Ledger* 52).[6] But the novel's popular and financial success was a key factor in achieving Fitzgerald's second primary goal. The destiny about which he had dreamed and boasted to Zelda now seemed a much more sure and attainable reality, and the newly acquired bankroll allowed him to make good on the promise that he could support Zelda through his success as a writer. Fitzgerald's gilded wallet in no insignificant proportion won her final acquiescence after shoring up belief that she would no longer have to sacrifice financial comfort for love. She reversed her previous rejection, relocated to New York City to marry Scott, and began to navigate her way in the new milieu where the circumstances turned and he held both the social and financial upper hand.[7] A residual sting remained for Fitzgerald, however, that finances had played a stronger role in his conquest of Zelda than his romantic ideals wanted to admit.

Fitzgerald would develop this sentiment—the conflict between romance's high ideal and the realities that tarnish it—in *The Beautiful and Damned, The Great Gatsby,* and *Tender Is the Night.* Although Scott won the prized southern belle for whom many suitors had competed, he later expressed fear that he had been "[t]he man with the jingle of money in his pocket" during the time of their engagement who, even after the passing years, was still unable "to stop thinking that at one time a sort of *droit de seigneur* might have been exercised to give one of them my girl" (*MLC* 147).[8] In a sense, this insecurity had begun with his first serious girlfriend, the wealthy and beautiful Chicago socialite Ginevra King, who ultimately rejected him and, perhaps inadvertently, imprinted upon him this angst. As James L. W. West III writes in *The Perfect Hour,* his account of the romance:

> Marriage into this world was only a distant possibility. If a prospective part-
> ner could bring something fresh into the family—new money, an old and re-
> spectable name, an inherited English title—then perhaps a marriage might
> be arranged. But good looks, an amusing line, and literary talent were not
> enough. For the very rich, these conventions of behavior carried through
> into adult life. They brought outsiders into their world for amusement
> and dalliance but were careful not to grant them full admission. (106–7)

During the summer of Fitzgerald's nineteenth year and at the height of his in-fatuation with Ginevra, his August journal entry reflects a sense that Chicago's exclusive Lake Forest elite saw him as an outsider lacking the proper membership qualifications. He provides a brief compilation of the month's soirées with beautiful young socialites but certainly suggests he either felt snubbed or perhaps actually was as he notes in quotation marks: "Poor boys shouldn't think of marrying rich girls" (*Fitzgerald's Ledger* 170). While the Sayres did not possess to any degree the level of the King family's wealth, they did hold the pedigree of Old South prominence that feigned similar economic ranking and potentially threatened to block Scott's path to marrying their youngest daughter, Zelda. Through his popular success, Fitzgerald overcame financial disparity and the rejection on which he felt it had largely been based, but the emotional scar remained from having lost one girl and fear that he might have lost another because his pocketbook lacked heft.[9]

Fitzgerald saw himself on the weaker side of the gender dynamic then, in part related to perceived financial insufficiency, and because he often felt out-powered by the romantic hold beautiful women had on him. He used this anx-iety deeply embedded in his sense of self by weaving it for artistic benefit in his fiction. In one sense, his perceived economic disadvantage energized him into action, but it also generated hostility. These confident young women's flippant demeanor belied awareness of the influence their beauty and social ascendency held, and for Fitzgerald, their willingness to use this upper hand seemed an un-fair advantage over helplessly moonstruck men. In the early stages of his fame, Fitzgerald called out such women for their ability to wound men's hearts, naming them baby vamps, his shortened term for vampires. He prescribed to them the negative connotations implied in such a moniker, inverting the famous Drac-ula image of a leering male preying on helpless females. In his version, women become the predators seeking out male victims susceptible to their feminine powers. Fitzgerald's vamp label comes across as a slightly less pejorative ver-sion of the classic femme fatale characterization condemning women for men's failings, and *The Beautiful and Damned*'s second chapter, "Portrait of a Siren" (33–67), solidifies the allusion. Perhaps feeling a bit too bold in making the point and remembering that Gloria Gilbert was in many ways a thinly veiled version of Zelda, Fitzgerald opted to move away from another of his early man-uscript titles, "The Beautiful Lady without Mercy," an obvious allusion to John Keats's poem "La Belle Dame sans Merci" (*Selected Poems* 171–73). But Keats strikes the right chord in Fitzgerald's affinity for the romantically bruised heart that might become forever rendered asunder. The poem's original 1819 opening line asks the question, "Oh what can ail thee, knight-at-arms" (*Selected Poems* 171), and ultimately exonerates him from any culpability except being duped by the maiden's trickery, a willful deceit leading to his death as the latest in the line of many knights who had succumbed to the temptress's deadly charms.

Even while disparaging these destructive females, Fitzgerald finds them mysterious and irresistibly alluring as fictional types, especially when their social and financial status rests above that of the male characters. And just as importantly, he does not portray his male protagonists as intellectual sim-pletons mindlessly lured by the Circean voices of women intent upon their demise. To see them in such light projects a strongly misogynist tone that does not sufficiently represent the scope of Fitzgerald's vision. Instead, his fiction embraces the dark but titillating feminine mystique to be experienced through a liaison with a woman who rises above the ordinary, and he honors his male questor's passion for the endeavor, even if it proves to be the suitor's undoing. It is precisely such a dynamic that piques Fitzgerald's artistic interest and his tragic sensibility, and at his best, his characters are far more complex than one-sided analysis allows. He is able to juxtapose contradictory qualities and to offer both empathy and disdain for his fictional progeny, the males as well as the females, encouraging nuanced responses that work against binary vindication or vilification. At one point, he goes so far as to confess an affinity for both the masculine and the feminine in himself saying, "I am half feminine—at least my mind is" (qtd. in Turnbull 259). Thus, critics miss a central depth in his work when they suggest that Fitzgerald sees gender relations only as a battleground between females preying on the males they willfully hope to victimize.

Sarah Beebe Fryer, in her 1988 study *Fitzgerald's New Women: Harbingers of Change*, calls out critics who gather along gender-biased lines. She identifies a tendency, particularly from the male perspective, to blame Fitzgerald's central female characters as the chief aggressors on love's battlefield (6). Gloria Patch, Daisy Buchanan, Nicole Diver, Rosemary Hoyt, and Zelda Fitzgerald serving as the sometimes thinly veiled fictionalized model, receive the largest reproach in Fitzgerald's work as the impetus for the men's downfall. Such an analytical bent sees women not just participating in love's failure or as equally wrecked lovers when the romance is lost; they are instead accused of being its central malevolent force as calculating, cold-hearted, manipulative predators overpowering the males victimized through their self-serving malice. Fryer notes Brian Way's observation that "Fitzgerald's young heroines assert their independent wills and exploit their sexual attractiveness with complete impunity" (11; Fryer 6). She also identifies James Tuttleton's reference to Fitzgerald and other male writers of the period as having created "versions of what might be called 'the young American bitch'" (204; Fryer 6). Fryer further cites Tuttleton saying, "Fitzgerald's memorable heroes all suffer at the hands of rich, bored, sophisticated, insincere women" (205). Not surprisingly, she offers contrasting responses from feminist critics such as Jacqueline Tavernier-Courbin, who remarks that "most of Fitzgerald's women have a down-to-earth practicality and a non-romantic view of life which make them far more enduring than his heroes" (22).

Fryer fails to identify, however, male critics who work against gender lines and have a fuller grasp of the complexity Fitzgerald allows. Scott Donaldson suggests a chronological shift in Fitzgerald's dynamics—youthful stories that "treated the conflict between the sexes more as a game" gradually becoming in later works a "war between the sexes" (*Fool for Love* 116, 120). He further notes that by the time Fitzgerald wrote *Tender Is the Night,* marital relations become martial conflicts, and it is clear that "in such wars no one emerged unscathed. Even the winners were losers" (*Fool for Love* 124). In terms of the fictional females, however, Donaldson believes, "if his readers condemn these women, they do so without any warrant from Fitzgerald himself, who seems to have admired them despite their failings" (*Fool for Love* 67). In his 1965 study *The Art of F. Scott Fitzgerald,* Sergio Perosa also expresses this egalitarian stance, equating it to *The Beautiful and Damned* in believing that the novel's "two people, husband and wife, are equally guilty of an excessive indulgence in illusions and dreams" (36). Both critics acknowledge Fitzgerald's gender sensitivity and ascribe blame and absolution as well as offer equal compassion to the lovers whose romance will inevitably result in suffering.

Anthony Patch, Fitzgerald's first protagonist in a novel to become a hus-band—Horace Tarbox beats him to that status in the short stories in 1920's "Head and Shoulders" (*F&P* 61–86)—enters the search for romantic conquest naively seeing himself as a well-equipped questor who does not seek to escape the siren's song but is willfully hoping to be possessed by it. Because he is a man of self-assurance and financial prowess, he feels confident in his ultimate victory. He rejects the "kaleidoscope of girls, ugly, ugly as sin," he encounters in Times Square (28), and he is equally disinterested in the "[t]hree dozen virtuous females of the first layer [who] were proclaiming their fitness, if not their specific willingness, to bear children unto three dozen millionaires" (33). Through his friend Richard Caramel, Anthony discovers the path to the *belle dame* who will capture his heart when Caramel introduces his cousin Gloria Gilbert and declares that she is "Good-looking—in fact *damned attractive*" (emphasis mine). The precursory adjective "damned" bears important weight here in solidifying the novel's title through its pairing of beauty with damna-tion, and in a second important pairing Anthony admits to himself that "any girl who made a living directly on her prettiness interested him enormously" (36). The suggestion of a female's livelihood having direct connection to her beauty is no accidental word choice and solidifies Fitzgerald's continuing em-phasis on beauty as the economy women employ.

In painting the picture of the young Gloria Gilbert, his intended love match, Anthony will say, "she belonged to a class a little superior" (64), possessing an aura "like a single flower amidst a collection of cheap bric-à-brac" (65), using both floral and monetary terms to establish her aesthetic and economic value. In a reversal of Fitzgerald's usual mode in selecting women from a higher financial rank, Gloria's family cannot claim the monetary caliber and social status Anthony's pedigree seems to promise. Having come from Kansas City, the Gilberts are "middle-westerners," Fitzgerald's phrase implying a tinge of condescension, but they are monetarily comfortable enough to sustain an apartment at the Plaza Hotel and well-enough placed in the city's socially respectable echelons that Gloria would be a sufficient catch. Anthony is quickly smitten, and once he feels certain he has acquired her affection, the book's narrative voice exclaims, "His soul thrilled to remote harmonies; he heard the strum of far guitars and waters lapping on a warm Mediterranean shore—for he was young now as he would never be again, and more triumphant than death" (110). He anticipates "the union of his soul with Gloria's, whose radiant fire and freshness was the living material of which the dead beauty of books was made" (129). This is precisely the Shakespearean rub. Romance achieves its transcendent rapture by contrasting poignantly with the inevitable rupture of that intensity followed by the realization of what has been lost. Knowing that beauty is relegated to become the past's remaining dust, Fitzgerald hails the loss as having been worth the price the lover paid for the height achieved rather than sacrificing to mediocrity.

Gloria Gilbert, like Anthony, has no interest in the men and women populating the unsavory workaday world, and she banks on her beauty's cachet as the commodity used to raise herself above this crowd. Anthony's relational guiding principle is romantic conquest and possession, albeit with a keen eye to her aesthetic value as well. Gloria similarly proclaims in her diary, "I want to marry Anthony, because husbands are so often 'husbands' and I must marry a lover," but she is also practical and carefully calculating. She does not hesitate to express her belief that a man who "works for a salary" is "Totally undesirable!" (127). Gloria also sees herself superior to the women she calls "grubworms" who "crawl on their bellies through colorless marriages!" Because Anthony's seeming promise of financial superiority is coupled with what she feels is his romantic proclivity—the two ingredients essential to her requirements—Gloria projects her journey as his wife to be a "live, lovely, glamourous performance, and the world shall be the scenery" (127). She mirrors here a description Anthony had felt earlier when seeing himself and Gloria as "stars on this stage, each playing to an audience of two: the passion of their pretense created the actuality" (116). Both passages reflect a sense of theatrical play or, again, the pas de deux where the dance represents the vying for dominance as each character relies on the other to be the object against which his or her own actions are supported or thwarted.

Book 2's "The Radiant Hour" (115–62), which represents the central portion of the pas de deux, begins Anthony and Gloria Patch's sojourn as the attractive and financially well-apportioned denizens of the *beau monde* for whom everything is in place to assure life's success. Fitzgerald conveys Anthony's immediate postnuptial emotion when, a "languorous and pleasant content settled like a weight upon him, bringing responsibility and possession. He was married" (134). The intrusive narrator's declarative tone is important in contrasting seemingly incongruous emotions—languorous contentment, a weighty sense of responsibility, and a feeling of possession. Fitzgerald underscores here his often-used triad of love, money, and power, in this case depicting the engagement, marriage ceremony, and brief weeks afterward. That he limits this timeframe to a single hour is telling because of its truncated scope in the framework of what is expected to be a full lifetime together. Fitzgerald has already embedded the seeds of romance's dismantlement and the failure to hold that radiant hour beyond its brief initial glow.

As Fitzgerald begins writing *The Beautiful and Damned*, he relies upon the lively details he and Zelda provide as they frolic through their own early months of matrimony. He identifies this period as "Revelry and Marriage," although it perhaps might be more appropriately sequenced as marriage begetting revelry (*Fitzgerald's Ledger* 174). And whether an intended or unintended consequence, he and Zelda supply fodder to the consumer media of the day as they romp through fountains, circle incessantly in revolving hotel doors, ride on the hood of taxicabs, and act out any number of antics that fan the flames of their rising popularity. Kirk Curnutt labels the newlyweds New York's "cosmopolitan carousers" during their tenure as the golden couple whom the tabloids often touted more for their reckless behaviors than for their artistic or intellectual contributions to the vibrant postwar era (*Cambridge Introduction* 19). This strong emphasis upon the cavalier over the intellectual served to make them stars, which both enhanced and impeded productive movement forward. Linda Wagner-Martin rightly points out that "[t]he 'talk of the town' columns that fueled readers' interest in these beautiful people marked them indelibly, without doing justice to their symbiotic balancing of individual against couple" ("Zelda in the Shadows" 145). Both observations correctly identify the conflict that would follow them throughout their lives together—the necessity of work countered by play, of Scott's achievements linked to, or in spite of, Zelda's help or hindrance.[10] What these New York months established was the balance the couple tried but often failed to maintain—what would thereafter inform their marriage as they came together or were torn apart in their interpersonal relationship and finance's ebb and flow.

In those early weeks and months, Scott and Zelda realized the toll their excesses exacted, and they sought to run away from themselves and their New York antics. Instead, the couple took their troubling behavior on the road to Westport, Connecticut, where Fitzgerald would fictionalize their escape to "the grey house, drably malevolent at last, licking its white chops and waiting to devour them" (196). The summer of 1920 comes to serve as the real and fictional chronicle of excess threatening to sabotage a productive path forward. In the two decades to follow and from ever-changing geographies, Scott and Zelda would carry on in the pattern they set from the start of their peripatetic lives. In each new setting, they hoped to escape themselves and what they either created through pleasure-seeking sprees or brought down upon themselves as consequence of personal, emotional, and sometimes financial bankruptcy. Fitzgerald's retrospective confession years later once again compares his personal and artistic failure and the "dark night of the soul" to a financial metaphor of "a man over-drawing at his bank" (*MLC* 145, 147). These tones of both self-loathing and sympathy would surface in the fiction throughout his lifetime, beginning with *The Beautiful and Damned*.

To some extent, high romance's loss is not personal or to be ascribed as the fault of either lover—it is simply a matter of fact. In the subchapter "Con Amore" (135–42), Fitzgerald references the end of Anthony and Gloria's first few months of marriage, simply describing what follows as a new phase:

> The breathless idyl of their engagement gave way, first, to the intense romance of the more passionate relationship. The breathless idyl left them, fled on to other lovers; they looked around one day and it was gone, how, they scarcely knew. . . . But magic must hurry on, and the lovers remain. . . .
>
> The idyl passed, bearing with it its extortion of youth. . . . But, knowing they had had the best of love, they clung to what remained. (135)

Fitzgerald's lack of editorial judgment here, his failure to indict either Anthony or Gloria, seems surprising given that the narrative voice intervenes in *The Beautiful and Damned* more than in any other of his novels. Instead, in this instance the passage simply notes the truisms of life and relationships. Gloria articulates her grasp of this reality with a reverent but matter-of-fact acknowledgment that "something's lost—something's left behind. You can't ever quite repeat anything" (145). Fitzgerald later highlights in *The Great Gatsby* the fallacy of believing one can recapture previous treasures now gone when Jay Gatsby fails in his attempt to repeat the past he had overdreamed in his reconstruction of Daisy Buchanan. Anthony and Gloria Patch perhaps function as a lesser Jay and Daisy, less romantically tuned to a "high star" than Gatsby, but they travel a similar path nonetheless and serve as Fitzgerald's first ode to the impermanence of "a promise that the rock of the world was founded securely on a fairy's wing" (*GG* 119). He would articulate this notion with growing artistic power in the novels to follow as his own experience substantiated its reality.

Fitzgerald introduces in book 2 another variant pas de deux—the interplay between meaningful work and time wasted through excessive self-gratification. Trepidation about his own future and the need to accomplish something of value, a literary legacy in particular, too often conflicted with the raucous antics that made Scott and Zelda popular icons of hedonism. Perhaps for his own benefit, Fitzgerald demonstrates through Anthony and Gloria Patch's story line the cost of such imbalance. The newlyweds at first view their dalliances as self-aggrandizing amusement, but when in book 2 Adam J. Patch arrives unexpectedly at one of their bacchanalian indulgences, grandfather and grandson clash. The senior Patch condemns Anthony's reckless actions as antithetical to his own puritanical conviction that morality and a strong work ethic bring about the kind of economic success that he himself has generated (230–31). Mr. Patch's rigid adherence to this prescribed notion results in his disinheriting Anthony. The swift, deterministic blow and its repercussive aftermath dramatically alter Anthony and Gloria's romanticized vision of a financially embellished future and set the stage for the downward spiral of nearly Dreiser-like proportion that informs the rest of the novel.[11]

The tragedy Fitzgerald draws out here is not the loss of finances so much as it is Anthony and Gloria's failure to launch themselves into responsible, wage-earning adulthood. After an argument about Gloria's wanting to audition for a role in film, followed by Anthony's objection, she emotes: "I hate to see you go to pieces by just lying around and saying you ought to work. Perhaps if I *did* go into this for awhile it'd stir you up so you'd do something" (182). The sardonic tone of the narrative voice then describes Anthony and Gloria's effort to overcome inertia with "a burst of gargantuan emotion" as each decides to write a letter: Anthony's to his grandfather and Gloria's to Joseph Bloeckman, who had suggested the film test. The action culminates in "a triumph of lethargy" (182), and they return to their well-established pattern of failing to progress toward a means of financial self-sufficiency. Gloria, without any epiphanic clarity, proclaims: "There's only one lesson to be learned from life. . . . That there's no lesson to be learned from life" (215).

With narrative design that is central to Fitzgerald's dual aesthetic, the author also underscores the tragedy of Gloria and Anthony's romantic decline. The title of book 2's last section, "The Broken Lute" (220–58), provides a nod to the Renaissance's romantic instrument of choice and the inability in this broken condition to mesmerize with its lilting tunes. Fitzgerald sets the stage for the long denouement as the gulf widens between romance and hard-shelled reality in the couple's marriage. Love's early ecstasy, based at least in part on the promise of fortune, crashes abruptly against the financial loss Anthony and Gloria experience, and they both begin to flirt with infidelity as their once-vibrant romance wains. Anthony had earlier understood that his wife "was disposed to like many men, preferably those who gave her frank homage and unfailing entertainment" (198), and his fear grows with financial confidence lost. He is especially aware that Bloeckman stands ready to steal Gloria away, and on his part, Anthony's drunken flirtations further destabilize the couple's bond. Both feel an increasing sense "of beauty gone foul and revelry remembered in disgust" (247), but as summer melts into fall, they cling to hope they can renew the blush of love, "when the money was theirs . . . when they would 'agree on things again,' for both of them looked forward to a time when love, springing like the phoenix from its own ashes, should be born again in its mysterious and unfathomable haunts" (257). Like the nation now heading into war with its own fearful sense of beauty turned to dust, Fitzgerald identifies Anthony and Gloria's life as having become a restless search for something elusive or once possessed but now lost.

At the beginning of book 3, Anthony's enlistment in the army signifies a lack of purpose more than patriotic fervor, and he likewise stumbles into the affair that ensues during his military training in the South.[12] Fitzgerald describes this relationship with Dorothy "Dot" Raycroft, a young woman clearly not his heart's replacement for his wife, as a result of Anthony's "increasing carelessness about himself" rather than sincere romantic fervor. We learn that he "did not go to her desiring to possess the desirable. . . . He merely slid into the matter through his inability to make definite judgments" (270). A song wafting from a nearby front porch one night while Anthony is visiting Dot only brings to his mind "another face, radiant, flower-like, upturned to lights as transforming as the stars," a woman he identifies in this vision as "*la belle dame sans merci* who lived in his heart" (274). The image is so apropos of Fitzgerald's fictional romantic playbook that he will repeat it in *The Great Gatsby* in only slightly altered language when a young lieutenant Jay Gatsby begins his romantic infatuation with Daisy Fay as he "kissed her. At his lips' touch she blossomed for him like a flower and the incarnation was complete" (*GG* 134).

When the war is suddenly over and Anthony returns home to Gloria, Fitzgerald moves the pas de deux to its coda by dramatizing the deepening corrosion of the Patches' financial status, the downward trajectory of their relationship, and their subsequent attempts to subsist in increasingly diminished circumstances. He intensifies the arc of decline in Anthony and Gloria's marriage as they "become like players who had lost their costumes, lacking the pride to continue on the note of tragedy" (334). Gloria, at the age of twenty-nine, auditions for a small film role, only to find out in a letter from Bloeckman that the director "seemed to think that for the part he had in mind he needed a younger woman" but that "there was a small character part supposed to be a very haughty rich widow" she might be able to play (333). With her hopes crushed, Gloria cannot finish reading the letter, and in an argument later with Anthony, she says, "I wasn't thirty, and I didn't think I—looked thirty" (352). Anthony is also increasingly concerned about his own lost youth, his failure to find an essential purpose, and his growing awareness that the confidence in monetary domination he had always assumed was now dependent on the court's decision about whether to reverse his grandfather's financial punishment from beyond the grave. In spite of potential ruin, the couple remain enervated and fail to find meaningful or profitable occupations, even while their future clings to the uncertainly of legal rescue. The culminating blow occurs when Anthony narrowly escapes his affair being discovered, but the shock of Dot suddenly showing up just before the court's decision in the Patches' favor causes an emotional and physical breakdown from which he never recovers (365–67).

Having written *The Beautiful and Damned* during his and Zelda's honeymoon phase with its emotional highs and lows, Fitzgerald made good use of that period's fertile grounds to inspire his affinity for fictional moralizing. He seems to be saying through the Patches' ensuing free fall that no victory can be celebrated when it rests on the refuse of a life not lived by high values and productivity. Even with the inheritance won, the Patches' future is bleak because youth, beauty, and the halcyon days where these qualities reigned are forever gone with no amount of fortune able to bring them back. In Fitzgerald's choice for the novel's epigraph—"The victor belongs to the spoils," his darker inversion of an earlier popularized quip, "To the victor belongs the spoils"—he solidifies a fictional critique of the wasteland his characters have made of their lives.[13] Though Anthony and Gloria Patch are his only essential fictional couple throughout his novels to remain married—the Buchanans' marriage is not central—their misery has been both individually and tandemly evoked, and the personal and relational failings compound to intensify their romantic implosion.

Perhaps precisely because Fitzgerald recognizes the fragile margins between success and failure resulting from one's choices—the ability for a misstep to bring the house of cards tumbling down especially along the narrow path where love, artistic success, and financial security abide—he heightens his focus on moral collapse but offers compassion for his protagonists who strive against odds in which they will no doubt fail or to which better judgment might induce them to concede. Fitzgerald articulates this perspective a decade and a half after his initial success, when writing his 1936 confessional "The Crack-Up":

> Life, ten years ago, was largely a personal matter. I must hold in balance the sense of the futility of effort and the sense of the necessity to struggle; the conviction of the inevitability of failure and still the determination to "succeed"—and, more than these, the contradiction between the dead hand of the past and the high intentions of the future. If I could do this through the common ills—domestic, professional and personal—then the ego would continue as an arrow shot from nothingness to nothingness with such force that only gravity would bring it to earth at last. (*MLC* 140)

Anthony Patch projects this effort in *The Beautiful and Damned* in a much less vital way than Fitzgerald himself or than Jay Gatsby, Patch's more intensely obsessed fictional successor; but both protagonists dupe themselves into believing they will be victorious in the conquest to attain money that will be employed in the pursuit of love. From Anthony's early exclamation of invincibility, his journey ends with financial victory, in which he announces, "I showed them. . . . It was a hard fight, but I didn't give up and I came through!" (369). He makes this patently hollow boast even though he is a broken man, who, from the platform of a wheelchair, whispers his victory speech to no one, just as Jay Gatsby's life ends with a bullet wrongfully meant for him while he waits for the lover's call that will never come. They have both come to represent the antithesis of Fitzgerald's proclamation by abandoning high intentions of the past and replacing them with the dead hand of the future. Romantic readiness thus gives way to tragic failure as an emblematic sign that the victory truly belongs to the spoils.

Fitzgerald draws his strongest narrative impetus from an ability to embrace complicated moral evaluations and contrasting character assessments to envision a less judgmental, more empathetically inclusive circle. He concomitantly praises and condemns both lovers for their initial engagement in unrealistic romanticism and their ensuing and inevitable destruction of its beautiful potential. In his system of value exchange where love and money are often actively intertwined agents, each player bears blame to a varying extent for failing to sustain the vision, and each pays a high emotional price for prioritizing personal victory at the expense of a unified plan. While writing *The Beautiful and Damned,* Fitzgerald could only have begun to understand the credence he would give to this guiding principle, but in retrospect he was able to attest to its legitimacy. In a 1930 letter "Written with Zelda gone to the Clinique" after her first serious mental breakdown, he acknowledged the relevance he had intuitively understood a decade earlier. Fitzgerald lovingly penned: "I wish the *Beautiful and Damned* had been a maturely written book because it was all true. We ruined ourselves—I have never honestly thought that we ruined each other" (*Letters* 189). His fictional tracking of the ultimately doomed journey he would chronicle many times in his life first began to solidify with Anthony and Gloria Patch and later spilled over into *The Great Gatsby* and *Tender Is the Night.* In all three of these works, the best of his five novels, Fitzgerald's poignant talent was to reveal beautifully the wreckage on the shoals that Matthew Bruccoli J. calls "projections of what Fitzgerald feared for himself" (*Some Sort,* 152), and he revisits this theme repeatedly throughout his fiction as he mourns losses and brilliantly conveys the powerful emotions those losses evoke.

NOTES

1. The *pas de deux* is defined as a suite of dances usually in classical ballet sharing a common theme, most often a love story or sensual tension drawing the dancers together through intense interaction. The structure consists of five parts: entrée, adagio, two solo variations (usually with a ballerina and a danseur), and coda.

2. Zelda would later write *Save Me the Waltz*, featuring Alabama Knight (née Beggs) as a would-be ballerina, and in 1936 Fitzgerald posed to Harold Ober three screenplay ideas centering around ballet, following an earlier synopsis, "Lives of the Dancers" (*Fitzgerald: A Life in Letters* 295–98). Scott's concept was never to be realized, and although Zelda's novel was published, not only was it not a financial success, but it also caused a serious if short-lived rift in their marriage. In Zelda's psychiatric treatment at Prangins in Switzerland, her obsession with becoming a ballerina at the age of thirty was a topic of serious discussion as a strong potential cause for her breakdown.

3. The drawing (reproduced on page 156 herein) ultimately was not used for the book jacket, no doubt because of the female figure's nudity and the blatant rejection of the nation's prohibitionist amendment, but it established a visual reference to the debauchery central to Fitzgerald's narrative arc (Bruccoli, *Romantic Egoists* 99).

4. *The Beautiful and Damned* had yet another early draft title, "The Diary of a Literary Failure," when Fitzgerald's early emphasis was on both Anthony Patch and Richard Caramel as they explored making writing their career.

5. Zelda's premarriage letter in February 1920 refers to her impatience with the "constant recurrence" of Scott's mentioning "the princess in her tower" (*Collected Writings* 447). In a nostalgic letter written while she was hospitalized at Prangins in Switzerland after her first serious mental breakdown, Zelda wrote more lovingly about Scott's fixation: "I hope you know they are kisses splattering you[r] balcony tonight from a lady who was once in three separate letters, a princess in a high white tower and who has never forgotten her elevated station in life and who is waiting once more for her royal darling" (Bryer and Barks 105).

6. Bruccoli is able to garner these details because Fitzgerald was a meticulous record-keeper, and in the ledger he kept throughout his lifetime, he noted his career earnings year by year (*Fitzgerald's Ledger* 52).

7. Although several biographies about Zelda have been published in the last decade, Milford's seminal work remains a worthy and reliable source about the Fitzgeralds' early relationship.

8. Actually called *droit du signor*, or right of the lord, Fitzgerald refers to a supposed medieval right allowing the lord of a manor to sleep with the wife of any of his vassals on the wedding night. The validity of this practice is uncertain, perhaps having more to do with taxes than sex, but the possibility of such a concept certainly appealed to Fitzgerald's heightened sense of romantic tragedy.

9. Bryer's "'Better That All of the Story Never Be Told'" provides never-before-published excerpts from a June 1950 letter Zelda's sister Rosalind sent to Arthur Mizener after reading the manuscript of his Fitzgerald biography. She felt compelled to provide commentary or to set certain aspects straight. Relevant here is her opinion concerning Zelda's cold feet about marriage. Rosalind states, "I do not believe that Zelda's hesitancy about marrying Scott was prompted by

any mercenary motive, but that it was rather her uncertainty about the wisdom of the step that restrained her" (Bryer, "'Better That All of the Story Never Be Told'" 6).

10. Scott's name sometimes appeared as sole author on pieces Zelda wrote. This was usually done with her permission because his popularity commanded a much higher price per piece. The diary, however, seems to substantiate Zelda's accusation that Fitzgerald had plagiarized whole passages for his own use in *The Beautiful and Damned.* She makes this accusation public in a 2 April 1922 published review of *The Beautiful and Damned,* where she says: "It seems to me that on one page I recognized a portion of an old diary of mine which mysteriously disappeared shortly after my marriage. . . . Mr. Fitzgerald—I believe that is how he spells his name—seems to believe that plagiarism begins at home" (*Collected Writings* 388).

11. I refer here specifically to Dreiser's *Sister Carrie,* where George Hurstwood's decision to take money from his company and run away with Carrie Meeber leads to his increasingly declining circumstances and ultimate death.

12. This is a clear nod to Scott's courtship of Zelda during his own military training at Camp Sheridan outside Montgomery, Alabama, Zelda's hometown.

13. This phrase is attributed to New York senator William L. Marcy from an 1831 congressional debate (Titelman 342).

TROUBLE ON THE HOME FRONT
MILITARISM, MASCULINITY, AND MARRIAGE
IN *THE BEAUTIFUL AND DAMNED*

Meredith Goldsmith

One might conclude that the marriage of Gloria Gilbert and Anthony Patch, the couple at the center of *The Beautiful and Damned* (1922), fails due to the selfishness and financial worries of both parties as the two await their anticipated inheritance from Anthony's grandfather, Adam J. Patch, who is both a millionaire and Civil War veteran. Fitzgerald's critique of marriage may be sharpest in this novel, which, as Michael Nowlin has argued, offers a "radically unsentimental view of heterosexual relations" ("Mencken's Defense" 105). This essay suggests that the Great War, even in the period immediately before America enters it in April 1917, disrupts the Patches' already fragile marriage by unsettling the gender norms on which it depends. Although wartime propaganda, as Jennifer Haytock has argued, depended on and attempted to perpetuate stable divisions of gendered labor (1), life during wartime often prompted women to claim forms of independence, even though women like Gloria remained on the home front, in a relatively domestic situation. In Fitzgerald's novel, the physical separation between Anthony and Gloria during wartime prompts a redefinition of their class and gender roles.

As Anthony is relocated to an exoticized, racialized, and sexualized South, he experiments sexually with the Other through his affair with the white, working-class, sexually experienced Dorothy Raycroft, or Dot; simultaneously, however, he also briefly inhabits the role of Other, as he is forced to live among—and against his wishes, to assimilate to the norms of—immigrant and working-class American soldiers. The class-leveling discipline of the military, which Anthony resists, would enforce a certain kind of masculinity as well—dependent on physical strength and authority within a hierarchy rather than intelligence or education. As we learn early in the novel, Anthony has been trained to associate masculinity with the Civil War (20–21). Rejecting this discipline, however, Anthony becomes feminized and conscious of his own frailty. Similarly, sexually and economically vulnerable Gloria hovers on the edge of middle-class New Womanhood during Anthony's absence; even as she resists opportunities for meaningful employment, she realizes her sexual agency in her flirtations with visiting officers. As the "False Armistice" that allows Anthony to flee his military post indicates, any truce between men and women would be premature and hardly built to last (355). Although *Tender Is the Night* (1934) is the work of Fitzgerald's most explicitly concerned with postwar trauma, *The Beautiful and Damned* articulates the effects of the war on the home front, and especially its ramifications for the relationships between generations and between men and women.

As Keith Gandal (5–6), Matthew J. Bruccoli (*Some Sort* 82), and James H. Meredith ("F. Scott Fitzgerald and War" 133–34) have argued, Fitzgerald's lack of active duty should not deter us from analyzing the military rhetoric in his fiction. If, until 1917, World War I was the war Americans experienced vicariously, the presence of military conflict nonetheless pervades Fitzgerald's fiction. Even early in the novel, Fitzgerald surveys early twentieth-century Manhattan in terms that evoke the Civil War and Great War simultaneously. As Anthony hears an elevated train rattling by, he is "reminded of a fantastic romance he had lately read in which cities had been bombed from aerial trains, and for a moment, he fancied that Washington Square had declared war on Central Park and this was a north-bound menace loaded with battle and sudden death. But as it passed the illusion faded; it diminished to the faintest of drums—then to a far-away droning eagle" (29). This dreamlike image blends the Civil War, in which neighbor was turned against neighbor (much as here, a park in Lower Manhattan is turned against its northern neighbor), with "battle and sudden death," and newly invented military technology (aerial bombings). Fitzgerald conjures a startlingly nationalist and martial description of a train running through Manhattan, replete with drums and eagle. The imagined scene establishes the extent to which, despite Anthony's aversion to conflict, war—and the "fantastic" narratives through which it is depicted—has informed his imagination, as well as that of the larger culture.

Such military undercurrents pervade the novel, the bulk of which takes place before America enters the war. As is typical of Fitzgerald's early work, *The Beautiful and Damned* attempts to pull together a number of divergent strands: gender conflict, ethnic representations, the blur between past and present, and the inability of the leisure class to make a meaningful place for itself within American society. Contextualizing the novel in this way helps clarify aspects of the novel that might seem extraneous. Similarly, the novel's episodes of Civil War nostalgia remind us that both the Civil War and World War I were seen as efforts to defend "civilization" rather than efforts to protect slavery or to advance imperialism and nationalism. In addition, although Japan sided with the Entente powers in the Great War (and thus, eventually, America), the Japanese servant Tana—otherwise simply a crude caricature—serves as a vessel for the growing paranoia Fitzgerald observed about non-American Others in the 1910s and early 1920s, when the United States' most restrictive immigration legislation was passed. Writing in the prewar years, Fitzgerald observed a mounting anti-immigrant climate, including hostility toward Chinese and Japanese immigrants as documented in the Exclusion Acts of the late nineteenth and early twentieth centuries.[1] These interrelated phenomena—fear of the Other, the defense of American "civilization," and the disruption of gender roles—come to mark Fitzgerald's depiction of the Great War.

From his youth, Anthony has been trained to associate war with masculinity and power. We learn early in the novel that Adam J. Patch, whose fortune fuels Anthony's dissolute existence in and after college, "left his father's farm in Tarrytown early in sixty-one to join a New York cavalry regiment" (12). That Patch's wealth is acquired in the "fuss, fume, [and] applause" of the postwar period suggests how military service could confer an air of authority. As we will see later in the novel, Adam Patch's Civil War experiences ultimately blur with Anthony's Great War experiences, and both conflicts are presented through similar rhetorical strategies. The war secures Patch's reputation, and he "charge[s] into Wall Street" (12) and, eventually, extraordinary wealth. Fitzgerald's narrator uses military imagery to describe Patch's Comstockian conservatism: he "directed against the enormous hypothetical enemy, unrighteousness, a campaign which went on through fifteen years" (12). When *The Beautiful and Damned* begins, Patch's "campaign had grown desultory; 1861 was creeping up slowly on 1895; his thoughts ran a great deal on the Civil War," alighting only occasionally on Anthony, his only living heir (12). As 1861 "creeps up" on 1895,

Fitzgerald describes a character partially living in the past, suggesting a lag between the historical moment of the Civil War and that of the later Gilded Age. The war is part of the family's past and central to Patch's narrative of male authority. For example, as Adam Patch hectors Anthony to "accomplish something" after graduation, he first suggests writing a "history" of the "Civil War" or the "Revolution" (21). Anthony's wish to write a history of the "Middle Ages" or the "Renaissance popes" instead emphasizes his disdain for and exclusion from narratives of American heroism and conflict: his grandfather counters, "Why not your own country? Something you know about?" (21). Anthony believes he can abjure such conflicts and the masculine roles they imply. However, as the novel will show, Anthony has internalized the equation between militarism and masculinity more than he is aware.[2]

As Gandal argues, World War I novels dramatize, and even advance, the clash between the genders and the rise of New Womanhood characteristic of the 1920s. In Gandal's view, novels such as *The Beautiful and the Damned*, *The Great Gatsby* (1925), Ernest Hemingway's *The Sun Also Rises* (1926), and William Faulkner's *The Sound and the Fury* (1929) evoke the war through their depiction of wounded masculinity and female sexual aggression. The rejection of weak—often physically injured or psychologically fragile—men by powerful women, Gandal writes, reflects the possible fear of rejection by military authority. These novels' portraits of independent women echo military anxieties about female sexual promiscuity. "Charity girls," as they were dubbed in military circles, were women who slept with soldiers but were not prostitutes (7, 109). The conflict between female sexual agency and male fragility shapes *The Beautiful and Damned,* and Anthony's efforts to claim a strong sense of hetero-masculinity falter in relation to both Gloria—a symbol of glory and, implicitly, military prowess—and, as we will learn later on, to his military service itself.

Anthony's courtship of Gloria and his search for meaningful work both take place against the backdrop of pre–Great War tensions in Europe. Although the action of the novel takes place shortly after Anthony returns from Europe in 1913, we receive only hints of the growing political distress of Europe in the immediate prewar years. For Anthony and his cohort, this distress is signaled, yet only obliquely recognized, in the rise of yet another wave of immigration. While Anthony dallies and imagines an appropriate career, Anthony's counterpart, Richard Caramel, works "with bewildered Italians as secretary to an 'Alien Young Men's Rescue Association.' . . . The aliens kept coming inexhaustibly—Italians, Poles, Scandinavians, Czechs, Armenians—with the same wrongs, the same exceptionally ugly faces and very much the same smells" (68). Anthony rejects the immigrants aesthetically, underscoring his own political naiveté when he suggests that all had suffered the "same wrongs" (68). Fitzgerald parodies, somewhat proleptically, the vogue of "service" among white, elite college students, which, as he notes, "has long rocked the colleges in America" (68). Although Dick Caramel can stomach living briefly among aesthetically displeasing immigrant men, he soon tires of the task of "making sow-ear purses out of sows' ears" (69), implying that these men are fundamentally unassimilable, or that their inherent characteristics will not change. With the privilege of well-traveled white Americans, Anthony and Dick are free to ignore these mounting conflicts. Dick leaves his social work to write and Anthony's only contact with non-native-born Americans, at this early point of the novel, is with Joseph Bloeckman, the German Jewish film director with whom he competes for Gloria's attention. The novel highlights these non-Anglo-American Others (though, significantly, very few African Americans), emphasizing their growing presence in the New York landscape. Anthony occasionally observes Jews on the streets of Manhattan (28, 237), and Rachael Jerryl, a minor character, is an "exquisitely dressed Jewess with dark hair and a lovely milky pallor" (76). Soon, he will engage in extensive interaction with the Japanese servant, Tana. As in *The Great Gatsby*, Fitzgerald will consider the question of whether immigrants can truly become Americans. Here, Fitzgerald distinguishes clearly between the white and nonwhite and the rich and the poor. While the immigrants might not discard their inherent ugliness, Bloeckman—typically characterized as physically strong and ultimately stronger than Anthony—by the end of the novel is a "well-conditioned man" who knows "something of sparring" (360) and bests Anthony in a fight. Bloeckman, as the final battle between him and Anthony shows, is on a distinctly upward trajectory. In contrast, Tana and the other immigrants seem to mar the landscape, aesthetically as well as politically detrimental.

Although Anthony and Gloria marry in June 1914 and return from their honeymoon two months later, "simultaneously with the fall of Liège" (144), the couple experience the war only as a series of "rumor-bulletins" on the radio (140). Yet the battle abroad prefigures and ultimately shapes the long-running "verbal battle" (142) that soon begins between the couple at home.

As the war begins, Fitzgerald blurs the boundary between the Civil War and the Great War even further. When the Patches return from their honeymoon trip to California, they stop for a visit to General Robert E. Lee's mansion in Arlington, Virginia. In this episode, which anticipates Daisy Fay Buchanan's youth in the South (*GG* 90–92) and echoes Zelda Fitzgerald's family affiliations (Milford 3–7), Lee's mansion serves as a pivotal example of the recycling of the Civil War to meet dominant-cultural concerns of the early twentieth century. Debates began with the turn of the century over the historical status of Arlington House, which had fallen into disrepair after the war, and whether it should be renovated as a monument to the Confederacy or as a symbol of Union victory (Hanna 120–23). When Gloria and Anthony visit in 1914, the mansion had not yet been renovated but was open to tourists. As the couple wander through the dilapidated mansion, Gloria "br[eaks] down" (143) upon seeing the way the home has been modernized for the public. Gloria, ostensibly a modern flapper (31), rails at the modernization of the home: "Do you think they've left a breath of 1860 here? This has become a thing of 1914" (143). When Anthony responds, "Don't you want to preserve old things?" (143), Gloria praises the romanticized past, saying that "just as any period decays in our minds, the things of that period should decay too, and in that way they're preserved for a while in the few hearts like mine that react to them" (143). As tourists "swarm" (143) through the Lee family mansion, they are encouraged to imagine the Confederate past as *past*; Gloria, in contrast, wants to "love the past" (143) by having it live around her.[3]

Gloria sees herself as one of the few emotionally qualified people to respond to the Civil War's past appropriately. Although Anthony is largely silent during this episode, it his grandfather who has an illustrious Civil War past; we learn little about Gloria's family, although she hails from the border state of Missouri. Anthony's early infatuation with Gloria thus anticipates his later romance with Dot. Southern women, as we see here, claim an exaggerated connection to the antebellum past. As Gloria exclaims in her disappointment at the transformation of Lee's mansion into a tourist site, "I want [the house] to smell of magnolias instead of peanuts and I want my shoes to crunch on the same gravel that Lee's boots crunched on" (144). As the sound of men's "boots crunch[ing] . . . on gravel" (144) reverberates in Gloria's memory, this militaristic image erases the distance between 1860 and 1914. Potentially, it erases distances based on gender as well as those of time; Gloria wants, quite literally, to walk in General Lee's footsteps. Only the privileged few, like Gloria, can see the past in the present. A racialized class distinction marks the difference between those who can envision the glory of the past and those who cannot, whom Gloria racializes as "*animals*" (144; emphasis original) and classes as "these people" (144).[4] Gloria's yearning for the past also intersects with ageism: rather than allowing the past to remain alive for those able to appreciate its "poignancy," "they've made it into a blondined, rouged-up old woman of sixty" (143–44). Gloria's flapper fear of aging intersects with her gendered essentialism; her Confederate nostalgia projects an image of the antebellum South as a site of eternal youth.[5]

The Patches' visit to the Lee mansion emphasizes the novel's retrograde pull, as the ostensibly modern Gloria craves antebellum romance and the only profession Anthony can imagine is that of a medievalist or a historian. Fitzgerald's placement of this scene is not accidental—the end of the Patches' honeymoon is simultaneous with the beginning of the Great War, displaced though it is onto the Civil War. Civil War and antebellum nostalgia will become even more prominent when Anthony relocates to South Carolina for his basic training. Memories of the Civil War function as a counterpoint to the modern conflict just initiated in Europe. Yet, in a sign of their elite status, Gloria and Anthony largely ignore the war early in their marriage.

However, Fitzgerald signals the mounting conflict through the displacement of immigrants, one of whom becomes a servant in the Patch household. The couple's Japanese servant, Tana, is one of Fitzgerald's few Asian American characters; analyzing his depiction of this character can deepen our understanding of ethnicity in his fiction.[6]

Once Gloria and Anthony are installed in their suburban home in Marietta, Tana comes to the household as their servant. Reflecting America's complex immigrant history, Tana replaces a "broad-hipped, broad-shouldered Swedish girl," who "weep[s] violently into her bowed arms on the kitchen table" one day (159). In this moment, Fitzgerald briefly acknowledges the exhaustion, low pay, and unhappiness of immigrant female workers, yet there is no communication between Gloria and her female servant. A white woman who might be able to transition into other forms of employment, or at least another domestic service position, the Swedish "girl" disappears, "g[iving] way" to "an exceedingly efficient Japanese" (165).[7] It is worth contextualizing Tana's presence in the eastern United States at that time. As Ronald Takaki reports, "Between 1885 and 1924, 200,000 Japanese went to Hawaii and 180,000 to the U.S. mainland" (45).

Although "the Japanese government promoted the emigration of women" (46), Tana is presented as an itinerant immigrant bachelor, not clearly part of any community.

Tana's race, gender, sexuality, and national identity "others" him from the white American landscape that he enters when working for the Patches. Some of the characteristics Fitzgerald associates with Tana could be linked to the bachelor stereotype—both hypersexualized and feminized, Tana carries "a collection of Japanese post cards"; in addition to the Japanese cards, though, he has "half a dozen [cards] of pornographic intent and plainly of American origin, though the makers had modestly omitted both their names and the form for mailing" (165). In addition, he sews his own clothes, including his underwear. Fitzgerald also emphasizes Tana's inability to discern differences between Asian and white: he makes a "rather good copy of an etching of Abraham Lincoln, to whose face he had given an unmistakable Japanese cast" (165). Similarly, he fails to discern the implications of a racist cartoon he encounters in the newspaper: "a facetious Japanese butler diverted him enormously, though he claimed that the protagonist, who to Anthony appeared clearly Oriental, had really an American face" (166). Both Anthony and Tana label the cartoon character as Other to themselves (to Anthony, Oriental; to Tana, white), but Fitzgerald emphasizes Tana's lack of discernment—the "facetious Japanese butler" is nothing like himself.

As Tana occupies the Patch household, bringing ethnic and racial otherness into their midst, Anthony and Gloria will come to experience the war even closer to home. Although Anthony and Gloria seem largely unaware of the conflict raging abroad, Fitzgerald demonstrates how the war begins to pervade their ostensibly carefree life. In one early sign of deterioration of their marital struggles, Fitzgerald depicts a fight between the couple that evokes the rhetoric of the Great War. As Anthony grips Gloria's arm while they argue on a train platform, "the bells distilled metallic crashes that were like physical pain, the smoke-stacks volleyed in slow acceleration at the sky, and in a moment of noise and gray gaseous turbulence the line of faces ran by, indistinct" (170). Metal, smoke, noise, and gas—imagery more common to the battlefield than to the Patches' elite suburb—come to characterize the humiliation of a public argument. Anthony simply wants to win, to "sustain his will with violence." Their argument briefly turns violent, as he tears her sleeve and she bites his thumb, drawing blood (170–71). Afterward, Gloria's appearance, replete with torn clothing, echoes that of a rape victim—"broken and dispirited, humiliated beyond . . . measure" (171). As Haytock shows, in the early years of the war, images of male sexual aggression and female victimhood were mapped onto the conflict between Germany and Belgium, with Belgium often depicted as a rape victim (4). The text implies that their reconciliation through sex, which follows the argument, results in a pregnancy (173), and then a possible miscarriage through an abortifacient. As the couple's difficulties increase, Fitzgerald will use the language of dominance, will, and violence—the language of military conflict—to characterize the interactions between Anthony and Gloria. Where Anthony and Gloria have enjoyed a passionate romantic relationship, despite their frequent disagreements, this militaristic moment highlights the gendered dynamic of marital relationships, despite Gloria's "Nietzschean" sense of power (172).

Whereas the Great War serves as an undercurrent to Gloria and Anthony's relationship, it is the object of "pious rage" for Anthony's grandfather. Adam Patch, the representative of the novel's older generation, views the war as something of an obsession: "Pin maps plastered his walls; atlases were piled deep on tables," and his reading involves the memoirs of war correspondents and soldiers (174). The novel's debate over meaningful work crystallizes in his excitement over the mounting conflict. Patch urges his grandson to "go over and write about these Germans . . . write something real, something about what's going on, something people can read" (174). He even offers to pay for Anthony's time abroad and to help him find a correspondent's position. However, Anthony's ambivalence has to do with the conflict between the image of a war correspondent ("He saw himself in khaki . . . leaning . . . upon a heavy stick, portfolio at shoulder" [175]) and the masculine dominance this role would of necessity provide: the very thought of such a role makes him envision "a world of harder men, more fiercely trained and grappling with the abstractions of thought and war" (175). Such a role would clarify the power dynamics between himself and Gloria, turning his wife into a "chance mistress, coolly sought and quickly forgotten" (175). Ironically, at the same time, Joseph Bloeckman offers Gloria an opportunity for a movie audition, which she links to Mary Pickford, "America's Sweetheart" (181). As Anthony rejects an opportunity for wartime labor and, at this point, Gloria rejects the film opportunity she will later seek, Fitzgerald emphasizes their complacency in the face of the mounting conflict in Europe: all three—Bloeckman, Gloria, and Anthony—"sat like over-oiled machines, without conflict, without fear, without elation, heavily enamelled little figures secure beyond enjoyment in a world where death and war, dull emotion and noble savagery were covering a continent with the smoke of terror" (181).

Gloria and Anthony's indifference in the face of the war abroad helps explain the representation of Tana, who begins to serve as less of a caricature and more of a repository of fears of cultural Otherness. In a moment anticipating *Tender Is the Night,* where Rosemary Hoyt is horrified by the dead body of an African American man on her hotel room bed (*TITN* 126), Gloria had "taken a strong dislike to Tana ever since the day when, returning unexpectedly from the village, she had discovered him reclining on Anthony's bed, puzzling out a newspaper" (199). Although the text emphasizes Tana's poor reading skills and not his status as a sexual threat, a hint of anxiety around miscegenation remains, inasmuch as Tana has taken Anthony's (and at times, Gloria's) rightful place. The text also emphasizes Tana's inscrutability: he attempts to build a typewriter (183). Maury Noble spreads the rumor that he is "a German agent kept in this country to disseminate Teutonic propaganda" (199), and goes so far as to prank him with falsified letters "addressed to the bewildered Oriental" under a German name and "adorned with an atmospheric double column of facetious Japanese" (199). And as Tana becomes a figure of fun for Anthony and his friends and a source of anxiety for Gloria, the household becomes increasingly centered on male bonds—Anthony, his "insensitive guests" (197), and Tana—and less so on the bond between Anthony and Gloria.

The increase in Anthony and Gloria's financial and emotional troubles parallels the continued conflict, even the stalemated trench warfare, of the war abroad. Gloria and Anthony, we learn, have been selling Adam Patch's bonds (226) rather than purchasing war bonds. A riotous evening in which Tana plays his Japanese flute coincides, disastrously, with a visit from the old man, who discovers the household and guests in extreme drunkenness (230–31). Patch, a teetotaler, shuns Anthony, and the couple is ultimately disinherited (245, 247). As Anthony runs short on options, he realizes that his fellow Harvard alumni have found meaningful work in the war: "a few, he found, were working constructively at jobs that were neither sinecures or routines" (239). For example, Calvin Boyd "had discovered a new treatment for typhus, had shipped abroad and was mitigating some of the civilization that the Great Powers had brought to Servia." Meanwhile, "Severance, the quarter-back . . . had given up his life rather neatly and gracefully with the Foreign Legion on the Aisne"

(239). Fitzgerald ironically emphasizes that the "Great Powers" brought typhus to the Balkans along with ostensible "civilization"; Anthony is also attracted to Severance's effective performance of death, rather than a death for honor. Although Anthony continues to vacillate, war is declared in April 1917, and it appears that the war will give him a concrete task of self-definition.

The declaration of the war also allows Fitzgerald to develop his critique of propaganda: with April 1917, "the press began to whoop hysterically against the sinister morals, sinister philosophy, and sinister music produced by the Teutonic temperament" (256). The propaganda machine is decisively gendered: "Any song which contained the word 'mother' and the word 'kaiser' was assured of a tremendous success" (256), echoing Haytock's observations that wartime propaganda affirmed stereotypical gender roles (4–5). Propaganda works, as Fitzgerald observes, by endorsing both masculinity and whiteness: "everybody was a fine fellow, and every race a great race—always excepting the Germans" (257). It appears that the dissipation of the Patches is briefly halted, as Anthony plans to join "an impossible caste of officers" drawn from the "more attractive alumni of three or four Eastern colleges" (256–57). The role of officer, Anthony believes, will offer him the masculine dominance he has never really had.

Yet the novel does not allow Anthony even this brief moment of "glamour" (257). He fails the medical examination for officers' training but is drafted soon after into the regular army. As Anthony and Gloria separate in Grand Central when his "contingent" (258) is sent south, the tone of the novel, as well as Fitzgerald's critique of militarism, changes markedly. The physical separation of the couple allows the novel's sustained narration from Gloria's point of view; eventually, Gloria transcends her role as a cosseted leisure-class wife, emerging as a complex, lonely, and vulnerable woman. Anthony, once a scion of the privileged class, is thrust among working-class and ethnic men and must redefine himself accordingly. If, in the first two sections of the novel, military rhetoric is a harbinger of things to come, in book 3, characters' identities are shaped and reshaped in relation to the military conflict. While Anthony and Gloria both yearn for and struggle with normative gender roles earlier in the novel, those roles are further unsettled once war is declared. And finally, while the legacy of the Civil War and Reconstruction resonates faintly through the beginning of the novel, its third section and its southern milieu allow that theme to emerge with greater clarity. If 1860 has been subsumed by 1914 early in the novel, as

Gloria claims at General Lee's house (143), the novel looks further backward into the past as Anthony descends southward.

As many readers know, Fitzgerald was "a poor soldier" who "regarded the army as an impediment to his writing" (Bruccoli, *Some Sort* 82). Fitzgerald's indifference to his own training is mirrored in Anthony, who is, at best, contemptuous of the regimentation of military life. Like Anthony, Fitzgerald was not sent overseas: "For the rest of [his] life 'I didn't get over' was an expression of regret" (Bruccoli, *Some Sort* 90), even inspiring a 1936 *Esquire* short story by that title (*LD* 15–22). Yet Fitzgerald's observation of military life allowed him to engage in a critique of the discipline the army attempted to impart. And, as Gloria and Anthony endure their yearlong separation, the war enacts changes on both of them and intensifies the rift between them. The structure of book 3, with its repeated deployments and deferral of the expected action—Anthony's belief that he will be sent abroad—mirrors Anthony's own suspensions of action. Thus, Anthony's efforts to claim a masculine identity through military service are perpetually delayed.

The title of the first section of book 3 of the novel, "A Matter of Civilization" (261–97), reminds the reader of the ideology driving American participation in the Great War: maintaining the civilization represented by France and Britain, and rejecting the ostensibly barbarian behavior of Germany and its Austro-Hungarian allies. Yet, throughout Anthony's almost yearlong experience in the training camp, the ideals of civilization—or indeed, the larger goals of the American alliance with France and Britain—are never mentioned. Instead, Fitzgerald emphasizes the role of the army as a disciplinary institution that would standardize men like Anthony, transforming him from a nonworking, individualist aristocrat to an anonymous soldier. As a Pullman car bears Anthony and his fellow soldiers south, Fitzgerald emphasizes the arbitrary and homogenizing nature of military discipline. Initially, a lieutenant first comes in to ban smoking on the train. However, the lieutenant returns shortly after to announce that smoking is permitted, at which point "everyone smoked—whether they had previously desired to or not" (263). As Anthony reads the newspaper, he notes an item about the "Shakespeareville [Kansas] Chamber of Commerce," which "had recently held an enthusiastic debate as to whether the American soldiers should be known as 'Sammies' or 'Battling Christians.'" Ultimately, the name chosen is "Liberty Lads" (263). Fitzgerald emphasizes how wartime propaganda, embodied in these labels, is at striking odds with the actual activities of soldiers.

As Anthony establishes himself in base camp, his attentions turn both to the "whimsicalities of all army administration" (264) and to the efforts of the military to reshape soldiers physically and psychologically. For the first time in his life, Anthony is subjected to a series of "inoculations and physical examinations," as well as "drilling" (265). Similarly, for the first time in his life, he is exhausted by physical labor. His days initially consist of marching in "the field . . . in ragged order . . . [making] listless efforts to keep in step" (265). It is not simply that Anthony is weak from passivity or lack of exercise; Fitzgerald emphasizes that Anthony's manhood is somehow different from that of the more robust soldiers. Anthony emulates those who are stronger, and Anthony admires the "sinewy and muscular" Lieutenant Kretching (265) and "follow[s] his movements faithfully" (266) as the soldiers perform calisthenics. Anthony's imitative masculinity does not pay off: Fitzgerald describes a culture of bullying as well, as the "officers and sergeants" who "walked about among the men with the malice of schoolboys, grouping here and there around some unfortunate who lacked muscular control, giving him confused instructions and commands" (266). Anthony, who has never felt the need for conventional masculinity embodied in physical strength, now realizes the currency implied by such strength. Anthony becomes more sensitive to class distinctions as well as masculine norms: "he suspected that the dim purpose of the war was to let the regular army officers—men with the mentality and aspirations of schoolboys— have their fling with some real slaughter" (266–67). Removed from his conventional milieu, this alternate setting offers Anthony some critical perspective on both his own aristocratic class status and masculine frailty.

Fitzgerald did his training first in Fort Leavenworth, and then at Camp Zachary Taylor, near Louisville, Kentucky. In April 1918, he was relocated to Georgia, and finally arrived at Camp Sheridan in June 1918. It was there, while Fitzgerald was encamped near Montgomery, Alabama, where he met and fell in love with Zelda Sayre (Bruccoli, *Some Sort* 82). Anthony first serves in South Carolina, after which his camp is removed to Mississippi. The southern milieu is essential to this section of *The Beautiful and Damned*. The forced conformity of the military combined with southern social conventions call Anthony's class superiority into question. While the southern environment allows Fitzgerald to engage in a deeper examination of class, book 3 provides a forum for the author to further explore issues of race and sex, particularly through Anthony's affair with the working-class local woman Dorothy "Dot" Raycroft.

Fitzgerald's first descriptions of the town emphasize its embedded racial, gendered, and class hierarchies. The South Carolina town where Anthony is stationed explicitly evokes the Civil War, replete with a hotel named the Stonewall (267). Anthony first finds the town "unexpectedly attractive" (267): he notes the "vividly dressed overpainted girls," the "dozens of taxi-drivers" with their drawling accents, and "an intermittent procession of ragged, shuffling, subservient negroes" (267). For Anthony, this sexualized and racialized environment epitomizes the "slow, erotic breath of the South" (267). The "indolent and exotic" (267) character of the town comes to compensate, briefly, for the discipline of the military. Anthony relishes this explicitly racialized environment, like the nightclub "where a tragic negro made yearning, aching music on a saxophone" (281). In such an environment, Anthony is not only a soldier to be respected but an empowered white man, even without the veneer of his aristocratic lineage.[8]

Anthony's affair with the local girl, Dot, is made possible by military displacement, which has separated him from Gloria and obscured his aristocratic background. Ironically enough, it is in this context that Anthony can act in the manner more typical of a man of his class. As he begins his relationship with Dot, he recalls the affair that he had with another working-class girl, Geraldine (277), before his marriage to Gloria. Dot, unlike Gloria, is sexually active and even somewhat liberated. Where Gloria, a "Nordic Ganymede," has "kissed . . . many men" (94, 155) and been involved in a number of scandalous engagements, Dot has had several lovers and sacrificed her "technical purity" (271) while still in high school. Her two subsequent affairs are linked to the mobility the war has afforded: she met a "naval officer, who passed through town during the early days of the war," and then becomes lovers with the "son of a local clothier" who leaves for "training-camp" shortly after their affair (272). Dot claims to herself that "the war had taken these men away from her" (272), justifying her continued amorous behavior. Similarly, Anthony can claim to himself that only the separations incurred by the war would justify his infidelity.

Fitzgerald racializes Dot as well. Her name implies a blemish or a stain, suggesting that she functions as a stain on Anthony and Gloria's whiteness. Fitzgerald's use of black/white imagery stops just short of connecting Dot to the trope of the tragic mulatta; she is characterized as a "dark, unenduring little flower" (271). Dot's "black hair" is in striking contrast with her "pale" face (334); her "cheap white dress" does not hide her "dark and injured heart" (284). Sexually active, inferior in social class, and marked by a strong southern accent, Dot seems the ideal mistress for a man bent on strengthening a fragile sense of masculinity, and an ideal counterpoint to the proud, disdainful Gloria.

Gandal argues that women like Dot served the role of "charity-girls" for men in camp, sleeping with soldiers out of choice rather than financial necessity (109). The name of Camp Hooker alludes to Civil War general Joe Hooker, who allegedly started the tradition of transporting prostitutes to Union soldiers' base camps.[9] Women like Dot thus exercised a measure of sexual agency, and Dot has been able to choose her lovers even though she is viewed as an object by the military men she encounters: "The soldiers she met were either obviously below her, less obviously, above her—in which case they desired only to use her" (273). Dot shows an unexpected strength, despite her frail appearance; upon choosing Anthony and continuing their affair, Dot comes to "dominate" (284) him. When Anthony's regiment is deployed to Mississippi, Dot insists that she accompany him, forces him to support her financially, and escapes from her claustrophobic home in South Carolina (286–89). Although it would be easy to view Dot as a victim, she manipulates Anthony into running to her side by feigning plans for suicide (289). Although Anthony briefly shifts into a more traditional gender role, Dot claims a measure of independence through their liaison, and, arguably, this independence must be tamed at the novel's end. Dot's brief episode of dominance harkens back to Gloria's earlier measure of control over Anthony. Both relationships can be linked to the novel's military contexts: as Anthony attains "glory" and a measure of authority through his relations with Gloria, his liaison with Dot echoes the fraught relationship between North and South. As in Gloria's outburst at the Lee mansion, the Great War period begins to blur with the Civil War era.

In addition to his efforts to shore up his masculinity, Anthony's adjustment to the military involves a temporary shift in class identity as well. Fitzgerald notes a series of minor deceptions Anthony makes as to his profession, never admitting his status as "member of the leisure class" (274). For the first time, Anthony's class identity is a deficit rather than an asset, particularly given the lack of his own immediate military background. Anthony's own critique of unearned class authority increases, as he notes the authority of the colonel, a

"West Pointer" who "circumnavigated the battalion drill-field upon a handsome black horse" (276), and the general, "who traversed the roads of the camp preceded by his flag—a figure so austere, so removed, so magnificent, as to be scarcely comprehensible" (276). Despite his cynicism, Anthony admires these images of authority and does not object when he is promoted to the status of corporal (279). The martial imagery of flags and stallions, of powerful officers on horseback, is strikingly less modern and more nostalgic than the battle images Fitzgerald uses earlier in the novel. "West Pointers," we recall, had faded from celebrity, and "began to be noticed for the first time in years" only in 1917 (257).

When Anthony is arrested for leaving the post without permission, his class status is negated, and he is sentenced to hard labor. Moving toward physical and mental breakdown, culminating in a diagnosis of influenza, he is sent to the base hospital, believing he will soon be sent to the "interminable massacre beyond" (293). Yet, when Anthony is deployed to Long Island and then returns to New York in the wake of the "False Armistice," his class identity is briefly restored, as he and Gloria reunite at the Armistice Ball.

Through the section narrated in Gloria's perspective, "A Matter of Aesthetics" (298–333), Fitzgerald emphasizes, as with Dot, the effects of the war on women with absent husbands. Gloria, too, has been destabilized by the war. Unlike Muriel, who volunteers for the Red Cross (276), Gloria has nothing to occupy her time. Typically, Gloria expresses her disdain for volunteer work in racist, classist terms: "What would Anthony think if *she* went into the Red Cross? Trouble was she had heard that she might have to bathe negroes in alcohol, and after that she hadn't felt so patriotic" (276). Although Anthony is sensitive to the presence of immigrants in his training camp, this is the only time the novel acknowledges the existence of African American soldiers. War makes Gloria imagine the breach of physical and racial boundaries, causing her anxiety that quashes her claims to "patrioti[sm]" (276). Throughout this section, Fitzgerald explores what roles are left to women who do not follow soldiers, as Dot does, and who do not find a meaningful role as volunteers, as does the "martial Muriel" (300).

Desperately lonely, Gloria is forced to rethink her commitment to her marriage as well. Gloria agrees to help entertain two officers after meeting an old friend, the former Rachael Jerryl, now Rachael Barnes. Rachael, although married, thinks it her duty to "do all we can to make [the troops' impending departure for Europe] attractive to them" (302). In this episode, the separation of men and women during wartime allows women a measure of sexual freedom. Rachael, whose husband is abroad, does not seem averse to a dalliance with an officer on the eve of his departure. The sheer casualness of the episode is worth comment. Gloria is the only one of the four not to view such improprieties as a matter of course; even as Captain Collins slips his arm around her shoulder and moves in for a kiss, "absurdity triumphed over disgust" (304) and she declines. Gloria is more bound to a traditional gender role, that of the faithful wife, than Rachael: "[T]he lure of promiscuity, colorful, various, labyrinthine, and ever a little odorous and stale, had no call or promise for Gloria" (305). When Gloria does enjoy a dalliance, she is more guided by nostalgia than attraction—the aviator she connects with, like the Civil War generals she admires, is "a relic of a vanishing generation" (306). Although the airman is killed in flight shortly after—the first of many aviation officers to perish in flight in both Fitzgeralds' fiction, a tragedy inspired by a wartime beau of Zelda's badly injured in a training crash at Montgomery's Taylor Field (Milford 33)[10]—eventually several other men find their way to Gloria, although she rejects their advances (307) and reminds them of her married state. For her, adultery would be a form of humiliation, borne of loneliness. However, this section emphasizes her potential sexual agency.

After their yearlong separation, Anthony and Gloria find that the war has complicated their relationship. Anthony has been unable to claim masculinity through his military service or to find a sustainable career after the war—jobs are reserved for veterans (312), and the "march of the returning troops along Fifth Avenue" (312) does not include noncombatants like Anthony, who are forced to pretend, during their trip to back to the camp after the false armistice, that "they were just returned from France, where they had practically put an end to the German army" (308). Anthony leaves the war with cynicism deepened rather than patriotism affirmed. This cynicism, coupled with their increasing financial woes, leaves the Patches bitter and hopeless.

Dot's reentry into the novel marks what could be the Patches' final step toward disaster. In a rarely analyzed scene, Dot confronts Anthony in his and Gloria's apartment, explaining that she has established herself in New York in the hope of finding him. The ambiguity, violence, and shifting power dynamics bespeak Anthony's failed efforts to establish his prowess through the military and with Dot. Similarly, although manipulative, Dot has established a measure of independence and is now employed and living alone. For the second time, Dot threatens suicide, and masochistically begs Anthony to beat her: "Oh, hit me, and I'll kiss the hand you hit me with!" (366). Anthony violently attacks Dot and throws a chair "with all his raging strength straight at the white, frightened face across the room" (367). While Anthony suffers a breakdown that finds him reverting to a childhood state, when Gloria and Richard Caramel return to the apartment, Dot is gone, and it is not clear whether a killing has occurred or whether Dot has simply fled (367). In Dot's unexplained disappearance, Fitzgerald removes the evidence of Anthony's sexual transgression, associated with the Great War and its displacements. As Fitzgerald erases the dot on Anthony's whiteness and his conscience, he also eliminates Anthony's association with working-class southern women, which the war made possible.

In August 2017, a little more than one hundred years after Anthony and Gloria's visit (144) to the Lee mansion, neo-Nazis and Klansmen marched on the town of Charlottesville, Virginia, in a protest of the scheduled removal of a statue of Robert E. Lee. Finally removed in the summer of 2021, the statue was one of many Civil War monuments erected during Reconstruction and up into the dawn of the Civil Rights movement. The statue—planned for installation in 1917, yet not completed until 1924—enforced white supremacy by invoking the Confederate past, serving as a warning to African Americans as well as immigrants. Historic preservation was a subset of this movement: in 1914 and through the early 1920s, a plan was implemented to restore Arlington House, the site of Gloria's Civil War fantasy and meltdown, to its antebellum glory (Hanna 132–33). The planned installation of the Charlottesville monument in 1917, like the intended restoration of the Lee mansion, paralleled America's involvement in the war and the move into the 1920s. While we conventionally consider the end of the Great War as ushering the rise of modernity, white supremacists of the 1920s fetishized the alleged glory of the previous era, as Gloria does during her visit to the Lee mansion and as white supremacists in Charlottesville did a century later. While Gloria expresses Civil War nostalgia—a retrospective glance at the codes of gender, race, and class of the antebellum South—Anthony, too, admires generals on horseback, symbols of authority steeped in the long nineteenth century as it verged on the twentieth. Patch's wealth, and thus his legacy, depends on his grandfather's ability to leverage his Civil War achievements. As the Great War separates Anthony and Gloria and forces them to live independent, modern lives, it at first destabilizes the nostalgia to which both are prone, yet ultimately mobilizes it even more powerfully.

Fitzgerald understood the destructive power of Confederate imagery. His intuitive understanding of symbols of American identity, coupled with his family's complicated relationship to the Civil War, make the allusion to the Robert E. Lee mansion and the novel's Civil War rhetoric uncannily prescient. While it is no surprise that virtually all of Fitzgerald's characters depend upon white privilege, the extent to which images of white supremacy occupy their imagination should command our attention.

Reading *The Beautiful and Damned* from the vantage point of the Great War helps restore the centrality of the military as a tool of identity formation for both the sexes in Fitzgerald's fiction. As we know, male military service— real, imagined, or embellished—courses through Fitzgerald's fiction, as Nick Carraway accounts for his service almost as an afterthought (*GG* 3), and Tom Buchanan, who never served, doubts Gatsby's military exploits (*GG* 124–25). In *Tender Is the Night*, Fitzgerald acknowledges the ubiquity of the war's effects, even for noncombatants. As Franz Gregorovius asks Dick Diver, shortly after his arrival in the neutral space of Switzerland: "Tell me of your experience in the war. Are you changed like the rest?" (*TITN* 138). And for women, the war allows a measure of sexual agency, as women were able to leave their homes in socially sanctioned ways through volunteer work, like Daisy Fay and Jordan Baker, and fall in love with the romantic heroism of soldiers. Before the arrival of Dick Diver, the fragile Nicole Warren had "never seen an American uniform" (*TITN* 139); later, she will fall in love with Tommy Barban, a mercenary soldier "who had worn the uniform of eight countries" by the age of eighteen (*TITN* 38). Daisy, Jordan, and Nicole choose and discard sexual partners based on their symbolic appropriation of military prowess, much as Rachael Barnes believes it her patriotic duty to sleep with departing officers. These symbols of gendered power underlie the romances in Fitzgerald's most important work.

Anthony's failure to attain such symbols haunts him as he and Gloria finally leave for Europe with their fortune restored. Despite the implications of their appearance—weak, debilitated, and, as an onlooker mentions, "unclean" (368)—their sense of entitlement is nonetheless back in place.[11] As Anthony reclaims the role of dissolute aristocrat, Gloria's narrative emphasizes her inability to claim the temporary liberation of wartime, whether through work, volunteerism, or even an affair. Dot, who does claim such independence, is rendered invisible by the novel's closure. The war disproportionately affects women without means; Dot can flourish only when soldiers move through town. After the war is over, her lack of cultural capital becomes apparent once more.

By the end of the novel, Anthony has internalized the military prowess he never really had, and this too contains an echo of the Civil War: when he and Gloria embark for Europe, he feels "much as a general" who "might look back upon a successful campaign and analyze his victories" (369).[12] In a wheelchair and a victim of a breakdown, Anthony's appearance faintly recalls that of a shell-shocked veteran, but Anthony Patch is no Septimus Warren Smith. Finally, Anthony becomes Adam Patch, lost in a dream of past glory; ironically, then, he echoes Gloria in her Civil War fantasies. Gloria's name—an allusion to the chorus of "The Battle Hymn of the Republic" ("Glory, glory Hallelujah")— ironically resonates against Adam Patch's Union victory. Even as Gloria dreams of an antebellum South, she and Anthony triumph through their attainment of Adam Patch's inheritance, the winnings of a capitalist postbellum North. Fitzgerald's final critique of military rhetoric emerges as Anthony, despite his fragility, imagines himself as a symbol of the authority he previously despised. *The Beautiful and Damned* provides a pivotal example of how "Over There" becomes "Over Here," how the war abroad shapes the war between the sexes at home. Anthony and Gloria may have reached an uneasy truce, but one senses that trouble on the home front will continue.

NOTES

1. See, for example, Theodore Roosevelt's "The Threat of Japan" (1909), in which he describes Japan as a "formidable military power" with "peculiar fighting capacity" who are nonetheless desirable as farmers and laborers, thus creating threatening competition with white laborers. For the exclusion acts enacted against Asians in the late nineteenth- and early twentieth-century United States, see Takaki 14.

2. On Fitzgerald's use of Civil War imagery more generally, see Irwin, 10–32. Fitzgerald came from a family of Civil War sympathizers and viewed himself as a mixture of his midwestern Anglo-Irish and southern Protestant heritage. North-South unions—typically between northern officers in training camps and local southern belles—appear in *The Beautiful and Damned, The Great Gatsby* (116), and in a number of short stories. As Irwin remarks, Fitzgerald's attraction to North-South conflict stems from his interest in the conflict between "money and breeding" in American life, and his knowledge that an ideology of "breeding" could not persist in the twentieth-century capitalist United States.

3. Significantly, the vista that would have been available to Gloria and Anthony from the Lee mansion also includes the graves of soldiers at Arlington National Cemetery. Fitzgerald also does

not refer to slave quarters that were still part of the touristic attractions of the property or to the Freedmen's Village that was built on the Arlington estate in 1862. Gloria's antebellum fantasies triumph over the realities of Civil War deaths, the lives of enslaved people, and the free African Americans who had claimed space on the former Lee property.

4. In *Artificial Colors: Modern Food and Racial Fictions*, Catherine Keyser explores how both Fitzgeralds used food imagery to explore racialized boundaries. The visit to Arlington is redolent with food imagery, garbage, and odors, all of which chip away at Gloria's composure. The bus the couple take from Washington to Virginia pauses at the zoo, causing Gloria to "call[] down the curse of heaven on monkeys" (144). At Arlington House itself, food waste litters the site in the form of "peanut-shells" and "banana-peels" (144). Gloria's teary outburst is prompted when she sees a sign for the ladies' room in the room where General Lee was married, creating an uncomfortable intermingling of the racial, marital, and excremental.

5. Fitzgerald's depiction of Gloria echoes the letters Zelda sent him from Montgomery in 1919. After visiting a graveyard, Zelda writes: "I wanted to *feel* 'William Wreford, 1864.'... Isn't it funny how, out of a row of Confederate soldiers, two or three will make you think of dead lovers and dead loves?" (Bryer and Barks 26). Zelda's remarkable letter conjoins sex, death, and antebellum romance. Despite the concurrence of themes, Gloria is more callous than Zelda, who ends her letter to Fitzgerald with the claim that "Old death is so beautiful—so very beautiful—We will die together—I know—Sweetheart." For an account of Zelda's family's Confederate affiliations, see Wagner-Martin, *Zelda Sayre Fitzgerald* 7–8.

6. Numerous critics have written about Fitzgerald's representations of African Americans and Jews, yet there has been little attention to his Asian representations. David Ullrich's essay in this volume addresses this lacuna. In the past few decades, the discussion of race in Fitzgerald's writing was initiated by Walter Benn Michaels in 1993 in *Our America: Nativism, Modernism, Pluralism* (23–26) and continued by Mitchell Breitweiser (17–70) and others. This work has focused largely on *Gatsby* but should be extended more thoroughly to other novels, as Catherine Keyser has done. For examples of this discussion, see Clymer (61–92) and my own essay "White Skin, White Mask: Passing, Posing, and Performing in *The Great Gatsby*" (443–68).

7. This brief insight into the inner life of a Scandinavian servant recalls Fannie Hurst's *Lummox* (1923), which delves into the inner life of a similar woman, characterized to the outside Anglo-American world only by her silence.

8. Camp Sheridan was seen as a major economic driver for Montgomery, which solicited consideration from the War Department to establish a military camp there. With thirty thousand soldiers, it almost doubled the population of Montgomery and included both white and Black segregated regiments. Soldiers' engagement with "charity girls" like Dot who willingly slept with men, as well as their contact with prostitutes, was a significant concern: Camp Sheridan, like most military bases, "suffered from an epidemic of venereal disease" (Newton 59). And much like Camp Hooker, where Anthony is based, Camp Sheridan was named for a Civil War general, further blurring the lines between the Civil War and the Great War.

9. Fitzgerald alludes to this legend in the short story "The Night at Chancellorsville" (*TAR* 44–49), which depicts a group of prostitutes sent southward on a train to a Union encampment during the Civil War. Told from the perspective of a sex worker, the story offers a woman's point

of view on the military conflict: the prostitutes have little sense of the difference between Union and Confederate soldiers, and although the train is attacked by Confederate soldiers, the story disappears from the papers. Although the story is slight, it is notable for Fitzgerald's effort to narrate from a female perspective and to articulate this unusual perspective on the war. When the soldiers on the train refer to the prostitutes as "General Hooker's staff," Fitzgerald characterizes prostitutes as critical, if unnameable, complements to the war effort. As Meredith notes of this story, Fitzgerald "appl[ies] a heavy coat of modernist irony to the Civil War in order to strip away" its connotations "of chivalric romance" ("Fitzgerald and War" 193).

10. The aviator story reappears in "The Last of the Belles" (*TAR* 54) and Zelda's *Save Me the Waltz* (*Collected Writings* 90–91).

11. Gloria and Anthony's physical frailty at the end of the novel should remind us that both characters have been touched by the flu pandemic of 1918–20, a subject I hope to explore in a subsequent essay. Anthony contracts the flu in the Mississippi camp, initiating a physical collapse that mirrors his growing psychic fragility (292–93). Similarly, Gloria's growing self-awareness and alienation from Anthony camouflage her physical illness; her illness also entails a growing fraying of and anxiety over racialized boundaries. First, she suffers a near-collapse and must depend on the "Martinique elevator boy [to] help[] her upstairs" (295). In the hallucination that accompanies her flu, which advances into "double pneumonia," Gloria may be revisiting the racially charged symbolic environment of Arlington House, as she imagines "millions of people, swarming like rats, chattering like apes, smelling like all hell . . . monkeys" (326).

12. In *Tender Is the Night,* Fitzgerald echoes this language as Dick thinks back to successful parties he has hosted: "He sometimes looked back with awe at the carnivals of affection he had given, as a general might gaze upon a massacre he had ordered to satisfy an impersonal blood lust" (*TITN* 35).

THE BEAUTIFUL AND DAMNED
AND THE JEWISH PEOPLE

James L. W. West III

The Beautiful and Damned (1922), like its predecessor *This Side of Paradise* (1920), is crowded with characters, incidents, and themes. It is difficult to single out individual themes and concerns in the novel, but I would like to attempt such an exercise here. I will discuss Jewish characters in the narrative and, more generally, the place of the Jewish people in American society of the early twentieth century. These concerns are not readily apparent on a first reading: there is too much else going on, too many ancillary matters, too many incidents and turns in the plot. But a close reading of the text brings the Jewish characters to the forefront and makes apparent their place in the story. These are assimilating Jews, interested in moving up in society and fitting into American life. They are successful in their endeavors; indeed, they more nearly represent the drive toward success and the capacity for adaptation than do Anthony and Gloria Patch.

The narrative arc of *The Beautiful and Damned* is complicated. Anthony stands to inherit a fortune from his grandfather, the vice crusader Adam J. Patch. Anthony graduates from Harvard, spends a year traveling in Europe, and then settles down in New York in a gentleman's apartment on East Fifty-Second Street. As a supremely eligible bachelor, he makes the round of tea dances and society balls, meeting the daughters of the haute bourgeoisie and contemplating marriage. Through his friend Dick Caramel he is introduced to Gloria Gilbert, also a child of wealth, although, in financial terms, not in Anthony's league. Gloria, however, has other attractions: her good looks, her insouciant manner, and her disregard for convention. She is being courted by more than one man but eventually chooses Anthony.

Although he has a degree from Harvard, Anthony has no qualifications for earning a living. He professes a vague desire to write but lacks the drive to produce steadily and so lives, idly and unproductively, on an allowance. Gloria, who is only very lightly educated, also has nothing to do. Indeed, one of the major themes of the novel is this problem of productive labor. In the absence of financial need, as one waits for an inheritance to arrive, how does one organize one's days and months and years? What gives shape and purpose to one's existence? Neither Anthony nor Gloria possesses the self-discipline to pursue a program of academic study or self-improvement; likewise, neither seems interested in helping the needy. They live in Manhattan, in the same apartment Anthony inhabited during his bachelor years. There are concert halls and museums and libraries and bookstores all around, but Anthony and Gloria engage only in popular diversions—the theater, the speakeasies, and the floor shows. The result is enervation and inertia, which lead to bickering and, in Anthony's case, to alcoholism (West, "Question of Vocation" 50–51).

Enter Joseph Bloeckman, a strong, vital Jewish man who wants to rise in society. He is "a dignified man and a proud one," Fitzgerald tells us (86). Bloeckman was born in Munich but came to the United States early in life. He speaks English without an accent; his hair is sandy, and his eyes are blue (108). He began his career as a peanut vendor, working in a traveling circus; later he became the manager of a circus sideshow and then set up as "the proprietor of a second-class vaudeville house" (86). Bloeckman began to invest in the movie business and caught the industry on the upswing, just as it was developing into a major attraction. Ambitious, focused, and lucky, he rose over nine years to a position of prominence in the cinema business.[1]

When we are introduced to Bloeckman he is already the head of his own movie company, "Films par Excellence."[2] He has connections with Gloria's father, who made his money in the manufacture of celluloid, essential to the production of films. Bloeckman meets Gloria several months before Anthony is introduced to her, and he courts her energetically. He proposes to her, but they both know that a marriage would be impossible; they laugh, and she rejects him. They remain friendly, and he continues his suit. He has no illusions about his social eligibility, no misconceptions about the place of a Jewish man in New York society; but he is persistent and confident, aware of his growing wealth and influence, and certain that he will eventually rise to social prominence—and that Gloria will accept his offer of marriage. When she instead chooses Anthony, he is angry. He and Gloria argue about the matter, but she will not change her mind. Bloeckman, who seems genuinely to want Gloria and to love her, disciplines himself and preserves his dignity. He resolves to wait, perhaps sensing that Gloria's marriage to Anthony will not turn out well.

Anthony is a good catch for Gloria, but not because of his lineage. His nose is long and sharp, but he is not an aristocrat. Fitzgerald makes this clear in the third paragraph of the novel: "Virginians and Bostonians to the contrary notwithstanding," he writes, "an aristocracy founded sheerly on money postulates wealth in the particular" (11). Old Adam Patch, Anthony's grandfather, was a farmer's son who joined the Union cavalry early in the Civil War, did well in the conflict, and emerged with the rank of major. He became a speculator on Wall Street, and "amid much fuss, fume, applause, and ill will he gathered to himself some seventy-five million dollars" (12). "Cross Patch," as he is nicknamed, used his money to become a moral crusader after the manner of Anthony Comstock, head of the New York Society for the Suppression of Vice. The targets for both men were "liquor, literature, vice, art, patent medicines, and Sunday theatres" (12). Adam's son, Adam Ulysses Patch, married a young Boston society woman named Henrietta Lebrune. Together they produced an heir, Anthony Comstock Patch, the protagonist of the novel. The only distinction to which Anthony's father can lay claim is that he was "the first man in America to roll the lapels of his coat" (13). Anthony is thus only two generations removed from agriculture, possessed of a veneer of sophistication from his years at Harvard but certainly not a high-blooded aristocrat.

Neither is Gloria of elevated birth. Her father, Russel Gilbert, is a graduate of "a small but terrifying Western university" (40). He has made his money in Kansas City. He and his wife, Catherine, are in New York to put Gloria on display, hoping that she will marry into the ranks of the socially prominent. The family lives in a suite at the Plaza Hotel, where Gloria receives invitations and entertains suitors, who are numerous. Mr. Gilbert has a mind that is largely vacant. "His ideas," Fitzgerald writes, "were the popular delusions of twenty years before; his mind steered a wobbly and anaemic course in the wake of the daily newspaper editorials" (40). His wife, bored and lacking stimulation, has become a follower of Biphilism—Fitzgerald's invented name for theosophy, a philosophical system promulgated in the United States by the formidable Madame

Helena Petrovna Blavatsky. The paranormal phenomena demonstrated by Madame Blavatsky were shown to be fraudulent as early as the 1880s, but Mrs. Gilbert, like thousands of other Americans, has remained a believer. Gloria, their daughter, is not given to deep thought. She vibrates to the city scene, to popular amusements and the pleasures available to those with money and leisure.

By 1922, when *The Beautiful and Damned* was published, Jews had become very much a part of the life of New York City. Between 1880 and 1920 their numbers grew rapidly, from about 80,000 in 1880 to around 1.6 million in 1920—fully 25 percent of the city's population. Jews established themselves in commerce and quickly gained a foothold in finance, law, medicine, and the other professions. They won positions on university faculties and took seats on the boards of libraries and museums. Fitzgerald, as a social chronicler, must have observed these developments and wondered how they would turn out, both for the city and for the country. Perhaps he was alarmed, as many people were, though he himself had no great regard for the old New York establishment that was being replaced.

Jews in *The Beautiful and Damned* are especially prominent in popular entertainment. Early in the novel Anthony and his friend Maury Noble attend a performance of a new musical comedy called *High Jinks*. This was an actual Broadway show, a "musical jollity" that opened on 10 December 1913 at the Lyric Theatre. The book for the show was written by Leo Ditrichstein, an Austrian American Jew who had found success as an actor and playwright; lyrics were by Otto Hauerbach (a name later adjusted to Harbach) and Rudolf Friml. The ingénue was played by Elaine Hammerstein, granddaughter of the producer Oscar Hammerstein (and a cousin of Oscar Hammerstein II). After the performance Anthony and Maury part ways, and Anthony walks back to his apartment alone. He passes through "a kaleidoscope of girls" and breathes "into his lungs perfume and the not unpleasant scent of many cigarettes." The passage continues: "Two young Jewish men passed him, talking in loud voices and craning their necks here and there in fatuous supercilious glances. They were dressed in suits of the exaggerated tightness then semi-fashionable; their turnover collars were notched at the Adam's apple; they wore grey spats and carried grey gloves on their cane handles" (28). A few pages later, in a description of New York in the autumn, we read: "Jewesses were coming out into a society of Jewish men and women, from Riverside to the Bronx, and looking forward to a rising young broker or jeweler and a kosher wedding" (33).

Later in the novel, as Anthony and Gloria ride into New York on a commuter train, Anthony contemplates the streets of the city. He notices the presence of Jewish shopkeepers: "Down in a tall busy street he read a dozen Jewish names on a line of stores; in the door of each stood a dark little man watching the passers from intent eyes—eyes gleaming with suspicion, with pride, with clarity, with cupidity, with comprehension" (237). Anthony knows that Jews are everywhere in the city: "New York—he could not dissociate it now from the slow, upward creep of this people—the little stores, growing, expanding, consolidating, moving, watched over with hawk's eyes and a bee's attention to detail—they slathered out on all sides. It was impressive—in perspective it was tremendous" (237). A few pages later Anthony is forced to give up the lease to his midtown apartment by a landlord named Sohenberg, who raises the rent beyond what Anthony can afford and, happy to get rid of Anthony and his noisy parties, will not budge on the figure, despite the fact that Anthony has paid for many improvements on the apartment out of his own pocket (240).

Bloeckman is not the only Jew with whom Gloria keeps company. Her friend Muriel Kane is also Jewish. Muriel is from "a rising family" in East Orange, New Jersey, a Jewish enclave: "She was short rather than small, and hovered audaciously between plumpness and width. Her hair was black and elaborately arranged. This, in conjunction with her handsome, rather bovine eyes, and her over-red lips, combined to make her resemble Theda Bara, the prominent motion-picture actress" (75).[3] Gloria's other friend, Rachael Jerryl, is "an exquisitely dressed Jewess with dark hair and a lovely milky pallor. . . . Her family were 'Episcopalians,' owned three smart women's shops along Fifth Avenue, and lived in a magnificent apartment on Riverside Drive" (76).[4] Anthony is not happy that Gloria associates with Muriel and Rachael; early in book 2 he challenges Gloria to explain why she likes them. She answers readily: "They're no exertion, those girls. They sort of believe everything I tell 'em—but I rather like Rachael. I think she's cute—and so clean and slick, don't you?" (117). Gloria seems free of prejudice, Anthony less so.

If Anthony is anti-Semitic, what about Fitzgerald? Several critics have taken up the question: Milton Hindus in 1947, Jeffrey Meyers in 1993, Alan Margolies in 1997, Suzanne del Gizzo in 2013, and Arthur Krystal in 2015. All find Fitzgerald to have been prejudiced against Jews, especially early in his career, but no one argues that Fitzgerald was a committed anti-Semite. In "F. Scott Fitzgerald and Literary Anti-Semitism" (1947), one of the first full-length articles on *The*

Great Gatsby (1925), Hindus finds Fitzgerald to be representative of "the modish anti-Semitism of the 20's" but concludes that "*The Great Gatsby* is nothing so simple as a piece of propaganda against the Jews" (510). Fitzgerald escapes condemnation in the essay; the real targets for Hindus are T. S. Eliot and Ezra Pound, especially the latter. Meyers, one of Fitzgerald's least sympathetic biographers, seems to have begun his investigation with the assumption that he would find anti-Semitism in Fitzgerald's published writings and would certainly find it in the author's letters and journals. Meyers, however, admits that he was mistaken. Fitzgerald, he believes, had a mixed opinion of Jews early on; as he matured, however, his view of the Jewish people became more complex and sympathetic, culminating in the luminous portrait of Monroe Stahr in *The Last Tycoon* (1941) (1, 10). Margolies, in a broad-ranging article, examines Fitzgerald's attitudes not only toward Jews but toward African Americans and immigrant groups of the 1920s and 1930s. Margolies's argument is that Fitzgerald rejected Nordicism (the eugenics-inflected thinking common in his time) and that he was appalled by the lynching of southern Blacks. Margolies discusses Fitzgerald's attitudes toward Jews and, like the other critics, does not find him markedly anti-Semitic. Margolies depicts Fitzgerald as inconsistent in his views—sometimes enlightened, sometimes not, and in no predictable pattern ("Maturing" 75–93). Del Gizzo agrees: she records the racial and ethnic slurs and the stereotypes that appear in Fitzgerald's fiction; she concludes that Fitzgerald was nervous about recent immigrants to the United States and about the effect they would have on American culture (224–33). Krystal's view is mixed: he notes that Fitzgerald had little experience with Jews during his boyhood in St. Paul and his college years at Princeton. Jews were a tiny minority in both places. As a young man, writes Krystal, Fitzgerald harbored an attitude toward Jews that was provincial but not malicious ("Fitzgerald and the Jews").

My own view is similar. Fitzgerald had an anti-Jewish streak that appeared from time to time in his public and private writings, but he was not truly anti-Semitic. He was conflicted in his feelings about Jews: he admired their intelligence and drive but was uncomfortable with their clannishness and, when he encountered it, their arrogance. The depiction of Bloeckman in *The Beautiful and Damned* is colored by his prejudice, though Bloeckman, who is a superior man to Anthony and to the other male characters, is allowed to win out in the end. Bloeckman is stronger, more self-disciplined, and more resilient than any other character in the novel.

Part of the problem about Fitzgerald's attitudes lies in the mode of narration employed in this novel. Fitzgerald tells the story in an omniscient voice but grants himself the ability, from time to time, to narrate through Anthony's consciousness and to reproduce Anthony's thoughts. But Fitzgerald also editorializes. Therefore, when anti-Semitic remarks appear on the page, one is never quite sure whether they represent Anthony's perceptions or Fitzgerald's. Of all the protagonists in Fitzgerald's novels, Anthony is the least autobiographical; one cannot necessarily ascribe his thoughts and general outlook to Fitzgerald. This is a problem throughout the narrative. For example, there are numerous passages in which Anthony, Gloria, and their friends profess a cynical but unconvincing nihilism. Anthony, for example, calls Gloria "a quaint little determinist" (61), and the omniscient narrator tells us that her central maxim is "Never give a damn" (172). Are we meant to take this attitudinizing seriously? Are these Fitzgerald's views or those of his characters? The same is true of the anti-Semitic passages: whose thoughts and observations are we reading?

Fitzgerald's opinions underwent change as he grew older. Evidence of his broadening views can be found in two stories from the middle period of his career, both of which have bearing on *The Beautiful and Damned*. These stories are "Two Wrongs" (1930, *TAR* 24–44) and "The Hotel Child" (1931, *TAR* 288–309), both published in the *Saturday Evening Post* and both with texts that were compromised by *Post* editors. Fitzgerald wrote "Two Wrongs" in October and November 1929 and sold it to the *Post* shortly thereafter. The story appeared in the issue for 18 January 1930. "Two Wrongs" is the story of Bill McChesney, a theatrical producer who has enjoyed a string of recent hits on Broadway. Bill is a self-made man but not a particularly admirable one. He has progressed from modest beginnings to success in the world of entertainment. He is brash and occasionally obnoxious; he is also anti-Semitic. Early in the story he calls one of his Jewish friends a "dirty little kyke" (*TAR* 24). The friend, whose name is Brancusi, seems to understand that Bill is socially insecure and clumsy with his attempts at humor. Brancusi lets the remark pass. But three years later, when Bill calls Brancusi a "lousy little kyke" (*TAR* 33), Brancusi takes offense. He resolves to have nothing further to do with Bill and to erase him "from his mind forever" (*TAR* 34). Bill loses his magic touch on Broadway and succumbs to alcoholism. His marriage, damaged by his infidelities, deteriorates and fails. At the end of the story he contracts tuberculosis and leaves New York for treatment at a sanitarium in the West. Bill's anti-Semitism was obvious in the typescript of the story that Fitzgerald sent to Harold Ober, his literary agent, but editors at the *Post* cut both "dirty little kyke" and "lousy little kyke" from the text, muting this aspect of Bill's behavior. Certainly one understands the motivation: the *Post* was aimed at a broad, middle-class readership and usually avoided ethnic slur words. An important aspect of Bill's character, however, was lost with the cuts.

Something similar happened to "The Hotel Child," an exuberant piece of short fiction from about a year later. Fitzgerald wrote "The Hotel Child" in November 1930 and published it in the *Post* for 31 January 1931. The story is about the casual anti-Semitism of a group of decadent British aristocrats in a Swiss resort city. The lead character, a young woman named Fifi Schwartz, is hurt by the comments of the British; her mother, accustomed to prejudice, is tougher. Fifi wins out in the end. She outwits her adversaries (in a zany plot) and emerges with her youth and beauty intact. The typescript that Fitzgerald sent to Ober has several references to drunkenness and indulgence in hashish; it also contains the word "Sheeny" (*TAR* 292), directed at Fifi by one of the British characters. All of this was scrubbed from the story by the *Post* editors. The anti-Semitism is still apparent in the *Post* text, but the reader must dig for it. Fortunately, the typescripts of "Two Wrongs" and "The Hotel Child," mailed by Fitzgerald to Ober from Europe, preserve these readings. They were restored to the texts of the stories in the Cambridge Fitzgerald Edition of *Taps at Reveille*, Fitzgerald's fourth and final short-story collection (1935).

One can trace influences on *The Beautiful and Damned,* and on its Jewish characters, from at least one other author of the period. I have in mind Edith Wharton, whose writing Fitzgerald very much admired. Her novel *The House of Mirth* (1905) was almost certainly a likely source for Fitzgerald. In the novel—which, coincidentally, was also published by Scribner's—Wharton tells the story of Lily Bart, a beautiful but impecunious member of New York society. Lily is connected by birth to one of the best families of the city, but she must marry advantageously if she is to hold her position. An eligible suitor named Percy Gryce appears, but he is stolid and unexciting. Lily refuses his offer. Her other possibility is Simon Rosedale, a Jew who has made a fortune in real estate and the stock market and who wants very much to be included in New York society. Lily, as his wife, could help him to gain admission. He seems to be genuinely fond of her (as Bloeckman is of Gloria), but Lily finds

him physically repellent and resists his advances. As the novel progresses, Lily
loses what little money she has and becomes involved in a matrimonial scandal. She is innocent of wrongdoing, but accusations from her rival Bertha
Dorset have a bad effect on her reputation. Rosedale offers to help by taking
care of Lily's debts, but she refuses. Later, and in desperation, she tells him
that she will marry him, but by this time her standing in society has further
deteriorated. Rosedale's conversation with Lily near the end of the novel, in
chapter 7 of book 2 (407–19), is a breath of fresh air in an otherwise stifling
narrative. Rosedale explains that breaking into New York society is a game for
him, a hobby. He is not emotionally invested in the outcome. He is confident
of his financial acumen and knows that, if he waits long enough, he will gain
leverage over the men who control entry to high society. He seems truly sorry
for Lily but speaks frankly to her, which no one else has been willing to do.
Bloeckman resembles Rosedale in many ways. Bloeckman is an observer who
quickly learns the rules of the contest; he is content to wait for his chance; he
is largely impervious to criticism and condescension; he is attentive and persistent. Eventually, he believes, he will get what he wants.

The other Wharton novel that bears a strong resemblance to *The Beautiful
and Damned* is *The Custom of the Country* (1913). In this novel we make the
acquaintance of Undine Spragg, one of Wharton's most memorable characters.
Undine is the daughter of Abner E. Spragg, who has made his money in Apex
City, a fictional municipality somewhere in the state of New York. Abner and
his wife, Leota, have brought Undine to New York City to find a husband. The
family has taken up residence in the Hotel Stentorian, a fictional establishment
on the Upper West Side. Undine receives suitors there in the same way that
Gloria entertains admirers at the Plaza. The goal for both young women is to
break into New York society through an advantageous marriage. Undine resembles Gloria: she has reddish-gold hair, is beautiful and spirited, and likes to
flout convention. As a consequence, she must be watched carefully: at one point
she is pursued by a handsome Austrian riding master who lets it be known that
he is of aristocratic birth (25). Undine finds him quite attractive, but her father
is suspicious and has the man investigated. He turns out to be a Jew named
Aaronson, suspected of financial improprieties in Europe. Undine, rescued
from this particular adventurer, marries Ralph Marvell, a dullish member of
the New York upper crust. They produce an heir, but the marriage fails, and
they are divorced. Undine moves on in search of the next husband. Both she

and Gloria have good survival instincts: both are conscious of the passage of time, the impermanence of their beauty, and the necessity of marrying well.

Now to Bloeckman. We first become acquainted with him in book 1, chapter 3, "The Connoisseur of Kisses." He joins Anthony, Dick Caramel, and Maury Noble for a dinner at the Biltmore Hotel with Gloria, Muriel, and Rachael. The Biltmore, at Forty-Third and Madison, is at the heart of the city, just across the street from Grand Central Station. The party is dining at the Cascades, a fashionable restaurant on the nineteenth floor of the Biltmore that features a twenty-eight-foot indoor waterfall. Anthony and his friends condescend to Bloeckman when they first meet him. They see "a stoutening, ruddy Jew of about thirty-five, with an expressive face under smooth sandy hair" (84). His speech is faintly coarse, his clothes tight-fitting, his neckties flashy. Bloeckman attempts to engage these three Harvard graduates in a conversation about college sports, specifically about a hockey game between Harvard and Princeton that he has probably read about in the newspaper, but they ignore him. Anthony, who is squeamish about a good many things, finds Bloeckman off-putting. The man is smoking a cigar and emitting "two slender strings of smoke from nostrils overwide" (84). Later in the evening Bloeckman will chew his cigar "back and forth in his mouth" and talk with "violent gestures" (89).[5] Bloeckman's expression "combined that of a Middle-Western farmer appraising his wheat crop and that of an actor wondering whether he is observed" (84). "I detest these underdone men," thinks Anthony. "Boiled looking! Ought to be shoved back in the oven" (84). Bloeckman, in conversation with Dick, discusses movie versions of popular novels. Bloeckman reveals himself to be a philistine. "The main thing in a moving picture is a strong story," he says. "So many novels are all full of talk and psychology. . . . It's impossible to make much of that interesting on the screen" (86). Worst of all for Anthony is Bloeckman's admiration for Adam J. Patch, his grandfather. "He's a fine man," intones the movie man. "He's a fine example of an American" (84).

Bloeckman is one among a good many Jews who were making a strong show in the field of entertainment. Their presence was especially apparent in popular music and on Broadway. About midway through the scene, for example, Maury and Muriel trade the titles of current Broadway hits that they have seen, giving us a cross-section of what was then popular. Many of these shows were headlined by Jewish performers, and much of the music in them was written and performed by Jews. For example, in the scene at the Biltmore,

Maury and Muriel dance (while Muriel sings the lyrics) to a tune called "He's a Rag Picker," from the 1914 musical *5064 Gerard.* The song was written by Irving Berlin, born Israel Isadore Beilin in Russia in 1885 to a father who was a Jewish cantor. The family immigrated to the Lower East Side; the son, now calling himself Irving Berlin, began his long career in 1911 with "Alexander's Ragtime Band." By the early 1920s he had become established as one of the country's premier songwriters, both for Broadway shows and, once sound came to Hollywood, for screen musicals.[6] Much of the other music that plays through *The Beautiful and Damned,* in fact, was written or sung by Jewish songwriters and performers: Leo Ditrichstein, Jerome Kern, Nora Bayes (née Eleanora Sara Goldberg), and Al Jolson (née Asa Yoelson). Many of the female stars of the period, some of whom were Jewish, got their start in the *Follies,* a leggy variety show presented on Broadway by the Jewish impresario Florenz Ziegfeld, who is mentioned several times in the novel.[7]

Not long after the dinner at the Cascades, Gloria accepts Anthony's proposal of marriage. Bloeckman, the rejected suitor, is missing from the narrative for the next year or so, but he reappears when he encounters Anthony, by accident, on a commuter train. Anthony and Gloria are living in the fictional suburb of Marietta in what they call the "grey house," and Anthony is taking the train in and out of New York. Anthony notices immediately that Bloeckman has changed: "It seemed to Anthony that during the last year Bloeckman had grown tremendously in dignity. The boiled look was gone; he seemed 'done' at last. In addition he was no longer overdressed. The inappropriate facetiousness he had affected in ties had given way to a sturdy dark pattern, and his right hand, which had formerly displayed two heavy rings, was now innocent of ornament and even without the raw glow of a manicure" (176). Nor are the changes confined to Bloeckman's looks and dress: "This dignity appeared also in his personality. The last aura of the successful travelling-man had faded from him. . . . One imagined that, having been fawned upon financially, he had attained aloofness; having been snubbed socially, he had acquired reticence" (176). This new version of Bloeckman is troubling to Anthony, who "no longer felt a correct superiority in his presence" (176).

Bloeckman inserts himself into Anthony and Gloria's married life. He appears unannounced at their door and begins to talk to Gloria about a career as a cinema actress. Gloria is willing: "I want to be a successful sensation in the movies," she tells him. "I hear that Mary Pickford makes a million dollars annually" (180). She also notices that Bloeckman has changed. He is "infinitesimally improved, of subtler intonation, of more convincing ease" (180). He makes a date with Gloria to take her riding in his imported sports car. Later in the chapter he and she go for a long drive "all over New York State" (184), a trip that she enjoys immensely. It was "the best jaunt" (184), she tells Anthony. Gloria is energized by Bloeckman, a successful man whose business ventures are prospering. Anthony, by contrast, has been wasting his days, talking about becoming a writer but doing nothing to begin a career in authorship. To pass the time and in response to their strained financial circumstances, he and Gloria have been nagging at each other, arguing about trivialities, and drinking more than they should. It is no surprise that a drive through the countryside with Bloeckman should be invigorating for Gloria.

She and Anthony have nothing of consequence to do, so they attempt to amuse themselves with Tana, their Japanese house servant. Tana is introduced as a figure of fun, but he is more than that. He has entrepreneurial ideas and wants to build an improved typewriter, which he calls a "typewutta" (182). His machine will have single keys for the most frequently recurring combinations of letters in English—for example, *-ing* and *-ed*. Most typewriters in 1922 were heavy, cumbersome, expensive, and noisy. Tana's insight is simple and efficient. Probably it will not be introduced commercially, but at least Tana (unlike Anthony) has ambition. All that Anthony can think of to do is to brood, criticize Gloria, and wait for Adam Patch's money to descend upon them.

Bloeckman next appears in the novel in "The Broken Lute," chapter 3 of book 2 (220–58). Adam Patch has appeared at the riotous party thrown by Anthony and Gloria at their house in Marietta. Not long after that Adam dies, and Anthony learns that the old man has disinherited him. Anthony challenges the will in the courts, but it will be several years before the case can be resolved. Bloeckman has been in England, expanding the reach of "Films par Excellence." When he reappears he is even more presentable: "Always he dressed a little better, his intonation was mellower, and in his manner there was perceptibly more assurance that the fine things of the world were his by a natural and inalienable right" (255). Bloeckman still seems to be interested in Gloria and offers again to arrange a screen test for her. She presents the idea to Anthony: "If I'm ever going to do anything I'll have to start now," she tells him. "They only want young women. Think of the money, Anthony!" (256). He is opposed, they quarrel violently, the idea is dropped.[8]

When we see Bloeckman next, several chapters later, his transformation is complete. He has changed his name to Joseph Black and has become a major entrepreneur in the film industry. Gloria and Anthony are at their lowest point. The Great War is over, he and she have reunited, but nothing has been settled. The lawsuit over Adam Patch's millions continues to creep through the courts. Anthony and Gloria, short of money, have moved to a flat on Claremont Avenue, near Harlem, then a racially mixed neighborhood. Black offers Gloria a screen test, and this time she takes him up without telling Anthony. The role Black has in mind is that of a "younger sister," though Gloria is by now approaching thirty. She takes the test but fails miserably. Black writes her a note, suggesting that she would be more suitable for "a small character part" playing "a very haughty rich widow" (333). Gloria is devastated. She examines herself in a mirror: "Yes—the cheeks were ever so faintly thin, the corners of the eyes were lined with tiny wrinkles. The eyes were different." Her grief is genuine: "Oh, my pretty face," she whispers. "Oh, I don't want to live without my pretty face!" (333).

Another year passes, during which Anthony falls in with dissolute companions and begins to drink heavily. "He hated to be sober," we learn. "There was a kindliness about intoxication" (343). Even Gloria drinks more than she has before. She desperately wants a grey squirrel coat, all the fashion that fall, but Anthony forbids it. They have only enough money to get by and to pay his bootlegger. Most of their friends have deserted them. Dick Caramel, quite successful with his novels and other writing projects, is solicitous about their welfare but reluctant to become involved. Maury Noble, who is making "*piles of money*" (337) and is engaged to a Philadelphia heiress, wants nothing to do with them. Muriel pays a visit to their flat and offers faint encouragement, but this only sparks a loud argument between Anthony and Gloria. Rachael Jerryl has married a man with a gentile name, Rodman Barnes, and has fallen out of touch.

The stage is set for the culminating scene in *The Beautiful and Damned*. It occurs in chapter 3 of book 3, a chapter appropriately entitled "No Matter!" (334–69). Anthony is drunk. He is down to his last few dollars and needs money. He is snubbed by his former friend Dick Caramel and cannot reach his broker, Mr. Howland. Anthony has learned of Gloria's unsuccessful screen test and is angry that she should have turned to Joseph Black for help. Impulsively, Anthony decides to confront his rival. He tracks him down at a faux-French dancing club called Boul' Mich, located on West Forty-Fifth Street. Anthony sends a messenger boy into the club for Black, who comes to the lobby and approaches warily. After a muddled attempt at pleasantries, Anthony throws an accusation at Black: "Un'erstand you kep' my wife out of the movies," he says. Black is incredulous. "Look here, Mr. Patch," he answers, "you're drunk. You're disgustingly and insultingly drunk." Black attempts to leave the lobby and rejoin his party in the club, but Anthony blocks his way. "Not so fas', you Goddam Jew," he says. Black is shocked. "Be careful!," he cries. Anthony starts to repeat the slur: "I'll say it again, you God—" he says, but this time Black answers with his fists: "Then Bloeckman struck out, with all the strength in the arm of a well-conditioned man of forty-five, struck out and caught Anthony squarely in the mouth. Anthony cracked up against the staircase, recovered himself and made a wild drunken swing at his opponent, but Bloeckman, who took exercise every day and knew something of sparring, blocked it with ease and struck him twice in the face with two swift smashing jabs" (359–60). Anthony is thrown out of the lobby and onto the street. With his mouth full of blood and his front teeth loose, he eventually makes his way back to the apartment he shares with Gloria. This is an oddly satisfying moment. Almost any reader will by now have lost patience with Anthony. His weakness, his complaints, and his lack of spine have put him beyond sympathy. Black has proven himself the better man.

Fitzgerald must end his novel. He presents a relatively abrupt denouement, which he brings about by manipulating the plot. Anthony undergoes a breakdown and is left mentally impaired. Almost simultaneously the lawsuit over Adam Patch's estate is settled—in Anthony's favor. Edward Shuttleworth, the reformed alcoholic who looked after Old Adam, and who was the other claimant to the money, locks himself in a room and commits suicide. Anthony and Gloria, worth some thirty million dollars, embark on a luxury liner for Europe. Anthony has not fully recovered from his breakdown; perhaps he never will. He is attended to by a private physician. Gloria, older but with vestiges of her beauty intact, wears "a Russian sable coat that must have cost a small fortune"—a considerable step up from the grey squirrel coat she had earlier coveted (368). We see Anthony and Gloria through the eyes of a young couple on the liner. Anthony looks "a little crazy" to them and Gloria seems "dyed and unclean" (368). They have been punished for their inanition, self-absorption, and inertia.

Ideally *The Beautiful and Damned* should show a progression from antipathy toward Bloeckman, and toward the other Jewish characters, to acceptance and admiration. We should not forget that Fitzgerald himself was a member of a minority and that he knew something about social ostracism. His Irish background and Irish looks were not a disadvantage in St. Paul, where many of the best families had Irish roots, but being Irish and Catholic had been marks against him at Princeton and elsewhere. He was temperamentally disposed to favor the underdog, the climber, but in *The Beautiful and Damned* he never warms to Bloeckman. Fitzgerald's respect for the man is grudging. He seems to admire Bloeckman's drive and persistence and, by extension, to admire the same qualities in upwardly bound Jews. But Bloeckman is not our hero. Most of the characters, and particularly Anthony and Gloria, are adrift—pursuing money and social position, amusing themselves with empty entertainment and drinking, doing little to move themselves or their society forward. Perhaps that is why, in the end, *The Beautiful and Damned* is not a more satisfying novel.

NOTES

1. Murray identifies the original for Bloeckman as J. Stuart Blackton (1875–1941), a film producer and director during the silent era. Blackton founded Vitagraph Studios in 1897 (182).

2. Among the names on the guest list in *The Great Gatsby* is "Newton Orchid, who controlled Films par Excellence" (*GG* 74).

3. Possibly Fitzgerald means nothing by the comparison, but the movie temptress Theda Bara (1885–1955) was born Theodosia Burr Goodman in Chicago in 1885, the daughter of Bernard Goodman, an immigrant Jewish tailor who had come to Chicago from Poland. In part to distract moviegoers from Bara's Jewish background, her publicists let it be known that she had been born in the shadow of the Sphinx and that her name was an anagram for "Arab Death."

4. Secular Jews of this period sometimes converted to Protestantism, usually to the Episcopalian or Presbyterian denominations, which were more welcoming than were the Methodists and Baptists.

5. The reference calls to mind, without too great a stretch, T. S. Eliot's "Burbank with a Baedeker: Bleistein with a Cigar," first published in the United States in 1920 in Eliot's *Poems* (17–18).

6. Still in the future was Berlin's marriage to Ellin Mackay, a Roman Catholic debutante who defied her father to marry Berlin in 1925. Fitzgerald mentions the Berlin-Mackay marriage in his essay "My Lost City," written in 1935 (*MLC* 109), and in his story "Three Acts of Music," written in 1936 (*LD* 5).

7. Fitzgerald would have known that Jews were making a mark in book publishing in 1922. Alfred A. Knopf, Horace Liveright, and Benjamin Huebsch had already begun their careers in 1922. Bennett Cerf, Donald Klopfer, Richard Simon, Max Schuster, Harold K. Guinzburg, and George S. Oppenheim would soon become prominent, challenging such established houses as

Scribner's, Harpers, Putnam's, and Holt. Jews were also advancing in medicine, law, and finance, but these fields are outside the concerns of the novel—or at least outside the interests of Anthony and Gloria.

8. One thinks here of Carrie Meeber and George Hurstwood in Theodore Dreiser's novel *Sister Carrie* (1900). Hurstwood, like Anthony, has been drifting, sitting in hotel lobbies and on park benches, thinking back on his years in Chicago, where he was the manager of a popular bar. Carrie, by contrast, has had a recent success in an amateur play and wants to become a professional actress. Eventually she succeeds.

A MATTER OF OVERCIVILIZATION
FITZGERALD'S CRITIQUE OF MODERNITY
IN *THE BEAUTIFUL AND DAMNED*

Joseph K. Stitt

F. Scott Fitzgerald's novels rest on the foundation of his philosophical and historical imagination. His romantic egoists—and their individual struggles with love, money, prestige, sexuality, beauty, self-expression, and mutability—exist in a time-bound universe, and Fitzgerald is very much aware of the role of the intellectual context of modernity in particularizing individual dreams and individual catastrophes. Fortunately, critics have increasingly come to recognize this in recent decades, rejecting a notion fostered early on by Edmund Wilson, Edna St. Vincent Millay, Malcolm Cowley, and others that Fitzgerald was a gifted stylist with a head almost utterly devoid of ideas (see Wilson, "Literary Spotlight" 20). The individual struggles of Fitzgerald's egoists are purposefully entangled in ideas about value and values, which are purposefully entangled in ideas about communities, nations, and civilizations.

Fitzgerald's thinking about modernity, decline, nihilism, and the problem of overcivilization plays a vital role in *The Beautiful and Damned* (1922) and the Fitzgerald corpus as a whole. Scholars have given considerable attention to the role racialist, and sometimes blatantly racist, declinism plays in *The Great Gatsby* (1925) and other works (see Turlish; and Margolies, "Maturing" 75–93), but the scope of Fitzgerald's concerns about modernity covers a much broader area than Lothrop Stoddard, Madison Grant, and questions about whether and to what degree Tom Buchanan's endorsement of *The Rise of the Colored Empires* is being satirized (*GG* 16).[1] Fitzgerald read Oswald Spengler enthusiastically (see Lehan 30–36; Moyer 238–56; and Bruccoli, *Some Sort* 201), and though his knowledge of Spengler would come too late to have a major influence on *Gatsby,* or any influence at all on *This Side of Paradise* (1920) or *The Beautiful and Damned,* his enthusiasm should come as no surprise. Fitzgerald was primed for Spengler by a preexisting interest in declinist and antimodernist thinking, a strong sense of historical pessimism, and a cultural context in which antimodernism had been a vital intellectual current for decades. The problem of decadence and decline, and of the moral crisis posed by modernity, is the rot within the heart of *The Beautiful and Damned,* and an appreciation of Fitzgerald's antimodern impulse can help decrypt aspects of the novel that readers often find difficult to crack.

The historian T. J. Jackson Lears has perhaps done more to trace the lineage of American antimodernism than any other scholar. His *No Place of Grace: Antimodernism and the Transformation of American Culture, 1880–1920* (1981) describes the multifarious resistance to modernity on both the political right and the political left, among artists, activists, and thinkers as well as ordinary Americans. As early as 1856, the art historian Charles Eliot Norton was already worried that his countrymen had "lost the capacity for moral suffering," seeking "relief from harass in self-forgetfulness among the delights of sensual enjoyment" (qtd. in Lears 27). From Walt Whitman to Theodore Roosevelt to the closing pages of *The Great Gatsby,* there is the fear that the "fresh, green breast of the new world" (*GG* 217) is receding farther and farther into the past, that the vitality (and virility) of the early republic is withering away, giving way to superficial pursuits, to corruption, to dandyism, to effeminacy (Lears 27). Neurologist George Miller Beard's *American Nervousness,* published in 1881, posited that modern industrial life, which Beard explicitly referred to as "all civilization," caused a condition he named "neurasthenia," a catchall diagnosis that he associated with indigestion, sleep loss, nocturnal emission, a "desire for stimulants and narcotics . . . fear of responsibility . . . fear of being alone, fear of fears, fear of contamination, fear of everything, deficient mental control, lack of decision in trifling matters, [and] hopelessness" (Beard 304, 7).

The American version of the Arts and Crafts movement, building on the critique of modern industrial capitalism found in John Ruskin and William Morris, rejected modernity by embracing the organicism and community-mindedness its adherents associated with the Middle Ages.[2] Brooks Adams's quasi-scientific, and transparently polemical, *The Law of Civilization and Decay* (1896) likewise favored the "the ecstatic dream" of the medieval world over the "mercenary quality" and commercialism of modern times (383, 381). Frank Norris, whose *Vandover and the Brute* (1914) was an influence on the deterioration-of-the-idle-rich-boy plot of *The Beautiful and Damned,* held that the only way the United States could alleviate the debilitating effects of overcivilization was to pursue a course of vigorous militarism through the conquest of the American West and the commercial subjugation of Asia (Piper, "Frank Norris and Scott Fitzgerald" 393–400; Lears 130–31). American Catholics and Catholic fellow-travelers (including many cultural conservatives as well as aesthetes in the tradition of Wilde, Pater, and Huysmans) were treated to a decades-long assault on modernity, from Pope Leo XIII's "Aeterni Patris" encyclical of 1879, which reaffirmed the superiority of Thomism over modern philosophy, to Pius X's antimodernist "Lamentabili sane exitu" decree of 1907, his antimodernist "Pascendi Dominici Gregis" encyclical of the same year, his attack on modern theology in his "Oath against Modernism" of 1910, and his 1914 inculcation of Thomism in all Catholic colleges through the Sacred Congregation of Studies (Boersma 18; Mettepenningen 25). And, of course, Thomism and antimodernism were of great importance to a writer and thinker who would have an enduring influence on Fitzgerald: Henry Adams.

Fitzgerald's interest in Adams, and especially *The Education of Henry Adams* (1907), is well established. Book 2 of *This Side of Paradise* is entitled "The Education of a Personage" (*TSOP* 155ff.) and "The Education of a Personage" was a working title for the entire novel. In a letter to Maxwell Perkins, Fitzgerald admitted that the character Thornton Hancock in the novel "is Henry Adams" (*Letters* 138).[3] David McKay Powell has argued that *Mont-Saint-Michel and Chartres* (1904) is also present in "the Gothic disposition" in *This Side of Paradise,* and both Powell and William Wasserstrom have detected reverberations of Adams in *The Beautiful and Damned* (Powell 104; Wasserstrom 297). This does not, of course, mean that Fitzgerald consistently parrots Adams's views. Amory Blaine's vision of the future in *This Side of Paradise* at least aspires to be an antidote to the kind of historical pessimism found in *The Education of Henry Adams,* and the lapsed Catholic Fitzgerald, like Amory, is not as enthralled with the centripetal grandeur of the High Middle Ages as Adams is. On the whole, though, Fitzgerald's quarrel with Adams, at least on the matter of the present state of civilization, disappears from his work after *This Side of Paradise.* The crisis of meaning that is at the heart of *The Education,* the crisis that for Adams is represented by the replacement of the Virgin with the dynamo (that is, with an unthinking nothing), the substitution of gold or glitter or coal or any mere substance for real value, will echo through the rest of Fitzgerald's career, as will the problem of the modern West's descent into spiritual entropy. Much more so than Adams, Fitzgerald will find himself drawn to the glamour of modern decline, to the exhilaration of iconoclasm and even desecration, to all those aspects of a cultural crack-up that feel like liberation, but he will also portray decline as a historical calamity.

The Beautiful and Damned investigates this calamity more directly than any of Fitzgerald's novels. All of the thematic threads in the novel—questions about genuine human connection, about artistic merit and integrity, about the masculine and the feminine, about war, about race and class, about regionalism, about intergenerational conflict, about addiction, about dreaming a worthwhile dream—can be traced back to the crisis of modernity. The central problem in the novel, which Fitzgerald sometimes articulates explicitly and sometimes embodies, is the problem of modernity and overcivilization, a problem that leads to nihilism, decadence, and dissolution.

Situating Fitzgerald's characters in relation to this problem offers an especially useful way of understanding what they represent, and provides even more clarity if we also consider the degree to which different characters exemplify Fitzgerald's distinctive conception of the romantic. In the following schematic, "modern" should be associated with sophistication, skepticism, overcivilization, and ultimately with nihilism, whereas "romantic" should be associated with yearning, an idealistic temperament, and emotional or artistic lyricism.[4]

	ROMANTIC	ANTI-ROMANTIC
MODERN	Anthony Patch (Nihilism, Agony)	Maury Noble (Nihilism, Resignation)
ANTIMODERN	Dorothy "Dot" Raycroft (Naiveté, Affirmation)	Adam J. Patch (Puritanism, Regression)

Representing the ideas in the novel in a visual way clarifies a number of patterns and relations. Anthony is not quite like Maury but is drawn to him. Anthony is not quite like Dot but will find himself romantically entangled with her. Anthony is almost perfectly antithetical to his reformist prig of a grand-father. Dot is almost perfectly antithetical to Maury. Adam J. Patch's position is the grayest, the dullest, the least lively. Anthony's position, of yearning for significance but being empty of belief, is the place of maximal agony. Examin-ing these patterns and relations can solve what might appear to be plot-related problems (notably, the mystery of Dot's role as Anthony's destroyer at the end of the novel) and help sketch out the intellectual architecture of *The Beautiful and Damned* as a whole.

Fitzgerald makes it quite clear very early on that Adam Patch is not the cure for what ails Anthony, much less the cure for what ails civilization:

> Emulating the magnificent efforts of Anthony Comstock, after whom his grandson was named, he levelled a varied assortment of upper-cuts and body-blows at liquor, literature, vice, art, patent medicines, and Sunday the-atres. His mind, under the influence of that insidious mildew which eventu-ally forms on all but the few, gave itself up furiously to every indignation of the age. From an armchair in the office of his Tarrytown estate he directed against the enormous hypothetical enemy, unrighteousness, a campaign which went on through fifteen years, during which he displayed himself a rabid monomaniac, an unqualified nuisance, and an intolerable bore. (12)

Adam Patch's stale puritanism is the enemy of the artistic impulse, the body, and the mind. The antimodern, anti-romantic position might intuitively seem to be good ground from which to repel the onslaught of decadence and de-cline, but this is not so. If these things can be repelled, it will not be by means of cultural sclerosis, or by the hand of a "pious ass" and "chickenbrain" (79).

It would also be a mistake to associate Adam Patch's Comstockery with the backward-looking element in Henry Adams. The medieval world Adams celebrates in *Mont-Saint-Michel and Chartres* is not a world of mildew and darkness but of motion and light, a world where swarms of human hands make great structures rise from the earth. Far from dismissing the body, Aquinas insists that "the intellectual soul," the quintessence of personhood, must be united with the body (*Mont-Saint-Michel* 501). Adams points admiringly to lines from *De rerum natura*, "perhaps the finest in all Latin literature," wherein Lucretius "invoked Venus exactly as Dante invoked the Virgin," and for Adams affection for the Virgin does not amount to advocating for virginity: "anyone brought up among [American] Puritans knew that sex was sin. In any previous age, sex was strength" (*Education* 384). Whether Adams retained any hope for redeeming civilization is uncertain. If he did, though, he would not have imagined the redemption issuing from the bossy, blinkered sermonizing of a figure like Adam Patch.

Maury Noble represents what civilization ought to be redeemed *from,* and he lies at the very center of the *The Beautiful and Damned,* curled up like a "large slender and imposing cat" (24). Before Gloria and before Dot, Maury is the focus of Anthony's affection. He plays the intellectual consort to Anthony's dissolution and represents the logical destination of modern skepticism and sophistication while remaining emotionally isolated from its consequences. Even if he is not one of Fitzgerald's more convincing creations, the ideas in the novel revolve around him, and every major character in the text should be considered, thematically, in relation to him.[5]

Maury looms large in Anthony Patch's life. He is "the only man of all his acquaintances whom he admires and, to a bigger extent than he likes to admit to himself, envies" (24). When Maury is unexpectedly home one Saturday, Anthony's spirits soar "faster than the flying elevator. This was so good, so extremely good, to be about to talk to Maury—who would be equally happy at seeing him. They would look at each other with a deep affection just behind their eyes which both would conceal beneath some attenuated raillery" (43). Anthony's "restless soul" feels warmth in the "glow" of Maury's "strong persuasive mind," bringing "him a peace that could be likened only to the peace a stupid woman gives" (44). As time passes and Anthony's life becomes more and more broken—shattered by drunkenness and, more fundamentally, an absence of purpose and a failure of the will—his estimation of Maury does end up falling somewhat. He tells Gloria he "used to think" Maury was "so brilliant," but "brilliant people don't settle down in business—or do they?" (337).[6] Still, Maury continues to have a hold on him. When Anthony resigns from all his clubs and finds new friends in Parker Allison and Pete Lytle, Fitzgerald depicts Anthony's time with them as a grotesque parody of his days with Dick and Maury. His new companions are "ape[s]" who think in phrases rather than complete sentences, have imaginations that are "almost incapable of sustaining a dialogue," live "thoughtless" lives, and only rise above "their muddled clauses" when they talk about food and booze and girls (342). In certain moments Maury's absence fills Anthony's life, especially the absence of his voice. Maury's last tangible appearance in the novel, when a drunken Anthony runs across Madison Avenue with the idea of asking Maury for money, is a conspicuously ineloquent scene, with Maury speaking barely twenty words, none of them memorable, before cutting Anthony, leaving him "standing there alone under the lights" in front of the Biltmore (356). And even if Anthony is no longer as dazzled as he once was by what he believed to be Maury's brilliance, he is still stung by Maury's turning away from him, "furiously aware that he had been snubbed" and "as hurt and angry as it was possible for him to be in that condition" (356). Maury remains with him, at least in Anthony's deranged mind, to the very end, appearing as one of the "friends [who] had deserted him" on the last page of the novel (369).

Maury's doctrine is, in some eyes, the height of sophistication, the ultimate conclusion of the skepticism of modernity, but it is also simple enough to compress into three words: Everything is meaningless. This idea and its consequences pound through *The Beautiful and Damned* like a drumbeat. It can be heard at least faintly in the first sentence of the novel, when the reader learns that "the Holy Ghost of this later day" is "irony," and is implicated even earlier, in the book's epigraph: "The victors belong to the spoils" (11, 3). Maury will suggest the idea more directly later in the first chapter: "And I shall go on shining as a brilliantly meaningless figure in a meaningless world" (27). Anthony justifies his idle existence, and unknowingly foreshadows his pitifully idle end, by invoking "The Meaninglessness of Life" (51). Gloria is described three times as a Nietzschean and adopts "Never give a damn" and "I don't care!" as maxims (139, 172, 233).[7] She later tells Anthony that he and Maury and "everyone else whose intellect" she has "the slightest respect for, agree that life as it appears is utterly meaningless," and though she is questioning her own disbelief as she says this, and justifying a passing interest in Bilphism, she admits that her motivation for believing in meaning has more to do with alleviating her unhappiness than it has to do with truth (254). Richard Caramel several times objects to Maury's nihilism, and to Anthony's—"I've always believed that moral values existed, and I always will," he insists (345)—but Fitzgerald refuses to allow Caramel to be articulate enough or formidable enough to develop his objections. Given his ineffectual nature, it could be that Caramel lacks conviction and is merely repeating the conventional wisdom of a previous era, not thinking so much as having an involuntary reflex that leads to an utterance. Whatever the reason for his failure, it is clear that he does not speak for the spirit of the age. Even though most of his contemporaries still nod their heads at the same utterances Caramel does, and even though some of those people might have actual conviction, the thinkers who are considered the most urbane, the intellectual victors of modernity, are those who are steering civilization in Maury's direction.

Fitzgerald considers the consequences of taking such a course, and of having taken one, in a very overt way. Maury describes them, in song, the same night he delivers his "Symposium" speech: "The—pan-ic—has—come—over us, / So ha-a-a-s—the moral decline!" (201). Later, not long before Adam Patch's unexpected visit to the party in "The Broken Lute" chapter, Maury will drink to "the defeat of democracy and the fall of Christianity" (229). On a more personal level, he recognizes that nihilism fails to pose a fatal threat to him only because of his emotional inertness. As he tells Anthony, "Nothing—quite—stirs me," even when he tries to let himself be stirred (49). He also tells Anthony, in the very same speech, that "it's you who are very romantic and young," an accurate observation that helps explain how two men following the same idea can end up having such different fates (48).

The distinguishing characteristic of romantics in Fitzgerald is that they are running after something, most likely in a desperate way. They yearn. They run. They have a direction and a desired end. They are all bound up in *telos*. Anthony's problem is that the central intellectual conviction he shares with Maury, that everything is meaningless, is not compatible with *telos*. If all ends are pointless, what is the point of running toward them? Anthony tries to rationalize his plight as being a universal aspect of the nature of desire when he tells Dot that desire "cheats you," that it must be an insubstantial "sunbeam" that "gilds some inconsequential object," and this does indeed follow logically if every object and every action is in fact inconsequential (284). The problem lies in arguing that every single object must be inconsequential by first assuming universal inconsequence, which begs the question.

Whether Anthony's nihilistic assumption is correct or not, it will remain in conflict with his romantic nature, and it is this internal tension that eventually pulls him apart. In time, his romantic yearning will be so worn down by inconsequence that he effectively runs out of objects to pursue. He still pursues the inheritance he hopes the lawsuit will bring him, but he pursues the inheritance so he can avoid doing anything, which for him amounts to pursuing a "way of life" that involves not pursuing anything (369). Caramel *almost* gets the final version of Anthony right when he tells him, "You don't do anything—so nothing matters" (346). He just has the causality reversed. Anthony has convinced himself that nothing matters, so he doesn't do anything.

Though an anti-romantic disposition prevents Maury from being ripped apart as Anthony is, it is worth noting that he does not escape unharmed. Early on in the narrative he seems a grand figure. He can fill "the room, tigerlike, godlike" (44). He has "accomplished the globe" as if he were "some predestined anti-Christ" (42–43). Gradually, though, he diminishes. He is not the *Übermensch* or Milton's Satan. Even to Anthony, he grows "rambling and inconclusive" (217). He makes money and gets married, every bit as conventional in deed as the ordinary people he despises. He foresees the rest of his life not long after delivering his long speech at the train station:

> He was wondering at the unreality of ideas, at the fading radiance of existence, and at the little absorptions that were creeping avidly into his life, like rats into a ruined house. He was sorry for no one now—on Monday morning there would be his business, and later there would be a girl of another class whose whole life he was; these were the things nearest his heart. In the strangeness of the brightening day it seemed presumptuous that with this feeble, broken instrument of his mind he had ever tried to think. (218)

Maury does have a heart, we learn, but his ultimate end is to settle for filling it with what he believes to be rats. His mind, despite producing so much talk and at times representing the culmination of civilization, placing him "among the saved," has *always* been a broken thing (24). When he makes the speech at the train station earlier, he is not clearly visible as a human being. Fitzgerald places him on "the roof of the shed, where he sat dangling his feet over the edge, outlined as a shadowy and fantastic gargoyle against the now brilliant sky" (211). The words he lets fall might have the power to infect other minds but are themselves insubstantial, and even as infection they have their limitations. However much harm his words might do, it is not Maury who blasts Anthony's mind to pieces in the end, but Dot.

Considering the relationship of Anthony Patch and Dorothy Raycroft in *The Beautiful and Damned* solely from an individual, personal perspective, without sorting through Fitzgerald's historicism, gives rise to more questions than it answers. It also points to an apparent problem that has not received enough critical attention. Why does Fitzgerald allow such an apparently inconsequential character to be so consequential at the close of the novel?

Dot is the focus of what might seem, given Dot's nature, to be a puzzlingly titled chapter, "A Matter of Civilization" (261–97). By the time she appears, a "soft-eyed girl in a lilac dress," the reader is almost three-quarters of the way through the novel (267). Though Anthony's dalliance with her is more substantial than his earlier relationship with Geraldine Burke, Dot never holds his attention in the way Gloria does, or even in the way Maury Noble does. Even in those moments when he seems to feel the greatest affection for her, once when the moonlight strikes her face and again when he recognizes that he "cared for her" after she threatens to kill herself, his mind almost immediately turns to Gloria (277–78, 289). Anthony never loves Dot, but "slid[es]" into the affair as a result of "his increasing carelessness about himself" (270). Dot is someone to whom things happen, neither weak nor strong, apparently insubstantial—in Anthony's mind, a "baby" (272, 278). Within a few months her company becomes "tedious, then almost intolerable" (287). When she sends him a letter after he collapses while shoveling gravel in Mississippi—"an incoherent, a tear-swollen scrawl, a flood of protest, endearment, and grief"—Anthony reads only a page before he lets it slip from his hand (292–93). Then Dot herself slips from his life, largely unmissed, until the very end of the novel.

Thus described, Dot would not seem to be in a position to have much of an effect on Anthony, and yet somehow, sometimes, she does, and does so quite powerfully. Early on in their affair, "[t]he little girl in the white dress dominated him, as she approached beauty in the hard symmetry of her desire" (284). It is her eyes that seem to be observing Anthony when he collapses in Mississippi, her voice that seems to call out to him (292). And what is most striking is her appearance in New York in the final pages of the book. Given that Anthony almost seems to have forgotten her, as surely some readers have, it seems very strange that Dot can walk in the door, gasp and sob her way through a few heartfelt platitudes, and break his mind. When next we see him, after he throws a chair at Dot and loses consciousness, Anthony sits on the floor with his childhood stamp collection, letting handfuls of stamps drift "down about him like leaves," threatening to "tell . . . grandfather" if Caramel and Gloria refuse to leave the room, unperturbed by the fact that grandfather is dead (368). It has taken years of determined drunken dissolution to transform

Anthony into a wretch. Dot, without meaning to, transforms him into a child and an imbecile in an instant.

It is of course possible that Dot's role in the end could be nothing more than a slip-up on Fitzgerald's part. The author needs a sparrow to fall and hurls Dot into the scene to fell him, *diabolus ex machina*, without thinking through Anthony's psychology or Dot's thematic function in an artistically rigorous way. It is much more likely, though, that Fitzgerald knows very well what Dot represents, and that he uses her to dramatize the precise nature of Anthony's failure as a human being—and the precise nature of Anthony's anguish—in the context of overcivilization.

Anthony's journey to Dot begins when he is newly drafted into the army, rattling toward South Carolina in "a sort of brummagem Pullman" (261). The journey is a movement away from the chill of the North, and also a movement into the past.[8] Anthony rattles toward a more primitive place, a less civilized place, an agrarian relic, but also a place that is less vulnerable to the infection of modernity. Fitzgerald does not idealize the South when he refers to the "yo-kelry of South Carolina," the "overpainted girls," "ragged, shuffling, subservient negroes," and "the pervasive lull of thought," but he is drawn quite strongly to what he perceives to be the region's feminine warmth and is charmed at times by its very backwardness (264, 267). The South is deeply entangled, sometimes morbidly so, in its past, and is both a younger and a more ancient place than the North. It is "more of Algiers than of Italy, with faded aspirations pointing back over innumerable generations to some warm, primitive Nirvana, without hope or care" (280–81). However many defects it might suffer from, overcivilization is not one of them. It does not teem with Maury Nobles.

Dorothy Raycroft, who is very nearly as dissimilar to Maury Noble as it is possible to be, blends into the southern landscape as if she were a well-placed brushstroke of lilac or violet. Like Maury, Dot resembles a cat, but not because of an agile or indifferent psyche. Instead, she "basked like a cat in the sun," drowsy and warm (281). She is poor, poorly lettered, and uncultivated. She walks naturally through a town in which it is "natural to be bound nowhere in particular, to be thinking nothing" (268). Though not slovenly, she is the sort of person who dresses "decently but shabbily," who might choose to wear "a somehow pitiable little hat adorned with pink and blue flowers" (365–66). She will never be a member of any smart set, will never flirt with George Jean Nathan or trade barbs with H. L. Mencken.

In short, Dot lacks sophistication, and though this would not normally be an enviable deficiency, in some respects it is highly enviable in the historical situation Fitzgerald depicts in *The Beautiful and Damned*. Because Dot is unsophisticated, she is free to desire things, and people, without being infected with the assumption that every object of desire, and every person, must be meaningless and thus valueless and thus not worth desiring. And despite being "bound nowhere in particular" much of the time, in the sense of not being someone who is inclined to calculation or planning, Dot is very much a creature of desire, of yearning, of *telos*. As a romantic, she will of course feel pain intensely, but her experience of pain will not be as excruciating, or at least as self-repudiating, as Anthony's because her pursuit of *telos* will not threaten to rip her apart from the inside. Unlike Adam Patch, she does not have to be a corpse. Unlike Maury, she can fill her heart with something other than rats. Unlike Anthony, she can be a romantic with an undivided soul.

Even if she often seems shabby, and often childlike, Dot can even be said to hearken back, however faintly, to the feminine ideals Fitzgerald found in Henry Adams, to both Venus and the Virgin. Dot loses her good reputation in high school after an "indiscretion" with a local clerk at a class picnic, and though she retains "her technical purity," in a year's time she will lose that as well, to a naval officer Dot is sure she is in love with, just as surely as she would have been in love with the clerk had he not skipped town for New York (271–72). Other men follow, and yet before she will give herself to Anthony she comes close, at least mentally, to restoring her virginity:

> Crying quietly she had confessed to him that he was not the first man in her life; there had been one other—he gathered that the affair had no sooner commenced than it had been over.
>
> Indeed, so far as she was concerned, she spoke the truth. She had forgotten the clerk, the naval officer, the clothier's son, forgotten her vividness of emotion, which is true forgetting. She knew that in some opaque and shadowy existence someone had taken her—it was as though it had occurred in sleep. (277)

Of course, Fitzgerald is lampooning Dot's naiveté here. This is the Eternal Virgin of comedy rather than theology. Pathetic as she is, though, and as delusional as she is, there is something admirable in her sincerity, especially if it is juxtaposed with the bad faith of Anthony or Maury or Gloria. In a sense, Fitzgerald presents Dorothy Raycroft as living up to her name, as someone who just might bear a resemblance to "a gift of God" if only the world she lived in had not fallen so much farther than she has.[9] Her value has been anticipated, in the form of the "stupid woman" who gives "peace," early on in the novel, and when she appears in the flesh, she promises Anthony the "rest" his ruptured soul desperately needs and alleviates the "inevitably futile poundings of his imagination" (44, 270). She offers Anthony the solace of the Dolorosa, of pity and sorrow, because she intuitively sees "her own tragedies mirrored in his face," and for a time he does "find himself increasingly glad to be alive," existing "in the present with a sort of animal content," finding in "her soft sighs and tender whisperings . . . the consummation of all aspiration, of all content" (273, 276, 281). Of course, it does not and could not last. What Dot has to offer fails to save Anthony partly because she is such a faded remnant of any kind of divine virgin or goddess of love, but most of all because Anthony can never be offered anything, or receive anything, that he will continue to value.

Fitzgerald makes Dot a remarkably inarticulate character. When she speaks, she almost never strings more than two sentences together and almost never says anything that is not a banality. Again, though, what is small about her points to what is substantial about her, and also suggests what is lacking in others. Her ineloquence reminds us that Maury and Anthony consist almost solely of words, and some of Dot's most perceptive words in the novel reproach Anthony for being overmuch about language: "I don't want just words. If that's all you have for me you'd better go" (284). When Anthony tries to respond, she interrupts him: "What's death to me is just a lot of words to you. You put 'em together so pretty" (284). Through modernity and possibly beyond it, from Frege to Saussure to Russell to Wittgenstein to Derrida, there has been a tendency to reduce thought and even life itself to language, but it is quite clear that Dot would be disinclined to follow the linguistic turn. The signifier will never be the ultimate end for someone like her. To reduce death to merely "death" would seem palpably insane.

Anthony finds himself troubled over words, and over their relation to the palpable, in the "No Matter!" chapter (334–69), after Dot appears on his doorstep in New York. He is in a state of high intensity, and is in fact speaking his final words to Dot: "'I'll kill you!' he was muttering in short, broken breaths. 'I'll *kill* you!' He seemed to bite at the word as though to force it into materialization" (367). These are also the last words Anthony will speak with anything like an intact mind. The "face of the world" is about to change for him forever, with a snap (367). What is at least as interesting as the bad thing about to happen, though, is what has been happening—what the face of Anthony's world has been made up of for quite a long time, perhaps since the Holy Ghost of irony descended on him in 1911 (11). To a great degree it has been a world of words, of detachment from matter as matter as well as matter as meaning, of semantic symbols being put together more cleverly and knowingly than they ever were before, of too often failing to appreciate the reality of another human being looking him in the face.

Although Dot might appreciate people a bit too enthusiastically at times, she is not guilty of failing to look, and Fitzgerald is even more interested in her eyes than he is in her tangible physicality. On the night she first meets Anthony, she seems to fade away as a corporeal being, with one telling exception: "It was so dark that he could scarcely see her now. She was a dress swayed infinitesimally by the wind, two limpid, reckless eyes" (270). Her eyes actually appear in the text one word before she does—"A soft-eyed girl in a lilac dress tittered to her companion" (267)—and eyes are ever-present in the pages devoted to her. In the Cambridge Edition of *The Beautiful and Damned*, some version of "eye," including "eyes" and "eyed" as well as "eye," appears about 0.52 times per page. In passages where Dot is present, either in person or by implication, some version of "eye" appears about 1.47 times per page, which means that eyes are almost three times as likely to appear on a page involving Dot than on a typical page in the novel.

Even more intriguing than the profusion of eyes is what Fitzgerald does with them. They can be pretty things to look at or windows to an emotional state, as is typical in fiction, but they play a crucial thematic function as well. Scrutinizing what Dot sees and fails to see, and how she makes Anthony see himself and think about being seen, helps solve the puzzle of Dot's power over Anthony at the end of the novel, and also helps further our understanding of Fitzgerald's ideas about civilization and value.

Dot, the "soft-eyed girl," peers through eyes as "soft as shadows," and softness is the first quality to which her eyes are coupled (267, 268). Softness can indicate weakness, and Dot's eyes are certainly weak, even "insensate," in the sense of being not especially perceptive (281). Time after time she misperceives people, and time after time lends her attention to men who will treat her poorly and make her miserable. Softness can mean more than weakness, though, and Dot's eyes are also soft in a positive sense. Instead of looking at people to perceive qualities and pull them toward her so she can comprehend them, she uses her eyes to project qualities outward, and the softness with which she imbues people, and also the softness she offers them herself, is tenderness, or love. Combining the two kinds of softness, poor eyesight and tenderness, leads Dot to grief and can make her seem to be a fool, but there is a kind of poetry in her foolishness—and also a resemblance to the body of belief that once stood at the center of Western civilization. Love that is undeserved is at the heart of Christian doctrine, described not as foolishness but grace. The grace Dot offers, the knowledge of love both as a commonplace and a fundamental truth, will of course not end up being a form of salvation to those she offers it to. She offers it nonetheless, and the main fault seems to lie not with the woman who makes the offer but with those who cannot comprehend the offering.

Anthony, or at least Anthony in modern mode, insists on the futility of love and of all other desires. He tells Dot he once got what he desired (Gloria) but that, once gotten, the object of desire "turned to dust in my hands" (283). He continues:

> I've often thought that if I hadn't got what I wanted things might have been different with me. I might have found something in my mind and enjoyed putting it in circulation. I might have been content with the work of it, and had some sweet vanity out of the success. I suppose that at one time I could have had anything I wanted, within reason, but that was the only thing I ever wanted with any fervor. God! And that taught me you can't have *any-*thing, you can't have anything at *all.* Because desire just cheats you. It's like a sunbeam skipping here and there about a room. It stops and gilds some inconsequential object, and we poor fools try to grasp it—but when we do the sunbeam moves on to something else, and you've got the inconsequential part, but the glitter that made you want it is gone— (283–84)

Dot's manner of seeing bears an uncanny resemblance to the sunbeam in Anthony's metaphor, except for the fact that she refuses to believe that the objects she sets alight with tenderness are inconsequential or merely gilded. "[S]tanding, dry-eyed, picking little leaves from a dark vine" (284), she pointedly rejects Anthony's attack on desire and insists that he has not provided her anything of substance, only words.

Dot's eyes begin to have a curious effect on Anthony as their affair continues. When Dot is on Anthony's mind, eyes appear even though she is not present. In his rush to get to her after she makes a suicide threat over the phone, Anthony runs toward the car that will take him to her after he sees its "two yellow eyes [appear] around a bend," and when he bursts into her dark room to check on her and strikes a match to see, "[t]wo wide eyes [look] up at him from a wretched ball of clothes on the bed" (288, 289). Just before Anthony collapses while shoveling gravel, he imagines eyes upon him:

> Then one afternoon in the second week he had a feeling that two eyes were watching him from a place a few feet beyond one of the guards. This aroused him to a sort of terror. He turned his back on the eyes and shovelled feverishly, until it became necessary for him to face about and go for more gravel. Then they entered his vision again, and his already taut nerves tightened up to the breaking point. The eyes were leering at him. Out of a hot silence he heard his name called in a tragic voice, and the earth tipped absurdly back and forth to a babel of shouting and confusion. (292)

He determines later that the voice he heard, or imagined he heard, was Dot's voice, almost certainly making the eyes hers as well. The scene does not make clear why being looked at by a backward "baby" of a girl, whose eyes are not cruel but filled with softness and charity, would terrify Anthony, threaten to break his nerves, and destabilize his world. It does, however, foreshadow Dot's appearance at the end of the novel.

Just before Dot arrives at his apartment in New York, and just after a self-pitying reflection that blames all "the sorrow and the pain" he has experienced on the women in his life, Anthony looks at himself in the mirror and sees a man in a wretched state, a "stooped and flabby figure," his "eyes with their crisscross of lines like shreds of dried blood" (365). This seems to be a continuation of his self-pity, of *what has been done to him* by a cruel and loveless world, but he hopes things will get better, or at least be "different," if only he can get hold of his grandfather's money. When Dot comes in and looks at him, her "violet eyes . . . red with tears," Anthony's fear is not the usual fear that eyes might provoke (366). He is not afraid she will see he is a wretch. Dot of all people seems to be least likely to notice this about him. In her *manner of looking*, though, with eyes projecting tenderness, "appallingly in earnest" (366), full of grace, she is a reminder that Anthony's manner of looking is not the only way to look, that it is possible to see value in the world rather than meaning-lessness, that at least once it was possible to live in a budding civilization that affirmed more than it critiqued, and that some people, some of whom might seem unimpressive otherwise, are capable of feeling adoration well after the adored object has been grasped. Dot's eyes are destructive because they are charitable. Anthony is not afraid of being seen, but of turning to the mirror again and recognizing that wretchedness is not something the world has made him suffer. The source of his wretchedness is himself, and Dot's manner of looking proves that his wretchedness is not inevitable. However pathetic she is, and however faint a shadow of the long-gone age she represents, Dot is a rebuke to Anthony's existence and to modernity itself. He suddenly senses that "all the civilization and convention around him was curiously unreal" (366). He threatens to kill Dot, and throws the chair at her, because her continuing existence suggests that some things might be true and valuable in ways he has never allowed himself to comprehend. Unfortunately for him, Dot's vanishing provides no relief. "[W]ith almost a tangible snapping sound the face of the world changed before his eyes," and the "impenetrable darkness" that descends on him as his mind breaks will be with him from now on (367).

The antimodern strain in Fitzgerald's work is much more prominent than is generally recognized, and amounts to something far weightier than the "anxiety" that has so long been associated with modernism. When he wrote his famous 1933 letter to his daughter, Scottie, about duty and virtue and not concerning herself too much with pleasure (*Letters* 3–4), Fitzgerald was being a hypocrite, or at least someone who had failed to live up to his own ideals, but he was not writing anything he did not believe. He thought he knew enough about decadence to know that it was dangerous, and dangerous not only on a personal level but on the level of a nation or civilization. Tellingly, *The Beautiful and Damned*'s depiction of New York's celebration of the triumph of the Allies provides little description of the actual celebration on Broadway beyond the appearance of light and faces, and consists primarily of historical examples and historical images that suggest a historical warning:

> Here surely the victory had come in time, the climax had been scheduled with the uttermost celestial foresight. The great rich nation had made triumphant war, suffered enough for poignancy but not enough for bit-

terness—hence the carnival, the feasting, the triumph. Under these bright lights glittered the faces of peoples whose glory had long since passed away, whose very civilizations were dead—men whose ancestors had heard the news of victory in Babylon, in Nineveh, in Bagdad, in Tyre, a hundred generations before; men whose ancestors had seen a flower-decked, slave-adorned cortège drift with its wake of captives down the avenues of Imperial Rome. (295)

In just three sentences, Fitzgerald transforms what seems to be a poignant victory, in fact a divinely ordained victory, into a procession of the dead. What appears to be triumph dissolves into hubris, luxury, the superficial distractions of the carnival, and almost casual cruelty and exploitation. We are reminded that a great rich nation can, as Charles Eliot Norton and Frank Norris feared, all too easily become soft and weak. We are reminded of the even bleaker vision of Henry Adams, in which the great rich nation descends into soulless commercialism and scientism, a spiritual entropy complemented all too well by the deification of "the meaninglessness of life." Like the antimoderns of previous decades, Fitzgerald fears that the historical cycle is now arcing in a downward direction. Even if Alexander is not yet at the gates demanding surrender from the money counters of Tyre, even if cruel Ninevah has some time to spare before its cruelty is paid back in kind, the decay has already set in. Babylon awaits its hour of judgment.

The historical pessimism in Fitzgerald is sometimes overlooked because he is far from consistent with his gloomy prognosis, especially in terms of tone and emotional resonance. He often finds himself carried along in the rush of a flower-decked existence, and from time to time even manages to find some pleasure in the experience. He has a gift for capturing the sharp intake of breath that so often proceeds from the superficial beauty—and the heart-breakingly fleeting beauty—of glittering faces and glittering things. The mania, or "panic," of the bustling world around him can feel exhilarating to the point of seduction, and he can be drawn to the irreverence of philosophical ideas that seem to be designed to shatter old icons rather than build anything new. Ultimately, though, Fitzgerald suggests we should see modernity as less dynamic than toxic. The poison of Maury Noble's words acts slowly but without ceasing. Desire in a world without meaning or ends can only lead to sickness. Anthony's weaknesses for alcohol and easy money further the progression of the illness, and by the time he achieves the false victory of an unearned inheritance, the disease has spread to his mind. *The Beautiful and Damned* is Fitzgerald's portrait of a civilization that is dying, in the usual manner, of self-inflicted ailments, and the damnation in the title of the novel is much, much more than a darkly pretty metaphor.

NOTES

1. Turlish argues convincingly for Stoddard's *The Rising Tide of Color*—a widely read declinist tract lamenting the waning dominance of white, and especially "Nordic," civilization—as the primary inspiration for *The Rise of the Colored Empires* in *Gatsby* (443–44). Margolies examines the complexities of Fitzgerald's views on race and racialist declinism, noting the often-troubling depictions of minority characters in his work but also the disdain Fitzgerald expresses for the sort of "Nordic theory" spewed forth by Tom Buchanan and writers such as Stoddard and Grant ("Maturing" 80).

2. Fitzgerald has Anthony Patch plan to write a history of the Middle Ages, just as in the mid-1930s Fitzgerald himself would write a series of medieval stories known as the Philippe, Count of Darkness series (Bruccoli, *Some Sort* 383–84; Brown 191–92). Moreland explains his attraction to the period: "Just as it had for Twain and especially Adams, the medieval setting provided Fitzgerald with a 'feeling of escape from the modern world,' as he notes in a 1934 letter to Max Perkins [Kuehl and Bryer 209]. . . . In escaping the modern world, he felt that he was escaping the breakdown of civilization, whose premonitory symptoms were manifested in world war, economic depression, and the immorality of the young" (132).

3. Fitzgerald also claimed to have met Adams as a boy. Whether he was telling the truth or merely trying to impress Perkins is not absolutely certain (Powell 93–94), though Bruccoli treats the meeting as actually having taken place (*Some Sort* 35).

4. "Nihilism" is used for brevity here, and it should be noted that many moderns would object to having the term applied to them. From the vantage of Henry Adams, or of St. Thomas Aquinas, modernity is nihilistic insofar as it accepts the disenchantment of the world. Some moderns have attempted to replace enchantment with humanism (Albert Camus) or art (Wallace Stevens), but the variety of modernity represented by Maury Noble in *The Beautiful and Damned* offers no such consolations—with the possible exception of hypocrisy.

5. Although based on George Jean Nathan, Maury too often reads like an understudy for Lord Henry Wotton in *The Picture of Dorian Gray*. Both are men of the spoken word more so than the pen, but Wotton is more incisive and less likely to hold forth at length. Lord Henry's ideas, like Maury's, corrupt others while leaving him largely untouched. As Basil Hallward observes, "You never say a moral thing, and you never do a wrong thing" (8). Maury's views are even more cynical than Lord Henry's, though, and his cleverness less successful than Fitzgerald intended.

6. The romantic Anthony has stayed true to Maury's ideas more than Maury has, and Anthony is naïve enough to expect an anti-romantic nihilist to "stay true" to his ideas instead of settling for moneymaking and bourgeois respectability.

7. Whether Nietzsche actually endorses the meaninglessness of life is not especially relevant. Fitzgerald is using him as a proxy for the idea, or at least a very similar idea.

8. In "The Ice Palace," written the year before Fitzgerald began *The Beautiful and Damned*, Sally Carrol Happer moves in the opposite direction, taking a northbound train to a place more rosy-cheeked and vigorous than her Georgia home, and less "hangdog, ill-dressed, [and] slovenly," but also a place of ice, a defeminized place where men "are the centre of every mixed group," a place so cold that Sally Carrol is afraid to cry because her tears might freeze (*F&P* 74, 80).

9. "Raycroft," which might gloss as "light farm," is also suggestive, as is the smallness and singularity of "Dot."

"NO MATTER!"

WORK AND THE EMPTY SPACES OF
THE BEAUTIFUL AND DAMNED

William Blazek

Consider the lilies of the field, how they grow:
they labour not, neither do they spin.

—Matthew 6:28

"He's a nihilist."
"That must be exhausting."

—*The Big Lebowski* (1998)

In both his introduction to the Cambridge Edition of *The Beautiful and Damned* and his essay in *The Cambridge Companion to F. Scott Fitzgerald,* James L. W. West III addresses the key theme of *vocation.* He notes that the text is in part "a novel of its times—a probing satire of the Jazz Age" but "also a meditation on the necessity for a vocation in life, a calling that will give purpose to one's hours and days" (Introduction xiii). "What does one do with one's life?" ("Question of Vocation" 50). Among the signs of their lack of purpose and inability to answer that question are that both Anthony Patch and Gloria Gilbert are largely ineffectual in their attempts to discover a useful occupation and usually confused in their conception of a vocation. Their stunted lives are often fraught with childlike anxieties and behavior. He has inherited from his grandfather, Adam J. Patch, "night-sweats and tears and unfounded dreads" (20), while she is addicted to chewing gumdrops and habitually bites the ends of her fingers. Anthony is, from the time of his mother's early death, "wedded to a vague melancholy" (14), while Gloria allows him to be "gracefully lazy" (60). Anthony's cultured friend Maury Noble at first seems to have found a way to deal with their world's existential confusion, saying, "I shall go on shining as a brilliantly meaningless figure in a meaningless world," to which Anthony replies: "On the contrary, I'd feel that it being a meaningless world, why write? The very attempt to give it purpose is purposeless" (27). Anthony is crippled in his attempts to write by this demotivating belief, and he easily diverts himself into wasting time. The characters' discussions about purpose and meaning in life, therefore, express a deeper philosophical dilemma at the heart of *The Beautiful and Damned,* one for which questioning the value of work is both a cause of the dilemma and its potential solution. Gloria and Anthony expend their variable reserves of energy in searching for (as well as avoiding) solutions to life's meaning. They arrive at transitory answers, yet in the end they mostly wait for an answer to be delivered to them. At best they find meaning only in the very act of living through the economic, physical, and moral declines that the narrative traces.

In their expectation of entering a fuller if not more fulfilling life once the legal wrangle over Anthony's multimillion-dollar inheritance from his grandfather's estate can be resolved, Anthony and Gloria exist in a Panglossian world (sprinkled with modernist irony) in which everything will turn out right in some marvelous way, however little the reader comes to believe that to "turn out right" means more than simply becoming extremely rich. Even in the acquisition of great wealth, and certainly all along the trail leading to that magical resolution to their search for meaning, Anthony and Gloria's lives are filled with boredom, nothingness, and emptiness. That theme of nihilistic futility in the novel can be examined in two different manifestations: firstly, an emptiness of spirit, exhibited in Anthony and Gloria's inability to find meaningful work or, more specifically, meaning in work; and secondly, an emptiness of space, Fitzgerald's textual device for illustrating the emptiness of spirit within them. The author merges a double sense of nothingness, then, in the combination of philosophical questioning of what constitutes a meaningful life, and the narrative spaces that reflect the failure of the characters' self-determination—especially interior spaces that are marked by artificiality or by severe enclosure. These spaces seem to be extensions of philosophical attitudes and moral judgments, spaces that act upon characters because the people have not earned their own place within those scenes. The key locations are rented properties of temporary or transitory possession—Anthony's Manhattan apartment with its solitary comforts of bath and bedroom, the grey country house in Marietta, ever-smaller and dingier apartments in New York City, farther and farther away from the social and financial heart of Manhattan, and steadily distanced from healthy lives that might have been satisfied by love or sustained by useful work.

Focused on the material substance and conceptual insubstantiality of the text's inhabited interior spaces, the novel's themes of inanition, disillusionment and unfulfilled dreams are framed within a dynamic interaction between individuals, settings, and textual representation. In general, interior scenes in Fitzgerald's second novel contain a miscellany of narrative devices, insights into social change, reflective analyses of characters and their current situations, comparative judgments about present status and future aspirations, and dramatizations of interpersonal relationships and emotional states. Apartment lounges, bedrooms, bathrooms, entrance halls, and barrooms, therefore, are among the physical, mental, and social environments of *The Beautiful and Damned*; and these interior spaces resonate not only with individual lives but with the nation as well, reflecting the social isolation and moral instability of modern life in America during the critical decade of the First World War, a decade prone to disillusionment as well as the coming lure of easy money and the pursuit of material desires over spiritual needs.

Drawing upon Henri Lefebvre's theories about the production of space and Walter Benjamin's concepts of image-space, I would also argue that labor and energy are presented in *The Beautiful and Damned* as essential elements in the construction of verifiable and sustainable selfhood. When these vital elements are replaced by the power of capital alone, the text reveals, the result is a dissipation of energy and dysfunctional modes of production. Thus, Anthony Patch inhabits a world of suspended capital acquisition and is maintained largely by a leaky tap of funds from what seems to be an almost inexhaustible reservoir of bonds. While waiting in limbo for his vast inheritance, he and Gloria spend well beyond the seven thousand dollars in annual income from his late mother's estate (18). They are forced to draw upon what are first itemized as forty-two thousand dollars in bonds, soon reduced as he regularly cashes in five hundred dollars' worth to meet their expenditures, penalizing the bonds' liquidity by selling the 10 percent investments for only fifty to eighty cents on the dollar, until finally calculating that he has "paper money worth eighty thousand dollars at par" that would bring only "about thirty thousand on the open market" (247, 322, 351). The shrinking assets are reflected in Anthony's limited prospects for meaningful work and in the steadily more confined social and spatial environments that he and Gloria inhabit. Yet because he is unwilling and unable to work for his livelihood, or to find purpose in the effort to work, Anthony remains in bondage to his inheritance and to his dissatisfactions.

"It seems to me . . . that the position of a man with neither necessity nor ambition is unfortunate," Anthony complains; and he regrets that the era has passed when "there used to be dignified occupations for a gentleman who had leisure" (98). In the "Men of Business" chapter of his highly influential book *Self-Help* (1859), the English writer Samuel Smiles advised: "On the whole, it is not good that human nature should have the road of life too easy. Better to be under the necessity of working hard and faring meanly, than to have everything done ready to our hand and a pillow of down to repose on. Indeed, to start life with comparatively small means seems so necessary as a stimulus to work, that it may almost be set down as one of the conditions essential to success in life" (224). One might add, the stimulus to work may lead to essential *meaning* in life.[1]

While his grandfather is still alive, Anthony must at least make gestures toward the prospect of starting a job and finding a career. But even in this early phase, the effort seems more of a performance than a real, defined goal. Without the family wealth to rule his future, the reader is led to believe, Anthony might have found his métier, or gained the self-knowledge that Amory Blaine seeks in *This Side of Paradise*. With his knowledge of Italy and European civilization, along with his elite Harvard education and cultured manners, Anthony would be well-suited to a career in the diplomatic service (147). However, he must instead act out the role of dutiful and worthy grandson and heir in America by trying out gainful employment rather than wasting his energies on social trivialities and illusory plans. This is not to say that he is mercenary but rather that his circumstances, like those of the farmer in Thoreau's *Walden* who is chained to the inheritance and unremitting toil of a farm (348–49), force upon Anthony's psyche an appalling burden. "He found in himself a growing horror and loneliness," the narrative reveals (52). "—If I am essentially weak, he thought, I need work to do, work to do. It worried him to think that he was, after all, a facile mediocrity. . . . It seemed a tragedy to want nothing—and yet he wanted something, something. He knew in flashes what it was—some path of hope to lead him toward what he thought was an imminent and ominous old age" (52). The words hold a universal truth, that he needs work to discover what he is capable of and who he is. They also foreshadow his failure to succeed in that goal or, more accurately, to care enough to have a goal.

At first, with his grandfather's stern encouragement for him "to *do* something . . . accomplish something" (20), Anthony considers his occupational options and decides, to Adam Patch's obvious disappointment, to try his hand at writing a history of the Middle Ages. The proposal will entail much reading and research, and over the next year it offers Anthony many opportunities for diversion and procrastination; yet, apparently for the first time, "work had come into his life as a permanent idea. . . . [B]ut not one line of actual writing existed at present, or seemed likely ever to exist. He did nothing—" (21). The notion of writing and his subsequent efforts are feebly sustained at intervals before and after his marriage to Gloria. He even manages a minor accomplishment, selling to the *Florentine* journal "a Chestertonian essay on the twelfth century by way of introduction to his proposed book" (161, 179). However, while ambition may be the parent of achievement, Anthony falters in the task, in part because his scholarly writing is simply another masque, concealing his real purpose to ingratiate himself with his grandfather (152). Even when he wills himself to action because of financial necessity, he fails to sustain momentum. Spurred by the need to pay bills, he attempts to write short stories for the growing popular magazine market, produces "six wretched and pitiable efforts" in short order but earns only thirty-one rejection slips and lacks both the conviction and the resilience to carry on (251–53). Anthony's later desperate attempt to sell his treasured Keats letter further reveals his meager devotion to the writer's craft (351).

Anthony is at first jealous of his friend and foil Richard Caramel's twenty-five-thousand-dollar boon for the movie rights following the popular success of Dick's first novel, *The Demon Lover,* but he later disparages the author for selling out to the commercial literary market—a route that Anthony's abhorrence of mediocrity could never allow him to take. Nevertheless, even while the corpse of Dick's critical reputation "was dragged obscenely through every literary supplement" and he "was accused of making a great fortune by writing trash for the movies" (347), late nights find this disdained writer "laboring over his trash far into those cheerless hours when the fire dies down, and the head is swimming from the effect of prolonged concentration" (348). The value of work to give Dick's life meaning here transcends any pecuniary or critical value that society may grant his toil.

The other player in the trio of male protagonists, Anthony's best friend, Maury Noble, finds a different path to fulfillment of being, perhaps more surprisingly so because he is initially the novel's most vociferous nihilist, expounding in the long "Symposium," chapter 2 of book 2, his philosophy. This stems firstly from "a ghostly dissatisfaction at being used in spite of myself for some inscrutable purpose of whose ultimate goal I was unaware—if, indeed, there *was* an ultimate goal," before confirming to himself that indeed there is no ultimate goal (214). However, Maury, too, chooses to create meaning in his life and avoid loneliness by following a schema that leads him to first "go on shining as a brilliantly meaningless figure in a meaningless world" (27), then to "attractive indolence" that nonetheless holds within it a "surprising and relentless maturity of purpose" (42), before contriving a solipsistic solution from the only lesson that life has taught him: "the tremendous importance of myself to me" (216). Maury and Dick both are given fresh direction when the United States enters the Great War, and both benefit afterward—Dick as a prosperous author of eight novels (347) and Maury as a businessman engaged to an heiress. Maury has told Anthony "that he was going to work so as to forget that there was nothing worth working for" (337), a modus vivendi that produces a form of wholeness.

Before the war, the chief ambition that Anthony and Gloria contrive in order to avoid the trap of meaningless existence is to be gracefully idle. If, as Stewart Goetz explains, "the irony of being human [is] that our lives are ultimately absurd or meaningless," then it is perfectly feasible to fashion a purposeful life even if the purpose is not to take life seriously (6). Gloria would at first accept a mate who has the conviction and means to be deliberately lazy, "if they're gracefully lazy"; but she wonders "Is that possible for an American?"—a challenge to which Anthony is willing to rise in order not to do "dull, unimaginative work, certainly not altruistic work" (60). The couple aim to use their already comfortable income (before the flush of the Patch inheritance) to be "efficient people of leisure" enjoying the satisfactions and existential ease of "the majesty of leisure" (178, 180). However, boredom becomes the close companion of nothing worthwhile to do, and when Anthony complains, "As a matter of fact I think that if I hadn't met you I *would* have done something. But you make leisure so subtly attractive—" he exposes the flaw in their plans.

Gloria, too, reveals a longing for something more fundamental when she later turns from "a violent affirmation of the negative principle 'Never give a damn'" (172) to be "haunted by the suggestion that life might be, after all, significant" (238).[2]

The unsettling sense of nothingness and consequent unhappiness in Gloria and Anthony's lives is expressed through their careless discussion of an abortion for Gloria and the subsequent induced miscarriage or phantom pregnancy (173, 177), her doubts and infrequent but persistent considerations about motherhood, and most dramatically in her lightning-storm-induced fright about "the thing" that drives her frantically from her bedroom in the grey house—with half of her bed rain-soaked from an open window, like a traumatic nightmare of a fetal termination. She runs out into the wind-tossed night to escape not only the confines of an increasingly sterile and fractious marriage but above all the oppressive fear of life's insignificance (203–9).[3] The insouciance of her initial attitude toward an abortion is also a factor here; for even considering a destructive invasion of her womb, the most elemental interior space, comes back to haunt her as an inescapable liminal desire for a real child, or a child reformulated from and into Anthony: "So her dreams were of ghostly children only—the early, the perfect symbols of her early and perfect love for Anthony" (324).

Anthony also suffers from uncertainties, not only about his future prosperity but also about his ultimate end. Thus, he experiences episodes of unprovoked fear. These are comparable to his grandfather's old-age-related "night-sweats and tears and unfounded dreads" (20) that are likely to have foundations in not only his fear of death but also guilt about the spurious accumulation of his fortune, earned in the aftermath of Civil War service, when he "charged into Wall Street, and amid much fuss, fume, applause, and ill will he gathered to himself some seventy-five million dollars" (12). Anthony exhibits an inherent nervousness that Gloria diagnoses as cowardice, sharply expressed to her in the tight atmosphere of a San Francisco hotel room not long after their marriage. He leaps from slumber into a panicked state, although he first says it is "Nothing," and the night clerk who comes to check the room for any intruder outside of the window declares conclusively, "Nobody out there" (136–37). The threat here is clearly related to the nothingness at the heart of Anthony and Gloria's existential insecurities, a present and a future with nothing out there.

Both of Anthony's parents die before his twelfth birthday, instilling his permanent fear of death (13–14) and a deep-seated insecurity that fulfilling work might help to soothe. The twenty million dead in the Great War and the random nature of death in the trenches of the Western Front reinforce the bleak view that nothing matters in an illogical world. However, instead of growing up to face their responsibilities and redirect their lives to match their nation's mobilized new energies, Anthony and Gloria struggle to deploy themselves to the kind of work that the friends in their social sphere are eager to take up. During America's neutrality, Anthony is indecisive about his grandfather's offer to set him up as a war correspondent, and Gloria only briefly considers going to Europe as a nurse. When the United States declares war, Maury and Dick both enlist and are accepted into officer's training, but Anthony's low blood pressure invalidates his own application (and links symbolically with the low expectations of an easy resolution to the inheritance that he expects from his bloodline). So when he is drafted, another decision is made for him. In such an indifferent and pointless world, he "wanted, above all things, to be killed," he tells Gloria (257–58). However, Anthony's drifting character and inability to direct himself to a meaningful occupation is superseded by the imposed service and ordered discipline of the Army. At first contemptuous of dull and dishonest officers who are not his social superiors, he learns to apply himself to enforced duties, rises to the rank of Sergeant Patch, and is about to be reassigned to officer's training, only to be stripped of his rank when he is caught lying about his identity in order to reenter camp after curfew (287–91).

Anthony's varied efforts to establish a genuine identity through work collapse under the weight of American commerce's demands for conformity and his dread of ordinariness. Before the war, as a precursor to Nick Carraway's foray into the bond business in *The Great Gatsby* with the Probity Trust (*GG* 68), Anthony tepidly enters the office pool of young men in the firm of Wilson, Hiemer and Hardy. His mentor, an energetic young man about Anthony's age named Kahler, aspires to rise from his position as assistant secretary and points Anthony toward the ultimate reach of assistant vice president or maybe president, secretary, or treasurer—a telling hierarchical sequence of responsible roles in the palpable handling of money. The new recruit Anthony squirms under the "uneasy suspicion that he was being uplifted," and he is appalled by the narrow vision of American aspiration based on rapid capital gains in the booming markets: "He felt that to succeed here the idea of success must grasp and limit his mind" (194). He quits abruptly, another "triumph of lethargy" (182) that yields ironic resonance throughout the novel because he simply waits for his fortune to arrive through the court contestation of Adam Patch's will, expending a great deal of worry but not tedious industry toward that result. After the war, a less secure opportunity in sales opens up for Anthony, the dodgy "Heart Talks" scheme of promoting the power of positive thinking to an ingenuous public. However, he is in the throes of alcohol addiction by this point, and he unwisely selects discerning and suspicious people for his sales pitch. Perhaps in this instance his instincts and his own initial doubts are right about the merits of engaging in what feels like a Ponzi scheme. Yet he is attracted by the dynamic speaker who first invites potential salesmen to a meeting, promising "that *you* and *you* and *you* have the heritage of money and prosperity waiting for you to come and claim it" (313). The words seem to speak from Anthony's own conviction of his rightful inheritance and the happiness it seems to promise.

The attentive reader will be prepared for the shortcomings of that promise because of the interior description of Anthony's Fifty-Second Street apartment early in the text: "There was a deep lounge of the softest brown leather with somnolence drifting about it like a haze. There was a high screen of Chinese lacquer chiefly concerned with geometrical fishermen and huntsmen in black and gold; this made a corner alcove for a voluminous chair guarded by an orange-colored standing lamp. Deep in the fireplace a quartered shield was burned to a murky black" (17). The relaxing and relaxed atmosphere of sybaritic indulgence is most evident, but note also the fishermen and huntsmen illustrated on the screen, men at work but fixed in Keatsian attitudes by the colors of moneymaking and money symbolism, black and gold. His secluded alcove contains a chair "guarded" by a lamp and the fireplace's "quartered shield," drawing upon military metaphors to reference Anthony's future half-hearted endeavors as a writer and as a soldier ("burned to a murky black"), the heraldic shield quartered in the generational division of the Patch inheritance. He neither toils "Nor Does He Spin," as the fourth subtitled section of book 1, chapter 1, announces (18), a section positioned between sections about place ("The Reproachless Apartment" [16]) and time ("Afternoon" [22]) that bookend Fitzgerald's concerns about meaning and being, between concrete locations for work and contemplation, along with the ability to understand one's place and purpose in the temporal world.

Fitzgerald indicates that a large calculation of Anthony and Gloria's failure to find gainful employment and thereby gain their own lives is that they both see work in terms of performance. John T. Irwin constructs his study of the author's oeuvre around the theme of theatricality, but he also notes "the way that all human values are in danger of collapsing when money becomes the single most precious thing in people's lives" (28). Anthony and Gloria's problem might, therefore, be insurmountable because their society endorses that concept and they feel that work is simply a matter of performing for money. Gloria's attachment to the movies is the most obvious indication of this condition, as she is distraught to find that the movie industry values her only in a specific component of its machinery, "a small character part supposed to be a very haughty rich widow" (333). In the aftershock of her recognition of the loss of her beauty, by which she had chiefly defined herself, "Anthony and Gloria had become like players who had lost their costumes, lacking the pride to continue on the note of tragedy" (334). Again, Fitzgerald reinforces the personal and the environmental state of their situation through the space given to Gloria's full realization of her lost chance to use her beauty and talent for performance in film-acting, work that would have captured if not preserved her youth on celluloid, and provided some evidence of her vibrant individuality.[4] Instead, in their down-market eighty-five-dollar-per-month apartment "in the dim hundreds" (334), she is depicted in existential straits, drinking whiskey and crying alone: "She wondered if they were tears of self-pity, and tried resolutely not to cry, but this existence without hope, without happiness, oppressed her, and she kept shaking her head from side to side, her mouth drawn down tremulously in the corners, as though she were denying an assertion made by someone, somewhere." And then the author adds a sentence with a suspicious word amid the philosophical epigraphy: "She did not know that this gesture of hers was years older than history, that, for a hundred generations of men, intolerable and persistent grief has offered that gesture, of denial, of protest, of bewilderment, to something more profound, more powerful than the God made in the image of man" (341). Readers will be wary of the repeated *gesture* involved here, and their sympathy for Gloria tempered because, beyond the sentimental hyperbole in that passage, the text earlier uses the device of a diary entry, with its presumably intimate insight into her thoughts and feelings, to provide some important information about her character before her marriage to Anthony: "What grubworms women are to crawl on their bellies through colorless marriages! Marriage was created not to be a background but to need one. Mine is going to be outstanding. It can't, shan't be the setting—it's going to be the performance, the live, lovely, glamourous performance, and the world shall be the scenery" (127). Besides the irony of situation that the novel pursues in proving her declaration wrong during the course of her marriage, the text also highlights an irony of location, in the steadily shabbier settings of her marriage to Anthony, the progressively smaller and more constricting rooms that they inhabit along with the narrower expectations that they have of each other and of their lives, as they eventually focus their sole hope and desire on the inheritance fortune.

Before that dramatic, late, and clearly staged textual reversal in their downward economic and moral spiral, the novel presents some revealing scenes in which the themes of nihilism and failed vocation are woven into the fabric of interior settings. A key example takes place in "the grey house" in Marietta, a colonial building that, fittingly, Anthony and Gloria accidentally discover for a summer residence when, as she explains to the real-estate agent with a tellingly irresponsible casualness: "We broke down. . . . I drove over a fire-hydrant and we had ourselves towed to the garage and then we saw your sign" (152). Besides the hopes that a loving marriage can flourish here in the grey house, the building also serves as the vortex for the political and social changes about to engulf the United States as it enters the Great War. Colonial and contemporary history as well as a transitory period in the young couple's lives meet here and tumble together afterward in a disappointment of hopes. Their conversation about his half-hearted desire to work is staged between shots of first Gloria and then Anthony relaxing on a hammock. He claims not to "have any moral compunctions about work" and has been happy to "loaf gracefully" (178) and lapse into idleness. "I have worked—some," he feebly claims to Gloria, before she delineates the observable truth:

> "Work!" she scoffed. "Oh, you sad bird! You bluffer! Work—that means a
> great deal of arranging of the desk and the lights, a great sharpening of pencils,
> and 'Gloria, don't sing!' . . . and 'Let me read you my opening sentence,' and
> 'I won't be through for a long time, Gloria, so don't stay up for me,' and a
> tremendous consumption of tea or coffee. And that's all . . . Then yawns—
> then bed and a great tossing about because you're all full of caffeine and
> can't sleep. Two weeks later the whole performance over again." (179)

Most literate observers will recognize these procrastinations as the perfectly normal routine of a writer, but Gloria also calls the activity a "performance," in line with the way that work is perceived throughout the novel. His futile attempts to achieve something real and lasting from his labor demonstrate not only, as he claims, how the distractions of life prevent him from using his mind for creative production; they also reflect America's association of hard work with either selfish prosperity or selfless denial for the sake of children and family, rather than hard work for the satisfaction of the concentrated effort itself. Work as an ideal, then, becomes confined within American prisons, like Hawthorne's Custom House (*Scarlet Letter* 1–42) or Willy Loman's mobile office (A. Miller).[5]

Work, spaces, and values converge in *The Beautiful and Damned*. Anthony becomes the black hole in the text where social and moral values collapse, and interior spaces exhibit his centripetal decline—whether in the bachelor apartment where he acknowledges his loneliness and plots his pursuit of beauty, in the party lounge of his rented summer house where his fate as a disinherited aristocrat is determined, or in bedrooms where his fears and disintegrations are exposed. "You don't do anything—so nothing matters," Gloria tells her husband, expressing the text's underlying critique of America's class structure, capital stratification, hollow idealism, and what may be a peculiarly metropolitan nihilism. But Gloria has it wrong, for Fitzgerald damns them for a deeper failure: for them nothing matters, so they do not or cannot do anything. The existential void suggested in her words is further represented in the offstage courtrooms where the Patch will and inheritance is decided, in the locked hotel room where Mr. Shuttleworth, the loser of the legal case, commits suicide. As a portrait of social exclusion, moral exhaustion, and mistaken ideals, the constricted spaces frame a key aspect of Fitzgerald's early fiction and reinforce the narrative design of a novel filled with emptiness and nothingness, a theme startlingly exhibited in the disabled mental and physical condition that Anthony Patch occupies just before the deus ex machina of the court verdict that unexpectedly settles the will in his favor.

Often childish in their carefree behavior leading to that settlement, the couple act "like bewildered babes in the wood" (148). Anthony's youthful hobby of stamp collecting is the equivalent of Charles Foster Kane's Rosebud sled, a happy combination of concentrated interest and joy. Vicariously traveling through the stamps' multicolored geographic variety and the solitary pleasure they offer to him, Anthony plays with them with an intensity that no other activity holds for him (14). Their value is later diffused somewhat by the dissipations of his early marriage but is recovered when he remembers at the last minute not to leave them behind when departing from the grey house (235). The final image of his philatelic obsession is in the penultimate section of the narrative, a scene of madness and physical collapse that finds him "sitting on a patch of sunshine on the floor of his bedroom. Before him, open, were spread his three big stamp books, and . . . he was running his hands through a great pile of stamps that he had dumped from the back of one of them" (367). The enclosed isolation of his possessive childlike enjoyment ends in a disorderly emotional spillage within the sunshine patch that will mark the boundaries of his defeat. Gloria, who "neither said so nor gave any show or sign of interest in children," becomes at thirty "a lonely, lovely woman . . . retrenched behind some *impregnable* inhibition *born* and coexistent with her beauty" (349; emphasis added); yet she buys and dresses a doll when loneliness penetrates her emotional armor (308), and the final image of her is of a barren woman serving as the nursemaid for her infantilized husband.[6]

Gideon Baker explains in *Nihilism and Philosophy* how the nihilist principle that truth does not exist was addressed by Martin Heidegger's exploration of "a truth not *of* the world but a truth *in* the world" (6). That pursuit defines the critical aspects of Nietzsche's influence on Fitzgerald, in the philosopher's radical "re-evaluation of all values," his efforts to diagnose the sickness of society and prescribe cures for the patient humankind. Fitzgerald's novel focuses on questions of truth *in* the world without providing even palliative care—except, perhaps, for the caustic depiction of the committed but wayward nihilist Anthony Patch, last shown in the text as "a bundled figure seated in a wheel chair near the rail" of the *Berengaria,* accompanied on board by his wife and a private physician, and last heard whispering to himself a pathetic defense of his determination *not* "to give in, to submit to mediocrity, to go to work" (369). Anthony's negation could be understood as a triumph of sorts, of will or willfulness, but it is a poor reflection of the capabilities of human intelligence and the capacity of the human spirit.

In the concluding chapter of Voltaire's *Candide* (1759), the surviving characters reflect upon the nature and meaning of life as they sit outside of their farmhouse near Constantinople.[7] One day, when their philosophical disputations had ceased,

the boredom was so intolerable that the old woman was provoked to remark: "I should like to know which is the worst, to be ravished a hundred
times by negro pirates, to have one buttock cut off, to run the gauntlet of
a Bulgar regiment, to be whipped and hanged at an auto-da-fe, to be dissected, to row in the galleys—in fact, to experience all the miseries through
which we have passed—or just to stay here with nothing to do?" "That's a
difficult question," said Candide. The old woman's speech produced fresh
reflections. Martin's conclusion was that man was born to suffer from the
restlessness of anxiety or from the lethargy of boredom. . . . Pangloss allowed that his sufferings had been uniformly horrible; but as he had once
maintained that everything would turn out right in some marvelous way,
he still maintained it would, however little he believed it. (140)

The etiological and ontological conundrums addressed in *Candide* resonate
in *The Beautiful and Damned* through the lives of Anthony Patch and Gloria
Gilbert Patch. Admittedly, neither experiences quite the same exotic range of
traumatic experiences as Voltaire's characters, but the novel's main protagonists
suffer from both the restlessness of anxiety *and* the lethargy of boredom. "The
Beating," set in the winter of 1920, is the antepenultimate section of Fitzgerald's
novel. Gloria and Anthony are living in their dingy flat on Claremont Avenue
in the Morningside Heights neighborhood of Upper Manhattan. "For hours
at a time he would sit in the great armchair that had been in his apartment,"
positioned within that single remaining vestige of his luxurious bachelorhood,
but he is now "lost in a sort of stupor—" (349). Dragging himself from that
tight space, he heads into the city with their last four dollars in cash to buy
some food and, more deliberately, a drink of alcohol. His journey to the bottom takes him waywardly from Sam's bar to a drunken meeting outside the
Biltmore Hotel with his old companion Maury Noble, who snubs him (356),
to the lower lobby of the Boul' Mich' dance club for an aggressive encounter
with the enterprising Jewish filmmaker Joseph Bloeckman (reincarnated as
Joseph Black), who punches him (360), and finally to the darkness of a taxi and
an unrecompensed fare that he pays for with a severe beating, with the moon
"shedding light down into Claremont Avenue as into the bottom of a deep and
unchartered abyss" (363).

Beyond the subsequent and lasting physiological and neurological damage to Anthony, the scene highlights the enfeebled nature of his intellectual

vision. "The Beating" is contained in book 3, chapter 3, which is entitled "No Matter!," a declaration that reflects Gloria's earlier "Never give a damn" (172) attitude toward life and signals Anthony's descent into the abyss of unknowing. He struggles to understand what can matter because of the perplexing and contradictory choices that life has offered to him: money from a cold and demanding grandfather, Gloria's beauty as a prize as well as an excuse for lethargy, the somatic comforts of his bathroom and apartment, the leisure of a dilettante gentleman adrift in America and Europe, the potential for creative endeavor through writing, the companionship of good friends. The philosopher Richard Hare writes (in a chapter he labels "Nothing Matters"): "There are real struggles and perplexities about what matters most," and falling into doubt or confusion about what we value most "introduces a shallow stagnation into our thought about values. We content ourselves with the appreciation of things, like eating, which most people can appreciate without effort, and never learn to prize those things whose true value is apparent only to those who have fought hard to reach it" (46–47). Yes, Anthony is able to proclaim in the text's closing words, "I showed them. . . . It was a hard fight, but I didn't give up and I came through!" But coming from a man wrecked physically and mentally, this is a pyrrhic victory, hard-fought but hollow. He has earned through pesky endurance and luck an empty inheritance but gained little of true value as the couple sail into the past of his boyhood dream to settle in Europe, a graveyard for his future, with only Gloria's doughty maintenance for company.

In the conclusion to *Candide*, the moral of the story is expressed in a three-way dialogue between Candide, Pangloss, and Martin. Candide says, "'we must go and work in the garden.' 'You are quite right,' said Pangloss. 'When man was placed in the Garden of Eden, he was put there "to dress it and to keep it," to work, in fact; which proves that man was not born to an easy life.' 'We must work without arguing,' said Martin; 'that is the only way to make life bearable'" (143–44). *The Beautiful and Damned* situates itself within this literary tradition of philosophical contemplation about the meaning and the value of work, the dangers of accepting life without purposeful labor, and the importance of work even if only as a necessary illusion of self-fulfillment or a confirmation of being. The compulsion to work drove F. Scott Fitzgerald to write three novels and more than three dozen short stories within the first five years of his professional career; and in the last year of his life, when meeting challenges to his confidence and productivity, he wrote to his daughter: "What little I've accomplished has been by the most laborious and uphill work, and I wish now I'd *never* relaxed or looked back—but said at the end of *The Great Gatsby:* 'I've found my line—from now on this comes first. This is my immediate duty—without this I am nothing'" (*Fitzgerald: A Life in Letters* 451). In writing *The Beautiful and Damned,* Fitzgerald most clearly expressed the absolute necessity of work as a vital measure of human worth.

NOTES

1. Benjamin Franklin's *Autobiography* and Thomas Carlyle's evangelization of the Gospel of Work contain similar promotions of the value of work in obtaining personal security, social unity, and moral goodness. On the virtue of industriousness, Franklin offers the precepts: "Lose no Time.—Be always employ'd in something useful.—Cut off all unnecessary Actions" (1385). Carlyle proclaims in *Past and Present* (1843): "For there is perennial nobleness, even sacredness in Work. Were he never so benighted, forgetful of his high calling, there is always hope in a man that actually and earnestly works: in Idleness alone is there perpetual despair (168). For Carlyle and further sources, see Bradshaw and Ozmet.

2. From at first hardly being capable of picking up her own dirty clothes to put in a laundry bag (140–42), Gloria does eventually acquire some practical lessons in subsistence, three years later, when their funds run dry and she has learned to make her own coffee and "prepared sometimes three meals a day" (349).

3. If "the thing" mainly has sexual and maternal overtones, it also relates to Arthur Schopenhauer's concept of the World Will, defined by Terry Eagleton as "a horrific rather than exalted truth, one which gives birth to havoc, chaos, and perpetual misery . . . like a malevolent caricature of the Almighty" (82).

4. Gloria contemplates working in the movies four different times, but with this actual attempt when she is approaching the age of thirty, "It cheered her that in some manner the illusion of beauty could be sustained, or preserved perhaps in celluloid after the reality had vanished" (325). The conditional words *could be* and *perhaps* are purposefully inserted, for this is not the Golden Age of the Hollywood studio system of the 1930s to 1950s, when iconic stars could have their images preserved for future generations. Produced on volatile nitrate-based celluloid film stock that easily deteriorated or caught fire, the films of the silent era were expendable, often discarded after their initial commercial run. Moreover, at the time in which the novel is set, the 35mm format had yet to be standardized and manufacturing of camera film was still in an experimental stage before the industry came to be dominated by the Eastman Company. In that manner, Mr. Gilbert loses his pioneering celluloid business because "the moving-picture industry had decided about 1912 to gobble him up" (40). Mr. Gilbert's death, therefore, is not incidental to the novel's depiction of instability and the themes of waste and decline. Gloria's father "had spent his last days in a small hotel" (253), reinforcing the novel's spatial imagery of physical constraint and thwarted ambition.

5. However, an alternative reading of the relationship between work and leisure can be found in the history of "play theory" as it developed at the turn into the twentieth century. The scientific

management methods of the era evolved into organized routines for Americans to relax and play, designed chiefly to enable more efficient work (see Gleason, *The Leisure Ethic,* for a historical analysis of the Gospel of Play).

6. In not giving birth to a child, Gloria might be consoled by David Benatar's argument in *Better Never to Have Been:* "Because there is nothing bad about never coming into existence, but there is something bad about coming into existence, it seems that all things considered nonexistence is preferable" (44).

7. The monastery "anachronistically known as St. Voltaire's" (81) features in Anthony's storytelling of the "Deplorable End of the Chevalier O'Keefe."

CONTRIBUTORS

WILLIAM BLAZEK is professor of American literature and modern culture at Liverpool Hope University. He is a founding coeditor of the *F. Scott Fitzgerald Review* and has served on the executive board of the Fitzgerald Society since 2008 and as the society's vice president since 2020. He is the coeditor of two essay collections, *American Mythologies* (with Michael K. Glenday, 2005) and *Twenty-First-Century Readings of "Tender Is the Night"* (with Laura Rattray, 2007). His recent publications include the new Oxford World's Classics edition of *The Beautiful and Damned* (2022) and essays on F. Scott Fitzgerald, Ernest Hemingway, Edith Wharton, and Anglo-American literature of the First World War.

JACKSON R. BRYER is professor emeritus of English at the University of Maryland, the cofounder and president of the F. Scott Fitzgerald Society, and an editor of the *F. Scott Fitzgerald Review*. Among the books he has authored, edited, or coedited on Fitzgerald are *Approaches to Teaching Fitzgerald's "The Great Gatsby"* (2009); *Dear Scott, Dearest Zelda: The Love Letters of F. Scott and Zelda Fitzgerald* (2002); *New Essays on F. Scott Fitzgerald's Neglected Stories* (1996); *The Critical Reputation of F. Scott Fitzgerald: A Bibliographical Study* (1967; 1984); *The Short Stories of F. Scott Fitzgerald: New Approaches in Criticism* (1982); *F. Scott Fitzgerald: The Critical Reception* (1978); *Dear Scott/Dear Max: The Fitzgerald-Perkins Correspondence* (1971); and *F. Scott Fitzgerald in His Own Time: A Miscellany* (1971).

KIRK CURNUTT is professor of English at Troy University. He is the author of *The Cambridge Introduction to F. Scott Fitzgerald* and the editor of *All of the Belles: The Montgomery Stories of F. Scott Fitzgerald*, which collects Fitzgerald's three stories about Tarleton, Georgia. Curnutt serves as managing editor of the *F. Scott Fitzgerald Review* as well as executive director of the Fitzgerald Society.

MEREDITH GOLDSMITH is professor of English and associate dean of academic affairs at Ursinus College. She has published on F. Scott Fitzgerald, Edith Wharton, Anzia Yezierska, Jessie Fauset, and Nella Larsen and is the coeditor of three anthologies of literary scholarship on late nineteenth- and early twentieth-century American literature.

BONNIE SHANNON MCMULLEN is an independent scholar in Oxford, England. She has published numerous scholarly articles on George Eliot, Edgar Allan Poe, F. Scott Fitzgerald, and other writers. She has contributed to *A Distant Drummer: Foreign Perspectives on F. Scott Fitzgerald,* edited by Jamal Assadi and William Freedman (2007); *Twenty-First-Century Readings of "Tender Is the Night,"* edited by William Blazek and Laura Rattray (2007); and *F. Scott Fitzgerald in Context,* edited by Bryant Mangum (2013). "Echoes of Poe in the Jazz Age: The Haunting of F. Scott Fitzgerald" is forthcoming in *Retrospective Poe,* edited by Jose Ibanez and Santiago Rodriguez.

WALTER RAUBICHECK is professor of English at Pace University in New York, where he teaches American literature, film, and college composition. He is the coauthor of *Scripting Hitchcock* (2011) and coeditor of *Hitchcock's Rereleased Films* (1991), both with Walter Srebnick. He also edited *Hitchcock and the Cold War* (2019). He has published essays on F. Scott Fitzgerald, T. S. Eliot, and Dashiell Hammett and on a number of crime fiction authors, including Arthur Conan Doyle, Dorothy Sayers, and G. K. Chesterton.

GAIL D. SINCLAIR, founding executive director and scholar-in-residence at the Winter Park Institute at Rollins College, teaches in the master of liberal studies program. She has served more than a decade on the F. Scott Fitzgerald Society board. Her publications include essays in *Approaches to Teaching Fitzgerald's "The Great Gatsby"* (2009) and *F. Scott Fitzgerald in Context* (2013), and reviews and commentary on Fitzgerald's life in the *F. Scott Fitzgerald Review,* in addition to publications on Ernest Hemingway, Edith Wharton, Norman Mailer, John Updike, and other modernist writers.

JOSEPH K. STITT is associate lecturer at Birmingham-Southern College. He also has worked as an online content coordinator and a humor writer for an America Online affiliate company. His fiction and poetry have appeared in the *Seattle Review, Aura Literary Arts Review,* and *Paumanok Review.*

DAVID W. ULLRICH is professor of English at Birmingham-Southern College. He has served as an editor on the *F. Scott Fitzgerald Review* since 2014 and has been an Aspen Institute Fellow. He divides his research interests between British romanticism and American modernism, having published on William Blake, Samuel Taylor Coleridge, and Maria Edgeworth in romanticism and Fitzgerald and Hemingway in American modernism. His most recent publication is on John Cheever's "The Swimmer."

RICHARD WEBB JR. has taught history for twenty-four years at both the secondary and college levels. A featured presenter in the Connecticut Public Broadcasting Prohibition documentary *Connecticut Goes Dry,* he coproduced *Gatsby in Connecticut,* a documentary about the Fitzgeralds' months in Westport, Connecticut. His companion book to the film, *Boats against the Current,* recounts Webb's own journey of making the film with fellow Westporter Robert Steven Williams.

JAMES L. W. WEST III is Edwin Erle Sparks Professor of English Emeritus at Pennsylvania State University. He is the author of *The Perfect Hour: The Romance of F. Scott Fitzgerald and Ginevra King* (2005) and the general editor emeritus of the Cambridge Edition of the Works of F. Scott Fitzgerald, complete in eighteen volumes, sixteen of them under his editorship. West's edition of *The Beautiful and Damned* appeared in the Cambridge series in 2008. He is editing a new volume of Fitzgerald's writings for the Library of America.

WORKS CITED

Adams, Brooks. *The Law of Civilization and Decay: An Essay on History*. Macmillan, 1896.

Adams, Henry. *The Education of Henry Adams*. Houghton Mifflin, 1918.

———. *Mont-Saint-Michel and Chartres*. Houghton Mifflin, 1913.

Anonymous. *Madeleine: An Autobiography*. Harper and Brothers, 1919.

Antolin, Pascale. "New York in *The Beautiful and Damned*: 'A City of Words.'" *F. Scott Fitzgerald Review* 7 (2009): 113–25.

Aquinas, Thomas. *Summa Theologica*. Trans. Fathers of the English Dominican Province. 1947. Archon, 1967.

Astro, Richard. "*Vandover and the Brute* and *The Beautiful and Damned*: A Search for Thematic and Stylistic Reinterpretation." *Modern Fiction Studies* 14.4 (1968–69): 397–413.

"Author on the Rocks." *Westporter-Herald* 25 June 1920, 1.

B., M.P. "The Meaninglessness of Life." *Harvard Crimson* 10 March 1922. https://www.thecrimson.com/article/1922/3/10/the-meaninglessness-of-life-the-story/.

Baker, Gideon. *Nihilism and Philosophy: Nothingness, Truth and World*. Bloomsbury, 2018.

Barron, James. "Finding the Background of 'Gatsby' in Connecticut, Not Long Island." *New York Times* 20 May 2018. https://www.nytimes.com/2018/05/20/nyregion/great-gatsby-setting-connecticut-long-island.html.

Bates, Anna Louise. *Weeder in The Garden of the Lord: Anthony Comstock's Life and Career*. UP of America, 1995.

Baym, Nina. *Novels, Readers, and Reviewers: Responses to Fiction in Antebellum America*. Cornell UP, 1984.

The Beach Boys. *Surf's Up*. Brother/Reprise, 1971.

Beard, George Miller. *American Nervousness: Its Causes and Consequences*. Putnam's, 1881.

The Beautiful and Damned. Dir. Sidney Franklin. Warner Bros., 1923.

The Beautiful and Damned. Dir. Richard Wolstencroft. Accent Film Entertainment, 2009.

Benatar, David. *Better Never to Have Been: The Harm of Coming into Existence.* Oxford UP, 2006.

Benjamin, Walter. *The Arcades Project.* Trans. Howard Eiland and Kevin McLaughlin. Belknap P of Harvard UP, 1999.

Benn Michaels, Walter. *Our America: Nativism, Modernism, Pluralism.* Duke UP, 1995.

Bennett, D. M. *Anthony Comstock: His Career of Cruelty and Crime.* Bennett, 1878.

Bergson, Henri. *Creative Evolution.* Trans. Arthur Mitchell. Holt, 1911.

Berman, Ronald. "Intellectual Influences." Mangum, *F. Scott Fitzgerald in Context* 56–65.

Berret, Anthony J. *Music in the Works of F. Scott Fitzgerald: Unheard Melodies.* Fairleigh Dickinson UP/Rowman and Littlefield, 2013.

Beuka, Robert. *SuburbiaNation: Reading Suburban Landscape in Twentieth-Century American Fiction and Film.* Palgrave Macmillan, 2004.

The Bible. Douay-Rheims Version, Challoner Revision. E-book, Project Gutenberg, 2020.

The Big Lebowski. Dir. Joel Coen. Working Title Films, 1998.

Bigelow, Frederick Southgate. *A Short History of "The Saturday Evening Post": "An American Institution" in Three Centuries.* Curtis, 1927.

Birkerts, Sven. "Reading in a Digital Age: Notes on Why the Novel and the Internet Are Opposites, and Why the Latter Both Undermines the Former and Makes It More Necessary." *American Scholar* 1 Mar. 2010. https://theamericanscholar.org /reading-in-a-digital-age/.

Bishop, John Peale, and Edmund Wilson. *The Undertaker's Garland.* Knopf, 1922.

Bodenheim, Maxwell. "Garbage Heap." *Double Dealer* 3.16 (Apr. 1922): 202.

Boersma, Hans. *Nouvelle Theologie and Sacramental Ontology: A Return to Mystery.* Oxford UP, 2009.

Boese, Alex. "The September Morn Hoax." 2015. hoaxes.org/archive/permalink/the _september_morn_hoax.

Boyd, Nancy [Edna St. Vincent Millay]. *Distressing Dialogues.* Harper and Brothers, 1924.

———. [Edna St. Vincent Millay and Norma Millay]. "Sentimental Solon." *Metropolitan Magazine* 54.3 (Oct. 1921): 15–16, 60–63.

Boyd, Thomas A. "Hugh Walpole Was the Man Who Started Me Writing Novels." *F. Scott Fitzgerald in His Own Time: A Miscellany.* Ed. Matthew J. Bruccoli and Jackson R. Bryer. Kent State UP, 1971. 245–54.

Bradshaw, David, and Susan Ozment, eds. *The Voice of Toil: Nineteenth-Century British Writings about Work.* Ohio UP, 2000.

Breitwieser, Mitchell. "*The Great Gatsby*: Grief, Jazz, and the Eye-Witness." *Arizona Quarterly* 47.3 (1991): 17–70.

Brooks, Van Wyck. *Days of the Phoenix: The Nineteen-Twenties I Remember.* Dutton, 1957.

———. *The Ordeal of Mark Twain.* Scribner's, 1920.

Broun, Heywood, and Margaret Leech. *Anthony Comstock: Roundsman of the Lord.* Literary Guild of America, 1927.

Brown, David S. *Paradise Lost: A Life of F. Scott Fitzgerald.* Belknap P of Harvard UP, 2017.

Bruccoli, Matthew J., ed. *As Ever, Scott Fitz—: Letters between F. Scott Fitzgerald and His Literary Agent, Harold Ober, 1919–1940.* With the assistance of Jennifer McCabe Atkinson. Lippincott, 1972.

———. "Bibliographical Notes on F. Scott Fitzgerald's *The Beautiful and Damned.*" *Studies in Bibliography* 13 (1960): 258–61.

———. *F. Scott Fitzgerald: A Descriptive Bibliography.* Rev. ed. U of Pittsburgh P, 1987.

———. *Some Sort of Epic Grandeur: The Life of F. Scott Fitzgerald.* 2nd rev. ed. U of South Carolina P, 2002.

Bruccoli, Matthew J., and Judith S. Baughman, eds. *Conversations with F. Scott Fitzgerald.* UP of Mississippi, 2004.

Bruccoli, Matthew J., and Jackson R. Bryer, eds. *F. Scott Fitzgerald in His Own Time: A Miscellany.* Kent State UP, 1971.

Bruccoli, Matthew J., Scottie Fitzgerald Smith, and Joan P. Kerr, eds. *The Romantic Egoists: A Pictorial Autobiography from the Scrapbooks and Albums of F. Scott and Zelda Fitzgerald.* Scribner's, 1974.

Bryer, Jackson. "'Better That All of the Story Never Be Told': Zelda Fitzgerald's Sister's Letters to Arthur Mizener." *F. Scott Fitzgerald Review* 15 (2017): 1–16.

———. *The Critical Reputation of F. Scott Fitzgerald: A Bibliographical Study.* Archon, 1967.

———. *F. Scott Fitzgerald: The Critical Reception.* Franklin, 1978.

———, ed. *New Essays on F. Scott Fitzgerald's Neglected Stories.* U of Missouri P, 1996. 23–34.

Bryer, Jackson, and Cathy W. Barks, eds. *Dear Scott, Dearest Zelda: The Love Letters of F. Scott and Zelda Fitzgerald.* Scribner, 2002.

Bryer, Jackson, et al., eds. *F. Scott Fitzgerald in the Twenty-First Century.* U of Alabama P, 2003.

Bryer, Jackson R., Alan Margolies, and Ruth Prigozy, eds. *F. Scott Fitzgerald: New Perspectives.* U of Georgia P, 2000.

Burroughs, Catherine B. "Keats's Lamian Legacy: Romance and the Performance of Gender in *The Beautiful and Damned.*" Bryer, Margolies, Prigozy, 51–62.

Burton, Robert. *Anatomy of Melancholy.* 1621–28. Introduction by William H. Gass. New York Review of Books, 2001.

Butler, Samuel. *The Notebooks of Samuel Butler.* Ed. Henry Festing Jones. Fifield, 1912.

Carlyle, Thomas. *Past and Present.* Chapman & Hall, 1843.

Carter, John F., Jr. "These Wild Young People." *Atlantic Monthly* Sept. 1926: 301–4.

Chambers, John B. *The Novels of F. Scott Fitzgerald.* St. Martin's P, 1989.

Chambers, Robert W. *The Younger Set.* Appleton, 1907.

"Charges Levy Heads Bootleggers' Ring." *Boston Globe* 19 Nov. 1920, 1.

The Chorus Girl's Romance. Dir. William C. Dowland, Metro, 1920.

Churchwell, Sarah. *Careless People: Murder, Mayhem and the Invention of "The Great Gatsby."* Penguin, 2014.

———. "'The Scandal Detectives': *Town Topics* and F. Scott Fitzgerald, 1916–1923." *F. Scott Fitzgerald Review* 18 (2020): 1–47.

Cline, Sally. *Zelda Fitzgerald: Her Voice in Paradise.* Arcade, 2003.

Clymer, Jeffory. "Mr. Nobody from Nowhere: Rudolph Valentino, Jay Gatsby, and the End of the American Race." *Genre* 29.1–2 (1996): 161–92.

Cochoy, Nathalie. "New York as a 'Passing Stranger' in *The Beautiful and Damned.*" *F. Scott Fitzgerald Review* 4 (2005): 65–83.

"Compo Beach Pavilion Scene of Midnight Orgies." *Westporter-Herald* 22 Aug. 1919, 1.

Comstock, Anthony. *Traps for the Young.* 1883. Introduction by J. M. Buckley. 4th ed. Palala P, 2015.

"Comstock Dooms September Morning." *New York Times* 11 May 1913, 1.

"Comstock Takes Hand in Physical Culture Show." *New York Times* 6 Oct. 1906, 9.

Conductor 1492. Dir. Charles Hines. Warner Bros., 1924.

Connolly, Cyril. *The Rock Pool.* Obelisk P, 1936.

Conrad, Joseph. Author's Note to *The Shadow-Line: A Confession.* 1920. Ed. J. H. Stape and Allan H. Simmons, Cambridge UP, 2013. v–x.

Cory, Herbert Ellsworth. "The Senility of the Short Story." *Dial* 62.3 (May 1917): 79–81.

Crane, Stephen. *Maggie: A Girl of the Streets.* Appleton, 1896.

Cross, K. G. W. *F. Scott Fitzgerald.* Grove, 1964.

The Curious Case of Benjamin Button. Dir. David Fincher. Paramount Pictures, 2008.

Curnutt, Kirk. *The Cambridge Introduction to F. Scott Fitzgerald.* Cambridge UP, 2007.

———, ed. *A Historical Guide to F. Scott Fitzgerald.* Oxford UP, 2004.

———. "Youth Culture and the Spectacle of Waste: *This Side of Paradise* and *The Beautiful and Damned.*" Bryer et al., *F. Scott Fitzgerald in the Twenty-First Century* 79–103.

Curtiss, Thomas Quinn. *The Smart Set: George Jean Nathan and H. L. Mencken.* Applause, 1998.

Davis, Laura L. "'Not So Much Art as Financial Operation': Conrad and *Metropolitan Magazine.*" *Conradiana* 41.2–3 (2009): 244–65.

Del Gizzo, Suzanne. "Ethnic Stereotyping." Mangum, *F. Scott Fitzgerald in Context* 224–33.

Dell, Floyd. *Mooncalf.* Knopf, 1920.

Donaldson, Scott. *Fool for Love.* Congdon and Weed, 1983.

———. *The Suburban Myth.* Columbia UP, 1969.

"Don't Read Trash." *Great Falls Daily Tribune* 19 Dec. 1916, 4.

Dos Passos, John. *Manhattan Transfer.* Harper and Brothers, 1925.

Douglas, Susan J., and Andrea McDonnell. *Celebrity: A History of Fame.* New York UP, 2019.

Dreiser, Theodore. *Jennie Gerhardt: A Novel.* Harper and Brothers, 1911.

———. *Sister Carrie.* Doubleday, 1900.

Dunton, James G. *Wild Asses.* Small, Maynard, 1925.

Eagleton, Terry. *The Meaning of Life.* Oxford UP, 2007.

Eastman, Max. *Enjoyment of Living.* Harper and Brothers, 1948.

Eble, Kenneth. *F. Scott Fitzgerald.* Twayne, 1963.

Elias, Amy J. "The Composition and Revision of Fitzgerald's *The Beautiful and Damned.*" *Princeton University Library Chronicle* 51.3 (1990): 245–66.

Eliot, Charles W. *Fifteen Minutes a Day: The Reading Guide.* Collier, 1916.

Eliot, George. *Daniel Deronda.* 1876. Penguin, 1967.

Eliot, T. S. *Poems.* Knopf, 1920.

———. *The Waste Land.* Liveright, 1922.

Ellis, Bret Easton. *American Psycho.* Vintage, 1991.

———. *Less Than Zero.* Knopf, 1985.

Enfield, Jonathan. "As the Fashion in Books Shifted: *The Beautiful and Damned* as Arc-Light Fiction." *Modernism/modernity* 14.4 (2007): 669–85.

Epstein, Joseph. *Book Business: Publishing Past, Present, and Future.* Norton, 2011.

Fahey, William A. *F. Scott Fitzgerald and the American Dream.* Crowell, 1973.

Faulkner, William. *The Sound and the Fury.* Cape and Smith, 1929.

"Finds Indecency Flaunting as Art." *New York Times* 12 Feb. 1922, 26.

Fitzgerald, F. Scott. *All the Sad Young Men.* Edited by James L. W. West III. Cambridge UP, 2010.

———. *The Beautiful and Damned.* Scribner's, 1922.

———. *The Beautiful and Damned.* PermaBooks, 1951.

———. *The Beautiful and Damned.* Scribner Library Edition, Scribner's, 1966.

——. *The Beautiful and Damned.* Scribner Paperback Fiction, Scribner's, 1995.

——. *The Beautiful and Damned.* Introduction by Jay Parini. Signet Classics, 1998.

——. *The Beautiful and Damned.* Introduction by Jay Parini. Afterword by Ruth Prigozy. Signet Classics, 2007.

——. *The Beautiful and Damned.* Penguin, 2010.

——. *The Beautiful and Damned.* Ed. James L. W. West III. Cambridge UP, 2013.

——. *Correspondence of F. Scott Fitzgerald.* Ed. Matthew J. Bruccoli and Margaret M. Duggan, with Susan Walker. Random House, 1980.

——. *Flappers and Philosophers.* Scribner's, 1920.

——. *Flappers and Philosophers.* Penguin, 2010.

——. *Flappers and Philosophers.* Ed. James L. W. West III. Cambridge UP, 2012.

——. *F. Scott Fitzgerald: A Life in Letters.* Ed. Matthew J. Bruccoli with Judith Baughman. Scribner's, 1994.

——. *F. Scott Fitzgerald's Ledger: A Facsimile.* Ed. Matthew J. Bruccoli. NCR/Microcard, 1972.

——. *The Great Gatsby.* Armed Services Edition, 1945.

——. *The Great Gatsby.* Bantam, 1949.

——. *The Great Gatsby.* Scribner Library Edition. Scribner's, 1960.

——. *The Great Gatsby.* 1925. Ed. Matthew J. Bruccoli. Cambridge UP, 1991.

——. *The Great Gatsby: A Variorum Edition.* Ed. James L. W. West III. Cambridge UP, 2019.

——. *The Letters of F. Scott Fitzgerald.* Ed. Andrew Turnbull. Scribner's, 1962.

——. *The Lost Decade: Short Stories from "Esquire," 1936–1941.* Ed. James L. W. West III, Cambridge UP, 2008.

——. *The Love of the Last Tycoon: A Western.* Ed. Matthew J. Bruccoli. Cambridge UP, 1993.

——. *My Lost City. Personal Essays, 1920–1940.* Ed. James L. W. West III. Cambridge UP, 2005.

——. *The Notebooks of F. Scott Fitzgerald.* Ed. Matthew J. Bruccoli. Harcourt Brace Jovanovich, 1978.

——. *Poems, 1911–1940.* Ed. Matthew J. Bruccoli. Foreword by James Dickey. Bruccoli Clark, 1981.

——. *The Short Stories of F. Scott Fitzgerald: A New Collection.* Ed. Matthew J. Bruccoli. Scribner's, 1989.

——. *Tales of the Jazz Age.* Ed. James L. W. West III. Cambridge UP, 2002.

——. *Tales of the Jazz Age.* Penguin, 2010.

——. *Taps at Reveille.* Ed. James L. W. West III. Cambridge UP, 2014.

——. *Tender Is the Night.* Bantam, 1950.

——. *Tender Is the Night: A Romance.* Ed. James L. W. West III. Cambridge UP, 2012.

——. *The Vegetable, or from President to Postman.* 1923. Scribner's, 1976.

——. *This Side of Paradise.* Scribner's, 1920.

——. *This Side of Paradise.* Ed. James L. W. West III. Cambridge UP, 1995.

Fitzgerald, Zelda. Scrapbook of Zelda Fitzgerald. Princeton University Digital Library, Princeton U, Princeton, NJ. http://pudl.princeton.edu/objects/x346d693p.

——. *Zelda Fitzgerald: The Collected Writings.* Ed. Matthew J. Bruccoli. Scribner's, 1991.

France, Anatole. *The Revolt of the Angels.* Trans. Mrs. Wilfred Jackson. Lane, 1914.

Franklin, Benjamin. "The Autobiography." 1793. *Writings.* Library of America, 1987. 1305–469.

Frederic, Harold. *The Damnation of Theron Ware.* Stone, 1896.

Freedman, Alisa. *Tokyo in Transit: Japanese Culture on the Rails and Road.* Stanford UP, 2011.

Frost, Robert. *The Poetry of Robert Frost: Collected Poems, Complete and Unabridged.* Ed. Edward Connery Latham. Henry Holt, 1979.

Frye, Steven. "Fitzgerald's Catholicism Revisited: The Eucharistic Element in *The Beautiful and Damned.*" Bryer, Margolies, Prigozy, 63–77.

Fryer, Sarah Beebe. *Fitzgerald's New Women: Harbingers of Change.* UMI Research P, 1988.

Gandal, Keith. *The Gun and the Pen: Fitzgerald, Hemingway, Faulkner and the Fiction of Mobilization.* Oxford UP, 2008.

Gatsby in Connecticut: The Untold Story. Dir. Robert Steven Williams. ATG Communications, 2019.

Gervais, Ronald J. "'Sleepy Hollow's Gone': Pastoral Myth and Artifice in Fitzgerald's *Beautiful and Damned.*" *Ball State University Forum* 22.3 (1981): 75–79.

Gillin, Edward. "Fitzgerald's Twain." Bryer, Margolies, Prigozy, 253–68.

Gingrich, Arnold. "Salute and Farewell to F. Scott Fitzgerald." Bruccoli and Bryer, 477–81.

Glaser, Madeleine. "Fitzgerald's *The Beautiful and Damned.*" *Explicator* 51.4 (1993): 238–39.

Gleason, William A. *The Leisure Ethic: Work and Play in American Literature, 1840–1940.* Stanford UP, 1999.

Glenday, Michael K. *F. Scott Fitzgerald.* Palgrave Macmillan, 2012.

Gluck, Carol. *Japan's Modern Myths: Ideology in the Late Meiji Period.* Princeton UP, 1985.

Godbersen, Anna. *Bright Young Things.* 3 vols. HarperCollins, 2010–12.

Goetz, Stewart. *The Purpose of Life: A Theistic Perspective.* Continuum, 2012.

Goldhurst, William. *F. Scott Fitzgerald and His Contemporaries.* World, 1963.

Goldsmith, Meredith. "White Skin, White Mask: Passing, Posing, and Performing in *The Great Gatsby*." *Modern Fiction Studies* 49.3 (2003): 443–68.

Grant, Madison. *The Passing of the Great Race: Or, The Racial Basis of European History*. Scribner's, 1916.

Grissom, Candace Ursula. *Fitzgerald and Hemingway on Film: A Critical Study of the Adaptations, 1924–2013*. McFarland, 2014.

Gross, Barry. "'The Dark Side of Twenty-Five': Fitzgerald and *The Beautiful and Damned*." *Bucknell Review* 16.3 (1968): 40–52.

Grundy, Mr. "Polite Society." *Atlantic Monthly* May 1920: 606–12.

Hamilton, Sharon. "Mencken and Nathan's 'Smart Set' and the Story behind Fitzgerald's Early Success." *F. Scott Fitzgerald Review* 4 (2005): 20–48.

———. "The New York Gossip Magazine in *The Great Gatsby*." *F. Scott Fitzgerald Review* 8 (2010): 34–56.

Hanna, Jennifer. *Arlington House: Robert E. Lee Memorial—Cultural Landscape Report: History, Vol. 1*. National Parks Service, 2001.

Hardy, Thomas. *Jude the Obscure*. Osgood and McIlvaine, 1895.

———. *Tess of the d'Ubervilles: A Pure Woman Faithfully Presented*. Osgood and McIlvaine, 1891.

Hare, Richard. "Nothing Matters." *Life, Death, and Meaning: Key Philosophical Readings on the Big Question*. Ed. David Benatar. Rowman and Littlefield, 2004. 43–51.

Hawthorne, Nathaniel. "The Birthmark." *Hawthorne's Short Stories*. 1946. Ed. Newton Arvin, Knopf, 2011. 177–92.

———. *The Scarlet Letter*. 1850. Introduction by Michael J. Colacurcio. Belknap P of Harvard UP, 2009.

Haytock, Jennifer. *At Home, At War: Domesticity and World War I in American Literature*. Ohio State UP, 2003.

Hemingway, Ernest. *The Sun Also Rises*. Scribner's, 1926.

Hindus, Milton. *F. Scott Fitzgerald: An Introduction and Interpretation*. Holt, 1968.

———. "F. Scott Fitzgerald and Literary Anti-Semitism: A Footnote on the Mind of the 20's." *Commentary* 3 (1947): 508–16.

Hinnant, Amanda, and Berkley Hudson. "The Magazine Revolution in America, 1880–1920." *The Oxford History of Popular Print Culture, Vol. 6: U. S. Popular Print Culture, 1860–1920*. Ed. Christine Bold. Oxford UP, 2011. 113–29.

Hook, Andrew. "Cases for Reconsideration: Fitzgerald's *This Side of Paradise* and *The Beautiful and Damned*." *Scott Fitzgerald: The Promises of Life*. Ed. A. Robert Lee. Vision, 1989. 17–36.

———. *F. Scott Fitzgerald*. Arnold, 1992.

Hughes, Rupert. *Excuse Me!* Burt, 1911.

Hurst, Fannie. *Lummox.* Harper and Brothers, 1923.

The Husband Hunter. Dir. Howard M. Mitchell. Fox Film Corporation, 1920.

"I'm Being True to Me." *Washington Herald* 28 June 1922, 5.

Irwin, John T. *F. Scott Fitzgerald's Fiction: "An Almost Theatrical Innocence."* Johns Hopkins UP, 2014.

James, Henry. *The Art of Criticism: Henry James on the Theory and Practice of Fiction.* Ed. William Veeder and Susan M. Giffin. U of Chicago P, 1986.

Johnson, Christiane. "F. Scott Fitzgerald et Hollywood: Le rêve américain denature." *Revue française d'études américaines* 19 (1984): 39–51.

Joyce, James. *Dubliners.* 1914. Viking, 1958.

——. *Ulysses.* Shakespeare and Company, 1922.

Jurca, Catherine. *White Diaspora: The Suburb and the Twentieth-Century American Novel.* Princeton UP, 2011.

"Just a Few Great Books Gave Him His Start," *Metropolitan Magazine* 54.2 (Sept. 1921): 39.

Kaestle, Carl F., and Janice A. Radway. Prologue. *The History of the Book in America. Vol. 4: Print in Motion: The Expansion of Publishing and Reading in the United States, 1880–1940.* U of North Carolina P, 2014. 1–30.

Keats, John. *Selected Poems and Letters.* Ed. Robert Gittings and Sandra Anstey. Heinemann, 1996.

Kerrigan, John. *Shakespeare's Originality.* Oxford UP, 2018.

Keyser, Catherine. *Artificial Colors: Modern Food and Racial Fictions.* Oxford UP, 2019.

Kim, Sharon. "The Lost Tycoon: Allan Dwan in the Works of F. Scott Fitzgerald." *F. Scott Fitzgerald Review* 14 (2016): 79–109.

Kirsch, Adam. "The 'Five-Foot Shelf' Reconsidered." *Harvard Magazine* Nov.–Dec. 2001. https://harvardmagazine.com/2001/11/the-five-foot-shelf-reco.html.

Klein, Woody. *Westport, Connecticut: The Story of a New England Town's Rise to Prominence.* Greenwood P, 2000.

Krystal, Arthur. "Fitzgerald and the Jews." *New Yorker* 20 July 2015. http://www.newyorker.com/books/page-turner/fitzgerald-and-the-jews.

Kuehl, John. *F. Scott Fitzgerald: A Study of the Short Fiction.* Twayne, 1991.

——. "Scott Fitzgerald's Reading." *Princeton University Library Chronicle* 22.2 (1961): 58–89.

Kuehl, John, and Jackson R. Bryer, eds. *Dear Scott/Dear Max: The Fitzgerald—Perkins Correspondence.* Scribner's, 1971.

Kruse, Horst. *F. Scott Fitzgerald at Work: The Making of "The Great Gatsby."* U of Alabama P, 2013.

LaBarre, Suzanne. "Wanted: F. Scott Fitzgerald Editions That Aren't Gauzy Watercolors of Flappers—Finally, a Publisher Gets Fitzgerald Right." *Fast Company* 8 Aug. 2010. https://www.fastcompany.com/1662143/wanted-f-scott-fitzgerald-editions -that-arent-gauzy-watercolors-of-flappers.

La Sorte, Mike. "Kosher Nostra." Rick Porrello's American Mafia. March 2010. http:// www.americanmafia.com/Feature_Articles_453.html.

Lefebvre, Henri. *The Production of Space.* Trans. Donald Nicholson-Smith. Wiley-Blackwell, 1991.

Leo XIII. Aeterni Patris, *The Holy See.* 4 Aug. 1879. http://www.vatican.va/content/leo -xiii/en/encyclicals/documents/hf_l-xiii_enc_04081879_aeterni-patris.html.

Lears, T. J. Jackson. *No Place of Grace: Antimodernism and the Transformation of American Culture, 1880–1920.* Pantheon, 1981.

Lehan, Richard. *F. Scott Fitzgerald and the Craft of Fiction.* Southern Illinois UP, 1966.

Levey, Matthew, professor of history, Birmingham-Southern College. Interview with David Ullrich regarding the railroad in late-Meiji Culture. 11 May 2018.

Le Vot, André. *F. Scott Fitzgerald: A Biography.* Trans. William Byron. Doubleday, 1983.

Lewis, Sinclair. *Babbitt.* Harcourt, Brace, 1920.

"Lightning Tears Its Way through Artist's House." *Westporter-Herald* 2 July 1920, 1.

Lofting, Hugh. *The Story of Doctor Dolittle, Being the History of His Peculiar Life at Home and Astonishing Adventures in Foreign Parts.* Stokes, 1920.

London, Jack. *The Call of the Wild.* Macmillan, 1903.

Long, Robert Emmet. *The Achieving of "The Great Gatsby": F. Scott Fitzgerald, 1920–1925.* Bucknell UP, 1979.

Lorimer, George Horace. "The Unpopular Editor of the Popular Magazine." *Bookman* 60.4 (Dec. 1924): 396–97.

MacGrath, Harold. *Hearts and Masks.* Bobbs-Merrill, 1905.

———. *The Man on the Box.* Bobbs-Merrill, 1902.

Maney, J. Bret. "Going South: Disaster beneath the Mason-Dixon Line in *The Beautiful and Damned." Romance and Regionalism in the Works of F. Scott and Zelda Fitzgerald: The South Side of Paradise.* Ed. Kirk Curnutt and Sara A. Kosiba. Lexington, forthcoming.

Mangan, Gregg. "The Many Layers to Onion Farming in Westport." Connecticut History. 4 Aug. 2019. www.connecticuthistory.org. https://connecticuthistory .org/the-many-layers-to-onion-farming-in-westport/.

Mangum, Bryant, ed. *F. Scott Fitzgerald in Context.* Cambridge UP, 2013.

———. "The Short Stories of F. Scott Fitzgerald." Prigozy, *The Cambridge Companion to F. Scott Fitzgerald* 57–78.

Margolies, Alan, ed. *The Beautiful and Damned: The Manuscript.* 2 vols. Garland, 1990.

———. Introduction. *The Beautiful and Damned*. By F. Scott Fitzgerald. Oxford UP, 1998. vi–xxvi.

———. "The Maturing of F. Scott Fitzgerald." *Twentieth Century Literature* 43.1 (1997): 75–93.

Mastandrea, Martina. *F. Scott Fitzgerald on Silent Film*. Brill, 2022.

McInerney, Jay. *Bright Lights, Big City*. Vintage, 1984.

McIntyre, O. O. "Village Home of Artists." *Kansas City Star* 25 Nov. 1925, 26.

McMullen, Bonnie Shannon. "Architecture and Design." Mangum, *F. Scott Fitzgerald in Context* 353–62.

Mencken, H. L. *The American Language: A Preliminary Inquiry into the Development of English in the United States*. Rev. ed. Knopf, 1921.

———. *The American Scene: A Reader*. Ed. Huntington Cairns. Knopf, 1965.

———. *George Bernard Shaw: His Plays*. Luce, 1905.

———. *Minority Report*. Knopf, 1956.

———. *My Life as Author and Editor*. Ed. Jonathan Yardley. Vintage, 1993.

———. *The Philosophy of Friedrich Nietzsche*. Unwin, 1907.

———. *Prejudices: First Series*. Knopf, 1919.

———. *Prejudices: Second Series*. Knopf, 1920.

Meredith, James. "F. Scott Fitzgerald and War." Mangum, *F. Scott Fitzgerald in Context* 133–44.

———. "Fitzgerald and War." Curnutt, *A Historical Guide to F. Scott Fitzgerald* 163–214.

Merrill, Robert. "'Dalyrimple Goes Wrong': The Best of the Neglected Stories." Bryer, *New Essays on F. Scott Fitzgerald's Neglected Stories* 23–34.

Messud, Claire. *The Emperor's Children*. Knopf, 2006.

Mettepenningen, Jürgen. *Nouvelle Théologie—New Theology: Inheritor of Modernism, Precursor of Vatican II*. Bloomsbury T&T Clark, 2010.

Meyers, Jeffrey. "F. Scott Fitzgerald and the Jews: From Bigotry to Sympathy." *Forward* 12 Feb. 1993, 1, 10.

Milford, Nancy. *Zelda: A Biography*. Harper and Row, 1970.

Miller, Arthur. *Death of a Salesman*. Viking, 1949.

Miller, James E. Jr. *F. Scott Fitzgerald: His Art and His Technique*. New York UP, 1964.

———. *The Fictional Technique of F. Scott Fitzgerald*. Folcroft, 1957.

Mizener, Arthur. *The Far Side of Paradise: A Biography of F. Scott Fitzgerald*. Houghton Mifflin, 1951.

Monk, Craig. "The Political F. Scott Fitzgerald: Liberal Illusion and Disillusion in *This Side of Paradise* and *The Beautiful and Damned*." *American Studies International* 3.2 (1995): 60–71.

"More Nude Bathers at Compo Beach." *Westporter-Herald* 5 May 1920, 1.

Moreland, Kim. *The Medievalist Impulse in American Literature: Twain, Adams, Fitzgerald, and Hemingway.* U of Virginia P, 1996.

Mott, Frank Luther. *A History of American Magazines. Vol. 4: 1885–1905.* Harvard UP, 1957.

———. *A History of American Magazines. Vol. 5: Sketches of 21 Magazines, 1905–1930.* Harvard UP, 1968.

Moyer, Kermit W. "Fitzgerald's Two Unfinished Novels: The Count and the Tycoon in Spenglerian Perspective." *Contemporary Literature* 15.2 (1974): 238–56.

Murphy, Bernice M. *The Suburban Gothic in American Popular Culture.* Palgrave Macmillan, 2009.

Murray, Edward. *The Cinematic Imagination: Writers and the Motion Pictures.* Ungar, 1972.

Nathan, George Jean. "Memories of Fitzgerald, Lewis and Dreiser: The Golden Boys of the Twenties." *Esquire* Oct. 1958: 148–49.

Nathan, George Jean, and H. L. Mencken. *The American Credo: A Contribution toward the Interpretation of the National Mind.* Knopf, 1921.

Newton, Wesley Phillips. "Tenting Tonight on the Old Camp Grounds: Alabama's Military Bases and World War I." *The Great War in the Heart of Dixie: Alabama during World War I.* Ed. Martin Olliff. U of Alabama P, 2015. 41–65.

Nolan, Jennifer. "May Wilson Preston and the Birth of Fitzgerald's Flapper: Illustrating Social Transformation in 'Bernice Bobs Her Hair.'" *Journal of Modern Periodical Studies* 8.1 (2017): 56–80.

———. "Reading 'Babylon Revisited' as a Post Text: F. Scott Fitzgerald, George Horace Lorimer, and the *Saturday Evening Post* Audience." *Book History* 20 (2017): 351–73.

———. "Visualizing 'The Rich Boy': F. Scott Fitzgerald, F. R. Gruger, and *Red Book Magazine.*" *F. Scott Fitzgerald Review* 15 (2017): 17–33.

Norris, Charles G. *Salt, or, The Education of Griffith Adams.* Dutton, 1918.

Norris, Frank. *Vandover and the Brute.* Doubleday, Page, 1914.

Nowlin, Michael. "Mencken's Defense of Women and the Marriage Plot of *The Beautiful and Damned.*" Bryer et al., *F. Scott Fitzgerald in the Twenty-First Century.* 104–20.

———. "Naturalism and High Modernism." Mangum, *F. Scott Fitzgerald in Context* 179–90.

The Off-Shore Pirate. Dir. Dallas M. Fitzgerald. Metro Pictures, 1921.

O'Meara, Lauraleigh. *Lost City: Fitzgerald's New York.* Routledge, 2002.

"Ooh, Skinnay! Bill Hart May Be Our Neighbor Soon." *Westporter-Herald* 31 July 1920, 1.

Orwell, George. *Keep the Aspidistra Flying.* Victor Gollancz, 1936.

Page, Dave, and Jeff Kruger. *F. Scott Fitzgerald in St. Paul: The Writer and His Friends at Home.* U of Minnesota P, 2017.

Parini, Jay. Introduction. *The Beautiful and Damned.* By F. Scott Fitzgerald. Signet, 1998. vii–xiv.

Perosa, Sergio. *The Art of F. Scott Fitzgerald.* Trans. Charles Matz and Perosa. U of Michigan P, 1965.

Petry, Alice Hall. *Fitzgerald's Craft of Short Fiction: The Collected Stories, 1920–1935.* UMI Research P, 1989.

Philostratus. *The Life of Apollonius of Tyana.* Trans. F. C. Conybeare. Harvard UP, 1911.

Piper, Henry Dan. *F. Scott Fitzgerald: A Critical Portrait.* Holt, Rinehart and Winston, 1965.

———. "Frank Norris and Scott Fitzgerald." *Huntington Library Quarterly* 19.4 (1956): 393–400.

Pius X. "Lamentabili sane exitu." Papal Encyclicals Online. July 1907. https://www.papalencyclicals.net/Pius10/p10lamen.htm.

———. "Oath against Modernism." Papal Encyclicals Online. 1 Sept. 1910. https://www.papalencyclicals.net/pius10/p10moath.htm.

———. "Pascendi Dominici Gregis," *The Holy See.* 8 Sept. 1907. http://www.vatican.va/content/pius-x/en/encyclicals/documents/hf_p-x_enc_19070908_pascendi-dominici-gregis.html.

Podis, Leonard A. "*The Beautiful and Damned:* Fitzgerald's Test of Youth." *Fitzgerald/Hemingway Annual* 5 (1973): 141–47.

Poe, Edgar Allan. "The Masque of the Red Death." *Tales and Sketches, vol. 1: 1831–1842.* Ed. Thomas Ollive Mabbott. U of Illinois P, 2000. 667–77.

Powell, David McKay. "Henry Adams's Gothic Disposition in Fitzgerald's *This Side of Paradise.*" *F. Scott Fitzgerald Review.* 10 (2012): 93–107.

Prigozy, Ruth, ed. *The Cambridge Companion to F. Scott Fitzgerald.* Cambridge UP, 2002.

———. "Fitzgerald's Flappers and Flapper Films of the Jazz Age: Behind the Morality." Curnutt, *A Historical Guide to F. Scott Fitzgerald,* 129–62.

Quirk, Tom. *Bergson and American Culture: The Worlds of Willa Cather and Wallace Stevens.* U of North Carolina P, 1990.

Raubicheck, Walter, and Steven Goldleaf. "Stage and Screen Entertainment." Mangum, *F. Scott Fitzgerald in Context* 302–10.

Rice, Diana. "Literary Bootlegging." *New York Times* 6 Aug. 1922, 1.

Roosevelt, Theodore. "The Threat of Japan." 1909. Papers of Theodore Roosevelt, Manuscript Division, Library of Congress. 120–26. https://www.mtholyoke.edu/acad/intrel/trjapan.htm.

Rosenfeld, Paul. *Men Seen: Twenty-Four Modern Authors.* Dial P, 1925.

———. *Port of New York.* Harcourt, Brace, 1924.

Roulston, Robert. "*The Beautiful and Damned:* The Alcoholic's Revenge." *Literature and Psychology* 27.4 (1977): 156–63.

Roulston, Robert, and Helen H. Roulston. *The Winding Road to West Egg: The Artistic Development of F. Scott Fitzgerald.* Bucknell UP, 1995.

St. Aubyn, Edward. *Bad News.* Picador, 1992.

———. *Some Hope.* Heinemann, 1994.

Schiff, Jonathan. *Ashes to Ashes: Mourning and Social Difference in F. Scott Fitzgerald's Fiction.* Susquehanna UP, 2001.

"Scientific Methods of Investing and Trading in Stocks." *Metropolitan Magazine* 55.3 (Mar. 1922): 11.

Seaman, Eric. "Indecency Seethes in Latest Spasm of Petting Apostle." *Capital Times* 13 Mar. 1922, 7.

Searles, George J. "The Symbolic Function of Food and Eating in F. Scott Fitzgerald's *The Beautiful and Damned.*" *Ball State University Forum* 22.3 (1981): 14–19.

Seiters, Dan. *Image Patterns in the Novels of F. Scott Fitzgerald.* UMI Research P, 1986.

Shakespeare, William. *Antony and Cleopatra.* Ed. Barbara A. Moawt and Paul Werstine. Simon and Schuster, 2005.

———. *A Midsummer Night's Dream.* Ed. Barbara A. Moawt and Paul Werstine. Simon and Schuster, 2004.

———. *Romeo and Juliet.* Ed. Barbara A. Moawt and Paul Werstine. Simon and Schuster, 2004.

———. *The Taming of the Shrew.* Ed. Barbara A. Moawt and Paul Werstine. Simon and Schuster, 2004.

———. *The Tempest.* Ed. Barbara A. Moawt and Paul Werstine. Simon and Schuster, 2004.

Shaw, George Bernard. *Mrs. Warren's Profession: A Play in Four Acts.* Grant Richards, 1902.

Shulman, Max. *Rally round the Flag, Boys!* Doubleday, 1957.

"Sixteen Stills Were Reported in Westport." *Westporter-Herald* 10 June 1920, 1.

Sklar, Robert. *F. Scott Fitzgerald: The Last Laocoön.* Oxford UP, 1967.

Solomon, Barbara Probst. "Westport Wildlife." *New Yorker* 9 Sept. 1996: 78–85.

Smiles, Samuel. *Self-Help; with Illustrations of Character, Conduct, and Perseverance.* Ed. Peter W. Sinnema. Oxford UP, 2002.

Stavola, Thomas J. *Scott Fitzgerald: Crisis in an American Identity.* Barnes and Noble, 1979.

Stern, Milton R. *The Golden Moment: The Novels of F. Scott Fitzgerald.* U of Illinois P, 1970.

Stevens, Wallace. *The Collected Poems: The Corrected Edition.* Ed. Chris Beyers. Vintage, 2015.

Stoddard, Lothrop. *The Rising Tide of Color against White World-Supremacy.* Scribner's, 1920.

Stuart, Henry Longan. *Weeping Cross: An Unworldly Story.* Doubleday, 1908.

Sweeney, Anna. *Comparing Cultural Context through New Historicism: The Impact of Form upon Content in the Serialized and Novelized Versions of F. Scott Fitzgerald's "The Beautiful and Damned."* MA thesis, Liberty U, 2018. https://digitalcommons .liberty.edu/masters/496/.

Takaki, Ronald. *Strangers from a Different Shore: A History of Asian Americans.* Little, Brown, 1998.

Takamiya, Yumi, assistant professor of Japanese, University of Alabama at Birmingham. Correspondence with David W. Ullrich regarding "Japanese Railroad Songs," 11 July 2018.

Tangedal, Ross. "'At Last Everyone Had Something to Talk About': Gloria's War in Fitzgerald's *The Beautiful and Damned.*" *Midwestern Miscellany* 44 (2016): 68–81.

Tarkington, Booth. *Penrod.* Doubleday, Page, 1914.

Tartt, Donna. *The Secret History.* Knopf, 1992.

Tate, Mary Jo. *Critical Companion to F. Scott Fitzgerald: A Literary Reference to His Life and Work.* Infobase, 2007.

Tateki, Owada. *Tetsudo Shoka Chiri Kyoiku* (*Geography education railroad songs*). Miki Sasuwke, 1900.

Tavernier-Courbin, Jacqueline. "Art as Woman's Response and Search: Zelda Fitzgerald's *Save Me the Waltz.*" *Southern Literary Journal* 11 (1979): 22–42.

Taylor, D. J. *Bright Young People: The Lost Generation of London's Jazz Age.* Farrar, Straus and Giroux, 2009.

Taylor, Kendall. *The Gatsby Affair: Scott, Zelda, and the Betrayal That Shaped an American Classic.* Rowman and Littlefield, 2018.

———. *Sometimes Madness Is Wisdom: Zelda and Scott Fitzgerald: A Marriage.* Ballantine, 2002.

Thoreau, Henry David. *A Week on the Concord and Merrimack Rivers, Walden; or Life in the Woods, The Maine Woods, Cape Cod.* Library of America, 1985.

"Thousands of Dollars Worth of Alcohol Found When Taxi Turned Turtle in Westport Last Evening." *Westporter-Herald* 20 July 1920, 1.

Titelman, Gregory Y. *Random House Dictionary of Popular Proverbs and Sayings.* Random House, 1996.

Townsend, Lee. Unpublished memoir of Westport, Connecticut. Westport Historical Society.

Traganou, Jilly. "The Tōkaidō—Scenes from Edo to Meiji Eras." *Japan Railway & Transport Review*, no. 13 (September 1997): 17–27.

"Trash Reading Matter." *St. Albans Daily Messenger* 2 Aug. 1916, 4.

Trower, Katharine B. "The Fitzgeralds' Letters to the Hoveys." *Fitzgerald Hemingway Annual*, 1978. 55–60.

Troy, William. "Scott Fitzgerald—the Authority of Failure." *F. Scott Fitzgerald: The Man and His Work.* Ed. Alfred Kazin. World, 1951. 187–93.

"Truck Carrying $17,000 Worth of Booze Held Up." *Westporter-Herald* July 10, 1920, 1.

Trumbull, Charles Gaudaudet. *Anthony Comstock, Fighter: Some Impressions of a Life-time of Adventure in Conflict with the Powers of Evil.* 2nd rev. ed. Fleming H. Revell, 1913.

Tunc, Tanfer Emin. "This Side of Sexuality: Reproductive Discourse in the Works of F. Scott Fitzgerald." *F. Scott Fitzgerald Review* 13 (2015): 184–201.

Turlish, Lewis A. "The Rising Tide of Color: A Note on the Historicism of *The Great Gatsby.*" *American Literature* 43.3 (1971): 442–44.

Turnbull, Andrew. *Scott Fitzgerald.* Scribner's, 1962.

Turnbull, Charles. *Anthony Comstock, Fighter: Some Impressions of a Lifetime Adventure in Conflict with the Powers of Evil.* Kessinger, 1913.

Tuttleton, James W. "'Combat in the Erogenous Zone': Women in the American Novel between the Two World Wars." *A Fine Silver Thread: Essays on American Writing.* Dee, 1998. 195–217.

Ullrich, David W. "'Mr. Fitzgerald—I Believe That Is How He Spells His Name—Seems to Think That Plagiarism Begins at Home': A Reading of Zelda Sayre Fitzgerald's 'Friend Husband's Latest.'" *F. Scott Fitzgerald Review* 19 (2021): 105–33.

Van Vechten, Carl. *Parties: A Novel of Contemporary New York Life.* Knopf, 1930.

Vanderbilt, Kermit. Introduction. *The Beautiful and Damned.* By F. Scott Fitzgerald. Penguin, 1998. vii–xxv.

Veblen, Thorstein. *The Theory of the Leisure Class: An Economic Study of Institutions.* Macmillan, 1899.

Voltaire. *Candide or Optimism.* Trans. John Butt. Penguin, 1947.

von Ziegesar, Cicely. *Gossip Girl* series. 13 vols. Little, Brown, 2002–9.

Wagner-Martin, Linda. "Zelda in the Shadows." Mangum, *F. Scott Fitzgerald in Context* 145–53.

——. *Zelda Sayre Fitzgerald: An American Woman's Life.* Palgrave Macmillan, 2004.

Wasserstrom, William. "The Goad of Guilt: Henry Adams, Scott, and Zelda." *Journal of Modern Literature* 6.2 (1977): 289–310.

Waugh, Evelyn. *Vile Bodies.* Chapman and Hall, 1930.

Way, Brian. *F. Scott Fitzgerald and the Art of Social Fiction*. Edward Arnold, 1980.

"Wearies of Waiting a Comstock Arrest." *New York Times* 15 May 1913, 7, 14–19.

Webb, Richard, Jr. *Boats against the Current: The Honeymoon Summer of Scott and Zelda: Westport, Connecticut 1920*. 2nd ed. Prospecta, 2020.

———. Eve Potts. Interview with Webb. Unpublished. 2015.

———. Lou White. Interview with Webb. Unpublished. 2015.

Welty, Eudora. *Delta Wedding*. Harcourt Brace, 1946.

Werbel, Amy. *Lust on Trial: Censorship and the Rise of American Obscenity in the Age of Anthony Comstock*. Columbia UP, 2018.

West, James L. W., III. Introduction. *The Beautiful and Damned*. By F. Scott Fitzgerald. Cambridge UP, 2008. xiii–xxix.

———. Introduction. *This Side of Paradise*. By F. Scott Fitzgerald. Cambridge UP, 1995. xiii–liii.

———. *The Perfect Hour: The Romance of F. Scott Fitzgerald and Ginevra King, His First Love*. Random House, 2005.

———. "The Question of Vocation in *This Side of Paradise* and *The Beautiful and Damned*." Prigozy, *The Cambridge Companion to F. Scott Fitzgerald* 48–56.

———. "The Second Serials of *This Side of Paradise* and *The Beautiful and Damned*." *Papers of the Bibliographical Society of America* 73.1 (1979): 63–74.

"Westport Now Home to Famous Movie Actors." *Westporter-Herald* 23 July 1920, 1.

Wharton, Edith. *The Custom of the Country*. Scribner's, 1913.

———. *Ethan Frome*. Scribner's, 1911.

———. *The House of Mirth*. Scribner's, 1905.

"Where Only Man Is Vile." *Los Angeles Times* 13 Apr. 1916, 16.

"Why Not Operate a Tabard Inn Library?" *Cosmopolitan* 42.6 (Apr. 1906): 718.

Wilde, Oscar. *The Picture of Dorian Gray*. 1890. Bantam, 1982.

Wilson, Annasue McCleave. "An Unseemly Emotion: *PW* Talks to Claire Messud." *Publishers Weekly* 29 Apr. 2013. https://www.publishersweekly.com/pw/by-topic /authors/interviews/article/56848-an-unseemly-emotion-pw-talks-with-claire -messud.html.

Wilson, Edmund. *Axel's Castle*. Scribner's, 1931.

———, ed. *The Crack-up*. New Directions, 1945.

———. *Letters on Literature and Politics, 1912–1972*. Ed. Elena Wilson. Farrar, Straus and Giroux, 1977.

———. "The Literary Spotlight: VI. F. Scott Fitzgerald." *Bookman* 50.3 (Mar. 1922): 20–25.

———. *The Shores of Light: A Literary Chronicle of the Twenties and Thirties*. Farrar, Straus and Young, 1952.

Wilson, Sloan. *The Man in the Gray Flannel Suit.* Simon and Schuster, 1955.

Wister, Owen. *The Virginian.* Macmillan, 1902.

Woolf, Virginia. *Jacob's Room.* Hogarth, 1922.

"W. S. Hart Coming Home." *Westporter-Herald* 16 Aug. 1920, 1.

INDEX

CPSIA information can be obtained
at www.ICGtesting.com
Printed in the USA
LVHW031940011222
734345LV00002B/266

9 780807 178577